MW01056183

CARIBBEAN RUM

Florida A&M University, Tallahassee
Florida Atlantic University, Boca Raton
Florida Gulf Coast University, Ft. Myers
Florida International University, Miami
Florida State University, Tallahassee
University of Central Florida, Orlando
University of Florida, Gainesville
University of North Florida, Jacksonville
University of South Florida, Tampa
University of West Florida, Pensacola

UNIVERSITY PRESS OF FLORIDA

Gainesville · Tallahassee · Tampa

Boca Raton · Pensacola · Orlando · Miami

Jacksonville · Ft. Myers

By Frederick H. Smith

CARIBBEAN

A Social and Economic History

Copyright 2005 by Frederick H. Smith
Printed in the United States of America on recycled, acid-free paper
All rights reserved

10   09   08   6   5   4   3   2

A record of cataloging-in-publication data is available from the
Library of Congress.
ISBN 978-0-8130-2867-5

The University Press of Florida is the scholarly publishing
agency for the State University System of Florida, comprising
Florida A&M University, Florida Atlantic University, Florida
Gulf Coast University, Florida International University, Florida
State University, University of Central Florida, University of
Florida, University of North Florida, University of South
Florida, and University of West Florida.

University Press of Florida
15 Northwest 15th Street
Gainesville, FL 32611-2079
http://www.upf.com

To Jane and Rachel

Contents

Contents

Figures

Figures

Tables

Preface and Acknowledgments

In the summer of 1996 I went to Barbados to prepare a historical archaeological field school in Bridgetown with my colleague, Dr. Karl Watson, and his students from the department of history at the University of the West Indies, Cave Hill. On the morning of Saturday, July 13, Watson called to say that construction workers in a part of the city known as the Pierhead had unearthed skeletal remains while preparing a site for the expansion of a local shopping mall. The skeletal remains turned out to be human, and further investigation revealed more burials at the site. We spent the day surveying this unmarked and forgotten cemetery and recording information about the site. Based on the absence of grave markers, the cemetery's location on the periphery of the town, and the presence of a mid-eighteenth century white kaolin clay tobacco pipe, which had been placed in the crook of the right arm of one of the deceased, we determined that the graveyard was the final resting place of Bridgetown's slave population.

Throughout the day, construction workers and residents from the nearby neighborhoods monitored our excavation and pondered our work. Some mentioned the ghosts of those buried at the site and the restlessness of *duppies*, the mischievous, and sometimes malicious, spirits of the dead. At the end of the day, we removed the skeleton with the tobacco pipe and began packaging it for proper storage at the University of the West Indies. About that time, someone in the crowd shouted that we needed to pour libations to those buried at the site, and within minutes a bottle of rum was produced for that purpose. The rum was poured on the ground and the pouring was punctuated by requests that the duppies "rest in peace" and "leave us alone."

This event was a major turning point in my academic career. Since 1991, I had conducted fieldwork in different parts of the Caribbean and during these visits had the opportunity to observe the central place of rum and other forms of alcohol in Caribbean society. In 1994, I was interested enough to write a short paper on the social history of Caribbean rum for David Geggus' course on Caribbean history at the University of Florida. During the excavations at the Pierhead cemetery in Bridgetown, however, I was an actual participant in an event that embodied and expressed centuries of alcohol-related traditions in the Caribbean, which inspired me to pursue further study.

This book explores the role of alcohol in the Caribbean from the sixteenth century to the present. Drawing on materials from Africa, Europe, and throughout the Americas, it contributes to the growing field of Atlantic studies and breaks new ground in using an interdisciplinary approach that incorporates documentary, archaeological, and ethnographic evidence. It investigates the economic impact of Caribbean rum on multiple scales, including rum's contribution to sugar plantation revenues, its role in bolstering colonial and postcolonial economies, and its impact on Atlantic trade. A number of political-economic trends determined the volume and value of rum exports from the Caribbean, especially war, competition from other alcohol industries, slavery and slave emancipation, temperance movements, and globalization.

This book also examines the social and sacred uses of rum and identifies the forces that shaped alcohol drinking in the Caribbean. While the enormous amounts of rum available in the Caribbean contributed to a climate of excessive drinking, levels of alcohol consumption varied among different social groups. The different drinking patterns reflect more than simply access to rum. For example, levels of drinking and drunken comportment conveyed messages about the underlying tensions that existed in the Caribbean, which were driven by the coercive exploitation of labor and set within a highly contentious social hierarchy based on class, race, gender, religion, and ethnic identity. Moreover, these tensions were often magnified by epidemic disease, poor living conditions, natural disasters, international conflicts, and unstable food supplies. While nearly everyone in the Caribbean drank, the differing levels of alcohol use by various social groups highlight the ways in which drinking became a means to confront anxiety.

As an interdisciplinary study of alcohol and drinking in the Caribbean, this book is geared toward multiple audiences. It is intended for social and economic historians of the Atlantic world, as well as historical anthropologists interested in colonialism, culture contact, the African diaspora, slavery, and plantation life. In addition, the book is meant for scholars in the growing field of alcohol studies.

I wish to thank David Geggus for his support, advice, and encouragement throughout the process of writing this book. Although initially skeptical about a comprehensive book on Caribbean rum, Geggus read numerous drafts of my work. He taught me how to seek out the nuances of alcohol use and the impact of rum industries on Caribbean economies, which strengthened my understanding of the forces that shaped rum consumption and rum making in the Caribbean. I would also like to thank Kathleen Deagan, Marley Brown, Norman Barka, and Kathleen Bragdon, who all have had a positive influence on my academic and professional career.

I wish to thank the Department of Archaeological Research at the Colonial Williamsburg Foundation, which largely funded my fieldwork. In particular, Marley Brown was instrumental in securing funds for my research projects in Barbados. The A. Curtis Wilgus Foundation at the Center for Latin American Studies at the University of Florida also provided seed money that made the early phase of my research possible.

Many people in Barbados played a prominent role in this project. Karl Watson has dedicated his life to protecting and preserving the natural and cultural resources of Barbados and has made many valuable contributions to our understanding of the history and archaeology of the island. Watson encouraged me to pursue my research in Barbados and laid the groundwork for my studies. I would also like to thank Kevin Farmer, curator of history and archaeology at the Barbados Museum and Historical Society, for his help and support over the years. Ingrid Marshall, Sherry Ann Burton, and the rest of the staff at the Barbados Department of Archives managed my many requests and located little-known documents that facilitated the completion of this project. I would also like to thank my other friends and colleagues in Barbados who made this project possible. Morris Greenidge, Mary Archer, Steven King, William Bain, and Richard Haynes provided support throughout my research. I am especially indebted to my dear friends Nicholas Forde and Milton Innis, who set the foundation for many of my endeavors.

Jerome Handler has also been supportive of this project. Handler's unique blend of historical and anthropological research has been an inspiration, and he provided several key references to alcohol use in early Barbados. I also wish to thank John Byram, Mac Griswold, Christina Kiddle, Dwayne Pickett, Mark Walker, Peter Mancall, Anthony Maingot, Harry Paul, Jeremy Cohen, Belkis Suarez, Michael Nassaney, Robert Ulin, Laurie Spielvogel, Ann Miles, Allen Zagarell, Emilie Castonguay, Karen Weinstein, Terry Weik, Sheila Dickison, John Arthur, Kathy Weedman, Matthew Smith, Jaunita DeBarros, Chris Crain, Brian Lee, Nicole Lukacyzk, and Brendan Weaver for their insights over the years. Richard Phillips, Justino Llanque-Chana, Paul Losch, and the rest of the staff at the University of Florida Latin American Collection also contributed to the success of this project. My drive and enthusiasm for this project came from William L. Smith and Mona Smith.

Most of all I am indebted to Jane Wulf. In 1995 and 1996, Jane assisted in the archaeological excavations in Barbados. In 1998 and 2000, she searched the Barbados Archives for plantation records and rum-making statistics. Above all, Jane has supported me throughout my academic and professional career and encouraged me to pursue this project. This book would not have been possible without her assistance.

CARIBBEAN RUM

CHAPTER 1

Introduction

THOUSANDS OF FOREIGN TOURISTS travel to the Caribbean each year seeking temporary escape from overwork, cold weather, fading love, and the drudgery of middle-class life. Yet, where do peoples of the Caribbean find escape? For the past 500 years, the Caribbean itself has been a scene of escape, and alcohol has often been the means through which escape was achieved. This book investigates the history of rum in the Caribbean from the beginnings of the rum industry to today. It seeks to understand why people in the Caribbean drank (or chose not to drink) and what contributions rum has made to the Caribbean economy. It argues that rum's social meaning and economic value arose from its ability to provide a temporary respite from the challenges of everyday life in the region.

Rum is the potable alcoholic beverage obtained by distilling sugarcane juice and the waste products of sugar making.[1] It was first produced in the Caribbean in the early seventeenth century by European and African colonists who sought to re-create the drinking habits they left behind in the Old World. More importantly, colonists drank to cope with the many anxieties they encountered on the colonial Caribbean frontier, especially unfamiliar surroundings, boredom, loneliness, epidemic diseases, a coercive labor system, an imbalanced sex ratio, and competing racial and class agendas. Drinking patterns also reflect the transfer of Old World beliefs about the social, spiritual, and medicinal value of alcohol. However, Christian missionaries and temperance advocates, who descended upon the Caribbean after slave emancipation in the mid-nineteenth century, challenged the meaning and escapist functions of alcohol use and began to reshape drinking patterns in the region.

While internal demand sparked the initial rise of rum making, a wide array of factors dictated the economic success of Caribbean rum industries. Regional forces, such as the rise and decline of sugar production, led to the expansion and contraction of rum industries in different regions of the Caribbean at different times. Outside forces, such as war, mercantilism, and competing alcohol industries in Europe and North America, also determined where and when rum making was economically feasible. As a result of these factors, rum making spread from its cradle in seventeenth-century Barbados to Jamaica, Demerara, Martinique, Cuba, and Puerto Rico.

For decades, Caribbean researchers have used the study of exotic commodities as prisms through which to view social and economic trends in the Atlantic world. Anthropologist Sidney W. Mintz, most notably, popularized the commodity-based approach in his study of the changing meaning of sugar in Europe.[2] Yet, while such studies emphasize the meaning of Caribbean commodities to consumers in Europe and North America, the meaning of these goods to the slaves, servants, peasants, and planters who produced them has often been overlooked. In part, the explanation for this metropolitan perspective lies in the fact that such commodities, especially sugar, were almost entirely exported for foreign consumption. The study of rum offers similar possibilities to discuss political-economic and social trends in the Atlantic world, but provides a special opportunity to explore the meaning of commodities in the societies that produced them. Unlike sugar, which was shipped to foreign markets, the primary market for Caribbean rum was the Caribbean, especially in the early years of rum making.

This is not the first study of Caribbean rum. In the 1970s, historian John McCusker wrote a meticulous study of Caribbean rum industries, which highlighted Caribbean rum's impact on North American trade just prior to the American Revolution.[3] It explored many nuances of rum making and estimated the value and volume of rum industries in the eighteenth century in order to gauge rum's economic impact on the balance of North American trade. Yet, it too emphasized the role of rum outside of the Caribbean. While this book explores the economic trends in Europe and North America that shaped the development of Caribbean rum industries, it also sheds new light on the economic impact of rum on the Caribbean estates that produced it. In short, the rise of rum making underscores the economic efficiency of Caribbean sugar planters, who turned the waste products of their sugar factories into a highly profitable alcoholic commodity.

Although the social history of alcohol has been investigated in a number of regional and cross-cultural settings, this is the first comprehensive study of alcohol in the Caribbean. In fact, researchers have explored the social history of alcohol in Europe, Africa, and South Asia—the Old World homelands of most Caribbean peoples. This rich body of alcohol studies literature outlines important alcohol-related themes, such as anxiety, accountability, power, identity, and vulnerability, which provide the foundation for the study of alcohol and drinking in the Caribbean. Alcohol studies research allows us to investigate how the drinking patterns of Europeans, Africans, and South Asians changed in the diverse social climate of the Caribbean, where alcohol was readily available and liberal attitudes toward drinking existed. Moreover, it allows us to investigate alcohol use among Carib Indians, a group whose drinking habits have never been addressed before. The theories and models developed in alcohol studies research also allow us to ask what Old World beliefs about the social, sacred, and medicinal meaning of alcohol survived and what were forgotten. Why did different social groups embrace different drinking habits? What was the impact of temperance reform on Caribbean peoples in the nineteenth century? And how have colonial and state governments shaped alcohol use in the region?

The answers to many of these questions lie in the economics of Caribbean rum. Access to rum played an important role in the opportunity to drink, and availability was often shaped by metropolitan decisions. What material and ideological factors led some governments in Europe to encourage rum making in their colonies and led others to restrict it? How did colonial assemblies, planters, and metropolitan officials contribute to the economic success of rum? At the beginning of the eighteenth century, few in the Atlantic world knew what rum was. Yet, at the beginning of the twenty-first century, rum is one of the world's most widely consumed spirits. How did rum evolve from a cottage industry in the small islands of the Lesser Antilles into a multibillion-dollar industry controlled by multinational corporations?

Various factors have hampered academic interest in alcohol in the Caribbean, especially rum's status as a secondary item of trade. Sugar has defined the Caribbean economy, while rum has generally been treated as a fortuitous by-product of sugar production. Perhaps, its secondary status has made it less appealing to Caribbean historians and anthropologists. In addition, rum catered to peripheral markets at the frontier margins of the Atlantic world. North and South America and Africa imported huge amounts of rum, while Europe, especially southern Europe, had relatively little exposure to rum until the nineteenth century. In addition, rum consumption was concentrated among poorer classes. Soldiers, seamen, Indians, poor whites, and slaves were the primary consumers of rum and, despite the efforts of West Indian lobbyists, it remained the drink of common folk well into the twentieth century. The study of rum, therefore, provides a special opportunity to address underappreciated aspects of the Atlantic economy, as well as explore the concerns of disenfranchised social groups who lived in the Caribbean.

Negative western attitudes toward drinking have also hindered scholarly interest in alcohol studies in the Caribbean. The emotional discourse emanating from nineteenth- and twentieth-century anti-alcohol campaigns deterred many scholars from pursuing the study of alcohol in society. Modern social fears continue to shape notions about alcohol studies. College binge drinking, drunk driving, alcoholism, and other problems associated with alcohol overshadow the more objective cultural and historical research. While the negative impact of alcohol on society is certainly an important facet of alcohol studies, decades of research have shown that drinking is more than simply a social ill or the basis for aberrant behavior. Alcohol has helped revolutionize world trade and shape the course of global politics. Drinking patterns distinguish social boundaries, reinforce group identities, and define the parameters of masculinity and femininity. Alcohol use enhances sociability, defines periods of leisure, and provides a temporary avenue of escape from various social pressures. The dual nature of alcohol also produces a complicated dichotomy whereby drunkenness is profane, yet alcohol has strong spiritual connotations. Overcoming the passionate rhetoric surrounding alcohol use has been a challenge for alcohol studies researchers.

The holistic type of inquiry that the study of alcohol in society demands has led to interdisciplinary research that often blurs the line between history and anthropology. The publication of several edited volumes on drink in a variety of cross-cultural and historical settings highlights the breadth of alcohol studies and the need for collaboration with colleagues in cultural, historical, psychological, economic, and health fields.[4] Alcohol studies have been strengthened by the exchange of ideas among members of the Alcohol Temperance History Group (ATHG), especially through its journal the *Social History of Alcohol Review*. The ATHG is an international group of scholars who represent a broad range of academic disciplines. Moreover, an increasing number of history and anthropology departments now offer alcohol-related courses, which suggests that alcohol studies research is becoming a more widely recognized subfield that will continue to grow in the future.

Rum was not simply an inevitable by-product of sugar production. In fact, many early sugar producers simply ignored the alcoholic potential of the waste products of their sugar factories. In the seventeenth century, however, growing knowledge about alcohol distillation, advances in distillation technology, and the increasing demand for alcohol in the Caribbean spurred the emergence of Caribbean rum.

CHAPTER 2

At the Margins of the Atlantic World

Caribbean Rum in the Seventeenth Century

THE COMMERCIAL PRODUCTION of rum began in the sugarcane-growing regions of the Americas in the seventeenth century and was fueled by colonists' desire for alcoholic beverages on the frontier margins of the Atlantic world. Separated from their customary alcoholic drinks, Europeans and Africans in the Caribbean searched for local alternatives and turned to rum at the start of the sugar revolution. Old World beliefs about the medicinal value of distilled spirits spurred local consumption. Rum also fed the traditional maritime demand for alcohol at a time when Caribbean colonization was increasing the frequency of long distance overseas trade. While the use of inferior ingredients and small stills limited the scale of rum production, early forays into rum making highlight the efficient economic strategies of Caribbean sugar planters and their attempts to capitalize on local and regional alcohol markets. Indeed, rum making became a profitable enterprise, and rum quickly found local and regional markets that helped nurture the growth of American trade. The inter-Caribbean rum trade created exchange networks that brought together disparate New World colonies, and the internal rum trade created links between diverse social groups. Continental merchants and traders in North and South America also began to accept Caribbean rum in exchange for much-needed provisions and plantation supplies. Yet, despite its growth, the early Caribbean rum trade remained at the margins of the Atlantic world and failed to fully penetrate the huge alcohol markets of Europe.

Replicating Old World Drinks

The Europeans and Africans who settled the Caribbean came from societies with strong traditions of alcohol use, and it was only natural that they would seek to secure alcohol once they arrived in the New World. Distance, shipping costs, and the demand for other necessary provisions made imported alcoholic beverages expensive and beyond the economic reach of most early colonists. These factors limited the availability of traditional drinks from the Old World and fueled the search for local substitutes.

Before the large-scale transition to sugar production in the 1640s, colonists in the Caribbean experimented with the alcoholic potential of various local plants. They even tapped the knowledge of Caribs, the indigenous Amerindians of the Lesser Antilles and the Orinoco Delta region of mainland South America, to meet their alcohol needs. For example, Richard Ligon, an English colonist who lived in Barbados between 1647 and 1650, wrote, "The first [drink], and that which is most used in the Island, is *Mobbie*, a drink made of Potatoes."[1] The term *mobbie* probably derives from the Carib word *mâ'bi*, meaning a red variety of sweet potato, or *mabi*, a generic term for an edible tuber.[2] In 1627, a Barbadian expeditionary voyage went up the Essequibo River, into what is today Guyana, and returned with sweet potatoes and 32 Caribs who knew how to produce a fermented alcoholic drink from them.[3] Colonists eventually became skilled at the art of making mobbie, and Ligon even described the ability to increase the concentration of alcohol with the addition of more sweet potatoes.[4] To make mobbie, colonists in Barbados boiled the potatoes until they were soft, mashed them into a pulp, and placed the pulp in a large earthenware vessel. They added water, molasses, and a bit of ginger to the mix, and placed the vessel in a warm spot to ferment. Fermentation usually took a day or two, after which the mobbie was drunk or placed in a cool cellar for storage, where it could remain fresh for up to five or six weeks.[5] In the French Caribbean, missionary Father Jean Baptiste Père Labat also described the production of *maby*. Labat noted that French colonists made mobbie by putting 20 to 30 pots of water into a large jar with two pots of clear molasses, a dozen red potatoes, and many oranges cut into quarters.[6] The use of mobbie appears to have been restricted to Carib centers of the Lesser Antilles.[7]

Cassava-based alcoholic drinks, made from the root of the manioc plant, were also common in the early Caribbean. In Martinique, for example, French missionary Father Jean Baptiste Du Tertre wrote, "the drink most ordinary is called *oüicou*.[8] Oüicou was a Carib word for an alcoholic beverage made from cassava.[9] In Barbados, cassava-based alcoholic drinks were called *parranow* or *perino*.[10] Ligon described perino as "wholsomer, though not altogether so pleasant" as mobbie.[11] As with mobbie, the consumption of cassava-based alcoholic drinks was concentrated in Carib centers in the Lesser Antilles.[12]

Carib women were responsible for making oüicou and perino. They grated the manioc root into a wooden canoe-shaped trough, added water, stirred it, and let it soak. It produced a thick, brown, gravy-like substance, which they strained through a coarse cloth called a *hibichet*. The juice that dripped from the hibichet, known as manioc water, was collected in a calabash, while the moist manioc flour was formed into round flat cakes. These cakes, called cassavas, were baked on a flat griddle. Carib women chewed the cassava cakes and then spit the masticated liquid into a large earthenware jar called a *canary*, where it was allowed to ferment.[13] In Barbados, at least, Carib women simply chewed the raw grated manioc root rather than going through the additional steps of straining the manioc flour and baking it into cassava cakes.[14]

Enzymes from the women's saliva helped convert the starches of the cassava and manioc root into simple sugars, which are of course the key ingredient in alcohol fermentation. The masticated concoction fermented in a canary for several days, and the Caribs may have heated the pulpy mash to accelerate the fermentation process. It produced an alcoholic beverage similar in strength to beer. In the French islands, other ingredients, such as potatoes, sugarcane juice, and bananas were sometimes added to the fermenting compound.[15]

The production of an alcoholic beverage from a masticated substance fascinated European colonists, who recorded details about its production. Ligon provided one of the most comprehensive accounts of perino production in early Barbados.

> [Perino] is made of the *Cassavy* root, which I told you is a strong poyson; and this they cause their old wives, who have a small remainder of teeth, to chaw and spit out into water, (for the better breaking and macerating of the root). This juyce in three or four hours will work, and purge it self of the poysonous quality.[16]

Manioc root is indeed poisonous. It contains linamarin, a hydrocyanic acid, which, when eaten raw, is converted to cyanide by the human digestive system. Early Caribbean colonists were aware of manioc's poisonous qualities, and they marveled at how a toxic plant could produce a potable alcoholic drink. Ligon struggled to explain what he called "these direct contraries."

XIIII. Capittel.

Wie sie ihre Getrencke machen daran sie sich truncken

trincken/vnd wie sie sich halten mit dem
truncken.

Als Weibßvolck machet die Gerräncke/sie nemen die Wurtzel Mandio-
ka/vnd sieden grosse Döppen voll/wen es gesotten ist/nemen sie es auß Tranck.
den Döppen/giessens in einander Döppen oder Gefeß/lassens ein we-
nig kalt werden/denn setzen sich die jungen Mägde darbey/vnd kewen es mit dem
Munde/vnd das gekewete thun sie in ein sonderlich Gefäß. Wenn die gesottenen
Wurtzeln alle gekewet seyn / thun sie das gekewete wider in das Döppen / vnnd
giessen es widerumb voll Wassers/ vermengens mit den gekeweten Wurtzeln/

L ij   vnd

Figure 2.1. *How the Tuppin Ikins make and drink their beverages.* Carib women of the
Orinoco Delta region of South America masticating cassava and producing *oüicou.* In
Hans Staden, *Americae tertia pars memorabilè provinciae Brasiliae historiam continès*
(Frankfurt, 1592). Courtesy of the John Carter Brown Library at Brown University.

the poyson of the old womens breath and teeth having been tainted with many several poxes, (a disease common amongst them, though they have many and the best cures for it,) are such opposites to the poyson of the *Cassavy*, as they bend their forces so vehemently one against another, as they both spend their poysonous qualities in that conflict.[17]

In reality, grating, soaking, and straining the manioc allowed the roots' natural enzymes to convert the linamarin into cyanide gas, which harmlessly escaped into the atmosphere. Saliva introduced additional enzymes that speeded up the conversion process.

Colonists fermented a variety of other local plants and fruits to make alcoholic drinks. Ligon described the production of a wine made from the pineapple, which he liked so much that he referred to it as "the Nectar which the Gods drunk."[18] In the French Caribbean, Labat also believed that pineapple wine had an "extremely agreeable" taste.[19] In addition, early Caribbean settlers produced alcoholic beverages from plantains, bananas, plums, oranges, limes, wild grapes, the fruit of the tamarind tree, and the apple of the mahogany.[20]

The colonists' desire for alcohol in the Caribbean led to experiments with a variety of available plant resources, and the new arrivals even exploited the Caribs' knowledge of alcohol production. Yet, despite the local production of these drinks, early colonial writers often compared them to European alcoholic beverages. For example, Ligon wrote that perino tasted "the likest to *English* beer," and he considered the taste of mobbie similar to Rhenish wine.[21] In 1661, Felix Spoeri, a Swiss medical doctor in Barbados, likened mobbie to European beer.[22] Father Du Tertre and Father Labat had similar opinions about oüicou.[23] These comparisons suggest that early colonials sought to recreate, as closely as possible, the alcoholic beverages they left behind in Europe.

The Emergence of Rum

Columbus carried sugarcane to the Caribbean on his second voyage in 1493, and a sugar processing plant was established on Hispaniola ten years later. Commercial sugar production was well under way in the island by 1520.[24] Small mills produced some molasses for local consumption, but it appears that Spanish colonials in Hispaniola had little interest in the by-products of sugar production. In 1535, Spanish colonial official Gonzalo de Oviedo y Valdes wrote, "The ships that come out from Spain return loaded with sugar of fine quality, and the skimmings and syrup that are wasted on this island or given away would make another great province rich."[25] Although sugarcane juice and the by-products of sugar making were readily available in the Spanish Caribbean in the sixteenth century, there is no clear evidence that colonists used these materials to distill rum. Nor were colonists in the sugarcane-growing regions of Brazil and New Spain [Mexico] distilling rum in the sixteenth century.[26] The absence of distilling in the sugarcane-growing regions of the New World in the sixteenth century is not surprising; the art of alcohol distillation in Europe was still relatively new.

Alcohol distillation was known in Europe as early as the 1200s. The first distillers were physicians and apothecaries, who distilled spirits for medicinal purposes. However, in the early sixteenth century, market forces began to reshape the meaning of alcohol. In France, in 1514, Louis XII permitted the vinegar manufacturers' guild to distill spirits and, in 1537, Francis I encouraged the same among French wholesale grocers.[27] By the mid-sixteenth century, French distillers organized themselves into a separate guild, and distilled wine (brandy) soon became a beverage of more general use.[28] Distilling expanded in the mid-sixteenth century as the publication of several books revealed the secrets of alcohol distillation to wider audiences.[29] Yet, despite the growing knowledge of alcohol distillation in sixteenth-century Europe, the high cost of base material for distilling and the inefficient technology made distilled spirits expensive and beyond the economic reach of most Europeans.[30] Moreover, the production of distilled spirits was still chiefly in the hands of physicians and apothecaries, and what little distilled spirits were available in Europe in this period were consumed for medicinal rather than recreational purposes. Commercial distilled spirits industries did not get under way in Europe until the early seventeenth century, and there is no evidence to suggest that they started in the Caribbean any earlier.

Although colonists in the sixteenth-century Caribbean did not distill rum, they did exploit the alcoholic potential of sugarcane. In the sugarcane-growing regions of the Caribbean, colonists used sugarcane juice and the by-products of sugar making to produce fermented alcoholic drinks.[31] The earliest evidence in the Americas for the use of sugarcane in the production of a fermented beverage is in Spanish Santo Domingo. In 1550, Spanish Dominican friar Bartolomé de Las Casas, describing the period 1511–1520, wrote of the African slaves

> For it is a fact that the Negroes, like oranges, found this land more natural to them than their native Guinea; but once they were sent to the mills they died like flies from the hard labor they were made to endure and the beverages they drink made from the sugarcane.[32]

11

Las Casas does not give a name to the drink implying that no name had yet been devised for an alcohol made from sugarcane juice. That is, despite the variety of names used to signify fermented and distilled grapes in Europe in the sixteenth century, there was no name for an alcoholic beverage made from sugarcane juice. The absence of a name suggests that the drink was new and uncommon.[33] However, in 1596, Dr. Layfield, a chaplain on an English privateering voyage, landed in Puerto Rico and reported that the Spanish colonists of the island drank a fermented drink called *Guacapo* made of molasses and spices.[34]

Guacapo, or more commonly *guarapo* in the Spanish colonies, was the first specific name for an alcoholic beverage made from sugarcane juice in the New World, and it was a fermented drink produced on a small scale for local consumption.[35] Regional variations of the name sprang up throughout the Americas. In Brazil, fermented sugarcane drinks were called *garapa*, and in the French Caribbean they were called *grappe*.[36] In Barbados, Ligon referred to a drink called *grippo*, which seems to be analogous to guarapo, garapa, and grappe. Although Ligon was familiar with a variety of alcoholic beverages, he never tried grippo and could not, therefore, describe its production, ingredients, or taste. However, in Ligon's list of alcoholic beverages available in Barbados, grippo was immediately followed by a drink called "punch . . . made of water and sugar put together, which in ten dayes standing will be very strong." It seems likely that Ligon confused punch, a drink usually consisting of distilled spirits and spices, with a fermented sugarcane-based alcoholic drink called grippo.[37]

The production of fermented sugarcane-based alcoholic drinks complicates discussions about the origins of Caribbean rum making. These were fermented alcoholic drinks that should not be confused with distilled rum. In some respects, they were prototypes of rum. Fermentation was the first step in rum making and, thus, the production of fermented sugarcane-based alcoholic beverages may have helped pre-adapt colonists to rum distillation when sugar making expanded in the Caribbean in the mid-seventeenth century.

African slaves may have played a key role in the manufacture of these fermented rum prototypes. In Santo Domingo, Las Casas' mid-sixteenth century reference to fermented sugarcane-based concoctions hinted that Africans were the primary consumers and, perhaps, producers of these beverages. African slaves, like Europeans, sought to reestablish traditional patterns of alcohol use in the Caribbean. For instance, Charles de Rochefort, a Protestant minister who traveled throughout the French Caribbean, reported that African slaves in the French Caribbean tapped palm trees in order to produce a type of palm wine, one of the most widely consumed alcoholic drinks in West and West Central Africa.[38] African slaves apparently had easy access to sugar industry waste since early sugar planters had little interest in it. In Martinique, at least, some planters allowed their slaves to collect the unwanted skimmings that spilled over the cauldrons during the sugar boiling process, which the slaves used to make "intoxicating drinks."[39] Although Europeans recognized the alcoholic potential of sugarcane, Africans also came from societies that produced a wide variety of fermented alcoholic drinks, and they, rather than the Europeans, may have conducted some of the initial experiments with fermented varieties of sugarcane juice in the Caribbean.

Historians have speculated about the origins of New World rum making and often assume that it emerged immediately alongside sugar production. Much of the confusion surrounding the origin of New World rum making stems from the gradual evolution of rum prototypes and the almost parallel ascent of rum distilling in the different sugarcane-growing regions of the Americas in the first half of the seventeenth century. Despite this confusion, evidence indicates that the British island of Barbados and the French island of Martinique were the cradles, if not the birthplaces, of Caribbean rum. The expansion of sugarcane agriculture in the Lesser Antilles and the increasing knowledge of alcohol distillation in the seventeenth century led to the rise of rum making in these two islands.

The British settled Barbados in 1627 and the French settled Martinique eight years later. Early colonists grew a variety of cash crops, including cotton, indigo, and tobacco. Yet, despite these efforts, economic development in these two islands languished. The stagnation ended in the 1640s when Barbadian and Martinican colonists embraced sugar making. The Dutch, who had ousted the Portuguese from the sugarcane-growing regions of northern Brazil in the 1630s, spurred the rise of sugarcane agriculture in Barbados and Martinique. In Barbados, Ligon wrote

> At the time we landed on this Island, which was in the beginning of *September*, 1647, we were informed, partly by those Planters we found there, and partly by our own observations, that the great work of Sugar-making, was but newly practised by the inhabitants there. Some of the most industrious men, having gotten Plants from *Fernambock* [Pernambuco], a place in *Brasil*, and made tryal of them at the *Barbadoes*.[40]

James Holdip and James Drax are often cited as the planters who brought sugarcane and the knowledge of how to produce sugar to Barbados from the Dutch controlled region of Pernambuco in the early 1640s.[41]

The Portuguese recapture of Pernambuco in the 1640s and '50s severed the Dutch West India Company's direct access to New World sugar. In order to survive, the company capitalized on the shipping needs of British sugar planters in Barbados and French sugar planters in Martinique. This foreign trade strategy benefited Caribbean sugar planters who, without the Dutch, relied on limited and unreliable national traders and merchants. The Dutch middleman strategy was successful.

Dutch migrants from Pernambuco, with support from the Dutch West India Company, also reestablished sugar plantations in the struggling islands of the Lesser Antilles and helped expand sugar production in the British and French settlements. Du Tertre, who lived in Martinique in the 1640s, believed that the development of Martinique's sugar industry was due to the arrival of Dutch refugees from Pernambuco who took up residence in the island.[42] Sugar making expanded in 1654, when the Portuguese finally recaptured Pernambuco, and a Dutch ship carrying Jews and citizens from the Netherlands was forced to stop at Martinique. The new migrants brought with them capital, the knowledge of how to properly make sugar as in Brazil, the utensils for sugar manufacturing, and African slaves.[43]

The Dutch refugees may have also introduced rum distilling into Barbados and Martinique. In the early seventeenth century, the Dutch were leaders in alcohol distillation in Europe, and they may have brought that skill to the Caribbean from the Netherlands.[44] Alternatively, the Dutch, who controlled the sugarcane-growing regions of northern Brazil in the 1630s and '40s, may have learned and perfected the particular art of distilling sugarcane juice and sugar-making by-products and disseminated this knowledge to the British and French colonists in Barbados and Martinique.

Distilling immediately became a central element of the French Caribbean sugar industry. In 1644, Benjamin Da Costa, a Dutch Jew from Brazil, introduced sugar making equipment and, perhaps, the first alembics, into Martinique.[45] Yet, a manuscript from Martinique dated 1640, when the colony was only five years old, stated, "the slaves are fond of a strong *eau de vie* that they call *brusle ventre* [stomach burner]."[46] Although brusle ventre sometimes referred to French brandy, the comparative use of the term hints at a locally made concoction other than imported brandy. In the context of the Caribbean, brusle ventre was likely a distilled sugarcane-based alcoholic beverage and suggests that rum distilling preceded Da Costa's arrival in 1644.[47]

Du Tertre provided an early account of rum making in Martinique in the 1640s. According to Du Tertre,

The spent and exhausted canes and also the skimmings [from the boiling process] are not unusable, because the skimmings of the second and third cauldrons, and everything that spills over in the stirring on to the cauldron platform run into a cistern where it is kept to make eau de vie.[48]

Du Tertre's illustration of a sugar factory in Martinique included a *vinaigrerie* [alembic], which indicates that distilleries were an integral part of the first French Caribbean sugar estates.[49] Rochefort also noted that, by the 1650s, the scum by-products from sugar making were distilled to make *eau de vie de cannes*.[50]

Early British Caribbean sugar planters also pursued the art of rum making. In 1631, only four years after British settlement of Barbados, traveler Henry Colt referred to Barbadians as "devourers upp of hott waters and such good distillers therof."[51] This is an intriguing statement since there was little, if any, sugarcane growing in Barbados in 1631. The Barbadian expeditionary voyage that traveled up the Essequibo River in 1627 searched for plants that could be brought back and commercially grown in Barbados. Sugarcane was among those plants. According to Dalby Thomas, a lobbyist for British Caribbean planters, Barbadian colonists "knew no other use of [sugarcane] than to make refreshing Drink for that hot Climate."[52] In the Caribbean, the term "refreshing drink" typically referred to a fermented variety of sugarcane juice. Distilled beverages, as Colt illustrated, were characterized as "hot" rather than "refreshing." It is possible that one of the early settlers possessed an alembic and distilled the "refreshing drink" into a concentrated spirit.[53] However, if Barbadian settlers were distilling sugarcane juice in the 1630s, the level of production would have been small, especially as planters had to import new sugarcane plants from South America when full-scale sugar production began in the 1640s.

Ligon made the first clear reference to rum distillation in the British Caribbean. In 1647, Ligon, along with his friend Colonel Thomas Modiford, who later became governor of Jamaica, traveled to Barbados fleeing civil war in England and seeking fortune in the developing Atlantic trade. Soon after their arrival, Modiford purchased half of Major William Hilliard's sugar plantation, which, at that time, already possessed a still house. Ligon also referred to a drink made from "the skimming of sugar, which is infinitely strong, but not very pleasant in taste."[54] By 1650, rum making in Barbados was well under way, and it was common for large sugar plantations to have still houses.

For decades, distilled drinks made from sugarcane juice and the waste by-

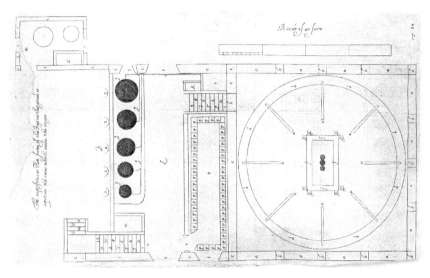

Figure 2.2. Plan view of a sugar factory and still house in Barbados in the mid-seventeenth century. In Richard Ligon, *A True and Exact History of the Island of Barbadoes* (London, 1673). Courtesy of the John Carter Brown Library at Brown University.

products of sugar production lacked a standard name. Ligon, for example, never referred to the drink as rum and, instead, called it "Kill-Devil." In the French Caribbean, Rochefort generically called distilled sugarcane-based drinks *eau de vie de cannes*. The modifier "de cannes" distinguished it from French brandy (eau de vie) made from grapes. The lack of a common name for a sugarcane-based alcoholic beverage in the seventeenth century underscores its novelty. The earliest document to specifically use the term *rum* is a plantation deed recorded in Barbados in 1650, which identified Three Houses estate in St. Philip parish as having "four large mastick cisterns for liquor for Rum."[55] The name *rum* originated in the British Caribbean in the seventeenth century and derived from the English word *rumbullion*. In 1651, Giles Silvester, an early resident in Barbados and the brother of Anglo-Dutch sugar planter Constant Silvester, one of the wealthiest and most politically powerful sugar planters in Barbados, made the only known reference linking rum and rumbullion. Silvester wrote, "the chiefe fudling they make in the Iland is Rumbullion, als Kill Divill, and this is made of Suggar cones distilled a hott hellish and terrible liquor."[56] *Rumbullion* was a word commonly used in Devonshire, England, to mean "a great tumult," and it was probably meant to convey the volatile effects of excessive rum consumption on early colonists. Its origin reflects the large number of West Country English who settled Barbados in the early seventeenth century.[57] By the early 1650s, *rumbullion* was shortened to *rum*. Planters in the French and Spanish Caribbean adopted *rum* as the term for a distilled sugarcane-based alcohol, translating it to *rhum* and *ron* respectively.

The Art of Early Rum Making

In the mid-seventeenth century, rum distillation was present on many Caribbean sugar plantations, especially in the British and French colonies. Ligon provided the earliest detailed account of rum making in Barbados, from 1647 to 1650, at the very beginning of Barbados' sugar revolution. According to Ligon, a good sugar factory was expected to have a "Still-house with two sufficient Stills, and receivers to hold the drink."[58] Ligon's description reveals that, at this early stage of the British Caribbean sugar industry, a still house was already considered an essential part of the sugar plantation complex. Although Ligon painted an ideal picture of sugar plantation efficiency, his companion, Thomas Modiford, did, in reality, purchase a plantation that already possessed buildings and equipment devoted to rum distillation.

In describing the art of rum making on early sugar estates in Barbados, Ligon explains,

> As for distilling the skimmings, which run down to the Still-house, from the three lesser Coppers, it is only this: After it has remained in the Cisterns, which my plot shews you in the Still-house, till it be a little soure, (for till then, the Spirits will not rise in the Still) the first Spirit that comes off, is a small Liquor, which we call Low-wines, which Liquor we put into the Still, and draw it off again; and of that comes so strong a Spirit, as a candle being brought to a near distance, to the bung of a Hogshead or But, where it is kept, the Spirits will flie to it.[59]

Ligon clearly emphasized the use of skimmings, the frothy scum that bubbled up during the sugar boiling process, while molasses, which is generally considered the most important ingredient in rum making because of its higher sucrose content, was, as Ligon stated in an earlier section of his book, reboiled to make lower-grade *peneles* sugar. In the French Caribbean, Rochefort reported that the skimmings from the first boiler are only good for feeding livestock, but that the sucrose-rich skimmings from the others could be used to make a drink for servants and slaves.[60] Du Tertre's discussion of rum making in Martinique also emphasized "the spent and exhausted canes and also the skimmings." According to Du Tertre, "molasses is enough good merchandise where it is used to make gingerbread in Europe."[61] In a later section of his work, however, Du Tertre incidentally mentions the use of molasses to make rum.[62] It appears that molasses was not widely used in rum distillation in the mid-seventeenth century and that sugar planters either sold it separately or continuously returned it to the cauldrons where it was reboiled to make low grades of sugar. However, by the late seventeenth century, Labat, as well as physician and Caribbean traveler Hans Sloane, both recorded the regular use of molasses in rum making.[63]

Besides relying on lesser ingredients, seventeenth-century Caribbean sugar planters employed small stills that restricted the level of output. Although Ligon did not mention the exact capacity of the stills illustrated in the still house, his plan showed that one still was slightly more than four feet in diameter and the second, probably used for the redistillation of *low wine*, was slightly less than four feet in diameter. Both stills fit into a still-house room no larger than 16 feet long, 10 feet wide, and 20 feet high. The capacity of the two stills probably reflected contemporary trends in Europe and held less than 100 gallons each.[64] The stills were probably made of copper. Copper was an important material in the Caribbean sugar industry and used for a variety of sugar-making utensils, including the series of deep cauldrons, or *coppers*, used to boil the sugarcane juice. In the seventeenth century, the Dutch imported raw copper ore from Sweden and developed a thriving copper industry in Holland. The ready availability of copper in Barbados, as well as other parts of the Caribbean, attests to the strength of Dutch merchants and traders in the seventeenth century.

The small still-house room also contained a fermenting cistern, or vat, where the rum-making ingredients were mixed. The fermenting cistern was seven feet by three feet and would have held several hundred gallons of fermenting *wash*. A century later, Barbados sugar planter William Belgrove recommended that a still house have 48 vats that could hold 300 gallons each.[65] The single fermenting cistern in Ligon's illustration reflects the small scale of early Barbadian distilling. Fermenting cisterns were usually made of coral stone blocks coated with a lime-based plaster. However, in the early years of Barbadian settlement, before the almost complete destruction of forests, wood was available and, in 1650, the four cisterns at Three Houses estate were made of mastic.[66] In the late eighteenth century, if not earlier, tall cone-shaped vats made of imported oak and pine replaced low square coral stone cisterns.

In the French Caribbean, Du Tertre and Rochefort made the earliest refer-

Maulin. 2. Fourneaux 3.Formes. 4.Vinaigrerie. 5.Cannee SVCRERIE 6 Gros 7.Latanir. 8 Pafomirioba 9.Choux 10.Cafe 11 Figuir . 131. et Chaudieres. de Juere Cocos . 11e r. 111. r. 32. Caraibes. de Negros .

Figure 2.3. An alembic in Martinique in the 1640s. In Jean Baptiste Du Tertre, *Histoire generale des Antilles* (Paris, 1667–1671). Courtesy of the John Carter Brown Library at Brown University.

ences to distilling apparatuses, which they called *vinaigreries*. The origin of the term appears to stem from Louis XII's 1514 decree, which gave *vinaigriers* [vinegar makers] the right to distill wine into brandy. *Vinaigrerie* derived from this guild's name and was probably the name given to the alembics in which they distilled their wine. The use of the term *vinaigrerie* to describe an alembic used for rum making demonstrates how French Caribbean rum makers adapted Old World mental models to help explain New World industries. However, in the eighteenth century, *guildiverie* replaced *vinaigrerie* as the term used for a French Caribbean alembic. *Guildiverie* is a corruption of the British Caribbean term *kill devil* and reflects the French Creoles' growing affinity for Caribbean, rather than metropolitan, culture.

Du Tertre provided the earliest drawing of an alembic in the French Caribbean. His mid-seventeenth-century illustration of a vinaigrerie in Martinique showed a small and simple alembic connected to a *worm* that ran through a wooden barrel of cool water to a *receiver*.[67] The alembic that Du Tertre sketched is very similar to some of those depicted in mid-sixteenth-century books on distilling.[68] Ligon's depiction of the still house contained two stills rather than the single distilling apparatus found in Du Tertre's illustration. While Ligon provided little information about the types and sizes of stills used in Barbados in the 1640s, the second still was probably used for the separate distillation of low wine, the spirit produced from the first distillation. The presence of a second still suggests a more advanced system of distilling and highlights the Barbadians' greater fascination with rum making.

Early alcohol distillation was a conservative art, and the level of distillation technology in the seventeenth-century Caribbean was probably comparable to that of distilleries in contemporary Europe. Other than the increasing capacity of stills, most major advances in distillation technology had been made by the 1550s. As early as the mid-fourteenth century, distillers in Europe used multiple distillations to improve their product. By the mid-sixteenth century, the important technological advances involving cooling and condensing systems, which provided better control over the separation of alcohol during distillation and speeded the distilling process, had also been introduced. In fact, distilling technology remained relatively unchanged between the mid-sixteenth and early nineteenth centuries.[69]

Despite the use of small stills and the heavy reliance on inferior ingredients, rum making in Barbados was not simply a cottage industry. Ligon's account of Barbados rum making suggests that it was already a specialized enterprise that employed skilled distillers who were learning to master the art of rum making. According to Ligon, Barbadian distillers had already established an important quality-defining characteristic of rum: the double distilling that produced a highly volatile and concentrated spirit. Even so, at the time of Ligon's account, the art of alcohol distillation was still relatively new, and its secrets had only recently been seized from the physicians and apothecaries of Europe. Yet, in the 1640s, Barbadian sugar planters constructed buildings and cisterns for the specific purpose of alcohol production, and Barbadian distillers double distilled their rum and made distinctions about its quality. This seemingly advanced level of rum production may have led Ligon to praise the business practices of Barbadian sugar planters and marvel at the output and profitability of rum making in Barbados.

The Volume and Value of Rum in the Seventeenth Century

The paucity of seventeenth-century plantation records and trade statistics makes it difficult to determine precise levels of rum production or rum's contribution to sugar estate revenues in this early period. However, the available evidence provides us with enough information to make some generalizations about the volume of rum production and the value of rum to sugar estates. Copies of two customs books from Barbados covering the period between August 1664 and April 1667 provide crucial information about the early Barbadian rum trade. Historian Gary Puckrein used them to show the volume and value of Barbados rum exports from August of 1664 to August of 1665.[70] Economic historian David Eltis used these records, as well as naval office shipping lists, to show the volume and value of rum exports from Barbados for three later periods of the seventeenth century.[71] While not a complete picture, these records furnish eight years of seventeenth-century export statistics. Table 2.1 shows that Barbadian rum exports increased dramatically from the mid- to the late seventeenth century, no doubt reflecting the growing importance of the rum trade.[72]

Ligon provided additional information about the volume and value of the early Barbados rum industry. Ligon calculated that rum contributed about 18 percent of sugar estate revenues showing that, by the late 1640s, the production of alcohol from sugarcane was already a lucrative enterprise.[73] According to Ligon, rum in Barbados sold for 2s. 6d. per gallon, while unrefined muscavado sugar sold for 3d. per pound. At this rate, a gallon of rum was equal in value to 10 pounds of muscavado sugar. Ligon clearly believed rum was cheap and sold "at easie rates."[74] Yet, he also wrote that Barbadian officials were "purposing to raise the price to a deerer rate." Price evidence from the Barbados customs books shows that 15 years later, a pound of muscavado was worth one-third less at about 2d., and a gallon of rum was equal in value to 12 pounds of muscavado.[75] Thus, the 1664–1667 figures suggest the price of rum fell to 2s. 1d. per gallon in that 15-year period. The 33 percent drop in muscavado sugar

Table 2.1. Volume and Value of Rum Exported from Barbados in Gallons

Year	Gallons	Value of total exports
1664–1665	102,744	4%
1665–1666	150,020	6%
1688, 1690–1691	382,242	24%
1699–1701	596,291	19%

Sources: For the period 1664–1665, see Puckrein, *Little England*, 60. For the periods 1665–1666, 1688, 1690–1691, 1699–1701, see Eltis, "New Estimates," 631–48.

prices and the 14 percent drop in rum prices was due to the increasing avail-ability of these products and Britain's imposition of mercantilist policies that restricted the colonists' commercial freedom.[76]

Scattered throughout Ligon's text are also clues to the amount of rum made on Barbadian sugar estates. According to Ligon, a 500-acre sugar plantation with two stills could make £30 from rum on a weekly basis.[77] Ligon also wrote that the "Drink that is made of the skimmings" brought in £120 per month or £1,920 during the 16-month crop cycle.[78] Using his estimate of a half a crown per gallon, Ligon's model plantation produced 15,360 gallons of rum during the 16-month crop cycle. At this rate, his plantation produced 2.6 gallons of rum per 100 pounds of muscavado sugar. Ligon also made calculations on a 20-month production cycle in order to show the economic benefit of produc-ing semirefined white sugar, which sold at twice the rate of muscavado. Under this more profitable system, the quantity of sugar decreased as more molasses drained away, and the proportional increase in rum, as well as the four addi-tional months of rum production, resulted in a ratio of 4.3 gallons of rum per 100 pounds of sugar. The molasses was reboiled to make low-grade peneles sugar. Had it been used to make rum, the ratio would have been even higher.

French Caribbean sugar planters also profited from rum, more commonly known as *tafia* and *guildive*. In the late seventeenth century, Labat considered a vinaigrerie an essential part of a Martinican sugar factory, and a sugar planta-tion was expected to have one slave as a distiller.[79] Labat estimated that a large sugar plantation of 750 acres would produce 238,000 pounds of sugar and 60 barrels of rum, about 4,042 gallons, in a 45-week crop cycle.[80] According to Labat, 10 percent of the rum was allocated to the plantation's 120 slaves to supplement their diet and reduce plantation costs.[81] The remaining 54 barrels were sold bringing 3,000 francs.[82] A gallon of rum was equal in value to 10 pounds of muscavado sugar, or 3 pounds of semirefined white sugar. Rum con-tributed about 7 percent of sugar plantation revenues, and the estate produced a ratio of about 1.7 gallons per each 100 pounds of sugar, mostly semirefined white sugar.[83] A comparison of Labat and Ligon suggests that Martinican sugar planters produced less rum and sugar per acre than sugar planters in Barbados, and the ratio of rum to semirefined white sugar was one-third of that Ligon identified in Barbados a half century earlier.

In the seventeenth century, rum making was largely confined to big sugar estates. In 1668, the Barbados Assembly passed an act that no one within the island was permitted to keep stills for distilling of rum "Except such Person or

Persons [who] have Land and Canes of their own, or such as keep Refining Houses."[84] Yet, despite the 1668 restrictions on rum making, smallholder-distilling operations probably existed in Barbados as they did in other parts of the British Caribbean. For example, in 1714, a visitor to Antigua wrote "the poorest sort . . . seldom make anything but rum, and ye trash and ye Cane after grinding serves for fewel under ye still."[85] In Montserrat, 17 rum works were in operation from 1678 to 1679. According to historical anthropologist Riva Berleant-Schiller, although the Montserrat Assembly encouraged the development of large sugar estates, wageworkers in the island managed to produce and sell rum.[86] Eltis's study of the 1664–1667 Barbados customs books shows that while 87 percent of all produce handled by the customhouse belonged to only the top wealthiest 20 percent of those entering produce, the remaining four-fifths "managed to supply some rum."[87] For the bottom 20 percent, however, rum was not economically significant, suggesting that it was probably acquired through the barter of rum for labor. Many of the remaining three-fifths may have entered rum acquired as payment for their services, especially the more expensive services of merchants, lawyers, and skilled craftsmen. Perhaps small-holders with modest distilling operations also entered some of this rum.

In the seventeenth century, most of the rum produced never left the islands. From 1665 to 1666, Barbados legally exported an annual average of 150,020 gallons of rum.[88] Ligon's plantation alone produced more than 7 percent of that amount. Ligon identified as many as 285 plantations on his map of the island covering the period 1647–1650. However, according to Barbadian historian Peter Campbell, the Ligon map was reproduced from an earlier map made in 1638 and, therefore, left off the names of many large sugar planters who arrived in the 1640s.[89] Richard Ford's map of Barbados provides a more accurate picture of the number of plantations for the 1665–1666 period. Published in 1674, Ford's map identified 844 plantations. About 350 were sugar plantations, but few of these were as big as 500 acres. According to historian Richard S. Dunn, a Barbadian sugar plantation "of 200 acres, equipped with two or three sugar mills and a hundred slaves, was considered the optimum size for efficient production."[90] Dunn also showed that 175 of the island's biggest planters owned an average of 267 acres each. If these big planters achieved the same per-acre level of rum making described by Ligon, then they alone could have produced more than one million gallons of rum per year. Thus, in the mid-seventeenth century, Barbados probably exported only 10 to 15 percent of its rum, and local consumption was enormous.

Rum Consumption and the Motivation to Drink in the
Seventeenth-Century Caribbean

A close reading of Ligon and Labat hints at the level of local rum consumption. According to Ligon, a plantation of 500 acres produced about 11,500 gallons of rum per year "besides what is drunk by their servants and slaves."[91] According to Labat, 10 percent of the rum made on his model Martinique sugar plantation was drunk by servants and slaves, which averaged out to an annual per capita consumption rate of about 3.4 gallons. Adding 10 percent to Ligon's rum production estimate and allocating that to the 130 servants and slaves he identified as the average for a 500-acre estate results in an annual per capita consumption rate of 8.9 gallons, not unusually high when we consider the greater number of white indentured servants in Barbados and their propensity to drink.

The tropical climate and new epidemiological environment of the Caribbean heightened European colonists' concerns about health. In order to alleviate their worries, they embraced long-standing traditions about the medicinal value of distilled spirits, which fostered a routine of heavy drinking. For example, fear of tainted, or potentially tainted, water was especially great in Barbados, which lacked sufficient mountain streams.[92] In the early settlement period, Colt complained, "Your water is thick and not of ye best . . . your rivers few or noone, except such as you account out of vaine glory rivers, beinge noe other then little pitts."[93] Ligon also noted "There is nothing in this Island so much wanting, as Springs and Rivers of water."[94] The capital of Bridgetown was particularly ill situated and the dangers associated with the consumption of tainted water were evident during a yellow fever epidemic that occurred in 1647. According to Ligon, the bodies of those who succumbed to the illness were thrown into the town's swamp "which infected so the water, as divers that drunk of it were absolutely poysoned, and dyed in a few hours after; but others, taking warning by their harms, forbear to taste any more of it."[95] Ponds were constructed on some plantations to water slaves and livestock,[96] and the people of Bridgetown relied on cisterns set on the sides of their houses for fresh water supplies. But while cisterns were sufficient for small families and individuals, they could not always adequately meet the water needs of a large population, especially after the rise of sugar production and the subsequent increase in numbers of African slaves and European migrants.

Even when water was available, it was not necessarily preferred. Negative European attitudes toward water, probably founded upon similar Old World concerns about tainted water, enhanced the desirability of alcoholic beverages in the Caribbean. Labat may have said it best when he wrote "only invalids and chickens drink water," when wine is available.[97] Such sentiments increased the demand for rum. Not every colonist, however, held negative views of water, and many considered the use of fiery spirits like rum in the hot climate of the Caribbean a dangerous combination. Colt believed that the tropical heat stirred animalistic impulses, which frequently led to fights and quarrels among the colonists. He warned, "Your younge and hott bloods, should nott have oyle [alcohol] added to encrease ye flame, but rather cold water to quench it."[98]

Early colonists also saw distilled spirits as a counter to chills, which made it a powerful antidote against damp weather. Drinking a shot of concentrated alcohol produces a warm feeling in the throat and stomach. Although alcohol actually dilates surface blood vessels and cools the skin, Europeans perceived it to be a hot fluid. The heat Europeans attributed to alcohol, especially distilled spirits, reveals their belief in Galenic principles of medicine, which operated on the premise that good health could be achieved and maintained by balancing the hot/cold and wet/dry dispositions of the body. Galenic principles governed medical treatment in Europe and spurred many colonists to use alcohol to prevent colds and chills. These beliefs, no doubt, encouraged Caribbean sugar planters to drink heavily and allocate rum to slaves and servants who worked in chilly and wet weather. Ligon wrote,

> for when [slaves] are ill, with taking cold, (which often they are) and very well they may, having nothing under them in the night but a board, upon which they lie, nor any thing to cover them: And though the daies be hot, the nights are cold, and that change cannot but work upon their bodies, though they be hardy people. Besides, coming home hot and sweating in the evening, sitting or lying down, must needs be the occasion of taking cold, and sometimes breeds sicknesses amongst them, which when they feel, they complain to the Apothecary of the Plantation, which we call *Doctor*, and he gives to every one a dram cup of this Spirit [rum], and that is a present cure.[99]

Ligon clearly expressed the widely held belief that illness was caused by an insufficiency of body heat. Thus, on cold damp days, after hours of sweating in the sun, the consumption of rum, a hot and fiery fluid, was considered an appropriate, as well as enjoyable, way to reintroduce heat back into the body.[100]

Rum was not only considered good for restoring body heat, but as a fiery fluid, rum was also believed to counter excessive internal body heat. Yellow fever epidemics spread through the early Caribbean and were generally characterized by high fevers. The Caribbean medical community embraced folk beliefs about the use of "fire to drive out fire" and employed rum for that purpose. Historian David Geggus shows that British troops in the Caribbean generally thought that a sober hour might give disease an opportunity to attack.[101] The demand for rum in the Caribbean, therefore, partly reflects the application of folk beliefs about the power of alcohol to regulate body temperature.

The high caloric value of alcohol may have also increased the demand for rum. An ounce and a half of 100-proof rum would have provided the consumer with 147 calories.[102] In order to cut plantation costs, some Caribbean planters supplemented their slaves' diets with rum.[103] However, while alcohol provided high numbers of calories, these were generally hollow calories, which lacked nutritional value and did not contribute to a healthy diet.

In one of the more unique explanations for excessive whiskey drinking in colonial North America, historian W. J. Rorabaugh argues that the diet of North Americans increased the desire for highly concentrated distilled spirits. According to Rorabaugh, a monotonous diet of "Heavy, oily foods, especially fried corn cakes and salt pork, left Americans in need of a complementary beverage, and the commonest turned out to be whiskey."[104] A similar argument can be made for the seventeenth century Caribbean, where a monotonous diet of heavily starched foods, such as potatoes, cassava, and maize was common. Meats consisted primarily of salted pork and salted fish.[105] As in North America, diet probably increased the demand for drinks with high alcohol content. In the Caribbean, rum was the most readily available.

The local demand for alcohol fueled the rise of an intra-island rum trade. In 1650, many small planters in Barbados continued to pursue nonsugar markets. Ligon pointed out that there were many small plantations,

> which are not able to raise a Sugar-work or set up an Ingenio, by reason of the paucity of acres, being not above twenty, thirty, or forty acres in a Plantation; but these will be fit to bear Tobacco, Ginger, Cotten-wool, Maies, Yeames, and Potatoes, as also for breeding Hoggs.[106]

These small planters relied on sugar planters for their rum. Ligon wrote that rum was sold "to such Planters, as have no Sugar-works of their own, yet drink excessively of it."[107] The high cost of distilling equipment and legal restrictions against smallholder distilling operations would have made it necessary for the vast majority of Barbadian colonists to get their rum from the large sugar estates with still houses. Big planters would have had great control over the flow of rum in the Caribbean, which they either sold directly to the community or doled out to slaves and servants on estates. These big planters also controlled the flow of rum in the Atlantic.

Rum in the Emerging Atlantic World

While local demand sparked the initial forays into rum making, the growing alcohol markets of the Atlantic world led to an expansion of Caribbean rum industries. In the same way that the grape wine trade gave rise to large-scale commercial networks between northern and southern Europe, rum helped fuel the growth of an Atlantic economy. The rum trade began at the most fundamental level—with the need to provision seamen—and quickly spread to new alcohol markets on the periphery of the Atlantic world. Although the markets for rum were largely restricted to the coastal margins of the Old and New Worlds, the rum trade helped nurture the growth of a more unified Atlantic economy. By the end of the seventeenth century, merchants and traders throughout parts of Africa, Europe, and North and South America began to accept Caribbean rum in exchange for much-needed plantation labor, provisions, and supplies.

In early modern Europe, alcohol was deeply ingrained in maritime communities, and seamen considered it a necessary provision on trading ventures. The potential disasters that could result from the limited availability of fresh water on long sea voyages made alcohol a critical store in long distance maritime trade. Moreover, many seamen considered alcoholic beverages healthy and nutritious. Christopher Columbus, for example, carried huge wine stores on his first voyage to the Americas—enough wine, in fact, that he was able to leave the crew of the grounded *Santa Maria* a year's supply. Dutch physician Franciscus Sylvius invented gin to combat maladies afflicting seamen of the Dutch East India Company.[108] In the seventeenth century, alcohol became a basic ration in the British Royal Navy: a tradition that would last for 300 hundred years.

Maritime traditions and beliefs about its salubrious qualities increased the demand for alcohol during the long voyages to and from the Americas. While wine, brandy, and gin filled the hulls of ships departing Europe, Caribbean sugar planters exploited the maritime demand for alcohol on the other side of the Atlantic and sold rum to traders for the return voyage. As early as the mid-seventeenth century, planters in Barbados sold rum to "Ships [where it was] . . . drunk by the way."[109] These seamen helped spread the taste for rum to other regions of the Atlantic.

In the seventeenth century, continental North America was a primary destination for Caribbean rum, especially from the British colonies. Merchants in
New England's seaport taverns, yeoman farmers, fisherfolk, Chesapeake planters, African slaves, Native Americans, and frontier fur traders all consumed
their share of imported Caribbean rum. The colder climate of North America
was conducive to beverages with high alcohol content and North American
colonists, as with their Caribbean counterparts, encountered tainted water,
disease, and a monotonous diet. These and other factors sparked the demand
for rum and the rise of the Caribbean-continental rum trade. Caribbean sugar
planters were eager to capitalize on this demand, and they refined methods for
turning the waste products of their sugar mills into a profitable alcoholic commodity.

As with early colonists in the Caribbean, colonists in seventeenth-century
North America experimented with locally made alcoholic drinks. Dandelion
wine and apple cider were common folk drinks in North America, and archaeologists have recovered evidence of beer-brewing operations at a number of
seventeenth-century British and French colonial sites.[110] Royal decrees and
parliamentary incentives encouraged British continental colonists in some regions to pursue grape wine making from local and imported vines.[111] Continental colonists also experimented with distilled spirits; archaeologists have
recovered distilling equipment from seventeenth-century settlements in North
America, including Jamestown, Virginia, the site of the first permanent English
settlement in North America.[112] The growing availability of imported rum,
however, reduced the continental colonists' need for the locally produced
alcohol.

In the seventeenth century, Barbados emerged as the leading supplier of
rum to the continental colonies. Eltis shows that in the period 1699–1701, Barbados alone exported an annual average of nearly 600,000 gallons of rum,
which represented 19 percent of the value of all Barbados exports.[113] Little of
this rum made its way to European markets. In 1700, for example, England and
Wales imported less than 2,000 gallons.[114] In the early eighteenth century,
Sloane still felt the need to explain to his readers in Europe that rum was made
from sugarcane juice.[115] The majority of the 600,000 gallons of Barbados rum
went to North America, particularly the Chesapeake and New England. In the
period 1699–1701, 9 percent of the value of all Barbados exports went to Virginia and Maryland. Since most of this was in the form of rum, the volume of
rum exports to the Chesapeake was probably in the range of 250,000 to
300,000 gallons annually. In this same period, New England also consumed 9

percent of the value of all Barbados exports, yet, as Eltis points out, molasses rather than rum probably represented most of the New England trade. Of course, by the end of the seventeenth century, New Englanders took it upon themselves to turn almost all of that molasses into rum.

Continental merchants were largely responsible for the rise of continental rum imports. As Rorabaugh put it, "Lacking hard money and fearful of credit, American merchants turned to barter. . . . Rum was the currency of the age."[116] For example, in 1682, Thomas Ashe, writing about conditions in the newly settled North Carolina colony wrote, "The Commodities of the Country as yet proper for England are Furs and Cedar: For Berbadoes, Jamaica and the Caribbee Islands, Provisions, Pitch, Tarr and Clapboard, for which they have in Exchange Sugar, Rumm, Melasses and Ginger, etc."[117] The rum trade between Barbados and the Carolinas reflects the strong ties that developed as a result of the great number of Barbadians who migrated to the Carolinas in the seventeenth century.

Trade between the Caribbean and the continental colonies often reflected family networks. For example, in the mid-seventeenth century, Constant Silvester, a wealthy and politically powerful sugar planter in Barbados, exchanged rum produced on his plantation for food, clothing, and barrel staves produced on his brother's estate in Shelter Island, New York.[118] The Hutchison family of New England, including cousin Peleg Sanford, a Rhode Island merchant with family connections in Barbados, exemplified this family-based trade strategy. By placing family members throughout the developing Atlantic world and catering to local demands, the Hutchison family constructed an elaborate commercial system that made them one of the most powerful forces in the emerging Atlantic economy.[119]

Merchants and shippers of the Dutch West India Company were important links in the Caribbean-continental rum traffic. The long history of the Dutch alcohol trade in Europe suggests that Dutch traders may have encouraged early rum making in the British and French islands in order to stimulate the North American trade. Historian Bernard Bailyn argues that Dutch traders helped New Englanders identify the needs of Caribbean plantations and acted as middlemen between the two regions.[120] In 1651, the British parliament imposed the first of a series of navigation acts meant to curb Dutch control of New World shipping and trading. These acts restricted the New England trade with Caribbean islands, especially with Barbados, which at that time was sympathetic to the Royalist cause. By the late seventeenth century, the navigation acts, the rise of New England's own merchant shipping business, and the continuing dominance of family trading networks reduced the Dutch influence. However, large quantities of Caribbean rum continued to enter New England through Dutch–New England smuggling operations based in Newfoundland and the Dutch entrepôt of Curaçao.[121]

In the seventeenth century, Caribbean rum fed the North American fur trade and helped place Native Americans squarely within the emerging Atlantic economy. Although Native North Americans had no prior history of alcohol use, they embraced alcohol for a variety of reasons, especially its unique physiological effects. Native Americans incorporated alcohol into traditional religious ceremonies and welcomed it as a sacred fluid that helped facilitate communication with the spiritual world. Moreover, historian Peter Mancall argues that alcohol provided Native Americans with an escape from the intense stress brought about by epidemic diseases and the rapid pace of cultural change.[122] Despite attempts by some colonial officials and religious leaders to curb the use of alcohol in the fur trade, alcohol was central to that business and remained so throughout the colonial period.

French North America also received its share of rum. In the late seventeenth century, French colonial administrator Jean-Baptiste Colbert implemented mercantilist trade policies known as the *exclusif*. The policies restricted French Caribbean trade with foreigners and sought to encourage direct trade between the French Caribbean and French provinces in Canada and Louisiana. French Canadians had lumber, fish, tar, and provisions that were much needed on Caribbean sugar plantations. In order to stimulate trade and facilitate a self-contained empire, Colbert's policies reduced import duties on rum entering French Canadian ports. As early as 1685, French Caribbean rum made its way to the northern French colonies.[123]

Much of the rum that entered northern French colonies fed the French fur trade. According to anthropologist R. C. Dailey, the fur trade assured the "solvency" of New France, and alcohol fueled the fur trade.[124] Jesuit missionaries in New France worried about the harmful effects of excessive drinking by Native Americans, but as in British North America, alcohol was an integral part of the French fur trade, and they were unable to abolish the alcohol-for-fur model. According to Mancall, the fur trade in New France "represented a clash of two dominant French ideologies in Canada, the churchmen's mission to spread the faith and the merchants' plans to increase trade."[125]

Clearly not everyone in the British and French continental colonies was pleased with the increasing quantities of rum. Throughout the early colonial period in North America, officials and religious leaders attempted to curb excessive drinking, which many blamed on the overabundance of Caribbean rum. Although Rorabaugh dismisses concerns about alcohol abuse in the early North American colonies, it is clear that many colonists in North America had great reservations about the ready availability of alcohol and the increasing levels of drunkenness. As early as 1654, the governor of Connecticut banned the import of "Rum, Kill Devill, or the like" and officials in Newfoundland frequently complained about the extent to which rum was responsible for the debauchery of fishermen and sought to restrict its use.[126] Early temperance advocates often couched their arguments in biblical terms. In 1708, for example, Reverend Cotton Mather warned the people of Boston of the "Woful Consequences" of the great "Flood of Rum" that was overwhelming their orderly society.[127] Colonial assemblies also considered the use of alcohol by Native Americans and African slaves a potentially volatile combination and attempted to restrict the sale of rum to these "dangerous classes."[128]

However, prohibitions against rum confronted the power of merchant capitalism. In particular, Boston merchants greatly benefited from the growing Caribbean rum trade. Rorabaugh argues that New Englanders preferred a barter trade based on rum, because "Unlike other goods, including molasses, rum shipped easily, could be warehoused cheaply, withstood any climate and improper handling, and increased in value as it aged."[129] In the seventeenth century, officials in Massachusetts enacted over 40 laws regulating and restricting colonial drinking. These laws were enacted to support clerical ideals of piety, as well as reinforce the paternal authority of colonial officials.[130] In 1661 and 1667, officials in Massachusetts declared rum a "menace to society" and attempted to ban its use.[131] In 1712, Boston officials banned the sale of rum in taverns, but the economic importance of the Caribbean rum trade meant that the "ban was a dead letter as soon as it was enacted."[132]

By the late seventeenth century, New Englanders began distilling their own rum from imported Caribbean molasses. Emmanuel Downing of Salem, Massachusetts, may have been distilling rum from imported Caribbean molasses as early as 1648, and a commercial rum distillery was operating in Rhode Island in 1684.[133] Historian John McCusker, a leading scholar on the North American rum trade, hints that King William's War (1689–1697) was the impetus for the expansion of rum distilling in New England. During the conflict, Britain prohibited imports of French brandy, which left an opening for rum in the British alcohol market. However, little, if any, rum made its way to England during this period.[134] It appears that local demand for alcohol in the British continental colonies—probably heightened by the decreasing availability of French brandy during King William's War rather than by attempts to crack British alcohol markets—spurred the expansion of New England rum making. New England merchants encouraged continental rum making because it reduced dependence on, and therefore the price of, imported Caribbean rum. New England merchants also became particularly adept at using New England–made rum to exploit trade with the fisheries of Newfoundland.[135]

In the seventeenth century, the Spanish American colonies were another primary destination for Caribbean rum. The high taxes imposed on imported Spanish wine and brandy, the unpredictability of wine shipments, and the fact that Spanish wine occasionally went bad on the long sea voyages to the Americas, led to experiments with alternative alcoholic beverages. For example, in New Spain, *pulque*, made from the maguey, was a principal alcoholic beverage enjoyed by Indian peasants living outside of urban centers.[136] In the viceroyalty of New Granada, *chicha* beer made from grain was popular.[137] Grape wine making operations (*bodegas*) also flourished in the Moquegua Valley of Peru.[138] In some parts of the Spanish Americas, alcohol production helped defray the cost of running local governments. For example, in parts of New Spain, officials encouraged pulque production, because liquor and tavern licenses helped fill local governmental coffers.[139] However, pulque production was only encouraged in rural areas where Spanish wine and brandy imports were unable to meet alcohol demands. In urban centers, such as Mexico City, Spanish officials aggressively discouraged local alcohol production, especially where it threatened colonial revenues from Spanish wine and brandy import taxes.[140] From the beginning of Spanish settlement, wine and brandy import taxes played a key role in keeping colonial governments solvent. In Hispaniola, for example, Columbus proposed a 15 percent tax on Spanish and Canary wine imports as a way to finance Spanish conquest of the Indies.[141]

In the sugarcane-growing regions of the Spanish Americas, colonists distilled rum, which they called *aguardiente de caña*. Yet, the sad state of sugar production in the Spanish colonies reduced the availability of rum-making ingredients and restrained the growth of the industry.[142] Officials also blamed rum for health problems and social disorder. The concentrated nature of rum probably compounded the fears of Spanish colonials, who typically consumed wines of relatively low alcohol content with meals and in Catholic religious contexts. As early as 1658, the Audiencia of Santa Fe de Bogotá complained about the destructive social impact of rum on Indian peasants.[143] Colonial officials in New Granada faced similar struggles. In 1694, the governor of New Andalusia [Venezuela] also considered rum harmful to the people of that region and urged illicit distillers to shut down their operations.[144] Prohibitions against rum making were also instituted in Cartagena and the kingdom of Guatemala.[145] By the end of the seventeenth century, Spanish and Spanish colonial officials were sufficiently concerned about the negative social and economic impact of rum that on June 8, 1693, the Crown instituted a comprehensive prohibition against rum making in the Spanish colonies.[146] Although the ban stifled the growth of Spanish Caribbean rum making, the frequent reiteration of the ban in the following century suggests the prohibition on distilling was often evaded.

The restrictions on Spanish Caribbean rum production, the limited nature of Spanish Caribbean sugar industries, and the high cost of Spanish wine and brandy imports reduced the availability of alcohol in the Spanish Americas. As a result, an illegal rum trade developed, which made the Spanish Caribbean a primary destination for British and French Caribbean rum. According to Ligon, rum was

> a commodity of good value in the Plantation; for we send it down to the *Bridge* [the capital port of Bridgetown], and there put it off to those that retail it. Some they sell to the Ships, and is transported into foreign parts.[147]

Ligon's reference to "foreign parts" suggests that the Spanish Caribbean was the likely destination. Jamaican traders also purchased cattle in Cuba with smuggled rum.[148] Labat wrote that French Caribbean traders also sold rum

> to Spanish on the coast of Caracas, Cartagena, Honduras, and the big islands where they don't produce it or use it to make a wine, and in exchange provide them with good English glass bottles with good mouths and corks with wire or cloth from Holland for 10 or 12 bottles.[149]

The Dutch island of Curaçao became an especially busy entrepôt for illegal shipments of rum to the Spanish mainland colonies.[150]

Rum and Island Caribs

Carib Indians of the Lesser Antilles also provided a good market for Caribbean rum. At the time of European contact, Caribs occupied the Caribbean from the Orinoco Delta region of mainland South America through the island chain of the Lesser Antilles, perhaps as far north as the eastern tip of Puerto Rico. Since before the arrival of Europeans, Caribs had a strong tradition of alcohol use, and they made a variety of fermented alcoholic drinks. Carib drinking centered on cassava-based alcoholic drinks, oüicou and perino, as well as the sweet potato–based mobbie, and their drinking habits received much attention from European chroniclers.

In the age of European exploration and settlement, foreign drinks entered the repertoire of alcoholic beverages available to Caribs. The wind and ocean currents of the Atlantic led many European sailing ships headed for the New World to Carib centers in the Leeward and Windward Islands. These islands represented the first landfall after weeks at sea, and they provided travelers with a place to rest and recover from long voyages. The hot springs of Dominica, for example, offered an especially pleasant respite for weary crews. As a result, an important trade developed between Caribs and Europeans in the early years of exploration and settlement. In exchange for iron axes, glass beads, and other goods, Europeans received fresh water and food provisions.

It was through this sort of informal exchange that Caribs were first introduced to European alcoholic beverages. Privateers, explorers, settlers, and missionaries usually carried huge stores of alcohol on their voyages. The Caribs esteemed European alcoholic beverages for their novelty, as well as for their high alcohol content. When English Dominican monk Thomas Gage arrived in Guadeloupe in 1625, the Caribs there greeted him in what had probably become a usual scene. According to Gage,

> some [were] speaking in their unknown Tongue, others using signs for such things as we imagined they desired. Their sign for some of our *Spanish* Wine was easily perceived, and their request most willingly granted to by our men.[151]

The Caribs also sought distilled spirits, especially French brandy. With the rise of sugar production in the Caribbean, rum, rather than European drinks, became increasingly common in the Carib-European alcohol trade. By the end of the seventeenth century, the ordinary Carib greeting in Dominica was *"Hello my friend, do you have rum[?]"*[152]

In order to tap this emerging trade, the Caribs increased their production of tobacco and cotton, two commodities prized in European markets. Du Tertre, for example, reported that Caribs had a strong penchant for French brandy, and that traders could purchase a great deal of cotton for a glass of eau de vie.[153] However, the Europeans wanted more than just the commodities that Caribs produced: they also wanted their land. In 1649, according to French claims, Kaierouane, the Carib chief of Grenada, sold the island for "a certain quantity of billhooks, crystal glassware, knives, other sundry items that they demanded, and two quarts of French brandy."[154]

Although alcoholic beverages were just one of many goods sold to the Caribs, they were a requisite part of the Carib-European trade. They played an especially crucial role in the gift-giving ceremonies that preceded trading. The use of alcohol as an entreaty to trade was also typical of the North American fur trade, as well as the West and West Central African slave trades.[155] Carib-European trading often began with a customary presentation of alcohol and the exchange of toasts. According to Labat, giving the Caribs something to drink was "an infallible way to gain their friendship," and the Caribs of Dominica received him especially well when he arrived "since it was accompanied by two bottles of rum."[156] In 1722, Barbados ship captain John Braithwaite described an incident in which his shore party was poorly treated and refused wood and water from the Carib chiefs of St. Vincent. According to Braithwaite, "Immediately after [the refusal], I sent ashore the sloop's boat with a mate, with rum, beef, bread, &c."[157] Such presents helped open lines of communication between Europeans and Caribs. They also helped British and French colonists build alliances with particular Carib groups and maintain their loyalties.

The success of the alcohol trade was enhanced by a preexisting Carib social structure that embraced alcohol use. From birth to death, alcohol played a central role in Carib ceremonial contexts. It helped facilitate communication with the spirit world, which made it a powerful link to spiritual assistance. The Caribs offered alcohol to gods (*zemis*) at public and private ceremonies. The offerings were called *Anakri* or *Alakri*, and they were placed on small wooden tables (*matoutous*) in their houses.[158] They helped the Caribs ward off evil and receive guidance in worldly pursuits. Oüicou was an important tool of Carib shamans; called *Piaye* or *Boyéz*, they used their power as intermediaries between the natural and supernatural worlds to invoke spirits who helped devotees recover from illness or exact vengeance against enemies.[159] The ritual of making alcohol offerings to spirits was so pivotal in balancing the relationship between the physical and spiritual realms that failure to observe it had serious consequences. In the seventeenth century, French Jesuit missionary Sieur de La Borde recorded Carib folklore that highlights the prominent place of these oblations in Carib thought.

What [Caribs] say about the origin of the sea, and about the Creation, and generally about all waters, relates in some manner to the flood. The great

Master of Chemeens who are their good spirits, angered and in a rage that the Caraibes at this time were very wicked, and no longer offered Cassava, nor Oüicou, made it rain many days such as great quantity of water that they were nearly all drowned, with the exception of a few who saved themselves in small boats and Pirogues on a mountain which was the only one left.[160]

This Carib legend explains the origins of the sea and perhaps the disastrous effects of hurricanes, which resulted from the Caribs' failure to supply their zemis with oüicou. Thus, alcohol offerings became, in effect, a vehicle for explaining and controlling major events in Carib society.[161] Apparently, mobbie never achieved the same spiritual importance of oüicou, perhaps because sweet potatoes were never as central as cassava to the Caribs' diet.

Carib rites of passage also necessitated the ritual use of alcohol. For example, in the seventeenth century, French missionary Raymond Breton observed the fundamental role of oüicou in childbirth in Dominica. According to Breton,

When the women give birth, the husbands withdraw from them, and they do not sleep together at all for five or six months from this point. And both undertake a fast, which is one of the most celebrated, especially when they have a boy for the first child. The man fasts more rigorously than the woman for fear that the infant should suffer by him. Father Raymond was at the house of Le Baron on Dominica, going to see one of these fasters, and as the Father was speaking to him of this fast, the savage told him that some abstained entirely from drinking and eating for the first five days after the confinement of their wives, and on the other days until the tenth, they take nothing but Oüicou. After this they eat nothing but cassava and drink Oüicou for the space of a month or two.[162]

Postpartum fasting and food taboos, known to anthropologists as the couvade, functioned to ensure the health and well being of newborn Carib children. Oüicou, a Carib drink with links to spiritual assistance, was exempt from such prohibitions.[163] Alcohol-laden ceremonies typified other rites of passage in a Carib child's life, such as the *elétuak* or *elétoaz* festivals held for children who were about to undergo the ritual piercing of the ears, nose, and bottom lip.[164] Naming ceremonies and puberty rites also gave rise to highly ritualized drinking bouts.[165] These were liminal periods when the physical and spiritual worlds were closely and precariously aligned. The befuddling effects of alcohol altered the senses and made the supernatural experience of these events all the more convincing.

Death marked the end of the physical life and a transition to the spiritual world. It therefore necessitated the assistance of a sacred fluid. Carib funerals prompted elaborate drinking binges, and family members were expected to leave offerings of oüicou on the graves of the deceased.[166] Such gifts helped ensure the successful passage of the dead to the spirit world. On the anniversary of a death, Caribs returned to the family member's grave where, according to Breton, they drowned their sorrows in an "abyss of *oüicou*."[167] The Caribs also drank the ashes of their deceased leaders in mixtures of oüicou.[168] Just as the Islamic prophet Mohammed's vision of paradise included rivers of grape wine, Caribs believed that heaven was a place where rivers of oüicou flowed without ceasing.[169] Europeans, recognizing the important relationship between alcohol and ancestors in Carib society, showed their respect and consideration for Carib funerary customs. In 1694, for example, Labat and his cohort sat down to dinner with the Caribs of Dominica and made the careless error of sitting on a Carib grave. Labat apologized, made a toast, and offered "drink . . . so as to make amends for the offence we had given them in sitting on their dead." After dinner, Labat and the Caribs lifted the mat and planks covering the grave, viewed the corpse, and drank to the deceased.[170] Labat was not simply indulging the Caribs' spiritual beliefs; the links between alcohol and spirituality were familiar to Europeans, whose Judeo-Christian beliefs called for the ritual use of grape wine.

At the same time, alcohol use in Carib society had a secular function. For example, the Caribs used alcohol to express internal social hierarchies. In 1596, George Clifford, an English privateer, landed in Dominica to resupply his expedition and refresh his crew. According to Dr. Layfield, a chaplain on the voyage who witnessed the drinking practices of the Caribs of Dominica,

> Their drinke is commonly water, but they make drinke of their Cassain [cassava], better of their Pines [pineapples] (and it should seeme that might be made an excellent liquor,) but the best and reserved for the Kings cup onely of Potatoes [mobbie].[171]

Carib gender divisions were probably also expressed in the choice of alcoholic beverages. In 1791, William Young, an absentee British sugar planter, went to visit his estates in St. Vincent. Young hosted a dinner party for Anselm and Brunau, two Carib chiefs on the island, and noted, "We treated them with *wine*, and afterwards about a dozen of their ladies were introduced, who preferred *rum*."[172] The Caribs may have also used drinking preferences to express their allegiance to particular European powers. For example, Braithwaite reported that the Carib chiefs of St. Vincent drank wine, but "scorned to drink rum."[173] While the preference for wine may have reflected class and gender divisions within Carib society, historians Peter Hulme and Neil Whitehead also argue that the Carib chiefs' insistence on wine over rum demonstrates their understanding of the deceptive tactics of the British who were there to explore the possibility of establishing a settlement.[174] The preference for wine suggests that the Caribs defined Europeans by the particular alcoholic beverages they drank, which, in this instance, may have allowed them to express their allegiance to the wine-drinking French rather than the rum-drinking British colonials of Barbados.

Oüicou, rum, and other forms of alcohol also played a central role at the Caribs' bacchanalian drinking festivals. The Caribs called these festivals *oüicous*, which was, of course, also the name for their cassava-based alcoholic drink. According to Du Tertre, "Our Savages make certain assemblies, which they call *Oüycou*, and since the arrival of the French, *Vin*."[175] Evidently, the Caribs obliged their French visitors by translating the name for these events to something the French could understand. Vins were held on a variety of occasions, but especially before raids on European settlements. According to La Borde, the Carib "never go to war without first holding a great *Vin*, and it is there that they hold counsel."[176] A village leader would call for a Vin and invite Caribs from two or three neighboring villages. These small Vins probably involved some fifty participants. However, larger gatherings, or *Grande Vins*, attracted hundreds of Caribs, and many traveled great distances from other islands to attend. Participants painted elaborate designs on their bodies with red and black paint, and they drank and danced all day and night without eating. They also made sure to "put aside a Canary, or calabashes for their Zemeen" at these events.[177]

French missionaries condemned the alcoholic excesses of Caribs because they saw drunkenness as an obstacle to Christian conversion. Carib men, women, and children were all known to get drunk on occasion.[178] La Borde believed that there were no people on earth "more inclined to drunkenness."[179] Missionaries were especially critical of the drunken debauchery that took place at Vins. According to Du Tertre, Caribs got "drunk like pigs" at these events.[180] Yet, missionaries failed to see that Vins were more than just drunken bacchanals. Vins were opportunities to express tribal concerns and settle old debts. They also provided the venue for the organization and planning of military campaigns. Alcohol stoked the fires of sociability, which helped remove barriers to social interaction and strengthen alliances between Carib villages. The physiological effects of alcohol, as well as its links to the spiritual world, may have also provided the intoxicated individuals with a momentary sense of power. Drinking, therefore, helped the Caribs speak like gods, which on these important occasions facilitated planning and problem solving.[181] Moreover, alcohol offerings to deities at these events ensured spiritual assistance in social and militaristic pursuits.

Indeed, the Caribs were not teetotalers. Although we lack information about the frequency of island Carib drinking binges, they probably drank as often as their mainland Carib cousins, who, according to the mid-sixteenth-century reports of German explorer, Hans Staden, held drinking festivals about once every month.[182] In the islands, the Caribs also enjoyed regular drinking festivals that entailed the consumption of copious amounts of alcohol. They were known, for example, to down ten to twelve barrels of oüicou at Vins, even at small Vins consisting of just two or three villages.[183] Evidently, the Caribs drank to get drunk on these occasions.

The Caribs' dynamic spiritual world may have increased their propensity to drink. Anthropologist James Schaefer found a strong relationship between drunkenness and societies with supernatural belief systems that include malicious and unpredictable spirits.[184] According to Schaefer, drinking helped reduce the anxieties brought about by the fear of malevolent spirits. Certainly, the Caribs' spiritual world included cruel and capricious spirits. In particular, the Caribs believed that evil spirits, known as *Maboia* or *Maboya*, brought death and illness upon the Caribs for even the slightest offenses. According to missionaries, constant torment by these evil spirits was responsible for the Caribs' melancholy and apathetic character.[185] Perhaps it was also responsible for their appetite for alcohol.

The long history of alcohol use in Carib society forestalled the kind of destructive impact that alcohol had on the indigenous peoples of North America. Despite their regular drinking binges, the Caribs' knowledge of and familiarity with the potentially disastrous effects of excessive drinking appears to have given rise to a philosophy of moderation. Outside of Vins, Carib drinking was probably not excessive. Rochefort, for example, praised the Caribs for their "ordinary sobriety."[186] The emphasis on ritualistic, rather than convivial, drinking may have also fostered restraint.[187] However, alcohol lost much of its spiritual, social, and ceremonial meaning within the context of European conquest. Europeans colonists set a "pernicious" example of drunken debauchery and vice, which the Caribs often imitated.[188] Moreover, European settlement and aggression disrupted Carib society, and the introduction of large quantities of rum into a context of epidemiological catastrophe accelerated the demise of the Carib family unit and other traditional social structures. Levels of alcohol use increased, and, rather than a doorway to sociability and spiritual guidance, drinking became a temporary means of escape from a world turned upside down.

Conclusion

In the seventeenth century, colonists in the Caribbean exploited a wide range of local alcohol resources and even tapped the alcoholic traditions of Carib Indians. Provision crops, such as cassava and potatoes, helped sustain early colonists in the Caribbean and provided them with raw material for alcoholic drinks. However, during the sugar revolution, these small-scale crops were pushed aside by planters who sought to maximize available land for sugarcane. The shift to sugar production made sugarcane juice and the waste products of the sugar industry abundant and, therefore, the practical choice to meet local alcohol demands. Decreasing reliance on provision crops, as well as the decreasing numbers of Caribs available to produce alcoholic drinks such as mobbie and oüicou, helped motivate the switch to the production of rum from sugarcane. Colonists at the margins of the Atlantic world embraced Caribbean rum. Although early rum making relied heavily on inferior ingredients and small stills, it bolstered sugar plantation revenues and stabilized sugar estates. Rum nurtured the growth of American trade and was a nursery for a new class of merchant capitalists on the American side of the Atlantic. In the seventeenth century, Barbados emerged as the leading rum producer. Rum fed local and regional demand, which was fueled by a variety of factors, including Old World beliefs about the medicinal meaning of distilled spirits. In the eighteenth century, advances in rum making, mercantilist policies, and the increasing demand for alcohol in Britain fueled the expansion of rum making, especially in the British Caribbean colony of Jamaica.

CHAPTER 3

Rum's Threat to Competing Alcohol Industries in the Eighteenth Century

NTHROPOLOGIST SIDNEY W. MINTZ describes Caribbean sugar production as a protoindustrial enterprise that combined the methods of factory and field.[1] There is little doubt that this characterization embraces, though not explicitly, the efficiency of an industry that turned its waste products into a profitable alcoholic commodity. In the eighteenth century, sugar planters experimented with new ways to extract high rum yields and improve their rum-making techniques. They speculated about the potential output of their still houses and left extensive records about distillation technology. Often, such speculation was based more on the optimistic guesswork of an overconfident planter class than on actual production figures. Despite the broad regional extent of rum making at the beginning of the eighteenth century, British Caribbean planters developed an especially sophisticated rum industry and pulled away from their French and Spanish rivals. Barbados and Jamaica, spurred by huge North American and metropolitan markets, emerged as the leading rum-making colonies. This chapter explores the methods of rum makers, especially in the British Caribbean, and examines the basis for their optimism.

Eighteenth century rum making was an art, but it was an imperfect art that relied heavily on rule-of-thumb principles and the skill of particular distillers. Antiguan sugar planter Samuel Martin explained,

> This art not having self-evident principles for its basis, is founded solely upon experience. The nature of fermentation (which is previously necessary to making rum) can be learned only by practice, and adjusted by exact

weight or measure; and even then great disappointments will happen to the distiller; either from imperceptible differences of heat and cold; or from some other latent causes not assignable.[2]

Eighteenth century rum making lacked standardization and quality controls, but the economic promise of rum drove planters to unlock the mysteries of rum production and make it a more scientific endeavor.

Numerous factors determined rum yields. At the most fundamental level, soil quality affected the amount of rum a plantation could produce. For example, Jamaican sugar planter Edward Long wrote that the "rich" soils on estates on the north side of Jamaica produced sugarcane juice "so viscid, that it often will not boil into sugar." However, according to Long, these estates produced "an extraordinary quantity of rum."[3] Jamaican sugar planter William Beckford also believed that sugarcane juice in the mountainous regions of Jamaica was too thick for sugar making, but well suited for producing rum.[4] What Long and Beckford observed may have been the result of the high salt content of soils in Jamaica's mountainous regions. Salt can reduce the recoverability of sucrose during sugar processing and increase the amount of molasses, as well as the sucrose level in that molasses, available for rum making.[5] Yet, the fermentation and distillation of sugarcane juice with a high saline content required great care because it fermented slowly and sometimes produced a "bitter" spirit.[6] Other qualities of the soil, including nitrogen levels, acidity, and drainage might also explain why the first few sugarcane crops planted on many newly cultivated lands were used only for rum.[7] Jamaican sugar planter Leonard Wray encouraged distillers to experiment with rum-making techniques and adjust them to the soils of their particular plantation.[8]

Humidity and seasonal change also governed rum yields. The tropical Caribbean climate consists of a wet and a dry season, and many planters warned about distilling in the wet season when the still house was likely to be cool and damp. Barbados sugar planter William Belgrove wrote, "I see no just Reason why [a] Still-House should be making Rum in the wet Season of the Year, when no good Fermentation can be expected or made equal to the Months between January and August."[9] An anonymous writer in St. Domingue also noted that the best fermentation occurred in the dry months of March, April, and May.[10] At a molecular level, alcohol and water have an affinity for each other and, thus, alcohol in a damp still house absorbs moisture from the air. When alcohol absorbs numerous water molecules, heat—an important catalyst for the conversion of sugar into alcohol during the fermentation process—is lost, the

Figure 3.1. *Holeing a Cane-Piece.* In William Clark, *Ten Views In the Island of Antigua, in Which are Represented the Process of Sugar Making* (London, 1823). Courtesy of the John Carter Brown Library at Brown University.

temperature falls, and fermentation slows.[11] During the wet season, a damp still house slowed the rate of fermentation, holding up work regimens; too much moisture prevented fermentation altogether.[12] In order to reduce moisture in the still house, some planters advised setting small fires to "dispel the chilly cold dampness of the fermenting part of the house."[13]

In the Caribbean, sugarcane was harvested every year, usually in the dry season months between January and May. Sugarcane spoiled quickly, so it had to be brought to the mill and squeezed of its juice soon after being cut. The juice was then boiled in large copper cauldrons. During the boiling process, impurities, known as scum, bubbled to the surface and were skimmed off. Lime, egg whites, and the blood of cattle were some of the ingredients added to the boiling cane juice to help bring impurities to the surface.[14] The skimming process continued as the juice was conveyed through a series of successively smaller cauldrons. Once the sugar boiler believed the juice had reached an appropriate viscosity, it was transferred to wooden barrels or earthenware molds in the purging house. There, remaining impurities—at this point called molasses—drained off, leaving a barrel of still-wet muscavado or a brownish loaf of sugar. Claying, a more common practice in Barbados and the French islands, consisted of capping the sugar mold with wet clay. Claying purged the loaf of more molasses and left a lighter semirefined sugar.

Rum begins as a *wash* compound, and the wash contained four basic ingredients: scum, molasses, dunder, and water. Scum from the bubbling cauldrons in the boiling house was carried in buckets or placed in gutters where it flowed into fermenting cisterns in the still house. The art of skimming was a specialized skill, and planters often worried that the sugar boilers responsible for skimming skimmed too deeply. Poor skimming techniques removed sugar rather than impurities alone, which decreased the amount of sugar produced.[15] As with scum, the molasses that drained from the sugar molds and barrels in the purging house was carried in buckets or dripped into gutters that channeled it to the fermenting cisterns in the still house. Claying further purged the sugar and provided more molasses for rum making. An extended purge time also increased the amount of molasses available for distilling. Dunder, the waste of previous distillations, was the third ingredient: it is simply the wash removed of much of its wet matter. Water was the fourth ingredient. There appears to have been no special treatment of water, although some planters may have preferred to use "pure spring water."[16] The need for water in rum making explains why distilleries were often located adjacent to rivers and streams.[17]

Figure 3.2. *Interior of a Boiling House.* In William Clark, *Ten Views In the Island of Antigua, in Which are Represented the Process of Sugar Making* (London, 1823). Courtesy of the John Carter Brown Library at Brown University.

The scum and molasses used in the wash were sometimes augmented by pure cane juice. During a visit to the Caribbean, physician Hans Sloane observed, "Rum is made of Cane-juice not fit to make Sugar."[18] These canes, called "rum canes," were set aside—usually because of some accident—for rum making. For example, in 1790, Beckford set aside rum canes that had been damaged by rats.[19] Hurricanes, droughts, fires, and other disasters damaged sugarcanes and made them useless for sugar making, but they were often fine for the still house.[20] Occasionally other ingredients were thrown into the fermenting wash. John Taylor, a visitor to Jamaica, wrote that sometimes the overseer would "empt his camberpot into it," but the purpose was apparently to keep the slaves from stealing it.[21]

The wash was the most important stage in rum making, and the combination of ingredients determined the amount of alcohol the wash produced. In fact, all of the alcohol made on Caribbean sugar estates occurred at this stage, and distillation merely extracted it from the wash. The proper mix of ingredients produced high rum yields, and planters, preoccupied with plantation efficiency, struggled to construct high yielding wash compounds. In recipe book fashion, colonial newspapers, planter guides, and estate journals sometimes listed wash compounds, but, in general, distillers tended to hold tight to trade secrets and conceal their rule-of-thumb methods from competitors.

In 1794, Jamaican sugar planter Bryan Edwards wrote that the average 100-gallon wash in the British Windward Islands contained equal parts scum, dunder, and water. After fermenting 24 hours, distillers added a three-gallon charge of molasses. A day or two later, distillers added a second three-gallon charge of molasses in order to further stimulate fermentation.[22] This practice appears general among rum distillers in the British Caribbean in the eighteenth century and was not confined to the Windward Islands.[23] However, Edwards wrote that the equal three parts wash was becoming an antiquated method in Jamaica and proceeded to lay out the "improved" Jamaican wash compound. In this new method, the average 100-gallon wash contained 50 gallons of dunder, 6 gallons of molasses, 36 gallons of scum, and 8 gallons of water. The difference is, of course, the use of less water and more dunder.[24]

Planters, including Edwards, recognized that something inherent in scum and molasses fermented to make rum. They referred to the concept of *sweets*. The use of this term suggests that they knew rum was produced from the breakdown of sucrose in the scum and molasses rather than from some other property or impurity in sugarcane juice. As Wray noted, "On the quantity of sugar contained in a wash, therefore, is the quantity of alcohol dependent."[25]

Planters adopted one fundamental principle for the wash compound: that it must contain 10–15 percent sweets. However, it appears that most rum makers agreed on an average of about 12 percent.[26] Molasses was the standard for sweets, and one gallon of molasses was considered equal to one gallon of sweets. Scum, on the other hand, represented some fraction of molasses. Edwards, for example, argued that the ratio of scum to molasses was 6 to 1. Thus, the average 100-gallon wash of 6 gallons of molasses and 36 gallons of scum provided the necessary 12 percent level of sweets.

Setting a wash was a dynamic process because the proportion of ingredients regularly changed throughout the distilling cycle. Despite the planters' attempts to establish standardized wash ratios, a wash could be made with or without scum or molasses and, sometimes, dunder alone was fermented.[27] The addition of water was sometimes unnecessary, and some planters argued entirely against its use.[28] Because the distilling cycle coincided with, and extended beyond, crop-over, the ideal average proportion of wash ingredients was rarely achieved on a wash-to-wash basis. For example, scum was abundant at the beginning of the sugar-making cycle, but ran out after the sugar boiling ceased. On the other hand, molasses, in limited supply at the beginning of the sugar-making cycle, was abundant at the end. This fact led Martin to write,

> when the wind blows fresh [at the beginning of the crop], and the boiling-house affords scum in abundance, then much of that, and little melosses, should make the composition [of the wash]. On the contrary, when there is but a scanty product of scum, the quantity of mellosses must be increased; and when at any time there is none at all, mellosses with water, and a large part of lees [dunder], must make the composition.[29]

The weekly still house records from York estate, Jamaica, highlight the dynamic nature of wash compounds over the course of the distilling cycle. Moreover, experiments with wash recipes led to regional variations among distillers, as well as changes in wash proportion trends over time.

The proper mixture of ingredients in the wash provided a healthy environment for yeasts, naturally present on sugarcane, to thrive and break down the fermentable sucrose into alcohol. The initial fermentation took about one day. After that, infusions of molasses further stimulated fermentation in the wash. While fermentation could cease within a few days, usually eight, some washes could ferment for several weeks.[30] Yeasts tend to die when sucrose runs out or when the level of alcohol in the wash reaches about 14 percent.[31] A fermentation lasting one to two weeks at a mild temperature was considered most desir-

Table 3.1. General Wash Proportions Versus Improved Jamaican Wash Proportions

General average wash	*Improved Jamaican average wash*
33.3 gallons scum	36 gallons scum
33.3 gallons dunder	50 gallons dunder
33.3 gallons water	8 gallons water
6.0 gallons molasses	6 gallons molasses
106.0 gallons wash	100 gallons wash

Sources: Edwards, *History, Civil and Commercial*, II:279–80; Long, *History of Jamaica*, II:560–61; Martin, *Essay Upon Plantership*, 55.

able because it ensured the greater conversion of sucrose into alcohol. Planters knew how to increase the length of fermentation by manipulating the proportion of ingredients in the wash, especially by the infusion of cold water to slow the process. During fermentation, the wash foamed and bubbled and was often described as a living organism.[32]

Once the wash settled, the sour smelling compound was "ripe for distilling." By the action of heat, distilling vaporized the alcohol and lighter substances in the fermented wash. This process removed water, salts, fusel oils, and other impurities that affected the proof and taste of the rum. The alcohol vapors collected in the *still head* and left through the *still worm*, where the vapors condensed and flowed out and into a receiver at the other end of the worm. After this first distillation, the liquid was a poor quality weak spirit called *low wine*. Although plantations could end the process after the first distillation, most British Caribbean distillers appear to have redistilled their low wine, either separately or by returning it to the subsequent wash. The second distillation removed more impurities, improved the taste, and increased the alcohol content of the rum. The second distillation reduced the total amount of low wine, but was necessary to make concentrated rum of a high proof.

In 1755, Belgrove wrote, "The Distilling House should have three stills to contain 900 gallons of Liquor, and a fourth big enough to contain the *low-wines* produced from the other three."[33] By the end of the eighteenth century, British Caribbean distillers were using even larger stills. For example, Edwards believed that plantations should employ stills of 1,000 to 3,000 gallons and wrote, "A still of two thousand gallons, with freight and charges, will cost but little more than one of one thousand five hundred gallons, and is besides worked with but little more fuel."[34] Edwards later indicated that the average

Table 3.2. Proportion of Wash Ingredients Used During the Distilling Cycle at York Estate, Jamaica, 1791, in Gallons

Weeks	Percentage of molasses	Percentage of scum	Percentage of dunder	Percentage of water
February 11–26	5	69	26	0
February 28–March 5	13	33	53	0
March 7–12	14	32	54	0
March 14–19	12	27	61	0
March 21–26	12	24	64	0
March 28–April 2	16	17	67	0
April 4–9	7	6	87	0
April 11–16	9	20	59	12
April 18–22	16	25	59	0
April 25–30	9	36	55	0
May 2–7	11	31	58	0
May 9–14	15	18	67	0
May 16–21	17	13	70	0
May 23–28	13	4	74	9
May 30–June 4	0	0	73	27
June 6–29	6	0	81	12
Average	11	23	63	3

Source: Gale-Morant Papers, Latin American Collection, George A. Smathers Library, University of Florida, Gainesville, Florida.

plantation would be more likely to possess two stills, one of 1,200 gallons and a smaller one of 600. In contrast, French distillers appear to have continued their seventeenth-century pattern of relying on small, antiquated stills. In 1768, for example, a distillery in Haut-de-Cap, St. Domingue, possessed two stills of about 300 gallons each.[35] In 1786, a series of articles published in St. Domingue's main newspaper, *Affiches Américaines*, described the use of 300-gallon stills of an inferior design. The anonymous author complained that in order for French Caribbean distillers to successfully compete with British Caribbean rum producers, they would have to follow the practices of British Caribbean distillers and increase the size of their stills, lengthen the necks of their still heads, and increase the length of their cooling worms.[36]

Rum is a highly volatile fluid, and loss of alcohol due to evaporation was a major problem for distillers. "The great object of the distiller," wrote Wray, was to produce as much rum as possible "loosing none, or as little as possible of it by evaporation."[37] The evaporation of alcohol began during the fermentation process, which led to design changes in fermenting vats.[38] For example, the low flat fermenting cisterns of the seventeenth century gave way to larger and taller fermentation vats that were made wide at the bottom and narrow at the opening. This design decreased the amount of air reaching the wash and, therefore, reduced evaporation. According to an anonymous author in St. Domingue, "The form of the *pièces à grappe* [fermentation vat] has to be a truncated cone, very large at the bottom and smaller at the top to make a quicker and better fermentation."[39] Fermenting vats, and for that matter all the utensils used to make rum, had to be thoroughly cleaned after every use, often with scalding hot water, to prevent them from souring the rum.[40]

The threat of evaporation continued after distillation. Historian John McCusker estimates that, despite the use of well-sealed "tight-casks," about 10 percent of rum shipped from the Caribbean to Britain and 5 percent of rum shipped from the Caribbean to North America leaked away or evaporated during the voyage. In some cases, a small crack meant that rum puncheons arrived at their destinations completely empty.[41]

Rum Making in Barbados and Jamaica in the Eighteenth Century

In the eighteenth century, Barbados and Jamaica emerged as the two leading rum producers in the Caribbean. A comparison of these colonies in Table 3.3 illustrates two contrasting approaches to rum making. The differences reflect distinct economic strategies that highlight broader themes of economic efficiency. Analysis of these two industries also offers insights into the issue of rum quality.

Sugar planters in Barbados clearly expected to produce a greater proportion of rum and believed that high rum yields were well within their grasp. Ligon estimated that a sugar planter in Barbados could expect to sell about 4.3 gallons of rum per 100 pounds of sugar, not counting the rum used by the inhabitants of the plantation, which represented a level comparable to that proposed by Edwards for Jamaica nearly a century and a half later. Even more astonishing, an anonymous writer in Barbados in 1737 believed that at least 20 gallons of rum per cwt. (one hundredweight or 112 pounds) of sugar was common. Belgrove also put his estimates in the double digits. The Barbadian repu-

Table 3.3. A Comparison of Expected Rum Yields in Barbados and Jamaica

Source	Years	Colony	Gallons of rum per cwt. sugar
Richard Ligon	1647–1650	Barbados	4.3
Anonymous	1737	Barbados	4.0–20.0
Richard Hall	1749	Barbados	9.1
William Belgrove	1755	Barbados	13.3–16.6
Edward Long	1768–1772	Jamaica	2.7–3.6
William Beckford	1790	Jamaica	4.0–5.0
Bryan Edwards	1794	Jamaica	4.2–5.1
Thomas Roughley	1823	Jamaica	3.4

Sources: Anonymous, "Some Observations," 2:242; Beckford, *Descriptive Account*, xxix, 146; Belgrove, *Treatise Upon Husbandry*, 44; Edwards, *History, Civil and Commercial*, II:284–85; R. Hall, *General Account*, 12–13; Ligon, *True and Exact History*, 112; Long, *History of Jamaica*, I:496, II:228–29; Roughley, *Jamaica Planter's Guide*, 386.

tation for high rum yields led many to conclude that Barbadians "think themselves the best distillers in all the sugar-islands."[42]

The Barbadian penchant for claying sugar is largely responsible for the higher rum yields. As mentioned earlier, claying consisted of capping the sugar molds with wet pads of clay. It leached out more molasses than purging alone and produced a whiter and more refined sugar loaf, which was in high demand in the British market. Clayed sugar took several months longer to produce and, as a result of protests from British sugar refiners, paid a much higher import duty than muscavado. However, because of the higher price of clayed sugar and the additional molasses for rum making, claying was profitable and Barbadians increasingly produced clayed sugars. Claying was especially common on larger estates. For example, between 1726 and 1730, managers at Codrington estate in Barbados clayed 83 percent of their sugar crop.[43] In contrast, Jamaicans rarely clayed their sugar and were content with exporting huge amounts of raw muscavado full of molasses.[44] The lower weight of clayed sugar and the increased availability of molasses for rum making largely explains the high rum to sugar ratio in Barbados.

It was generally estimated that a Jamaican hogshead lost 25 percent of its total weight in shipment to Britain.[45] Thus, a 16 cwt. (1,792-pound) hogshead of muscavado sugar described by Edwards in Jamaica contained over 448 pounds of molasses. This molasses, which could have been distilled into rum, drained away at sea. However, this does not mean that the Jamaican muscavado arrived in Britain looking like clayed sugar. Even after the 25 percent loss, British sugar refiners still complained that Jamaican sugar was crude and difficult to refine due to the high amounts of molasses still in the sugar.[46]

Every 142 pounds of muscavado sugar produced 100 pounds of clayed sugar.[47] The extra 42 pounds represented molasses, which the Barbadians turned into rum. According to Edwards, 200 hogsheads of muscavado weighed 358,400 pounds. Had this muscavado been clayed, Edwards would have received 252,394 pounds (141 hogsheads of 16 cwt.) of clayed sugar and 106,006 pounds of molasses. How much more rum could that molasses have produced? One simple approach is to base rum production on the weight of molasses. A gallon of molasses weighs about 11 pounds, and it was widely accepted that a gallon of molasses could make a gallon of rum.[48] Thus, the 106,006 pounds of molasses would have provided the still house with an additional 9,637 gallons of rum. The increasing amount of rum and the decreasing weight of clayed sugar would have boosted Edwards' ratio from 4.5 to 10.7 gallons of rum per cwt. of sugar. Thus, had claying become a common practice in Jamaica, the ratio of rum to sugar would have been similar to that achieved by rum makers in Barbados. Instead, Jamaican planters exported muscavado and accepted a reduced level of rum production.

An abridged purging process also brought Jamaican sugar planters lower rum to sugar ratios. The earliest runoff of molasses was watery material that contained little sucrose.[49] The Barbadian penchant for claying, therefore, produced molasses with a high level of sucrose, while the expeditious purge time in Jamaica produced a weak molasses that contained less sucrose. The Jamaican method contributed less sucrose to the wash and, as a result, Jamaican rum makers received less rum per gallon of molasses. In contrast, the molasses separated from the clayed and extensively purged Barbados sugar would have increased levels of sucrose in the wash and produced greater quantities of alcohol.

Many Caribbean sugar planters also believed that the high rum yields in Barbados reflected a problem endemic to Barbados of sugar boilers skimming too deeply into the boiling sugar juice.[50] According to Martin,

> The boasters [Barbadians] in the art of making much more rum than their neighbors, give room to suspect that they defraud the boiling-house; and so by diminishing the quantity of sugar, may easily increase the quantity of rum, which is by no means equivalent; and therefore all such fraud must be prevented by strict prohibition, and narrow inspection.[51]

Edwards also warned that "the boiling-house is defrauded of the cane-liquor by improper scumming,"[52] and McCusker accused sugar boilers in Barbados of committing this "ultimate transgression."[53] The basis for McCusker's argument was that, because rum could be sold locally to help pay plantation expenses, Barbadian plantation managers had a propensity to "bilk" their absentee planters of sugar in favor of increased rum yields. Others suggested that because plantation managers were often paid in rum, they increased rum production as a way to augment their salaries. For example, an anonymous writer in 1737 warned the planters of St. Kitts, "For the Overseer, who gets the Business upon the sole Credit or Promise of making a deal of Rum, will be sure to do it, tho' he makes the less Sugar."[54] Although Barbadians put a great deal of time and effort into refining their sugar and producing as much as they could, they may indeed have practiced deep skimming. Belgrove estimated that sugar boilers at his estate skimmed 10.4 gallons of scum per cwt. of sugar, while Edwards estimated that boilers in Jamaica skimmed 8.8 gallons of scum per cwt. of sugar.

Jamaican sugar planters may have also had a greater propensity to discard scum. McCusker reconstructed Jamaican wash ratios and estimated that Jamaican rum makers used about half of the available scum to feed plantation livestock.[55] In contrast, some believed that "No Scummings are ever given to Stock in Barbados."[56] Barbadian planters were thrifty and used almost every ounce of molasses and scum in rum making. They also had fewer cattle to feed. The Jamaican propensity to allocate substantial amounts of scum to livestock would have further reduced rum yields.

Alcohol content may also explain the discrepancy between Barbadian and Jamaican rum yields. Barbadian and Jamaican distillers adopted different methods of rum distilling, which led to differences in alcohol concentration. In 1765, Martin addressed the different techniques in Barbados and Jamaica and their effect on alcohol content.

> Whether the best method of distilling low-wines is by returning them into the subsequent still of liquor, or by drawing them off separately, experience must determine. The first method will certainly produce a cooler spirit, more palatable and wholesome; but the latter seems more profitable for the London-market, because the buyers there approve of a fiery spirit which will bear most adulteration; and certain it is, that the oftener a spirit is distilled, the more fiery it will be. This is evidently the ground of preferring Jamaican-rum to all other, not only because it is of a much higher proof, but also more

hot, and capable therefore of more adulteration: but it may be doubted whether the Jamaican-planter does not loose more by double distillation and over-proof than he gains by the price at London. If that be a fact, (as experiment will soon determine) it will be for his profit to draw more proof-rum from the wash, and a less quantity of low-wines, as expert distillers do in Barbados: but most certainly the spirit drawn from the wash is more cool, palatable, and wholesome, than that extracted from low-wines, by double distillation.[57]

To judge from Martin's observations, Jamaicans distilled a wash and the result-ing low wine was redistilled separately to produce a "hot" spirit with high alco-hol content. In contrast, Barbadian distillers ran off a single wash and the re-sulting low wine was returned to the next wash compound. The entire batch was, then, redistilled to produce a "cool" proof spirit.

The term "double distillation" is somewhat misleading, and the impact of distillation method on alcohol concentration is not entirely clear: both Jamai-cans and Barbadians distilled the same amount of fermented wash material, yet produced different concentrations of rum. Why should Barbadian rum be less concentrated? Alcohol has a lower boiling point than water, and distillation merely extracts the alcohol from the wash. As a result, the first runnings to flow from the still worm contained more alcohol. Thus, simply cutting off the flow of liquid from the still before the weaker spirit reached the receiver could raise the proof of the final product. For example, Jamaican sugar planter Thomas Roughley wrote that once the runnings of low wine from the still fell below 61 percent alcohol "the remainder of the spirit, which comes from the still worm, should be thrown up into the subsequent low wine butt" for redistillation.[58] Thus, distillers who paid close attention to the alcohol flowing from the worm could regulate the alcohol concentration of their rum regardless of whether the low wine was distilled separately, as was the case in Jamaica, or returned to the subsequent wash, as was done in Barbados. Yet, because the low wine batch started out with a higher alcohol content, it may have been easier and more expeditious to regulate the strength of the spirit using the Jamaican method.

Martin indicated that Barbadians produced weak rum, but the evidence for such generalizations about alcohol content is unclear for the late eighteenth century and certainly does not reflect early rum making in Barbados. As early as the 1640s, Barbadian distillers "double distilled" their rum to make high proof spirits. Ligon clearly described the practice of separately distilling the low wine to such a high alcohol content that the resulting rum would catch a flame.[59] In fact, Barbadian planters were so concerned with the strength of their rum that the Barbados Assembly passed an act in 1670 that fined planters £100 for producing rum that would not catch fire.[60] This probably refers to the old practice of gauging the strength of spirits by mixing them with gunpowder. Gunpowder, steeped in a spirit that contained more than 50 percent alcohol, will ignite. In the 1730s, an anonymous author from St. Kitts hinted that some Barbadians make rum "nine Degrees upon the Proof," or 54.5 percent absolute alcohol.[61] In the mid-eighteenth century, Belgrove's Barbados distillery was apparently also set up for the separate distillation of low wine.[62] In short, some distillers in Barbados, particularly in the early years of the Barbadian rum industry, did produce highly concentrated rum.

Although Martin described the production of highly concentrated rum in Jamaica, the practice was not universal in the late eighteenth century. For example, in 1774, Long wrote, "Some [Jamaican] planters draw the runnings too long, from a mistaken thrift of making the most they can, and thus perhaps depreciate the whole of their distillation."[63] Allowing the running to go on too long permitted more water to enter the batch and weaken the rum. It also allowed heavier fusel oils and other impurities, known as *congeners*, to enter the batch, which sometimes resulted in a bad-tasting product known as "still-burnt" rum. However, it appears that Jamaicans were increasingly producing concentrated rum. Edwards' account of double distilling in Jamaica refers to the production of "oil-proof rum," rum consisting of more than 50 percent absolute alcohol in which oil will sink.[64] Moreover, when Edwards noted, "it is the practice of late, with many planters, to raise the proof of rum; thus gaining in strength of spirit what is lost in quantity," he indicated that, although concentrated rum making was still a relatively recent trend in Jamaica, it was becoming more common.[65] The large-scale shift toward concentrated rum making in Jamaica occurred in the nineteenth century. In 1832, Roughley described the production of concentrated Jamaican rum above 61 percent absolute alcohol, or 122 proof.[66] In the 1840s, Wray observed that the standard Jamaican rum contained 60–65 percent absolute alcohol, at 120–130 proof.[67] By the end of the nineteenth century, Jamaican rum was generally exported at 78 percent absolute alcohol.[68]

The practice of raising proof was a rational economic strategy. It allowed the planter to increase the amount of alcohol shipped without increasing shipping costs. A puncheon of 120–130 proof rum contained 10–15 percent more absolute alcohol than a puncheon of proof rum, but the shipping cost and space used were the same. As Martin indicated, the increased strength of Jamaican rum made it more popular on the London market. McCusker's meticulous study of price records from the eighteenth century seems to confirm this. However, concentration does not necessarily correlate with quality. In fact, Martin believed Barbadian distillers produced "a cooler spirit, more palatable and wholesome" than the "fiery spirit" produced in Jamaica. According to Martin, the higher price of Jamaican rum simply reflected its higher alcohol content and, thus, greater potential for adulteration; in terms of quality, Martin argued, "it may be doubted whether the Jamaican-planter does not loose more [presumably in taste and quality] by double distillation and over-proof than he gains by the price at London." Quantity, not quality, as Martin argued, was "evidently the ground of preferring Jamaican-rum."[69]

In a 1778 report to a Parliamentary Committee of Extraordinary Services, William Knowlys, a broker in the Caribbean trade, ranked the different British Caribbean rums. McCusker embraces Knowlys' ranking of rum quality and argues that the higher alcohol content of Jamaican rum made it a better spirit. In addition, McCusker devises models of rum making for each Caribbean colony, which seek to confirm Knowlys' sequence. The model is based on the amount of molasses used in the production of rum (Table 3.4). Jamaican distillers, according to McCusker, used 100 gallons of molasses to produce only 94 gallons of rum, while, in Barbados, 100 gallons of molasses produced 145 gallons of rum. McCusker argues that the greater proportion of molasses used in Jamaican rum making meant that Jamaicans produced higher quality rum.

Table 3.4. John McCusker's Estimate of Molasses to Rum Ratios and Rum Prices, 1768–1772

Colony	Molasses : Rum	Average price per gallon in shillings
Jamaica	100 : 94	3.250
Grenada	100 : 94	2.500
St. Kitts	100 : 105	1.960
Antigua	100 : 120	2.875
Montserrat	100 : 120	2.250
Dominica	100 : 130	1.875
Nevis	100 : 130	1.835
Barbados	100 : 145	1.875

Source: McCusker, Rum and the American Revolution, 128–228.

In the French colonies, distillers made distinctions about rum quality based on the ingredients used in rum making. For example, sugar planter Joseph Francois Charpentier de Cossigny differentiated between *guildive*, drawn from the distillation of pure sugarcane juice [*vesou*], and *tafia* made from scum and molasses.[70] Guildive, sometimes called *rhum*, was apparently the preferred beverage because pure cane juice was less likely to introduce an acidic taste.[71] Distillers in Martinique relinquished the distinction between rhum and tafia in the nineteenth century, but distillers in Guadeloupe and Haiti maintained it until the early twentieth century.[72] In the modern French Caribbean, *rhum agricole* indicates rum made from pure cane juice, while *rhum industriel* indicates rum made from molasses and scum.

Unlike their French Caribbean counterparts, British Caribbean distillers appear to have made no distinction between rum made from sugarcane juice and rum made from molasses and scum. While molasses may have been a preferred ingredient for its high sucrose content, British Caribbean distillers had no problem using large amounts of scum to make their rum. The most important criterion of British Caribbean rum making was that the wash contained the proper amount of fermentable sucrose; whether sucrose entered the wash in molasses, scum, or pure cane juice did not matter. In fact, at the beginning of the crop, planters relied entirely on scum to produce rum, while at the end they relied heavily on molasses. Pure cane juice from "rum canes" was also occasionally set aside for rum making. In the British Caribbean, the quality of the rum produced was the same regardless of the source of sucrose.

The Destinations of Caribbean Rum in the Eighteenth Century

At the beginning of the eighteenth century, Caribbean rum began to leak across the Atlantic and threaten the traditional grape-based alcohol industries of southern Europe. Wine and brandy interests in Spain and France quickly corked Caribbean rum in a mercantilist bottle. In the Spanish Caribbean, colonial officials outlawed rum making and forced Spanish Caribbean rum makers underground. French Caribbean rum makers fared somewhat better. Although France prohibited rum from entering metropolitan ports, French Caribbean rum makers continued their seventeenth century pattern of supplying markets at the margins of the Atlantic world. At the opposite end of the spectrum, British Caribbean rum making flourished. British officials saw rum as a potential ally in their own battle against foreign alcohol, especially wine and brandy from southern Europe, and they actively encouraged British Caribbean rum imports.

Aguardiente de Caña: Cane Brandy

Spain developed a robust wine industry in the early Christian era, and in the fifteenth century wine production began in the Spanish Canaries. Spanish wine and brandy were widely consumed in the Iberian Peninsula. Huge amounts were also exported to northern Europe. In the 1690s, nearly two-thirds of all wine shipped from the Spanish Canaries went through London.[73] Trade records, travelers' accounts, and the ubiquitous Spanish olive jars often used to transport alcohol (recovered from Spanish colonial archaeological sites) attest to the fact that Spanish wine and brandy found substantial markets in the Spanish American colonies.[74] Spanish wine and brandy were also widely consumed in the foreign Americas. For example, among the numerous alcoholic beverages served at a dinner party held by Barbadian sugar planter James Drax in the late 1640s were "Sherry, Canary, Red sack, wine of Fiall [Faial, Azores]."[75] Moreover, Spanish wine and brandy fueled trade between the Spanish and the Carib Indians in the Lesser Antilles, the Taino Indians in Hispaniola, and Native Americans in Florida and South and Central America.[76]

The wine and brandy trade was central to Spain's economy, and any threat to that industry was immediately quelled. In 1625, English Dominican monk Thomas Gage traveled between Vera Cruz and Mexico City and noted Spanish opposition to colonial alcohol production. In the town of Segura de la Froutera Gage wrote,

> Here ... were presented unto us Clusters of Grapes as fair as any in *Spain*, which were welcome unto us, for that we had seen none since we came from *Spain*; and we saw by them, that the Country thereabouts would be very fit for Vineyards, if the King of *Spain* would grant the planting of Vines in those parts; which often he hath resented to do, lest the Vineyards there should hinder the Trading and Trafick between *Spain* and those parts, which certainly had they but Wine, needed not any commerce with *Spain*.[77]

In the sixteenth century, Spanish colonists in the Americas made fermented alcoholic beverages from sugarcane juice, and, by the mid-seventeenth century, colonists were distilling rum in sugarcane-growing regions of the Spanish Caribbean. Spanish and Spanish colonial officials expressed concern about rum, which competed with Spanish wine and brandy and, thus, threatened colonial import revenues. In addition, many colonial officials perceived excessive rum consumption, especially by African slaves and Indians, as the cause of social disorder. Throughout the second half of the seventeenth century, Spanish colonial officials instituted local ordinances that sought to curb the production and use of rum. The Real Cédula of June 8, 1693, prohibited rum making in all the Spanish colonies. However, the constant reiteration of the prohibition suggests that officials were unable to control illicit distilling.[78]

In the eighteenth century, Spanish Caribbean rum makers continued to face resistance. The War of the Spanish Succession (1701–1714) severely damaged Spain's wine and brandy trade. British imports of Canary wine dropped from 2,695 tuns in 1702 to only 75 tuns the following year. Also, British imports of Spanish wine dropped from 3,718 tuns to only 660 tuns in the same period.[79] The war preoccupied Spanish officials and weakened Spain's ties with her American colonies. After the conflict, Spain tightened commercial control over her colonies, which included tough enforcement of laws designed to curb Spanish colonial rum making. The Real Cédula of August 10, 1714, reiterated the Real Cédula of June 8, 1693. The Crown ordered that all rum-making materials be confiscated and broken. The owners were fined 100 pesos for the first offense and 2,000 pesos for the second; a third offense brought a 3,000-peso fine and exile. One-third of the money collected from the fines and confiscations went to judges and two-thirds went to the royal coffers of the Consejo de Indias in Spain.[80] The ban exemplified mercantilist thinking in eighteenth-century Spain and was evidently aimed at increasing exports of metropolitan wine and brandy to the Spanish American colonies.

After the war, Spanish wine and brandy exports recovered. In the eighteenth century, Britain alone imported over 111 million gallons of Spanish wine and over 10 million gallons of Canary.[81] Protecting this valuable national industry meant that prohibitions against *aguardiente de caña* remained strong. Nonetheless, the demand for Spanish wine and brandy in the Spanish Americas outweighed supply and, as a result, wine and brandy making expanded in Peru.[82] In the seventeenth and eighteenth centuries, Peruvian *bodegas* [wineries] helped satiate the demand for wine and brandy in distant and marginal areas of the Spanish American world. While Spanish and Peruvian wine and brandy helped meet some of the colonial alcohol needs, especially those of the elite who could afford them, the illicit production of *aguardiente de caña* filled the void.

In the eighteenth century, Spanish colonial officials proved too weak to control illicit rum making. They were forced to reiterate rum-making prohibitions and impose harsher measures to achieve compliance. In Cuba, a decree of 1739 gave distillers 15 days to cease operations or face fines and the destruction of their property.[83] Illicit distilling continued and, in 1754, Cuban officials ordered the destruction of stills and the impoverishment of illicit distillers; those caught distilling were forced to work on public fortifications without salary until they had become beggars.[84]

A series of events in the mid-eighteenth century helped stimulate Spanish Caribbean rum making. The Seven Years War (1756–1763) disrupted American trade and, in 1762, British forces captured Havana, Cuba. The occupation force introduced large numbers of slaves. They may have also brought distilling equipment and knowledge of advanced rum-making methods. Following the occupation, Spain's Bourbon reforms liberalized Spanish American trade. In 1764, open trade between French and Spanish Caribbean colonies increased the flow of French Caribbean rum, rum-making equipment, and knowledge of advanced rum-making techniques to the Spanish Caribbean.[85] Spain also experimented with free trade zones, like the entrepôt at Monte Cristi in northern Santo Domingo, which probably also increased access to foreign Caribbean rum and information about advanced rum-making techniques. These more open trade policies emphasize Spain's growing concern about the economic viability of her Spanish Caribbean colonies and new attempts to spur colonial growth and development.

In 1764, shortly after the British occupation, officials lifted the prohibitions against rum making and use in Cuba and Puerto Rico.[86] The inability to stop illicit rum trafficking probably hastened this decision. Opening the rum industry also meant increased revenues from distilling licenses. In the 1770s, Cuban rum was exported to New Spain, Cartagena, New Orleans, and Florida, where rum making was still prohibited.[87] Cuban rum exports jumped from less than 50,000 gallons in 1778 to an annual average of more than 100,000 gallons in the 1780s.[88]

Despite the removal of legal restrictions, rum making in the Spanish Caribbean remained, at the end of the eighteenth century, a relatively undeveloped industry. Decades of prohibition had stifled Spanish colonial rum making, and few had knowledge of advanced or commercial distilling techniques. In addition, prohibitions against aguardiente de caña ensured that wine and brandy imported from the Canary Islands and Spain, as well as from Peru, continued to be the preferred drink, especially among the elite. Local markets were also saturated with alternative alcoholic beverages, including maguey-based *pulque* and grain-based *chicha* beer, which thrived in the outlying regions of the Spanish Americas.[89] However, the main factor inhibiting the growth of Spanish Caribbean rum making was the lack of a metropolitan market.

In the eighteenth century, as in the seventeenth century, Spanish America remained an important destination for foreign Caribbean rum. French Caribbean traders carried substantial amounts of foreign rum to Spanish colonists. For example, between 1733 and 1752, Martinique exported an annual average of 1,457 *barriques* of tafia, or about 167,000 gallons, to the Spanish mainland colonies.[90] In 1786, St. Domingue, Martinique, and Guadeloupe exported just over 100,000 gallons of tafia, as well as another 200 *boucauts* (about 22,000 gallons) of higher quality rhum to the same destination.[91] French Caribbean traders also exported rum to other parts of the Spanish Americas. Santo Domingo, bordering the wealthy French colony of St. Domingue, relied heavily on the illegal smuggling of French Caribbean tafia. M.L.E. Moreau de St.-Méry, a Creole lawyer from St. Domingue, wrote a detailed account of Spanish Santo Domingo, but made no reference to rum production in the colony. He concluded,

> The temperance of these islanders is again remarkable in their drink, which is generally water. . . . They are fond enough of *taffia*; but, as they have none, except what is smuggled to them, it is at once very scarce and dear, selling so high as thirty French sous a pint.[92]

British Caribbean rum traders also benefited from the demand for rum in the Spanish colonies. Long estimated that in the period 1768–1771, Jamaicans shipped an annual average of about 120,000 gallons of rum to "South America, and other Parts."[93] Most of this rum, according to Long, went to Spanish America in exchange for "mules and horned cattle." The Dutch entrepôt of Curaçao was a jumping-off point for much of the rum illegally shipped to the Spanish mainland colonies. The British Free Port Act of 1766 opened four ports in Jamaica to foreign shipping, which probably increased rum trading between Jamaica and Cuba.[94] One drawback to the Jamaican free-port system, however, was that Spanish and French brandy was easily smuggled into Jamaica "to the great prejudice of the rum market."[95]

The American and Haitian Revolutions stimulated the Cuban rum industry. The first big rise in Cuban rum exports occurred after the American Revolution. Cuban rum exports jumped from less than 50,000 gallons in 1778 to an annual average of nearly 150,000 at the height of hostilities in 1781 and 1782.[96] According to Jamaican Congregational minister W. J. Gardner, British trade restrictions following the American Revolution forced U.S. ships to Cuba, where they obtained rum for U.S. lumber and provisions.[97] Cuban rum helped feed the great American drinking binge that followed the Revolution. However, the United States also made its own rum from imported molasses and, in the 1780s, the volume of Cuban molasses and rum exports were nearly equal.

The second jump in Cuban rum exports occurred during the Haitian Revolution. In the 1790s, the Haitian Revolution disrupted the rum and molasses trade from the French Caribbean to North and South America. Many French colonials fled to Cuba bringing with them slaves and sugar- and rum-making equipment. In 1790, the year before the slave uprising, Cuba exported about 178,000 gallons of rum. By the first decade of the 1800s, rum exports averaged almost 900,000 gallons per year. Cuban rum exports peaked at the height of the conflict in 1802, reaching more than 1.6 million gallons—a level that would not be achieved again for another half century.[98] The peak in rum exports also coincided with the last year of the U.S. whiskey tax. Regional rum exports probably also helped satisfy the alcoholic needs of the huge numbers of European soldiers and sailors converging on the Caribbean at this time. Although rum production was expanding, molasses exports were still more important to the Cuban economy. In the first decade of the 1800s, the volume of Cuban molasses exports was two and a half times greater than rum exports. St. Domingue was the largest exporter of molasses to the United States, and after the Haitian Revolution, Cuba emerged to fill the void.

Tafia

In the French Caribbean, rum making emerged in the early years of settlement alongside sugar production. Rum was widely consumed in the French Caribbean and exported to markets at the fringes of the Atlantic world. By the eighteenth century, French wine and brandy interests began to see rum as a potential threat, and they persuaded French officials to take action. In 1713, France closed its ports to rum. However, unlike the situation in the Spanish Caribbean, the restrictions did not prohibit French Caribbean rum making or force distillers underground.

French wine and brandy met the alcoholic needs of the French people, who imbued French alcohol with classical symbolism and nationalistic pride. The French wine trade, especially with England, had been huge since the early Middle Ages, and this trade was central to the French economy. However, in the sixteenth century, France began to lose important markets in northern Europe to sweet wines from Spain and Portugal. Conflict between France and England in the late seventeenth century also disrupted French wine exports.[99]

The most significant threat to the French wine trade to Britain, however, may have been wine producers and merchants from Oporto and the Atlantic island of Madeira. The British Navigation Act of 1663 allowed Portuguese wines to be exported directly to the British Americas without having to pass through English ports. The privileged position of Portuguese wine was expanded in 1703 when it was given favorable trade status in the British Empire in exchange for the right to sell English cloth to Portugal duty-free.[100] Wine from Portugal and Madeira was well liked in Britain. For example, during the eighteenth century, in what represented its largest wine import, Britain imported more than 295 million gallons of port, an Oporto wine of high alcohol content. Britain also imported in the same period at least another 13 million gallons of wine from Madeira.[101] Portuguese wine was especially popular among elites in the British American colonies. In 1740, Jamaica visitor Charles Leslie wrote, "The common Drink here is *Madera* Wine . . . [which] is used by the better Sort."[102] In 1732, Barbados imported £30,000 worth of wine from Madeira, which represented nearly 9 percent of the value of its total imports.[103] Even French colonials had a favorable opinion of Madeira.[104]

French wine and brandy interests could not defeat their Portuguese competition, but they could remove the threat of French Caribbean rum. They argued that guildive, a corruption of the British Caribbean *kill devil*, had deleterious health consequences. In contrast, French wine and brandy were touted as salubrious beverages, and the name given to French brandy, *eau de vie* or water of life, strengthened that image. In 1680, sugar refiners in France petitioned the government for the right to distill *eau de vie de mélasse* produced from the waste, or *syrup*, of sugar refineries. They were unsuccessful, however, which suggests that by the late seventeenth century the French government already opposed the production of non-grape-based alcohols. On January 21, 1713, Louis XIV issued a royal decree that prohibited the home production of non-grape-based alcoholic beverages, including those made from pears, grains, and the waste of sugar refineries.[105] The decree also prohibited—except for the ports in Normandy—the import of French Caribbean rum. The declaration specifically argued that rum was pernicious to health and threatened to compete with French wine and brandy.[106]

Despite war-related setbacks throughout the eighteenth century, as well as competition from wine and brandy makers in Spain and Portugal, the French wine and brandy trade, particularly to northern Europe, remained central to the French economy. The British continued to like French alcohol and imported more than 48 million gallons of brandy and 18 million gallons of French wine.[107] French wine and brandy also fed significant markets in Ireland, Africa, and the French and foreign Americas.[108] As a result, the 1713 ban against French Caribbean rum imports remained in effect throughout most of the eighteenth century. Yet, despite the restrictions, French Caribbean rum makers were more successful than their Spanish Caribbean counterparts. The ban may have limited the growth of French Caribbean rum making, but French Caribbean rum makers continued to supply a large share of the Atlantic markets.

According to French distilling technologist D. Kervégant, during the first half of the eighteenth century, Martinique produced about 250,000 to 500,000 gallons of rum annually and exported about half of its produce.[109] Annual tafia exports from Martinique between 1743 and 1745 reached about 490,000 gallons. Yet, despite a fairly substantial tafia export trade, the value of tafia exports from Martinique in this period represented only about 2 percent of the value of sugar exported to France.[110]

In the late seventeenth and early eighteenth centuries, France implemented Jean-Baptiste Colbert's mercantilist policies. The *exclusif* system restricted French Caribbean trade with foreigners and sought to spur the same type of positive trade relationship between the French Caribbean and French North America that existed between the British Caribbean and the British continental colonies. As a result, French North America became a main destination for French Caribbean rum. Until 1763, rum was a chief item of trade in New France, where it fueled the North American fur trade. At French bases in Newfoundland, Royal Island, and St.-Pierre and Miquelon, rum was exchanged for codfish, which helped feed the growing slave populations of the French Caribbean.[111] French Canada also supplied much-needed plantation supplies, including timber, tar, and livestock. The French colony of Louisiana received its share of tafia. According to French colonial historian Guy Josa, in 1744, Martinique shipped about 350,000 gallons to French colonies in North America.[112]

Although the *exclusif* prohibited trade with foreigners, the British continental colonies were an important destination for French Caribbean goods. This illicit trade highlights the vigor of the barter economy in the Americas. In the seventeenth century, New Englanders purchased cheap French Caribbean molasses at French, Dutch, Danish, and British American ports, which they carried home and used for their own rum industries. French Caribbean rum was less important than molasses in the North American trade and, in fact, French wine and brandy reexports from the French Caribbean often exceeded those of French Caribbean rum.[113] French Caribbean sugar planters, who had

no home market for rum, had plenty of molasses for the North American traders. Sugar planters in Martinique and Guadeloupe had an especially large
amount of molasses available since they clayed nearly all of their sugar.[114] However, the molasses trade between British North America and the French Caribbean was problematic for British sugar planters. A Barbadian explained,

> The French, unacquainted with the principles of distillation, furnished the
> Americans with considerable quantities of molasses, for the support of their
> distilleries, which, but for that intercourse, must have been thrown away.
> Hence the consumption of West Indian spirits was materially lessened on
> the American continent, to the manifest injury of the planters of Barbadoes,
> with whom rum was an important staple.[115]

If North Americans produced rum from cheap foreign molasses, then the
value of British Caribbean rum decreased. British Caribbean planters relied
on their rum to help cover the cost of plantation supplies, much of which they
purchased from North America.

North American imports of French Caribbean molasses raised the price of
provisions in the British Caribbean and led to great controversy in the British
Empire. French colonial administrator Georges Marie Butel-Dumont wrote,

> the people of New England exercise with the French Caribbean a commerce
> of contraband in which they buy our rum, molasses, and sugar for their use
> and in exchange we get horses and provisions. The problems that this traffic
> causes the British Caribbean has led Parliament to restrict the Americans'
> right to trade with foreigners.[116]

In 1733, British Parliament passed the Molasses Act, which imposed a six-
pence-per-gallon tax on foreign molasses entering British North American
ports. The tax was especially aimed at curbing importation of the French Caribbean molasses, which New Englanders used to produce rum. However, the
Molasses Act was rarely obeyed or enforced, and New Englanders found numerous ways of circumventing the tax through bribes and smuggling. Despite
restrictions imposed by the exclusif and the Molasses Act, French Caribbean
molasses continued to flow into New England ports.

The Molasses Act also barred French Caribbean rum from ports in Ireland.
In the early eighteenth century, a thriving trade developed between Ireland and
the French Caribbean. The Irish exchanged provisions, such as salted beef,
pork, fish, butter, and tallow for French Caribbean rum. Parliament specifically
targeted the French trade. Portuguese traders, for example, were not prohib-

ited from the Irish market, although their goods paid higher duty. Despite the restrictions, smugglers continued to supply Irish markets with French Caribbean rum.[117] However, as with the French Caribbean trade to North America, French Caribbean rum probably represented a small portion of Irish imports. French wine and brandy, reexported to Ireland from the French Caribbean, occasionally surpassed French Caribbean rum imports.[118]

In 1763, at the end of the Seven Years War, New England traders had easier access to French Caribbean molasses. After the Treaty of Paris, France was forced to give up control of French Canada and, as a result, the French Caribbean lost a crucial market for its goods and a major source of plantation supplies. In order to compensate for the loss, the French government loosened restrictions on French Caribbean trade. French colonists were allowed to ship their goods to neutral ports in St. Eustatius and the free port at Monte Cristi in northern Santo Domingo. In 1763, admiralty ports were opened to foreign traders in Martinique and Guadeloupe. Imports were restricted to codfish, lumber, livestock, and other goods that French metropolitan merchants could not adequately supply. In exchange, the French Caribbean could export molasses and rum only. Hundreds of foreign ships, especially from New England, entered these ports and took advantage of the opening French Caribbean trade.[119]

However, the opening French trade increased the frustrations of British Caribbean sugar planters. Martin encouraged British Caribbean sugar planters to reduce their dependence on North American goods by setting aside plantation lands for provisions.

> Besides the advantage of having a large product of our provision, independently of casual supplies, we may by that means prevent the monopoly of corn, and in some measure the constant drain of our current cash, which the New-England traders now carry to St. Eustatius, for the purchase of French sugar, rum, and molasses, and other foreign manufactures. A base, destructive trade, which (if not effectually prevented) will infallibly exalt the French islands upon the ruins of these [British] colonies. This illicit trade is audaciously carried on in the face of the sun, by the most flagitious race of men; by parricides who stab their country to the heart, that they may suck their subsistence from its vital blood.[120]

After the peace in Paris, Britain's parliament, swayed by British Caribbean interests in London, took a more interventionist role in developing the economy of the continental colonies. The Sugar, or American Revenues, Act of

1764 established greater metropolitan judicial control that strengthened enforcement of the Molasses Act. The 1764 act lowered the duty on foreign molasses to three pence per gallon in an attempt to discourage bribery and smuggling, but it also levied an equal tax on British Caribbean molasses. The continental colonists' reaction was to boycott all British goods. Within two years, the Sugar Act was repealed and a reduced duty of a penny per gallon was levied on all imported molasses. At the same time, the French government extended open trade. In 1767, free ports were opened at Carenage in St. Lucia and Môle St.-Nicolas in northern St. Domingue. The following year, a British naval commander complained,

> The more I consider the new Settlement and Freeport of the French at Cape Nicholas [Môle St.-Nicolas], of the more consequence it appears to me. In time of Peace it inveigles the whole North American Trade to them, which supplies them with lumber and Provisions at a low sale and drains us of Cash, and at the same time supplies North America with Sugar, Molasses, and Rum to the great distress of our West India Islands.[121]

French Caribbean trade with the Spanish mainland also steadily increased during the eighteenth century, making it one of the largest markets for French Caribbean tafia. Between 1733 and 1752, Martinique exported an annual average of about 167,000 gallons to the Spanish mainland colonies. In 1749, Martinican tafia exports to the Spanish mainland colonies peaked at nearly 300,000 gallons.[122] According to French colonial historian Jean Tarrade, exports from Guadeloupe to the Spanish colonies increased from 103 barriques of tafia in 1766, to 134 barriques in 1776, to 100 barriques and 200 boucauts of higher quality rum in 1786. In 1786, Tarrade estimated that St. Domingue exported over 54,000 gallons of tafia to the Spanish mainland colonies.[123]

The growing economic importance of the French Caribbean colonies in the eighteenth century weakened metropolitan opposition to rum. In 1752, French Caribbean interests won the right to place rum in bonded warehouses in France for reexport to Africa.[124] The ports of La Rochelle, Nantes, and Bordeaux—all key departure points for French slavers—benefited from this policy.[125] French wine and brandy interests continued to resist, and they even appealed to French class and racial consciousness. In 1764, a concerned spokesman for French wine and brandy merchants wrote,

> Self-interest, that passion which nature seems to have placed in man's heart only to degrade him, has inspired some residents in our colonies to make a

branch of commerce out of the invention of types of eau de vie made from sugar that are as pernicious to health as they are unpleasant to taste. As this strong liquor is cheap, the blacks use it, since their poverty will not allow them to numb themselves with a more satisfying brew. If there were no need to profit from the product of their labors and if human and divine laws did not order one to watch over their conservation, perhaps it would be an act of humanity to let them hasten the end of their days by its usage; but at least it is incontestable that one cannot excuse the effort to introduce this poison into our lands and climes, where the inhabitants, true men, enjoy the favors of humanity.[126]

In 1759, at the height of the Seven Years War, British troops captured the French Caribbean colony of Guadeloupe, and in 1762 they took Martinique. The capture of these islands fueled the expansion of French Caribbean rum making. In Guadeloupe and Martinique, British troops introduced slaves and distilling equipment and taught French colonials improved methods of rum making. According to Josa, before the conquest, Martinique had a small number of distilleries, and most foreigners refused to buy what was perceived as poor quality French Caribbean tafia.[127] The British occupation helped rectify some of these problems, and when Martinique was returned to France in 1763, the production of rum attracted the attention of the judges of the Council of Nantes, who demanded the admission of rum into France and a lifting of the 1713 ban. French Caribbean interests argued that rum did not have adverse consequences for health and pointed out that the people of Normandy and Britain, where rum had been legally traded for decades, were healthy.

Despite resistance from wine and brandy interests, the growth of rum making in Martinique and Guadeloupe, along with the need to bolster the French Caribbean economies after the Seven Years War, helped expand the French Caribbean rum trade. After 1763, open trade policies increased the rum trade between the French Caribbean and foreigners. In 1768, trade restrictions were further relaxed to permit French Caribbean rum into France for reexport to any place that would sell codfish in exchange—a policy that may have been especially aimed at spurring trade between the French Caribbean and British colonials in New England and Newfoundland after the collapse of the American Revenues Act in 1765.[128] An earthquake at Port-au-Prince in 1771 destroyed much of the city, and the demand for food and building materials further stimulated French Caribbean rum and molasses trades with British North America. In France, the Council of Commerce met at the end of 1775 to address the issue of relaxing metropolitan restrictions on the rum trade. After strong lobbying from French Caribbean interests, the ban on Caribbean rum exports to France was lifted the following year.[129]

French Caribbean sugar planters attempted to capitalize on the opening in the French market. In the late eighteenth century, they wrote numerous treatises on rum distilling that show a growing interest in the economic potential of this industry.[130] Some French Caribbean distillers mastered the art of rum making, including the famous distiller, Sir Loubery of Martinique, who may have perfected his skills during the British occupation of the island from 1762 to 1763.[131] However, the British Caribbean remained the center of rum making, and sugar planters in St. Domingue occasionally hired experienced Jamaican distillers to help them improve their rum-making techniques.[132] Yet, despite the growing interest in rum, the late-eighteenth-century French Caribbean rum makers could not penetrate the huge French alcohol market.

In 1767, French lawyer Michel René Hilliard d'Auberteuil reported that less than 1 percent of St. Domingue's administrative revenues came from tafia duties; in fact, he did not even feel the need to list it among the colony's major exports.[133] Prior to the Haitian Revolution, exports were less than 300,000 gallons per year.[134] In the mid-eighteenth century, much of the rum exported from St. Domingue was probably shipped to Louisiana, New England, French Canada, the Spanish mainland colonies, and entrepôts in the Dutch Caribbean. In the late eighteenth century, the metropolitan market for French Caribbean rum remained small and, in 1791, nearly 40 years after the initial relaxing of restrictions, St. Domingue's rum export to France was only 303 barrels. To judge from the colonial censuses, as well as the 1791 export statistics, rum production was concentrated in the colony's south and west provinces. As it clayed almost all of its sugar, the north province produced relatively more molasses; but this it shipped to North America, with which it enjoyed extensive relations, producing rum mainly for local consumption. In the mid 1780s, the north province housed 37 percent of the colony's sugar factories but only 25 percent of the distilleries.[135]

Although not a major export item, tafia augmented French Caribbean sugar plantation revenues. In the period from 1742 to 1762, accounts from Galbaud du Fort sugar plantation in Léogane, St. Domingue, show that the plantation's two *guildiviers* sold enough rum to contribute 10 to 20 percent of plantation revenues in these two decades.[136]

Tafia makers in Martinique and Guadeloupe were probably more successful than their counterparts in St. Domingue. In 1785, Martinique had 316 sugar factories and 215 guildiveries, which suggests that nearly 70 percent of sugar plantations distilled their sugarcane juice and the waste products of sugar making. In that same year, Guadeloupe had 415 sugar factories and 128 guildiveries, implying that 31 percent of plantations were involved in rum making.[137] In contrast, St. Domingue had proportionally far fewer guildiveries. In 1789, Moreau de St.-Méry estimated that at the height of production on the eve of the Haitian Revolution, St. Domingue had 793 sugar factories, but only 182 rum distilleries. So it appears that less than a quarter of St. Domingue's sugar plantations were distilling sugarcane juice and sugar industry waste products into rum.[138] This figure accounts for plantation-based distilling operations, as well as independent urban distilleries such as Fort Sainte-Claire, a "seaside" distillery in Port-au-Prince, which, in 1768, was advertised for sale in the colonies' main newspaper, *Affiches Américaines*.[139]

Although it had a smaller sugar industry, Martinique supplied 40 percent of the tafia sold to the Spanish mainland colonies in 1786.[140] Almost all of the higher quality French Caribbean rhum exported to the Spanish mainland colonies came from Guadeloupe, suggesting that distillers there may have been trying to carve out a particularly elite market. The disproportionately high number of distilleries in Martinique and Guadeloupe indicates the positive effects of both the British occupation during the Seven Years War and the islands' closer proximity to the Spanish mainland colonies. In addition, Martinique and Guadeloupe, unlike their counterparts in St. Domingue, clayed a greater proportion of their sugar, which provided them with a great deal more molasses for distilling. While St. Domingue exported large quantities of molasses to North America, Martinique and Guadeloupe developed solid rum industries. In the late eighteenth century, St. Domingue even became a destination for rum from Martinique and Guadeloupe![141]

As trade restrictions on French Caribbean rum were being lifted, French Caribbean rum makers began to embrace new opportunities. The lifting of the 1713 ban in 1776 coincided with the American Revolution, which temporarily had a positive effect on French Caribbean rum making. In 1778, the French entered the fight on the side of the Americans and evidently hoped to take over the huge North American rum market. Martinican rum exports to the United States increased during the height of the war, jumping more than fivefold between 1771 and 1777. Martinique also exported hundreds of barriques of tafia to St. Martin and St. Barts in this period, most of which were probably reexported to North America.[142]

The American Revolution led to the expansion of rum making in St.

Domingue. Historian Jacques Cauna's study of the Fleuriau plantation in western St. Domingue shows the surge in rum production during the American Revolution. Between 1777 and 1787, according to Cauna, the plantation produced 2,254 barriques of tafia for an annual average of 205 barriques, about 24,000 gallons. In some years, tafia contributed 20–25 percent of the plantation's revenues. In 1783, Fleuriau produced more than 35,000 gallons of rum, as well as a high rum-to-sugar ratio of 8.9 gallons per cwt. of sugar. Rum making declined after the Revolutionary War, however, and by 1787, the rum-to-sugar ratio fell to 1.2 gallons per cwt. of sugar. Between 1788 and 1791, Fleuriau produced no rum, but generated an increasing amount of molasses.[143]

Peaks in tafia exports from Martinique, as well as the increase in tafia making at Fleuriau plantation in St. Domingue, coincided with the height of the American Revolution. During the conflict, distilling industries in the rebellious continental colonies lost access to steady supplies of rum and molasses, especially from the British Caribbean. New York and Boston, centers of North American distilling, were both occupied by British forces. French Caribbean rum helped fill that void during the conflict. However, North American traders had always preferred to exchange provisions for cheap molasses, which they could distill themselves, and after the war, French Caribbean rum exports to the United States dropped.[144] This decline probably also reveals the decreasing American demand for rum. During the war, large amounts of rum were needed to provision European and continental soldiers. Rum and molasses from Cuba also began to penetrate the U.S. market, and after 1783, the rum trade between the British Caribbean and the United States resumed, albeit under restrictive conditions. In addition, rum was associated with colonial dependence and, therefore, "suffered from rising nationalism."[145] Once a universal spirit in the continental colonies, by 1790, rum represented only two-thirds of the hard liquor consumed. In the late eighteenth and early nineteenth centuries, whiskey, made from American-grown corn, replaced rum as the national drink, especially after the repeal of the whiskey excise tax in 1802.[146]

In the second half of the eighteenth century, France began to lift restrictions on the French Caribbean rum trade. In a comparative sense, French government policy toward the French Caribbean rum industry was less restrictive than Spain's. French Caribbean rum was extensively consumed within the French Caribbean and was an important item of trade with foreigners. As a result, French Caribbean tafia distillers were not forced to make dramatic changes in their industries once trade restrictions were lifted. Nevertheless, metropolitan restrictions on the French Caribbean rum trade and the lack of a substantial metropolitan market resulted in the stagnation of distillation technologies, especially in St. Domingue, which did not benefit from British influence during the Seven Years War. In 1786, a series of articles in St. Domingue's newspaper described the relatively underdeveloped state of the island's tafia making.

> The rum factories are rather important for our commerce and for our colonies, and we should address them seriously. America consumes a great deal of rum, and the British islands cannot give them sufficient quantity. As they are not able to get it from our colonies, which do not distill much, the Americans come and take our molasses and distill it themselves.[147]

Despite the growing number of treatises on rum making, fifteen years after France lifted the ban against rum imports into French ports, a slave rebellion erupted in St. Domingue, and by 1804, France had lost its potentially most productive rum-making colony.

Rum

In the seventeenth century, British Caribbean sugar planters developed strong rum industries that catered to the alcoholic needs of colonists on the Atlantic frontier. Moreover, and in contrast to the situation in the Spanish and French Caribbean, rum also found a place in the British metropolitan market. British officials welcomed British Caribbean rum as an ally in their war against foreign spirits that had drained England of capital for centuries. They opened the home market to British Caribbean rum and offered incentives to British Caribbean rum makers. As a result, rum sales boosted the revenues of British Caribbean sugar estates.

Amphorae vessel shards litter early archaeological sites in England and attest to the popularity of southern European wine in England prior to the Roman conquest.[148] Roman conquerors attempted to establish viticulture in southern England, but it was probably not until the tenth or eleventh centuries that viticulture was regularly practiced there. The Norman conquest of 1066 increased English contact with northern France and spurred the rise of early English viticulture. However, the cold climate prevented the large-scale production of wine in England and, in order to meet demand, English merchants continued to import huge amounts of wine from southern Europe.[149]

In the Middle Ages, most wine entered England through Anglo-Gascon merchants based in Bordeaux. In the first decade of the fourteenth century, wine exports from Gascon ports averaged more than 20 million gallons per year, and England represented the main market. Bad grape harvests, plague, and the commencement of the Hundred Years War disrupted British wine imports for the next century. By the time Bordeaux fell to the French in 1453, the Anglo-Gascon wine trade had been greatly curtailed.[150] The fall of Bordeaux undermined English alcohol supplies and substantiated concerns about England's dependence on foreign alcohol. Spanish and Portuguese wine helped fill the void, and the English penchant for sweet wines from the Canaries and Madeira magnified the role of Spain and Portugal in the English wine market. However, conflict between England and Spain during the sixteenth century, and conflict in Europe throughout the sixteenth and seventeenth centuries, reexposed England's vulnerability and renewed fears about alcohol supplies.

England's goal was clear: reduce its dependence on foreign wine and brandy imports, which siphoned away substantial amounts of English capital. This objective fueled the search for alternative alcohol sources at the beginning of English New World exploration and settlement in the Elizabethan age. Thomas Hariot, a member of the original Virginia colony (1585–1586) wrote,

> There are two kinds of grapes that the soil yields naturally; the one is small and sour, of the ordinary bigness as ours in England, the other far greater is luscious sweet. When they are planted and husbanded as they ought, a principal commodity of wines by them may be raised.[151]

James I encouraged the search for alternative alcohol sources during the first permanent English settlement in the New World at Jamestown in 1607.[152] Although colonists in Jamestown produced wine as early as 1609, their endeavors largely failed because the fragile vines imported from southern Europe were unable to withstand the harsh North American climate.

King William's War at the end of the seventeenth century curtailed British imports of French wine and brandy. At the first sign of conflict, parliament passed an act prohibiting the import of French alcohol. Although the act was repealed in 1685, parliament placed heavy duties on French wine and brandy imports four years later during the Grand Alliance against France in 1689. These duties remained in effect until the end of the seventeenth century. King William's War was soon followed by the War of the Spanish Succession. It was in 1703, during the third year of that conflict, that England instituted the Methuen Treaty, which allowed imports of Portuguese wine at less than one-third the rate imposed on alcohol from France.[153]

These conflicts revived fears about the vulnerability of British alcohol markets and stimulated interest in British Caribbean rum. England's limited success with viticulture precluded the implementation of protectionist policies against rum like those found in the southern European grape-growing nations of Spain and France. While England and Wales imported a mere 22 gallons of rum in 1697, that figure jumped to more than 22,000 gallons in 1710. By the 1730s, rum regularly surpassed most fermented alcohol imports, including French, Spanish, and Madeira wine.[154]

Brandy, however, proved to be a more formidable competitor. The British imported brandy from France, Portugal, and Spain. Like rum, brandy was a distilled alcoholic beverage made for those seeking a concentrated spirit. But brandy was expensive and consumed primarily by the British elite, who perceived it to be a superior drink. British Caribbean interests attempted to defeat brandy consumption in Britain by appealing to nationalistic sentiment.

> The notion of the superiority of Brandy to Rum ... has done mischief to our West-Indian colonies; and been injurious to our balance of trade, and political interest, by augmenting the consumption of a foreign commodity, purchased for money of our rivals, to the exclusion of one produced in our own dominions, and supplied in exchange for our manufactures and domestic products.[155]

In 1719, British imports of rum surpassed those of brandy for the first time. After 1741, rum imports regularly exceeded those of brandy for the rest of the century (Figure 3.3).

The use of distilled spirits increased in Britain during the seventeenth century as the secrets of distillation became common knowledge and the availability of distilled spirits grew.[156] The increased access to syrup from sugar refiners also provided huge amounts of cheap base material for distilling.[157] In the mid-seventeenth century, British soldiers stationed in the Low Countries of western Europe were introduced to gin, the invention of a Dutch physician. Gin, otherwise known as "Dutch courage," quickly became a popular spirit in Britain. Although the Dutch made their gin from barley, British distillers soon began producing their own version from corn [wheat] and syrup. Both Dutch and British distillers added the juice of juniper berries to give gin (the word derives from the Dutch word *jevener* [juniper]) its distinctive taste.

Compared to imported brandy, locally made gin was cheap and met the increasing alcohol needs of the British working classes. British grain interests supported gin making because it kept grain prices high and provided a

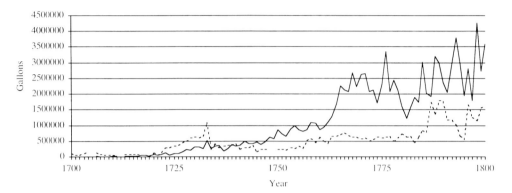

————— Volume of Rum Imports into England and Wales

- - - - - Volume of Brandy Imports into England and Wales

Figure 3.3. Rum and brandy imports into England and Wales. Graph by author. *Source*: Schumpeter, *English Overseas Trade*.

profitable outlet for surplus crops. Gin cut reliance on foreign spirits and, as a result, farmers appealed to British officials for support. In 1690, parliament imposed restrictive duties on foreign spirits and passed a series of statutes aimed at promoting the distillation of spirits from English grain.[158] That same year the London Company of Distillers, which under Charles I had been given exclusive rights to distill spirits in a 21-mile radius around London and Westminster, crumbled, and anyone able to pay excise duties could establish themselves as a distiller.[159] In 1688, "an excise duty was levied on half a million gallons of British spirits; by 1720 the amount was 2.5 million gallons and growing." In 1730, there were 1,500 distillers in London, and by 1735, excise duties were paid on 6.4 million gallons of gin.[160]

Conversely, in 1733, Britain imported about 500,000 gallons of rum.[161] Rum did not threaten British metropolitan alcohol industries. British grain distillers, who produced cheap gin, were more concerned about poor grain harvests and high bread prices than heavily taxed rum imported from the colonies. The British were huge consumers of foreign and domestic alcoholic beverages, and rum simply fit into the wide array of drinks available to the British public.

The growing use of spirits worried some British officials. In particular, gin drinking was seen as the cause of a variety of social and health disorders. Gin was given the name "mother's ruin," and it was widely accepted that one could get "drunk for five farthings, and dead drunk for two-pence half-penny."[162] Some attributed high mortality and low fertility rates in eighteenth-century

London to excessive gin drinking.[163] Starting in the late 1720s, parliament passed a series of Gin Acts, which were meant to curb the excessive use of distilled spirits, especially gin. The laws increased licensing fees and retail taxes on spirits-sellers. The Gin Act of 1736 included financial rewards to those who informed on illegal and unlicensed retailers.[164] Fearing its impact on rum exports to Britain, the West Indian planter lobby petitioned against the Gin Act. Their fears were justified. In 1737, rum imports into England and Wales fell to about half what they had been the year before.[165] The Gin Act, however, was impossible to enforce and, in the 1740s, per capita consumption of foreign and domestic distilled spirits soared.[166] Imports of British Caribbean rum also rebounded. In 1743, the Gin Act was repealed and replaced by more liberal controls.[167]

British Caribbean rum could not compete with the cheapness and national appeal of home-produced gin. However, poor grain harvests in the 1750s, especially in 1756, helped spur British Caribbean rum imports. The poor harvests increased grain prices, and in an effort to stave off the rising cost of bread, parliament passed legislation that forbade the distillation of grain. In the late 1750s, British Caribbean interests in parliament, led by William Pitt and William Beckford, introduced legislation that prohibited grain distilling. British port towns with the strongest connection to the West Indian trade, such as Liverpool, Bristol, and Lancaster, supported the prohibitions.[168] Parliament may have also seen the grain crisis and the resulting legislation as a way to further reduce social disorder and the public health consequences associated with excessive consumption of cheap gin. In 1760, parliament passed an "act for encouraging the exportation of rum and spirits of the growth, produce, and manufacture, of British sugar plantations." The act lowered tariffs on British Caribbean rum. The ban on grain distilling combined with various parliamentary incentives and public demand for all sorts of alcohol helped British Caribbean rum penetrate the huge British alcohol market and embed itself deeply in the British psyche. Rum, which had already conquered brandy, was encroaching on gin.

British Caribbean rum makers greatly benefited from another official policy: rum contracts with the national navy and army. The prevention of illness among sailors was a major concern of British naval officers, who viewed alcohol as a prophylactic against the many diseases that afflicted seamen. The growth of the British navy in the seventeenth century, due in large measure to the settlement of New World colonies, increased the demand for alcohol rations. British Caribbean interests argued that rum was healthier than other forms of alcohol, and they convinced British officials to adopt rum contracts for the Royal Navy. Britain, eager to support her colonies and, at the same time, reduce her dependence on foreign alcohol, could only benefit from such a situation.

Sidney W. Mintz refers to Britain's rum contracts with the Royal Navy as "much-needed creeping socialism for an infant industry."[169] Yet, by the eighteenth century, rum making was far from its infancy. Still, the British Royal Navy had no standard regulations for rum rationing until 1731, and any rum rationing prior to this time was dependent upon availability and the preference of the ship's captain. In 1731, the first official naval alcohol regulations were implemented. A gallon of beer a day was the standard, but a half-pint of rum could be used instead.[170] Although rum did not become the sole alcoholic beverage of the Royal Navy in the eighteenth century, victualing commissioners in London, under contract with the Royal Navy, helped make rum a more common beverage, especially for forces stationed in the Caribbean. Government-backed commissary agents in the British Caribbean purchased rum and, according to military historian Roger Buckley, the British government profited so much from the sale of contracts and licenses to alcohol distributors at military commissaries and canteens at home and abroad that the system was nothing less than "state-sponsored alcoholism."[171] In 1775, parliament passed an act making rum an integral part of naval rations. This act remained in effect until 1970.[172] British soldiers stationed in the Americas also received their share of rum. According to military historian Paul Kopperman, by the time of the American Revolution, rum rations were a fixed and regular practice in the British army.[173] Buckley estimates that, after the American Revolution, British troops regularly received about three and a half gallons of rum each month.[174]

British rum contracts with its navy and army highlight the efforts of the British Caribbean planter lobby to secure these markets. The need to provision alcohol to large numbers of soldiers and sailors in the Caribbean stimulated the growth of British Caribbean rum industries, and colonial assemblies were more than willing to encourage the practice of rum rationing. For example, in Jamaica, soldiers were "allowed to buy their rum free of the island duty, which is a saving of from 1s. to 1s. 6d. per gallon; an advantage purposely given them by the legislature."[175] There were also less formalized ways of supplying rum to troops. Planters stored rum for traveling troops, especially during times of civil unrest. During Tacky's slave rebellion in Jamaica in 1760, Thomas Thistlewood, the manager of Egypt plantation, broke open casks of stored rum made on his plantation "for to make grog for the troops."[176] This strategy may have helped ensure military protection during such uncertain times. The British Caribbean planter lobby probably also understood that military personnel were the driving force behind metropolitan trends in alcohol use. Thus, in the same way that British soldiers and sailors stationed in the Low Countries in the mid-seventeenth century brought home a taste for gin, British soldiers and sailors stationed in rum-laden posts and on rum-laden ships acquired a taste for rum and nurtured the British Caribbean rum trade to Britain once they returned from duty.[177]

The increasing use of rum in Britain suggests more than the desire of the British working class for drunken escape or the success of mercantilist policies aimed at bolstering the British Caribbean economy. Rum benefited from other forces, especially the traditional link between alcohol and health in Europe. Arnau de Villanova introduced the art of distilling to France in the 1300s and promoted distilled spirits as medicinal. Dutch physician Franciscus Sylvius invented gin to combat maladies afflicting seamen of the Dutch East India Company. Whether the result of postmedieval fears of plague or a consequence of the self-indulgence that accompanies prosperous societies, eighteenth-century Britain was preoccupied with matters of health. Rum helped alleviate those worries.

However, the excessive use of alcohol, especially gin, was of growing concern. British Caribbean rum interests exploited British health insecurities and took advantage of gin's weakness. They promoted the traditional links between alcohol and medicine, but manipulated rising fears about gin. In 1760, an anonymous writer proclaimed, "Since the [1750s] Suppression of Gin the Consumption of Rum has been greatly increased, and yet Dram Drunkenness, with all its dreadful Effects, has entirely ceased." According to the author, "Gin is vastly more destructive to the Human Frame than the Sugar Spirit."[178] In fact, the writer advocated the use of rum for "weak and depraved appetites and Digestions, and in many other Distempers of the declining sort," backing these claims with authoritative recommendations from physicians. The anonymous writer argued against lifting the ban on grain distilling and claimed,

> Gin is a Spirit too fiery, acrid, and inflameing for inward Use—But . . . Rum is a Spirit so mild, balsamic, and benign, that if its properly used and attempered it may be made highly useful, both for the Relief and Regalement of Human Nature.[179]

In Britain, temperance movements were still ill defined in this period, and campaigns against excessive drinking were top-down efforts spurred by clerics and sections of the landed gentry and sanctioned by parliament. In the 1730s, members of the Societies for the Reformation of Manners and the Society for Promoting Christian Knowledge were leading advocates of the Gin Acts.[180] In 1751, artist William Hogarth's "Gin Lane" illustrated growing public fears about excessive gin consumption and the abuses of cheap spirituous liquor, especially among the working classes. That same year, author Henry Fielding wrote *An Enquiry into the Causes of the Late Increase of Robbers*, which attributed rising crime rates to the excessive use of gin.[181] The specific attacks on gin, rather than rum, may simply reflect the greater availability of that cheap spirit and the fear of social disorder by upper-class wine and brandy topers. Because of its more limited presence, rum remained relatively safe from criticism.

Yet rum was not entirely exempt from attack. Increasing levels of alcohol use in the seventeenth and eighteenth centuries led to physician-based sanctions, which sought to curb excessive alcohol use in general. For example, in the 1780s, Philadelphia physician Benjamin Rush began the first research-supported and scientifically based campaign against excessive drinking. Rush's famous work *An Inquiry into the Effects of Ardent Spirits upon the Human Body and Mind* targeted excessive spirit drinking among North Americans and was particularly critical of Caribbean rum.[182] Rush's assault on rum no doubt reflected the greater use of that spirit in North America. In Britain, rum was largely a target of reformers in the antislavery movement rather than temperance advocates and physicians. In the late eighteenth century, enlightened reformers in Britain espoused progressive social beliefs about the virtues of ascetic living and human rights. Temperance and abolitionism were often joined at the heart of these movements. In the 1790s, abolitionist William Fox produced a series of pamphlets denouncing the use of slave-made British Caribbean products, including rum.[183] Among the images abolitionist Andrew Burns conjured up was a cask of Jamaican rum in which was found "The whole body of a roasted Negro lay stretched out, and fastened down in the bilge of the Cask, opposite the bung-hole." Burns wrote,

> Now far be it from me to insinuate from hence, that any such methods are used to meliorate West India Rum; I will only take upon me to affirm, as a certain fact, that the Carcase of a Dog, Cat, Sheep, Goat, Man or Woman, thoroughly burnt, and put in the bottom of a large vessel, full of Spirits of any kind, will greatly tend to meliorate and soften them.[184]

Temperance and antislavery crusades were not enormously successful in the eighteenth century, and British Caribbean rum imports continued to climb.

Figure 3.4. *Gin Lane* by William Hogarth. In *The Works of Hogarth, with Sixty-Two Illustrations* (London, 1874). Courtesy of the John Hay Library at Brown University.

The British elite's desire for fashionable and exotic goods may help explain the growth of rum consumption in Britain in the eighteenth century. According to Mintz, the demand for sugar in Britain reflected attempts by the working class to emulate elite tastes and consume products symbolic of wealth.[185] Yet rum, unlike sugar, was typically a product of common folk in the Caribbean and North America. Sailors, slaves, servants, pirates, and Native Americans consumed rum, and competitors in rival alcohol industries sought to emphasize that connection. The strategy of French wine and brandy makers, for example, was to regard rum as the drink of slaves rather than the drink of "true men." There is some indication, however, that British Caribbean interests attempted to market rum as an exotic drink of the nouveau riche British Caribbean planter and merchant.

In the seventeenth and eighteenth centuries, British upper classes imbibed expensive brandy imported from France, while rum typically vied with gin as the drink of the British working masses. The objective of West Indian interests was to wean the British elite off of French brandy and substitute instead British Caribbean rum. British Caribbean interests appealed to nationalism and, like their attacks on gin, accentuated health concerns. As early as 1690, Dalby Thomas, an advocate for British Caribbean sugar planters, wrote,

> [Rum is] wholesomer for the Body [than brandy], which is observed by the long living of those in the Collonies that are great Drinkers of Rum, which is the Spirits we make of *Mellasses*, and the short living of those that are great Drinkers of *Brandy* in those parts.[186]

In 1690, little, if any, rum entered Britain, which is probably why Thomas felt compelled to explain to his British audience that rum was made from molasses. Within five decades, British imports of rum regularly surpassed those of brandy. Yet, despite rum's success, brandy remained a target of British Caribbean rum interests. In 1770, physician Robert Dossie wrote, "the drinking of Rum in moderation is more salutary, and in excess much less hurtful, than the drinking Brandy."[187] In a fifty-page essay supported by medical evidence, Dossie argued that the volatile oils of rum acted as a corrective to the noxious qualities of pure alcohol, while brandy, according to Dossie, had no such corrective and was highly acidic. Dossie even performed experiments, including one, which showed that animal flesh steeped in rum remained plump and retained its softness better than flesh steeped in brandy.[188] Support for these arguments included physicians' accounts and comparative chemical analysis of various distilled spirits.

Although French brandy remained the preferred alcoholic beverage of the British upper class, rum punch offered an alternative. The term *punch* probably derived from the Hindu word *panch*, meaning *five* and denoting the number of ingredients used in punch making.[189] In the early seventeenth century, Dutch and English sailors returning from trading ventures in the East Indies probably introduced the term into England. Early punch concoctions were made with brandy, but the use of rum became increasingly popular in the eighteenth century. Rum punch was a mixture of rum and various exotic tropical ingredients, such as limes, lemons, sugar, and nutmeg. Only the rich could afford to combine and consume such expensive commodities. In addition, the display of ornate Georgian punch bowls, silver ladles, and other fashionable serving items enhanced the sociable art of upper-class punch-drinking performances. Jamaican interests, including absentee planters living in London, may have been especially good at marketing Jamaican rum as a fine quality spirit well suited for punch.

British Caribbean Planters and Rum

What were the impacts of British mercantilist policies and the increasing levels of rum consumption on British Caribbean rum producers? In the eighteenth century, Jamaica and Barbados were leading rum-making colonies, and sugar planters in these islands depended on rum revenues to help cover the cost of running their estates. Jamaica largely fed the metropolitan rum market, while Barbados relied more heavily on markets in North America and Ireland. During a brief period in the mid-eighteenth century, Barbados exported a disproportionate amount of rum and, although it still produced sugar, essentially became a rum-making island. However, new competition from foreign and British Caribbean rum makers and the disruption of North American trade after the American Revolution removed outlets for Barbadian rum and reduced the profitability of rum making. In the late eighteenth century, rum making in Barbados was on the decline.

Eighteenth century British Caribbean rum import and export statistics show that Jamaica dominated the British rum market. In the first two decades of the eighteenth century, less than 100,000 gallons of rum ever entered England and Wales in a single year. In the 1720s, however, rum imports averaged nearly 150,000 gallons annually. By 1724, England and Wales regularly imported more rum from Jamaica than from any other colony. In the 1730s, Barbados captured about 8 percent of the British rum market. In the period 1768–1771, Jamaica exported an annual average of two million gallons of rum to the British market, which represented 86 percent of all Jamaican rum exports and 81 percent of all British rum imports.[190] Jamaican rum was apparently preferred on the British market because of its higher alcohol content.[191]

Barbados also exported huge amounts of rum in the eighteenth century, yet relatively little Barbadian rum entered the British alcohol market. At first glance, import statistics suggest that Barbadians took advantage of the mid-

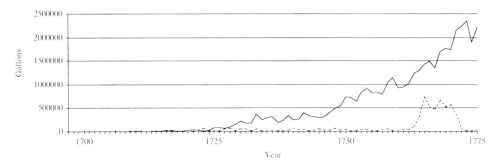

Figure 3.5. Rum exports from Barbados and Jamaica to England and Scotland. Graph by author. *Source*: McCusker, *Rum and the American Revolution*, 960–61, 974–75.

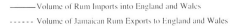

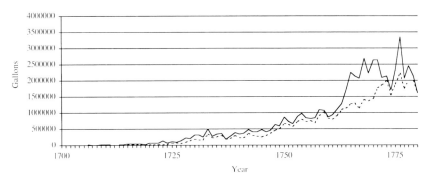

Figure 3.6. British imports of Jamaican rum. Graph by author. *Sources*: British imports from Schumpeter, *English Overseas Trade*; Jamaican exports from McCusker, *Rum and the American Revolution*, 960–61.

eighteenth-century bans on grain distilling and the parliamentary incentives toward British Caribbean rum (see Figure 3.7). Imports of Barbadian rum into England and Wales jumped from an average of about 30,000 gallons in the 1750s to about 230,000 gallons in the 1760s, an almost eightfold increase.[192] In the 1760s, rum from Barbados represented 13 percent of the British rum imports. However, most of the rum imported from Barbados appears to have fed the reexport trade. Rum reexports from Britain jumped from less than 1 percent of imports in the decade 1751–1760 to more than 45 percent in the following decade, while the amount of rum remaining in Britain held relatively steady at about one million gallons per annum. These statistics suggest that Jamaican rum remained in Britain, while rum from Barbados was reexported.

Some of the reexported rum went to northern Europe where the Seven Years War had disrupted northern European access to southern European wine and brandy. Unlike Britain, northern Europeans did not possess substantial rum making colonies to help fill the void. Africa also received its share of this reexported rum, where it was used to fuel the African slave and commodities trades. Nevertheless, it appears Ireland was the major recipient of this reexported rum.

The mid-eighteenth-century jump in rum imports coincides with the growing reexport trade to Ireland, which was emerging as a major consumer of Caribbean rum. The Irish exported provisions, especially salted beef, pork, and fish that helped feed Caribbean colonists. John Oldmixon, a colonial historian familiar with the British Caribbean trade, blamed the "pernicious" sugar, rum, and molasses trade between the French Caribbean and Ireland for strengthening foreign Caribbean sugar colonies.[193] In order to remedy the situation, parliament passed the Molasses Act, which, among other things, prohibited French Caribbean imports into Ireland.[194] Parliament also encouraged direct trade between Ireland and the British Caribbean. However, according to historian Richard Sheridan,

> The boom in the Irish market began in 1763, when, in consequence of a decision to drawback all duties on reexported West India rum, it became cheaper for Irish merchants to get their rum from England than to import it directly from the sugar colonies and pay the Irish import duty.[195]

In 1768, Barbadian planter George Frere wrote that 1.4 million gallons of Barbados rum had been "shipt to London, Bristol, Liverpool, Lancaster, Falmouth, Whitehaven, and most other parts of Great Britain; [but that] the rum is usually re-shipt to Ireland."[196] As a result of the new measures, the Irish increasingly became a nation of rum drinkers. Between 1763 and 1772, Ireland imported an annual average of about 1.4 million gallons of rum.[197] Between 1768 and 1777, the value of rum imports annually averaged £49,000, about 35 percent of the value of all Irish imports from the Americas.[198] The decline in Barbados rum exports to England and Wales in 1771 coincides with the cancellation of drawbacks. Thus, the sharp increase in rum imports into Britain in

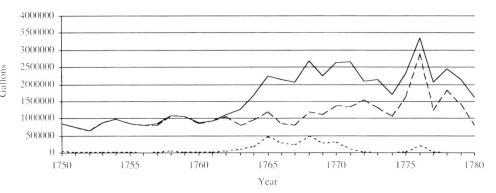

Figure 3.7. British imports of Barbadian rum and British rum reexports. Graph by author. *Sources*: British imports and reexports from Schumpeter, *English Overseas Trade*; Barbadian exports from McCusker, *Rum and the American Revolution*, 974–75.

the mid-eighteenth century shows the extent to which Barbados fed the Irish rum market, and the sharp drop in Barbados rum imports into Britain is misleading because rum from Barbados continued to flow into the large Irish rum market directly after the termination of drawbacks in 1771.

Although Ireland was an important market, North America was the primary destination for Barbadian rum. The barter trade between Barbados and North America arose in the early years of British settlement, and by the mid-seventeenth century, North America imported rum from Barbados in exchange for plantation supplies, such as barrel staves, provisions, and livestock. Barbadian sugar was largely intended for the profitable British market, and North Americans were forced to return home with rum as the only other major product of the island.

Customhouse records for Barbados in 1748 provide some interesting insights into the extent of the Barbados–North American rum trade.[199] In 1748, Barbados exported 12,884 hogsheads of rum, about 1.4 million gallons. Two-thirds of this rum was exported to the British continental colonies. The greatest portion of it went to Virginia and Maryland, followed closely by New England and Philadelphia (Table 3.5). Twenty years later in 1768, the destination of Barbados rum exports remained relatively unchanged (Table 3.6).[200] In fact, almost the same trade pattern between Barbados and the continental colonies had existed nearly 100 years earlier.[201]

While Barbados fed the demand for rum in the continental colonies, Jamaica sent a much smaller portion of its rum to North America. Jamaicans, unlike Barbadians, encouraged the development of provision grounds, thus, making them less dependent on North American food supplies.[202] Moreover, livestock were often acquired through illicit trade with Cuba.[203] Long estimated that in the period 1768–1771, Jamaica annually exported 200,000 gallons of rum to North America, about 7 percent of its total production. Yet, Long appears to have understated the volume of the export trade to North America. Edwards showed that Jamaica exported more than 400,000 gallons of rum to British North America in 1768 and more than 900,000 gallons in 1774, suggesting that while Jamaica exported a smaller percentage of its rum to British North America, the volume of Jamaican rum exports to British North America was similar to that of Barbados.[204]

The extensive Barbados rum trade with Virginia and Maryland demonstrates the importance of British Caribbean rum exports to southern plantations. For example, in 1790, Virginia planter Robert Carter ordered his agent at Nomini Hall plantation to pay "Mr. F. Smith for 8 gallns. W.I. Rum for the people to drink while making hay."[205] Unlike New England, the American South lacked a substantial distilling industry. In the 1780s, there was one rum distillery operating in Charleston, South Carolina, but the poor taste of its product was infamous and even criticized on the other side of the globe by a sugar planter in Bengal.[206] Moreover, planters in North Carolina and Virginia apparently preferred British Caribbean rum to that from New England.[207]

Since the seventeenth century, the British colonies in Canada were a main destination of British Caribbean rum. As early as 1677, the 8,000 gallons of rum imported into Newfoundland already accounted for nearly 20 percent of all alcohol imported through St. John's harbor.[208] Barbados was a main supplier of rum to British Canada and, in 1748, Barbados exported more than 100,000 gallons of rum, almost 10 percent of its total export, to Newfoundland (Table 3.5). In 1770, Newfoundland, Quebec, Nova Scotia, and Prince Edward Island imported nearly 600,000 gallons of rum. New England rum makers largely controlled these markets, but British Caribbean rum, especially from Barbados, continued to enter Canadian ports, either directly or as reexports via New England.[209]

Rum was valuable to the British Caribbean sugar planter. Jamaican sugar planters reckoned that a puncheon of rum was worth about two-thirds the price of a hogshead of sugar.[210] Accounts produced by Jamaican estates corroborate this late eighteenth century trend.[211] In Barbados, the value of a pun-

Table 3.5. Barbados Rum Exports in 1748

Destination	Gallons	Percentage
Britain	490,860	35.2
Philadelphia	146,988	10.5
Virginia/Maryland	268,380	19.2
New England	212,220	15.2
New York/New Jersey	47,844	3.4
North and South Carolina	86,724	6.2
Newfoundland	117,720	8.4
Bermuda	20,736	1.4
TOTAL	1,391,472	100.0

Source: R. Hall, General Account, 12.

Table 3.6. Barbados Rum Exports in 1768

Destination	Gallons	Percentage
Britain	600,000	39.7
Philadelphia	165,000	10.9
Virginia/Maryland	258,000	17.1
New England	202,000	13.3
New York/New Jersey	10,000	.6
North and South Carolina	105,000	6.9
Newfoundland	150,000	9.9
Bermuda	18,000	1.1
TOTAL	1,508,000	100.0

Source: Frere, Short History of Barbados, 114.

cheon of rum was equal to about a third of the value of a hogshead of sugar, no doubt reflecting the higher price of refined Barbadian sugar.[212]

In the period 1768–1771, Long estimated that rum brought in 18 percent of Jamaica's total revenues and one-third of sugar estate revenues.[213] Two decades later, Edwards also estimated that rum contributed about 30 percent to Jamaican sugar plantation revenues, and an anonymous writer in St. Domingue jealously made similar observations.[214] Jamaican plantation records support this widely held belief. For example, in 1798, rum represented 20 percent of the revenues from sugar and rum at Nightingale Grove estate, Jamaica, while in 1799 rum represented 29 percent. In 1798, rum represented 20 percent of the revenues from sugar and rum at Williamsfield estate, Jamaica, while in 1799 it represented 24 percent. Yet, rum as a percentage of revenues from sugar and rum at these two estates sometimes jumped to nearly 40 percent.[215] Analysis of early nineteenth century plantation records from thirty sugar estates in Jamaica led historian Barry W. Higman to conclude that rum, as a percentage of sugar estate revenues, rarely fell below 15 percent and occasionally rose above 25 percent.[216]

Rum revenues were more important to Barbadian sugar planters than to their Jamaican counterparts. In the 1720s, rum at Codrington estate, Barbados, constituted about 27 percent of the revenues from sugar and rum. However, in the 1760s, the value of rum as a percentage of revenues from sugar and rum jumped to an average of 43 percent. The profitability of rum at Codrington led to major still house renovations in the eighteenth century.[217] Rum revenues at Turner's Hall estate followed a similar pattern and in the 1750s and 1760s achieved an average of more than 30 percent. The additional molasses from claying increased the relative importance of rum to Barbadian estate revenues.

While sugar was often considered net profit, rum was expected to defray the cost of running the sugar plantation. The records of York estate, Jamaica, show that only a small percentage of rum was immediately shipped to London, while the majority was usually first sold within Jamaica or never left the plantation (Table 3.7). Much of the rum sold within the island went to local merchants to cover the cost of plantation expenses. The physician at York estate, for example, was also annually paid in rum.[218] Planters and plantation managers also cut down on plantation provision costs by using rum to supplement the diet of their slaves and servants. However, some planters were less optimistic about rum's ability to cover plantation costs. Edwards, for example, wrote, "nor is any opinion more erroneous" than that which supposes that plantation expenses are covered by rum.[219]

The pattern of using rum to help defray plantation expenses existed in other parts of the Caribbean. In Martinique, Labat promoted rum making as a way to cover plantation costs .[220] In Barbados, the agent for Codrington estate sold rum in Bridgetown to cover the cost of plantation supplies and workmen. Rum produced on Codrington estate was sold to local merchants, and in 1715 more than 15,000 gallons of Codrington rum was sold locally.[221] Rum also cov-

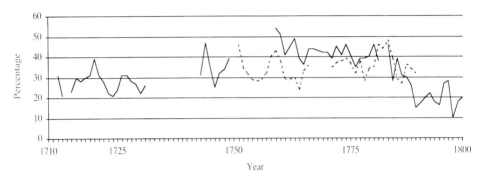

Figure 3.8. Rum as a percentage of revenues from sugar and rum at the Codrington and Turner's Hall estates in Barbados. Graph by author. *Sources*: Barbados Department of Archives, Codrington plantation records and FitzHerbert Papers.

ered the cost of hired labor. In the late eighteenth century, the president of Codrington College was given an annual supply of 90 gallons of rum, and in 1832 the plantation manager at Turner's Hall estate allocated 400 gallons of rum to "negroe carpenters."[222]

Plantation accounts show that rum yields and the ratio of rum to sugar varied from year to year. Accounts from Codrington also indicate that plantations made dramatic increases in rum production from the 1710s to the 1760s, no doubt reflecting a growing global demand for rum in the eighteenth century. The mid-eighteenth-century peaks at Codrington and Turner's Hall reveal attempts by Barbadian planters to dominate Irish and North American markets. Barbados had become a rum island. Relatively steady increases in rum production also took place at Worthy Park plantation and York estate in Jamaica. The changes in rum yields largely reflect the economic strategies of different sugar planters, but outside events also shaped levels of rum production.

In 1774, on the eve of the American Revolution, North Americans threatened to cut off commercial ties with the British Caribbean if Britain refused to lift trade barriers and remove oppressive taxes. In retaliation, Britain imposed a series of resolutions that further restricted North American trade. In January 1776, Britain began enforcing the Prohibitory Act, which severed commercial relations between the British Caribbean and the rebellious continental colonies. Several months later, the Continental Congress opened North American ports to foreign shipping and closed them to most British and British colonial traders. During the American Revolution, British Caribbean traders still had access to ports in areas loyal to Britain or under the control of British forces. North Americans and British Caribbean traders also found ways to circumvent controls through loopholes and smuggling. Although some British Caribbean rum continued to flow into North America, British Caribbean planters saw the writing on the wall and realized that food and provision shortages were imminent.

British Caribbean planters searched for alternative sources of food and plantation supplies. Some planters allocated commercial acreage to provision grounds. Many turned to merchants in Scotland. Expensive goods from England also helped fill the void for necessary provisions and plantation materials. In 1778, parliament lifted restrictions on British Caribbean trade with Ireland in order to relieve the planters' distress. British North American colonies in Canada also absorbed greater amounts of British Caribbean produce and increased production of plantation supplies and provisions, which helped stabilize rum revenues in some sugar colonies. British Canada imported an annual average of more than 800,000 gallons of British Caribbean rum in the mid-1780s, and imports averaged around 400,000 gallons per year in the following decade.[223]

Table 3.7. Gallons of Rum Sold, Used, and Stored at York Estate, Jamaica

Year	Shipped to London	Sold in Jamaica	Estate use	Estate stores	Total	Percentage remaining in Jamaica
1785	4,677	6,963	585	—	12,225	62
1786	3,631	10,285	847	1,331	16,094	77
1787	2,661	8,448	812	348	12,269	88
1788	1,180	21,196	850	—	23,226	95
1789	10,030	10,765	708	—	21,503	53
1790	3,769	20,828	700	—	25,297	85
1791	7,866	13,859	800	—	22,525	65
1792	8,702	11,621	800	—	21,123	59
1793	12,889	7,899	800	—	21,588	40
1794	12,000	7,200	800	—	20,000	40
1795	19,380	—	600	—	19,980	3

Source: Gale-Morant Papers, Latin American Collection, George A. Smathers Library, University of Florida, Gainesville, Florida.

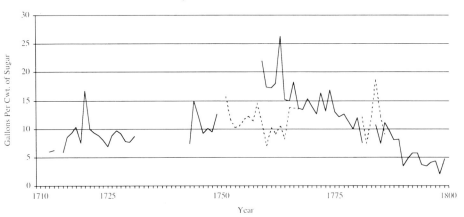

Figure 3.9. Rum production at the Codrington and Turner's Hall estates in Barbados. Graph by author. *Sources*: Barbados Department of Archives, Codrington plantation records and FitzHerbert Papers.

Despite these efforts, the British Caribbean rum trade suffered. The loss of the continental colonies meant the loss of one of the largest markets for British Caribbean rum. English, Scottish, British Canadian, and Irish markets could not replace the huge North American market. High wartime import duties also reduced rum consumption. Between 1780 and 1783, Ireland—once one of the largest markets for British Caribbean rum—annually imported less than 150,000 gallons. The threat of privateers and the conscription of ships to the war effort during the American Revolution reduced shipping in the British Caribbean. Freight and insurance rates also increased.[224] As a result, British Caribbean sugar planters shipped their most profitable item, sugar, rather than rum.

Rum makers in the Danish Virgin Islands (St. Croix and St. Thomas) were the biggest beneficiaries of the American Revolution. Since the mid-eighteenth century, the Danish Virgin Islands had been an important link in the North American rum chain. Although St. Thomas and St. Croix were Danish possessions, estates in these islands were often owned and run by British Caribbean planters. In the late 1760s and early 1770s, St. Thomas and St. Croix illegally smuggled about 500,000 gallons of rum per year to the thirteen continental colonies, mainly through ports in Connecticut.[225] During the American

Revolution, the Danish Virgin Islands served as a key base for smuggling operations. Between 1777 and 1807, their rum exports jumped to an annual average of more than 900,000 gallons.[226] It is unlikely that rum makers in St. Thomas and St. Croix had the ability to produce all of this rum from local sugarcane juice, scum, and molasses. Instead, they probably fed their stills with raw materials imported from Puerto Rico and the French Caribbean. Some of the rum may have been produced in the Spanish, French, and British colonies and reexported to North America via Danish Caribbean ports.

Bermuda and, until 1781, St. Eustatius also smuggled goods to the rebels in North America. However, rum was often secondary to arms and ammunition for North American forces. In 1781, British Admiral Sir George Rodney's fleet captured St. Eustatius, which had been an entrepôt for the North American purchase of French goods. It also supplied arms and ammunition to the Revolutionary armies in North America and was a symbol of North American economic and political independence.[227] Rodney's forces captured the heart of North American foreign trade, much of it rum based, which had initially helped spark the American Revolution.

The American Revolution was a setback for British Caribbean rum makers. British Caribbean rum exports to the thirteen continental colonies dropped from an annual average of about three million gallons in the period 1770–1773 to about 1.7 million gallons in the period 1783-1787.[228] English imports of British Caribbean rum, however, only fell from an annual average rate of about 2.4 million gallons in the period 1770-1773 to an annual rate of about 2.1 million gallons in the period 1783-1787.[229] British Caribbean rum makers in Barbados and the Leeward Islands were especially hard hit, while rum makers in Jamaica, who had dominated the rum markets of England, fared much better. To make matters worse, Barbados was devastated by a major hurricane in 1780, which killed more than 4,300 people and essentially destroyed sugar and rum production for the following year. In 1781, rum production at Codrington plantation dropped 78 percent from the previous year.[230] In 1780, plantation managers at Turner's Hall estate noted the loss of 400 gallons of rum "in the storm" and, in 1781, the full effect of the hurricane was felt as the value of the estate's produce dropped 80 percent.[231] The recovery was slowed by the arrival of another devastating hurricane in 1786.[232]

In 1783, trade resumed between the United States and the British Caribbean under restricted conditions. American traders were allowed to export only lumber, livestock, grain, flour, and bread in exchange for British Caribbean goods. However, ships from the United States were excluded from the trade and all products had to be shipped in British bottoms.[233] In retaliation, some American ports prohibited entry to British vessels or imposed heavy duties on British and British colonial goods. In 1787, the inspector general's account shows that Jamaica exported about 300,000 gallons of rum to the United States, about one-third the amount exported to North America in 1774.[234] In 1788, Barbados exported about 200,000 gallons to the United States, about one-fifth the amount exported two decades earlier.[235] Perhaps the less dramatic drop in Jamaican exports shows the Americans' growing appreciation for concentrated Jamaican rum. The new triangular trade route—from Britain to North America to the British Caribbean and back to Britain—only served to further strengthen Jamaican and weaken Barbadian rum making. In 1794, Americans temporarily banned all trade with the British Caribbean in retaliation against British sea captains impressing Americans into service. These trade restrictions extended the damage to British Caribbean rum making caused by the American Revolution. A planter in St. Vincent complained that British Caribbean rum makers were switching places with the French.

> We are compelled by the events of War and the rigors of Government to exchange situations with the French; for these materials which they formerly used to throw away, or to vend in a unwrought stage, they now manufacture into rum and dispose of more profitably at a price of 2/9 to 3/6 currency per gallon whilst the British Planter, in consequence of the discouragement he labours under will be compelled to discontinue his distillery and to dispose of his raw material as the French did formerly.[236]

Yet, despite these obstacles, some British Caribbean rum continued to flow into the United States. Parliament opened free ports in Bermuda and the Bahamas to U.S. shipping. British Caribbean governors frequently used their powers to allow American vessels to enter and trade in British Caribbean ports for emergency purposes.[237] French, Spanish, Danish, and Dutch ports also provided links for indirect trade between the United States and the British Caribbean.

In the late eighteenth century, rum markets in Britain also stabilized. Although there was a sharp increase in brandy imports, Jamaican rum makers greatly benefited from their control of British markets. In 1802, Britain imported more than four million gallons of rum, mainly from Jamaica.[238] British Caribbean interests in London also tried to raise the demand for rum in Britain in order to reduce British Caribbean dependence on American rum markets. According to Sir William Young, an advocate of British Caribbean trade, the inability of British Caribbean rum to secure a larger share of the British alcohol market was largely due to its "disuse." Young believed that increasing rum contracts with the British military would remedy the situation.

> If, in national policy, as well as in justice to its colonial and mercantile interests, the British Government would exclusively purchase rum for the supply of the soldiers and sailors [rather than brandy], then, with the habits and growing taste of so numerous a class, the liking and use would spread to every village and house; the import of rum to Great Britain would proportionally and yearly increase; the return per export of British produce and manufactures to the West Indies, would in a great measure supersede the necessities of intercourse and trade between America and the islands; and also put a stop to the national disputes arising in consequence; and in every view of national interest, the mother-country would be amply repaid for the protection and preference given in the sale of this article of colonial commerce.[239]

Competition in the U.S. market from foreign rum makers reduced the profitability of Barbados rum production.[240] During the Revolution, rum making expanded in Cuba, St. Domingue, and the Danish Virgin Islands, and rum from these islands penetrated the U.S. market. In addition, rum making started in the ceded islands of Dominica, St. Vincent, Grenada and Tobago, which, because they desperately needed provisions and supplies from the United States, could easily justify to British administrators the entrance of American ships to help meet emergency needs.

Although U.S. rum imports returned to pre-Revolutionary levels by 1800, Barbadian rum made up a much smaller slice of the pie. Between 1786 and 1792, Barbados exported an average of less than half a million gallons of rum per year, much of it to British Canada.[241] Moreover, Barbadian rum also faced the rise of U.S. whiskey drinking and a growing U.S. nationalism, which equated Caribbean rum, especially from the British colonies, with colonial dependence. Rum prices dropped considerably, and Governor Parry of Barbados wrote, "for want of vent, rum . . . is now a mere Drug upon the hands of the planters."[242] Rum production figures from Turner's Hall and Codrington show the immediate impact of these events (Figure 3.9). Molasses, a basic ingredient in rum making, appears in the accounts of Turner's Hall and Codrington for the first time in the early nineteenth century and highlights the decline of the Barbados rum industry.

Conclusion

At the beginning of the eighteenth century, mercantilist policies shaped the growth of Caribbean rum. While officials in Spain and France sought to restrict the colonial rum trade, officials in Britain saw rum as a potential ally in their war against foreign spirits. The Seven Years War was a turning point for French and Spanish Caribbean rum makers. The war spread knowledge about advanced distilling techniques, and the free trade reforms that followed the conflict helped release rum from its mercantilist bottle. British Caribbean rum, on the other hand, found a substantial home market and fed Britain's growing demand for alcohol during its industrial revolution. British Caribbean rum replaced many foreign alcohol imports and, as a result, rum revenues helped stabilize British Caribbean sugar estates.

However, Britain and North America were not the only major markets for Caribbean rum in the eighteenth century. The African slave and commodities trades also fueled the expansion of Caribbean rum. The novelty of distilled spirits, the spiritual value of alcohol in many parts of West and Central Africa, and the appreciation for slave-made products from the Caribbean fueled the African rum trade.

CHAPTER 4

Ancestors and Alcohol in Africa
and the Caribbean

B Y THE END OF THE SEVENTEENTH CENTURY, rum began to penetrate the West and West Central African slave and commodities trades. Rum was added to the wide array of indigenous alcoholic beverages and European trade spirits already available to African consumers. In the eighteenth century, African imports of rum grew and often replaced other foreign alcohol, especially in areas under British and Portuguese control. The social and sacred importance of alcohol to Africans stimulated demand, and rum was quickly absorbed into preexisting alcohol-based rituals. The fact that rum was a product of African slave labor in the Americas probably increased its symbolic value. The rum trade to Africa expanded throughout the slavery period, and although rum never became the sole article of trade, it played a crucial role in gift giving and as a secondary item of exchange.

Alcohol was familiar to newly arrived African slaves in the Caribbean, and the spiritual meanings slaves attached to drinking reflect the continuity of African cultural beliefs. Despite occasional efforts by colonial officials to restrict slave drinking, slaves had easy access to rum and other alcoholic beverages. The ready availability of alcohol sparked the creation of new African-oriented drinking practices, which, at the level of the lowest common denominator, combined the social and sacred alcohol-based traditions of diverse African ethnic groups. As it did in Africa, alcohol helped foster slave spirituality and promote group identity. The construction of new drinking styles also strengthened resistance ideologies, which challenged European efforts to suppress African customs. Understanding of slave alcohol use provides a prism through which to view underlying principles that helped shape slave life and highlights the ways Africans and African slaves maintained cultural links across the Atlantic.

Alcohol and the Atlantic Trades

Alcoholic beverages played a prominent role in the African slave and commodities trades. English slave trader John Atkins, for example, described the specific demands at different trading regions along the West African coast, but believed alcohol was "every where called for."[1] African historian Lynn Pan argues that the only exception to the European alcohol trade to Africa was in the northern stretches of the slave trade where Islam was strongly entrenched.[2] Yet even in Muslim controlled areas, alcohol use and the alcohol trade were strong. In the early sixteenth century, for example, Portuguese traveler Valentim Fernandes described the Wolofs, a partially Muslim group from the Senegal region, as "great drunkards who derive pleasure from our wine."[3]

Much of the alcohol introduced into the African trades entered through gift giving. European traders were expected to make regular presents of alcohol to kings, chiefs, and all those involved with securing slaves and goods. The Dutch may have been to blame for what many traders considered a "disagreeable and burdensome custom." According to slave trader John Barbot,

> Their design at first was only to draw off the *Blacks* from trading with the *Portugueses*; but those people having once found the sweet, could never be broke of it, tho' the *Portugueses* were actually expelled [from] all the places of trade they had been possessed of on the coast; but it became an inviolable custom for all *Europeans*.[4]

Dashee, *dassy*, and *bizy* became standard terms along the African coasts for gifts of alcohol dispensed prior to trading, and they were a requisite part of the trade protocol.[5] On the Gold Coast, Atkins wrote, the African trader "never cares to treat with dry Lips."[6] At Ouidah, Dutch slave trader William Bosman reported, the Africans were great lovers of strong liquors who expected their dassy, and "he that intends to Trade here, must humour them herein."[7] Gift giving, which often involved elaborate rules, was implemented to appease state leaders and integrate even peripheral African social groups into the Atlantic trade.[8]

Rum and other alcoholic beverages also entered Africa as part of larger trading packages. In the 1680s, alcohol represented about an eighth of West African imports and a century later about a tenth.[9] This ancillary use of alcohol is evident among all major slave-trading nations. In the 1720s, brandy was reported to be one of the principal commodities imported by the French at the slave-trading port at Ouidah, and documents of the Dutch Middelburgsche Commercie Compagnie show that more than 10 percent of trading packages consisted of alcoholic beverages, perhaps gin.[10] By the late eighteenth century, slave traders from New England and Brazil were each annually exporting about 300,000 gallons of rum to West and West Central Africa.[11]

The modern western view of alcohol as a profane fluid has often been evoked to underscore the insidiousness of European slave trading. According to Cuban anthropologist Fernando Ortiz, rum "was always the cargo for the slaver's return trip, for with it slaves were bought, local chieftains bribed, and the African tribes corrupted and weakened."[12] Similarly, historian Eric Williams explains,

> Rum was an essential part of the cargo of the slave ship, particularly the colonial American slave ship. No slave trader could afford to dispense with a cargo of rum. It was profitable to spread the taste for liquor on the coast. The Negro dealers were plied with it, were induced to drink till they lost their reason, and then the bargain was struck.[13]

Modern attitudes about the vulgarity of alcoholic beverages have helped magnify the evils of the slave trade. Yet, the reality of alcohol's part in the trade is more mundane than the images so passionately depicted. Before the arrival of European explorers and traders, West and West Central Africans had a long history of alcohol use. Already familiar with the potentially disastrous effects of regular excessive drinking, they were spared the type of social devastation that accompanied alcohol trade to peoples with no prior history of alcohol use, including Native North Americans and Australian Aborigines.[14]

The African Background of Caribbean Slave Drinking

Foreign alcoholic beverages entered a preexisting African social structure where the use of alcohol was widespread. The accounts of early explorers, traders, and missionaries in West and West Central Africa attest to the popularity of indigenous alcoholic beverages prior to the expansion of the transatlantic slave trade in the mid-seventeenth century. Like ethnographic field notes, these reports detailed the production of alcoholic beverages from various local sources, including honey, plantains, and various species of millet. However, palm wine, produced from the *raphia* variety of palm, appears to have been one of the most ubiquitous drinks found along the West and West Central African coasts.

An examination of alcohol use among the Akan, Igbo, Kongo, and Aja-Fon [the people French slave traders referred to as Arada] highlights the social and symbolic value of alcohol in the African trade and helps explain African demand. In addition, exploring alcohol use among these four African groups provides a foundation for understanding African slave drinking in the British and French Caribbean. The Akan and Igbo were central to the British transatlantic slave trade, while the Kongo and Aja-Fon Arada were the most significant to the French.

Alcohol use in Akan and Igbo societies predated European intervention and the rise of the transatlantic slave trade. As early as the eleventh century, Al-Bakri of Cordoba referred to "intoxicating drinks" served at the burial of the king of the ancient kingdom of Ghana.[15] Oral traditions collected and recorded in the late nineteenth century intimate a long history of palm wine use on the Gold Coast dating back to the Asante's initial migration into the region in the early sixteenth century.[16] Palm wine was also available in Igbo lands prior to the seventeenth century. In 1588, trader James Welsh wrote that in the Bight of Biafra "there are great store of palme trees, out of which they gather great store of wine."[17]

Alcohol use among the Kongo of West Central Africa and Aja-Fon of the Slave Coast also predated the rise of the transatlantic slave trade. In 1570, Portuguese missionary Baltasar Alfonso noted that the people of Luanda drank *walo*, a beer made from fermented grain, and in 1648, Portuguese missionary Jean-François de Rome described beer brewed from flour among the Kongo.[18] Palm wine was also present.[19] Grain-based beer, sometimes called *pitau*, and palm wine were also popular among the Arada of the Slave Coast.[20] According to Bosman, there were many types of grain at Ouidah, including "the great *Milhio*, . . . which the Negroes don't make Bread of it, but use it in the brewing of Beer."[21] Arada women played a central role in beer brewing.[22] Palm wine was less esteemed on the Slave Coast, but slave trader Derick Ruiters described the availability of at least two types of "sour Palm wine" in that region.[23]

With the expansion of European trade along the African coasts, foreign alcoholic beverages supplemented indigenous drinks. Africans valued imported alcoholic beverages for their newness, especially distilled spirits, which were much more concentrated than their usual fermented drinks. African elites may have also viewed the consumption of foreign alcohol as a way to help confirm status. For example, at Ouidah, Bosman noted that "The Richer Sort" preferred brandy.[24] The extent of the European trade, however, made foreign alcoholic beverages widely available, and Bosman believed that excessive brandy drinking was "the innate Vice of all *Negroes*."[25]

Some parts of West and West Central Africa appreciated rum more than others. Obviously those areas of West and West Central Africa with the greatest amount of direct trade with rum making regions, areas such as Angola and the Gold Coast, had greater access to rum. Historian David Eltis estimates that in the late seventeenth and early eighteenth centuries the Gold Coast, which carried on a considerable amount of direct trade with rum-laden British American traders, received about 48,000 gallons of rum annually.[26] African states, like those on the Gold Coast, usually contained 20,000 to 30,000 people, suggesting a considerable level of per capita rum consumption.[27]

Foreign spirits were integrated into traditional West and West Central African cultural festivals, such as the Igbo yam festival, the Akan *odwira* festival, and the Ga *homowo* festival.[28] Their use of foreign spirits in traditional cultural ceremonies indicates the flexibility with which indigenous groups met the political and economic changes that were occurring on the African coasts in the seventeenth century.

More importantly, however, was alcohol's unique ability to facilitate communication with the spiritual world. In Akan, Igbo, Kongo, and Arada religions, as well as in the religions of many other West and West Central African groups, the physical and spiritual worlds are closely aligned. Ancestors and deities played an active role in the daily lives of the living. Through revelation and divination, devotees gained access to the messages of a spiritual world that guided them through life.[29] As with sleep deprivation, fasting, and other mind-altering activities, the physiological effects of alcohol helped bring about human interaction with a supernatural realm. Historian Emmanuel Akyeampong argues that the Akan considered alcohol a sacred fluid that "bridged the gap between the physical and spiritual worlds."[30] According to Akyeampong,

> Rites of passage illustrated the conception of life as a progression from the spiritual world, through the living world, and back into the spiritual world. Naming, puberty, marriage, and funeral ceremonies represented different epochal stages in life's journey. The human perception of the relative intimacy of the spiritual and living worlds associated with each phase was reflected in a minimal or profuse use of alcohol.[31]

Akyeampong's analysis of the role of alcohol in Akan religion applies equally well to the Igbo, Kongo, and Arada. For each of these groups, alcohol helped link the physical and spiritual worlds, thereby ensuring the natural progression of life for individuals and communities.

Through libations and offerings, alcohol mediated physical and spiritual domains. Individuals and family groups poured libations and made alcohol offerings to seek favor from ancestral spirits and deities. They performed these acts to protect the community from evil, propitiate angry spirits, and accelerate an individual's recovery from illness. Libations and offerings, therefore, created a path to a spiritual world that secured community needs.

The Akan poured libations and made alcohol offerings to ancestors and deities before most significant undertakings.[32] In 1602, slave trader Pieter de Marees described an Akan drinking occasion in which the first drops of palm wine were poured on the ground in reverence for the ancestors. If the participants wore fetishes, they spit the first mouthful of palm wine on these. Failing to do so risked the possibility that partakers would not be allowed to drink together in peace.[33] Atkins and Barbot recorded similar ceremonies on the Gold Coast a half century later.[34] One of the most powerful Akan spiritual symbols is the ancestral stool, a sacred representation of a deceased relative. Several times a year, the Akan brought out their ancestral stools, placed alcohol offerings on them, and followed this ritual with the pouring of libations. In return, the living received ancestral blessings.[35]

The Igbo also poured libations and made sacrificial offerings of alcohol to their ancestors and deities in public and private ceremonies. Barbot wrote of them, "none drink without spilling a little of the liquor on the ground, for his idol."[36] In his famous narrative, Igbo slave Olaudah Equiano recalled that as a child growing up in a region subjugated by the kingdom of Benin his family poured libations to ancestral spirits before each meal.[37] Like the Akan stool, the Igbo *ofo-stick* embodied an ancestral spirit, and it too received regular oblations.[38]

Similar practices existed among the Arada and Kongo. Bosman wrote that worshipers in the serpent cult at Ouidah commonly left "drink offerings at the snake house."[39] In the nineteenth century, British colonial administrators, recognizing the importance of alcohol to the serpent cult at Ouidah, annually visited the "Boa Temple" and left offerings of rum with the priest.[40] Anthropologist Melville Herskovits noted that in 1930s Dahomey, alcohol continued to be the proper sacrificial offering for *vodou* deities.[41]

Alcohol also had a strong spiritual component in West Central Africa. Countering misconceptions of Kongolese alcohol use as base indulgence, anthropologist Georges Balandier argued that "social necessity signified more than the pursuit of alcoholic stimulation; *malafu* [palm wine] was required

on many occasions [especially at] rituals and ceremonies honoring the ancestors."[42] In the late nineteenth and early twentieth centuries, missionary Karl
Laman also recorded the spiritual role of alcohol among the Kongo.

> Here and there one still finds special houses for the safe keeping of the *nkisi*,
> idols and ancestral images. One also comes across small well-built ancestral
> houses in which there is only one mug, into which one pours palm-wine that
> is sacrificed to the ancestors.[43]

Alcohol libations and offerings marked major events in Akan, Igbo, Kongo,
and Arada societies, including birth, naming, and marriage. The abundantly
documented status of alcohol in funeral rites illustrates most clearly its profound spiritual value. Marking the end of physical life, death meant a return or
transition to the spirit world, and alcohol was central to this transition. Proper
Akan and Igbo funerals included generous quantities of alcohol, which helped
ensure the successful passage of the dead to the spirit world. Offerings of alcohol also guaranteed that the dead would give assistance and prosperity to the
family and community left behind. The Akan, according to de Marees, put
food and drink on the graves of the dead, believing that they "live on it, and
[thus] Pots of water and Palm Wine are constantly renewed."[44] Barbot noted
that in the Gold Coast,

> As soon as the corps is let down into the grave, the persons who attended
> the funeral drink palm-wine, or rum plentifully, out of oxes horns; and what
> they cannot drink off at a draught, they spill on the grave of their deceased
> friend, that he may have his share of the liquor.[45]

The Igbo also made copious use of alcohol at funerals. Alcohol was sprinkled
on the corpse prior to burial, and during the important second burial feast,
unlimited amounts of palm wine were consumed.[46] The Igbo made offerings
of alcohol to their ancestors at funeral ceremonies to ensure that the ancestral
spirits would welcome the newly departed soul.[47] After burial, relatives made
regular gifts of alcohol to their dead.[48]

Libations and offerings also characterized Arada and Kongo funerals. In
West Central Africa, in the late sixteenth and early seventeenth centuries, the
people of the Kongo were known to "bury their dead on the mountains in cool
pleasant places . . . [and to] leave wine and food."[49] According to historian Joseph Miller, in the seventeenth century the Imbangala of West Central Africa
"made extensive use of palm wine in their rituals . . . pouring the wine over the
graves of their ancestors in an attempt to contact the dead."[50] At Ouidah funerals, wrote British naval captain Frederick E. Forbes in 1851, "Much rum is dis-

tributed, and all night there is shouting, firing, and dancing."[51] Similarly, in the 1930s, Herskovits detailed alcohol's role in opening lines of communication with the ancestral world at burial wakes in Dahomey.[52]

Perhaps this widespread funerary use of alcohol reflects a need to bring the community through an anxious period of spiritual liminality. The transition of death marked a time of community stress when the terrestrial and spiritual worlds were closely but precariously aligned. The pacifying effect of alcohol on individuals, and indirectly on ancestors and deities, may have produced a perception of order and control that helped stabilize the community during uncertain and unpredictable phases.[53]

Communal drinking also strengthened the cohesiveness of the group. Social gatherings required the participation and economic assistance of individuals and families. Describing a communal naming rite, de Marees observed that when an Akan woman gives birth,

> all the people—Men, Women, Boys and Girls—come to her. . . . They give the Child a name upon which they have agreed and swear upon it with the Fetissos and other sorcery . . . on which occasion they make a big feast, with merry-making, food, and drink, which they love.[54]

Community events celebrated a shared identity and reaffirmed social commitments, and the liberating effect of alcohol helped remove obstacles to social discourse.[55]

The use of alcohol as a trade good for slaves developed in the early years of the African-European trade. Although West and West Central Africans had access to a variety of indigenous alcoholic drinks, they embraced rum and other foreign alcoholic beverages, which were distributed in gift-giving ceremonies and integrated into a larger trading package. The social and sacred value of alcohol increased the African demand. However, the heavy emphasis on rum in the African slave trade may also reflect a special appreciation for African slave-made products and symbolic respect for brethren stranded overseas. In the 1930s, Herskovits recorded Dahomean oral histories pertaining to the slave trading days. Included among these was a chant that the Dahomeans performed to their ancestors and to kin sent across the Atlantic.

> The English must bring guns. The Portuguese must bring powder. The Spaniards must bring the small stones which give fire to our fire-sticks. The Americans must bring the cloths and the rum made by our kinsmen who are there, for these will permit us to smell their presence.[56]

Access to Alcohol in Caribbean Slave Societies

If slaves were not already familiar with rum in Africa, they were quickly introduced to it during the Middle Passage or upon their arrival in the Caribbean.[57]
Dr. Collins, a planter and physician in St. Vincent, advised that, as part of the
seasoning process, newly arrived slaves should be given rum "for it is the business of the Planter to conciliate them by many compliances with their humour."[58] Rum, therefore, was used as a salutation to try to ease the transition into
Caribbean slavery.

British Caribbean sugar planters provided large amounts of rum to their
slaves as part of weekly plantation rations.[59] In the late eighteenth century, for
example, managers at the York estate, Jamaica, set aside 800 gallons of rum
each year for use on the plantation.[60] If this rum was reserved entirely for the
estate's slave population, which at that time was about 450, the rate of per
capita rum consumption would have been about 1.8 gallons. At Worthy Park,
Jamaica, plantation managers annually distributed seven or eight puncheons of
rum, which between 1784 and 1813 would have provided each of Worthy Park's
slaves with about 2.5–3.0 gallons per year.[61] Some planters and plantation managers dispensed rum even more liberally. Plantation managers at the Halse Hall
estate, Jamaica, for example, were known to distribute one pint to one quart of
rum a week to each adult slave, or 6.5 to 13 gallons per year.[62]

French Caribbean sugar planters also portioned out rum to their slaves. In
Martinique, French missionary Father Jean Baptiste Père Labat recommended
that 10 percent of the rum produced on his model sugar plantation, or about
402 gallons, should be annually set aside for the plantation's 120 slaves, which
gave an annual per capita rum consumption rate of about 3.4 gallons.[63] Some
French planters used rum as a dietary supplement in their efforts to cut plantation costs. In 1685, the French government passed the Code Noir, which was
meant to standardize and improve the treatment of slaves in the French Caribbean. Article 23 of the Code Noir specifically forbade sugar planters to substitute rum for substantive food in their slaves' diets.[64] Yet, despite these regulations, French planters continued to dole out rum as a dietary supplement.[65]

Slaves also received rum allotments as part of rewards and incentives systems. For example, in 1797, an anonymous author in Jamaica wrote,

> In the country where rats are numerous, and destructive to the canes, they
> make basket traps and catch them in abundance, for which on some planta-
> tions they receive a quantity of rum, proportioned to the number taken,
> which is known by the number of tails they produce.[66]

Jamaican vistor Charles Leslie indicated that slaves received a bottle of rum for every 50 rat tails collected.[67] This practice of exchanging rat tails for rum was apparently widespread and existed for many years. Rum was also given as a reward for good work. Jamaican sugar planter Thomas Roughley wrote that, as an incentive to the principal headman to do his duty well, "a weekly allowance of a quart or two of good rum . . . will be found of salutary effect."[68] Evidently, planters attempted to devise an effective incentives system, which used rum to improve discipline and elicit a favorable slave disposition.[69]

Slaves also received rum as an incentive to perform particularly difficult and unpleasant tasks. Labat, for example, advised giving slaves rum for doing backbreaking work, such as dunging and cane holing.[70] Some planters in St. Croix dispensed rum to their slaves two or three times a day during the arduous planting season.[71] In Dominica, sugar planter Thomas Atwood wrote,

> The field negros, when digging cane holes, have usually, in the afternoon, half a pint of rum and water, sweetened with molasses, given to each of them, which is a great refreshment in that labour, and causes them to work with chearfulness.[72]

In addition, Atwood believed singing "has a good effect in softening their labour, and is much promoted by giving them their rum and water." Sugar plantation work in general was grueling, and some planters simply distributed shots of rum to their slaves each morning before they headed out to the cane fields, in the middle of the afternoon, and when they returned at the end of the day.[73]

Slaves also got rum through barter and purchase. Jamaican sugar planter Matthew Gregory Lewis wrote that among his slaves were

> some choice ungrateful scoundrels . . . [including] a young rascal of a boy called "massa Jackey," who is in the frequent habit of running away for months at a time, and whom I had distinguished from the cleverness of his countenance and buffoonery of his manners, came to beg my permission to go and purchase food with some money which I had just given him, "because he was almost starving; his parents were dead, he had no provision-grounds, no allowance, and nobody ever gave him anything." Upon this I sent Cubina with the boy to the store-keeper, when it appeared that he had always received a regular allowance of provisions twice a week, which he generally sold, as well as his clothes, at the Bay, for spirits.[74]

Lewis also noted that some of his slaves sold their provisions to "wandering higglers" for the same purpose.[75] Many such transactions occurred at Sunday markets and, as a result, some planters began distributing food and drink allowances in the middle of the week rather than the end, for as Dr. Collins remarked "as Sunday is their holiday and market-day, they are apt to carry their allowance to market, and to barter it for rum."[76] The exchange of rum for sexual favors provided another opportunity to get rum, an opportunity that Jamaican plantation manager Thomas Thistlewood frequently gave to the female slaves under his supervision.[77]

Planters and plantation managers dispensed rum on holidays and special occasions. Lewis, for example, gave his slaves a holiday when he first visited his estate. According to Lewis, the slaves "were allowed as much rum, and sugar, and noise, and dancing as they chose."[78] Similar distributions of rum occurred in 1792 when absentee sugar planter William Young visited his estates in Antigua.[79] John Stedman, an Anglo-Dutch mercenary, reported that the plantation owner at one estate in Surinam gave his slaves a rum-laden holiday when he fired a cruel overseer who was responsible for the deaths of several slaves on the estate. At crop-over, Thistlewood served 15 quarts of rum to his slaves "to make them merry."[80] Planters also doled out extra rations of rum at Christmas, New Year's, and Easter.[81]

Although planters had great control over the distribution of alcohol, slaves also procured rum on their own. In the mid-seventeenth century, French missionary Father Jean Baptiste Du Tertre wrote "I have seen one of our negroes slaughter five or six chickens in order to accommodate his friends, and spend extravagantly on three pints of rum in order to entertain five or six slaves of his country."[82] Slaves also found clandestine ways of securing alcohol. In the 1788 British parliamentary inquiry into slavery, Governor Parry of Barbados believed that many health problems associated with slaves were attributable to rum "which they steal."[83] Henry Drax, a wealthy and prominent sugar planter in Barbados, wrote, "The blacks are commonly addicted to Thieving . . . [and if] they are taken stealing Sugar, Molasses, or Rum they must be severely handled."[84] A young domestic slave at Newton plantation, Barbados, was executed for just such an offense.[85] In Jamaica, "pilferage" may have accounted for as much as 5 percent of all the rum produced on the island.[86] Theft was also a problem in the French Caribbean. Labat believed that the rum sold by slaves at Sunday markets in Martinique was often stolen from their masters and neighboring estates.[87] Planters recognized that, in order to prevent theft, "due attention to the distillery, assisted by good locks and bars" was required.[88]

Taverns and rum shops were important institutions in the colonial Caribbean, and slaves were known to frequent them. In Barbados, concerns about slave drinking led to the enactment of laws that prohibited tavern keepers from selling rum to slaves.[89] The reiteration of these laws, however, suggests that they were rarely obeyed and hard to enforce. In the Danish Caribbean, officials tried to regulate the presence of slaves in taverns and encouraged tavern owners to serve slaves from the backyards.[90] In Jamaica, there were rum shops kept for the slaves' "entertainment, where they have a meal of coarse bread, salted fish and butter, and a bowl of new rum and water."[91] Archaeologists working at Drax Hall estate in Jamaica excavated an eighteenth-century tavern that, according to the researchers, was probably little more than a centrally located dirt-floor shack where slaves would gather to drink.[92] As with rum shops in the Caribbean today, taverns were places to get snacks and drinks, enjoy a variety of games, exchange gossip, debate current events, receive loans, sell goods, and advertise availability as a sexual partner. Sometimes taverns provided a safe place to fence stolen rum.[93]

Entrepreneurial freedmen and women seized part of the rum shop trade. In the 1770s and '80s, Rachel Pringle-Polgreen, a freedwoman, ran one of the most popular taverns in Bridgetown, Barbados, which catered to the colonial and military elite.[94] George Pinckard, a military physician who visited Barbados in the late eighteenth century, wrote, "taverns are commonly known by the names of the persons who keep them," and among the two taverns "most frequented, at Bridge Town, are those of Nancy Clarke, and Mary Bella Green; the former a black—the latter a mulatto woman."[95] A visitor to Kingston, Jamaica, noted, "many of the free negroes, especially the women, keep lodging-houses and taverns."[96] According to Jamaican sugar planter Edward Long,

> The most wholesome beverage [for newcomers] would be sugar and water, with or without a moderate allowance of old rum; what is still preferable is the cool drink [fermented sugarcane juice] prepared here by many of the free Negroe and Mulatta women, who vend it cheap to the soldiers.[97]

Close relations between slaves and freedmen and women probably facilitated slave drinking in taverns and rum shops. In Trinidad, some officials believed that slaves supplied stolen rum to freedmen and women, who were considered the primary retailers of stolen goods.[98]

Indeed, slaves took advantage of local rum markets and sometimes became crucial links in the local distribution chain. According to Du Tertre, slaves in Martinique collected skimmings that spilled over during the sugar boiling process and made "intoxicating drinks from it, which do a good trade in the island."[99] Nearly two centuries later, St.-Just, an enterprising slave on the sugar estate of Pierre Dessalles in Martinique, sold rum with his common-law wife in a shop set up on the plantation.[100] Dessalles apparently encouraged the commercial pursuits of his slaves, and in 1823 he took his slave Madeleine to his coffee plantation, Caféière, where she too sold rum.[101] Among the runaways advertised in St. Domingue in 1790 was an enterprising 28-year-old Mozambique man who bought rum at the gates of sugar estates and sold it in the mountains.[102]

Figure 4.1. Tavern owner Rachel Pringle of Barbados. Illustrated by Thomas Rowlandson and published by William Holland (London, 1796). From the collection of the Barbados Museum and Historical Society.

Social and Sacred Uses of Alcohol
in Caribbean Slave Societies

Historical ethnographies of slave life commonly stress the survival of African cultural traits in the Caribbean. Beginning with the pioneering work of Herskovits, historically minded anthropologists have sought to connect Caribbean slave traditions to Africa. Although Herskovits used broad culture-area concepts of West Africa to reconstruct African survivals, his research also illustrated the specific origins of particular cultural influences.[103] For example, Herskovits linked Haitian vodou and the religion of Fon-speaking peoples of Dahomey and identified the Yoruba roots of the Shango cult in Trinidad.[104]

In the 1970s, Sidney W. Mintz and Richard Price revised the Herskovitsian model in an attempt to explain commonalities across the African diaspora despite the cultural heterogeneity of slave societies.[105] Mintz and Price's model emphasized the creolization of African slave culture rather than the identification of specific West and West Central African cultural traits. They believed that the randomized nature of the slave trade, the violence of the Middle Passage, and the brutality of plantation slavery prevented the direct transfer of African cultural traditions and forced slaves to construct a new African American culture. The creolization process began between shipmates on the very ships that transported slaves to the Americas and continued once they arrived at their destination on American plantations. According to Mintz and Price, the birth of African American culture represents a dialectic between the shared mental constructs of enslaved Africans and the colonial social contexts in which slave societies developed. For example, they argued that shared beliefs about the active role of ancestral spirits led to syncretic religious adaptations that transcended cultural differences on the plantation. Thus, Jamaican *obeah* and Haitian vodou combined underlying principles of West and West Central African belief systems. Moreover, the "additive" nature of West and West Central African cultures encouraged syncretism in slave religions.[106]

More recent work on the Atlantic slave trade has returned to earlier emphases on the impact of particular African ethnic groups on particular parts of the Americas.[107] In turn, slave trade evidence has renewed the search for specific cultural influences in the Americas. Historian Robin Law, for example, identified the influence of Arada slaves from the Dahomean region of West Africa in the famous Bois Caïman ceremony that preceded the Haitian Revolution. Based on the oaths taken there, Law argued that the "ceremony at Bois Caiman in 1791 is clearly interpretable as a Dahomean-type ritual oath."[108] Historian Douglas Chambers used slave trade data to hunt for "igboisms" in Jamaican slave culture. According to Chambers, some of the most celebrated Jamaican slave cultural practices, such as *jonkonu* and obeah, represent Igbo customs.[109]

Do the drinking practices of Caribbean slaves reflect the direct transfer of particular African drinking customs or the construction of new drinking behaviors based on the shared beliefs of various African ethnic groups? Answering this question is difficult because most of our information about both African and African slave drinking comes from Europeans who often failed to explore the nuances of complex drinking customs. Moreover, African and African slave drinking rituals were usually private events conducted away from the eyes of Europeans. Thus, we may simply lack the raw evidence that would allow us to make a strong link between the drinking practices of particular African nations with those observed among African slaves in the Caribbean. However, the evidence does show that, at the level of the lowest common denominator, African slaves in the Caribbean created drinking customs that embraced their shared West and West Central African beliefs about the spiritual meaning of alcohol.

John Thornton's study of the rise of the Afro-Atlantic world provides a good model for exploring the drinking practices of Caribbean slaves.[110] Thornton argues that Mintz and Price overstated the randomized nature of the Atlantic slave trade. Rather than seeing a heterogeneous mix of West and West Central African cultures, Thornton, like Herskovits, focuses on broad bundles of cultural traits and sees West and West Central Africa as very homogeneous. Thornton identifies three cultural zones, which he believes shared a great deal in common. Moreover, Thornton argues that West and West Central Africans became increasingly homogeneous as a result of the rise of large African states and the expansion of European trade. Although Thornton concedes that differences between culture zones were obstacles to the transfer and recommencement of particular ethnic practices on American plantations, they did not prevent the construction of a new African-oriented culture in the Americas. Thornton stresses the cultural flexibility of Africans who were able to merge their beliefs and ideas with those from various parts of Africa and Europe. Most original in Thornton's argument is the idea that the processes that led to the rise of this new Afro-Atlantic culture emerged in colonial Africa and began to shape Africans long before they arrived in the Americas.

Thornton's examination of the rise of Afro-Atlantic religion is particularly germane to the study of alcohol use among Caribbean slaves. At a basic level,

Africans and Europeans shared similar beliefs about the nature of religion, especially the belief in a spirit world that was home to ancestors. Africans and Europeans also believed that the spirit world revealed its demands and desires through revelations. As a result of increasing interactions between Europeans and different African groups, a new Afro-Atlantic religion emerged "that was often identified as Christian, especially in the New World, but was a type of Christianity that could satisfy both African and European understandings of religion." According to Thornton,

> This new African Christianity allowed some of the African religious knowledge and philosophy to be accommodated in a European religious system and represented a merger of great significance, similar to the creation of Chinese (or East Asian) Buddhism or the Indianization of Islam.[111]

African priests, brought to the Americas as slaves, produced new revelations that helped build Afro-American cosmologies from various African beliefs. Like a lingua franca, African Christianity functioned as the link that brought together slaves from various nations.

One cultural similarity that Thornton overlooks in his analysis of Afro-Atlantic religious systems is that most Africans shared similar beliefs about the spiritual importance of alcohol. West and West Central Africans—excepting those at the northern margins of the slave trade who closely followed the teachings of Islam—believed that alcohol facilitated communication with the spirit world. Through libations and offerings, Africans opened lines of communication to the spirit world and showed reverence for ancestors and deities. Moreover, these practices were not entirely unfamiliar to Christian Europeans who used sacramental wine to strengthen their own sense of spiritual attachment. Common beliefs about the spiritual importance of alcohol merged in Africa and on the slave plantations in the Caribbean and helped unify Africans from various nations. The sacred uses of alcohol observed among African slaves in the Caribbean highlight the construction of new African-oriented drinking customs based on their shared beliefs.

Whether we accept the continuity argument of cultural bundlers, like Herskovits and Thornton, or the creativity argument of cultural splitters, like Mintz and Price, the millions of slaves transported to the New World in the sixteenth through nineteenth centuries came from diverse West and West Central African cultural backgrounds. Historical evidence from travelers' accounts, mission reports, and trade records indicates that alcohol figured prominently in precolonial West and West Central Africa and that most slaves came from societies with strong traditions of alcohol use. While the argument advanced here emphasizes the braiding of shared West and West Central African beliefs about alcohol, the recent work on the Atlantic slave trade has shown that certain African ethnic groups were concentrated in particular regions of the New World. These slaves presumably had a major impact on the drinking behaviors that developed within those regions. Moreover, we must concede that European writers may have simply failed to provide us with enough information to pinpoint particular African influences. In order to account for the new evidence and strike a balance in the debate over the emergence of slave culture, I focused above on the drinking patterns of the Akan, Igbo, Kongo, and Arada, four African culture groups viewed by many historians as having the greatest impact on British and French Caribbean slave life. As that discussion showed, all shared similar views about the basic spiritual importance of alcohol.

The Igbo from the Bight of Biafra and the Akan from the Gold Coast assuredly had a greater cultural impact in the British Caribbean than other African groups. According to Chambers, between 1700 and 1809, the Igbo represented as much as a third of all slave arrivals in the British Caribbean, a higher percentage than any other African ethnic group in this period.[112] The Akan also greatly influenced slave life in the British Caribbean due to their seventeenth-century presence in the region. This early presence suggests that Akan slaves probably had a profound socializing impact on later slave arrivals from other West and West Central African cultures.[113] There are good grounds for believing that the drinking practices of Igbo and Akan slaves significantly shaped drinking behaviors in the British Caribbean.

Slave societies in the French Caribbean were in the same way deeply influenced by particular African ethnic groups. In the eighteenth century, more than 75 percent of Africans brought to the French Caribbean came from the Bight of Benin and the Congo/Angola region of West Central Africa. In the first half of the eighteenth century, and probably before, most Africans destined for the French Caribbean departed from the Bight of Benin.[114] A series of wars in the early eighteenth century during the rise of the Dahomey kingdom produced numerous slaves and helped make Ouidah the main slaving station of French traders. In the mid-eighteenth century, the Congo/Angola region of West Central Africa became the major departure point of African slaves. European competition in the Bight of Benin forced French slavers to move south to the Portuguese-controlled regions along the Congo/Angolan coast.[115] Africans transported to the older French colony of Martinique disproportionately came from the Bight of Benin, reflecting the early settlement and development of that colony.[116] The French slave traders' shift to West Central Africa in the mid-eighteenth century and the increasing demand for slaves in St. Domingue meant that Kongos were the most numerous ethnic group in that colony and dominated the coffee sector that expanded after the mid-eighteenth century.[117]

Beliefs in the sacred nature of alcohol in these four African societies survived the violence of the Middle Passage and took hold in the slave societies of the British and French Caribbean. The ready availability of alcohol during the slavery period allowed African slaves to continue traditional African drinking practices. In the late eighteenth century, Moreau de St.-Méry, a Creole lawyer in St. Domingue, wrote that newly arrived slaves were not terribly surprised at the natural products of the island for they resembled what they knew in Africa.[118] Rum was among those products. Under the harsh conditions of Caribbean slavery, slaves used rum to help maintain a symbolic connection to Africa and the ancestral world. For those slaves who were not already familiar with rum in Africa, the ability to incorporate new varieties of alcohol into traditional forms of spirituality underscores the cultural adaptability of African slaves in a changing Afro-Atlantic social environment.

The religious practices of British and French Caribbean slaves demonstrate the continuous link between alcohol and the spiritual world. In the British Caribbean, obeah was a common form of slave healing and spirituality that integrated ancestor worship and a traditional system of doctoring. Although some early researchers linked the practice of obeah to Akan religious practices, Chambers claimed that the term *obeah* stemmed from the Igbo *dibia*, meaning a doctor or diviner who had close contact with the spirit world.[119] In all likelihood, obeah represented a mixing of various West and West Central African religious practices that venerated ancestors and sought spiritual assistance in worldly endeavors. According to anthropologist Jerome S. Handler, "For whites, Obeah became a catchall term for a range of supernatural-related behaviors that were not of European origin."[120]

Obeah rituals relied heavily on the sacred use of alcohol. As in Africa, alcohol was used to protect individuals and the community from harm and to appease malevolent spirits. Devotees, with the help of obeah priests, poured libations and made alcohol offerings before most major undertakings. Equiano found the healing practices of obeah doctors in the Caribbean similar to those he left behind in Africa.[121] Colonial whites saw obeah as a threat to the stability of the colonies and tried to outlaw its practice. The laws identified the use of alcohol in obeah fetish oaths and ancestor ceremonies. For example, in 1782,

Neptune, a slave, was transported off Jamaica "for making use of rum, hair, chalk, stones, and other materials, relative to the practice of Obeah, or witch-craft."[122] According to Jamaican sugar planter Bryan Edwards, colonial officials detected obeah practitioners by their fetishes, which typically included rum.[123] The use of rum in obeah practices reveals the transfer of African beliefs, especially Igbo and Akan beliefs, about the sacred nature of alcohol.

Alcohol also helped facilitate communication with the spiritual world in the French Caribbean. Moreau de St.-Méry wrote, "The Negroes' belief in magic and the power of their fetishes follow them from overseas."[124] The sacred uses of alcohol followed as well.

Vodou has become a blanket term for African-oriented religions in the French Caribbean, especially in Haiti. In the 1930s, Herskovits wrote vodou "is a complex of African belief and ritual governing in large measure the religious life of the Haitian peasantry."[125] It is accompanied by dances, spirit possession, and ceremonial rituals. The term *vodou*, meaning deities, comes from the Aja-Fon people of the Bight of Benin where, in the eighteenth century, Dahomey became the most important state. Known to the French as Arada, they worshiped the principle of sinuosity and snake deities.[126] Dahomey invaded and conquered the kingdom of Allada in 1724, which resulted in the shipment of many Arada to the French colonies in the New World. Similarly, slaves from Ouidah, conquered by Dahomey in 1727, also significantly influenced vodou in Haiti.[127] More recently, scholars have reevaluated the impact of West Central Africans in St. Domingue and challenged notions about the purity of Arada and Ouidah influences in vodou. Historian David Geggus, for example, showed "a very strong Kongo content in what eighteenth century colonists called voodoo."[128]

Vodou and ancestor worship transferred to the Americas, where they continued to play an active role in the daily lives of French Caribbean slaves. Moreau de St.-Méry provided a rare description of the use of alcohol in a vodou dance among the slaves of St. Domingue.

> If by mischance the excess of his [the dancer's] transport makes him leave the circle, the chant ceases at once, the Voodoo King and Queen turn their backs on him to avert misfortune. The dancer recovers himself, reenters the circle, begins anew, drinks, and finally becomes convulsive. . . . The delirium increases. It is even further aroused by the use of spirituous liquors which in the intoxication of their imagination the devotees do not spare, and which in turn keeps them up.[129]

Moreau de St.-Méry also mentioned a variety of vodou ceremony, known as *petro*, in which devotees consumed drinks of rum and gunpowder.[130] Perhaps these were oath-drinks meant to bind participants to silence and loyalty. Herskovits described rum and gunpowder offerings to vodou deities in Dahomey.[131] However, the use of rum and gunpowder in petro ceremonies in eighteenth-century St. Domingue may also reflect Kongo influences. Geggus, for example, examined the case of Jérôme Poteau, a mulatto slave in St. Domingue, who attracted large gatherings of slaves and sold *maman-bila* (small chalky stones) for ritual purposes. According to the eighteenth-century reports on the case, these stones were placed in rum and gunpowder "to make them angry" and, thus, to intensify their power. Participants also consumed mixtures of rum and crushed maman-bila during vodou ceremonies. Geggus points out that several aspects of the maman-bila rituals reflect Kongo magic and religious influences, including the use of chalky white stones.[132]

Modern ethnographic reports have also captured the essence of alcohol use in vodou ceremonies. Alfred Métraux's extensive study of Haitian vodou describes numerous instances in which devotees used alcohol to facilitate communication with the spirit world. In fact, followers contact their particular *loa* [spirits or supernatural beings] by making drink offerings.[133] Herskovits described vodou dances in Haiti in which it was the obligation of the family giving the dance to provide *clarin* (raw bush rum).[134] Alcohol-induced spirit possession also characterized vodou ceremonies, and according to anthropologist Erika Bourguignon, "it is the spirits, rather than the cult members, who drink."[135] Failing to make the proper oblation prevented devotees from being "mounted" or "saddled" by their loa.[136] Anthropologist Seth Leacock identified similar instances among Afro-Brazilian cults in which spirits possessed cult members at curing rituals and public ceremonies. According to Leacock, these ceremonies functioned to integrate members of the cult, relieve anxiety, and help problem-solve through spiritual guidance.[137] Besides its role in vodou rites and ceremonies, rum was an important ingredient in witchcraft and as a *garde* in many protective charms.[138]

As in Africa, alcohol figured prominently at slave funerals. According to Long, "drinking, dancing, and vociferation" characterized the funerals of British Caribbean slaves.[139] In 1688, John Taylor, a visitor to Jamaica, recognized the central role of the ancestors at funerals and observed that, after offerings, including rum, had been placed in the grave, they "fill up the grave, and eat and drink thereon."[140] Hans Sloane noted that slaves in Jamaica put rum and food into the graves of their deceased comrades "to serve them in the other world."[141] In 1740, Leslie wrote that slaves were buried with a pot of soup at the head, and "a Bottle of Rum at the Feet."[142] In 1791, Atwood described the role of alcohol at slave funerals in Dominica. "Their superstitious notions with respect to their dead are truly ridiculous, for they suppose that the deceased both eat and drink in their coffins; and for that purpose, they put therein articles for both."[143]

To date, evidence from graves of the use of alcohol has been hard to come by in the few slave cemeteries that have been excavated in the Caribbean. For example, in the early 1970s, Jerome S. Handler and Frederick W. Lange excavated more than 100 burials at Newton plantation, Barbados.[144] They recovered a large number of tobacco pipes used as grave goods, but recovered no bottles associated with any of the burials. A tobacco pipe, too, was recovered from a burial at an unmarked eighteenth-century slave cemetery in Bridgetown, Barbados. The grave contained shards of green wine-bottle glass, but the fragmentary and incomplete nature of the glass suggests it entered the burial accidentally and not as a grave good.[145] Despite Leslie's claim that British Caribbean slaves buried bottles of rum with the deceased, the lack of bottles recovered from slave burials indicates that the demand for bottles among the living outweighed the need for bottles in slave funerary rites. Bottles were prized for practical purposes, and slaves probably modified West African customs to meet local conditions. Perhaps slaves merely sprinkled alcohol on the graves of the dead rather than relinquish useful bottles. This was evidently the case at the annual celebrations to the dead in Dominica that typically occurred at the Christmas holiday when alcohol was widely distributed to slaves.

> At this time too, they perform their offerings of victuals on the graves of their deceased relations and friends; a piece of superstition which all negros are addicted to, and which, were they to neglect doing, they firmly believe they would be punished by the spirits of the deceased persons. This offering consists of meat, whole kids, pigs, or fowls, with broth, liquors, and other matters; and is performed in the following manner: a man or woman accustomed to the ceremony, takes of each meat laid in dishes round the grave, and pulling some of it in pieces, throws the same on the grave, calling out the name of the dead person as if alive, saying, "Here is a piece of such a thing for you to eat; why did you leave your father, mother, wife, children and friends? Did you go away angry with us? When shall we see you again? Make our provisions to grow, and stock to breed; don't let anybody do us harm, and we will give you the same next year;" with the like expressions to

everything they throw on the grave. After which, taking a little of the rum or other liquors, they sprinkle it thereon, crying out in the same manner, "Here is a little rum to comfort your heart, good bye to you, God bless you;" and drinking some of it themselves to the welfare of the deceased, they set up a dismal cry and howling, but immediately after begin to dance and sing round the grave.[146]

In the French Caribbean, the successful return to the spirit world at death also necessitated the use of alcohol. Historian Lucien Peytraud wrote "the dead drink, eat, enjoy, like the living; therefore they offer them food and liquors."[147] According to Herskovits, clarin was a central element of a Haitian funeral and, "When drinks are passed, the recipients must make three libations before drinking."[148] Alcohol was not given to the dying or put in the mouth of the deceased for fear that he or she might become drunk and not reach the spirit world. After the individual had died, however, libations were poured to aid his or her transition to the spiritual world.

As in West and West Central Africa, a small ruling class, who held the land and labor necessary to produce rum, largely controlled the flow of alcohol in the Caribbean.[149] Sugar planters, therefore, like African tribal chiefs and elders, had possession of a powerful fluid that was essential for opening communication with the spiritual world, receiving spiritual guidance, and ensuring successful transformations during rites of passage. Moreover, the sugar planters' distribution of alcohol at births, funerals, and other important events mirrored the pattern of alcohol distribution found among chiefs and elders in West and West Central Africa.[150] This hierarchical control of alcohol would have been familiar to African slaves in the Caribbean and may have helped legitimate the power of the planter class.

Slaves, however, also took initiative in getting alcohol for spiritual events and rites of passage and, according to an anonymous writer in Jamaica, "the best victuals and some liquors are procured [by slaves] in great plenty" on these occasions.[151] Feasts and ceremonies like those described above reinforced social ties on the plantations. Drinking spurred sociability at these events, which helped create a more unified slave community. One of the primary functions of alcohol in African-oriented religions in the Caribbean was the facilitation of social intercourse and the integration of community members. Community building would have been especially important to newly arrived African slaves in the Caribbean, which perhaps increased the social and spiritual value of rum.

Conclusion

Shared West and West Central African beliefs about the sacred nature of alcohol and the active participation of the ancestors in daily life took root in the slave societies of the British and French Caribbean. As in Africa, libations and alcohol offerings helped African slaves build bridges to the spiritual world and learn the desires of ancestral spirits and deities. Within the diverse African cultural context of the slave plantation, alcohol became a catchall substance for all dealings with the spiritual world. Even today, the spiritual importance of alcohol is evident in the short generalized rituals found throughout the Caribbean, such as when rum shop patrons pour the first capful of a newly opened bottle of rum on the ground for the ancestors.

Why did highly volatile rum operate in the same spiritual manner as traditional alcoholic beverages in Africa? The physiological effect of alcohol, especially a potent spirit like rum, altered consciousness and made it a vehicle for escape to the spiritual world. Moreover, since the seventeenth century, West and West Central Africans had welcomed rum as a sacred fluid and used it in place of indigenous alcoholic beverages. Many slaves, therefore, were already familiar with rum's spiritual dimensions when they arrived in the Caribbean. The anxieties generated by the hostile social environment of the Caribbean sugar plantation motivated African slaves' ongoing embrace of alcohol as a temporary means of escape to the spirit world and, symbolically, to Africa. The use of rum in spiritual contexts by diverse ethnic groups in Africa and their representatives and descendants in the Caribbean also underscores the adaptability of the Afro-Atlantic community. Like the rise of Afro-Atlantic Christianity, rum became a unifying feature of the Afro-Atlantic world. Just as the consumption of slave-made Caribbean rum helped Africans in Africa make a symbolic connection to their brethren overseas, it also helped Caribbean slaves form a link to their African homelands.

CHAPTER 5

Alcoholic Marronage

Identity, Danger, and Escape in Caribbean Slave Societies

FRICAN SLAVES IN THE CARIBBEAN embraced rum as a sacred fluid that enhanced connections to the spiritual world and strengthened ties to African culture. Of course, alcohol had secular as well as spiritual uses. Rum was a commercial commodity produced in a divisive social climate subject to the harsh conditions of slavery for a distant market. It was also a highly volatile fluid, considerably more powerful than the fermented beverages of low alcohol content typically encountered in Europe, Africa, and the pre-Columbian Caribbean. This vulgar side of rum made it an effective tool for advancing secular and immediate goals. The use of alcohol to confront worldly concerns is evident in group-defining patterns of drinking and in the increasingly aggressive aspects of alcohol use reflected in links between drunken violence and individual vulnerability. Over the long history of secular alcohol use, drinking became a means to release social pressure, circumvent authority, and challenge social-structural inequities, which occasionally made alcohol a powerful symbol of permanent escape through the overthrow of the existing social order. Understanding such patterns of alcohol use enables us to view underlying and overt conflicts that existed within Caribbean slave societies.

Alcohol and Identity in Caribbean Slave Societies

Drinking is a social behavior loaded with symbolic meaning. The type of alcoholic beverage consumed, levels of alcohol consumption, preparation of drinks, drunken comportment, and context of drinking performance convey messages that distinguish social groups. As a result, drinking is often integrated into broader strategies that have helped define boundaries between self and other in a number of historical and cross-cultural settings. While it may be apparent that different classes use alcohol to signal and reaffirm distinct identities, the separation of social groups in the Caribbean was very complex, incorporating not only economic class differences and cultural diversity, but also racial hierarchies and institutionalized legal statuses. Caribbean peoples had access to a wide range of alcoholic beverages. They produced alcohol from various local resources and, during the sugar revolution, turned to rum as the staple alcoholic drink. Imported alcoholic beverages from Europe were also available. As a result, the construction of unique drinking styles became a principal means of expressing social group affiliation.

Caribbean historians and archaeologists have made alcohol use a defining feature of Carib Indian society. Carib drinking centered on the cassava-based oüicou, a drink that permeated the foundations of Carib spirituality and sociability. The process of making oüicou, which entailed masticating the cassava, fascinated Europeans, who frequently recorded details about its production. Oüicou use was fundamentally Carib, and early writers all noted that oüicou was a Carib drink. For example, Barbadian colonist Richard Ligon wrote that perino, the Barbadian word for oüicou, was "a drink which the *Indians* make for their own drinking."[1] Although oüicou use was essentially Carib, curiosity led Ligon and other Europeans to try it. British colonial historian John Oldmixon wrote, "Tis a very beastly Preparation, and one would think by its fine Taste that it had been some more delicate Drink."[2] Yet, while European colonists may have occasionally imbibed oüicou, it is unlikely that they did so on a regular basis. They probably considered the consumption of a masticated beverage strange. Other Europeans simply found it repulsive.[3] Slaves also drank their share of oüicou and, in the late seventeenth century, French missionary Father Jean Baptiste Père Labat even considered it one of the "ordinary" drinks of slaves in Martinique.[4] If seventeenth-century colonists drank oüicou in any great amount, such use was largely confined to poorer classes in areas with dense Carib populations.[5]

Mobbie, the sweet potato–based fermented beverage originally produced by Caribs, became a common drink in the British and French Caribbean. In the early settlement period, Ligon wrote that the drink of the servants in Barbados was "nothing but *Mobbie*."[6] The use of mobbie, however, was not restricted to servants. For example, Henry Whistler, a traveler to Barbados in

1654, believed that the Barbadians' usual "drink is mad of petatoe routes."[7] Even elites appreciated the taste of mobbie. In 1652, Heinrich Von Uchteritz, a German indentured servant in Barbados, noted "the genetry make a drink from the potato root," and in 1654, French priest Antoine Biet described a dinner at the home of a wealthy Barbadian sugar planter that included "sweetened mauby" for those who did not want wine.[8] The French also liked the taste of mobbie. According to Charles de Rochefort, a French colonist, mobbie was one of the most popular drinks in the French Caribbean.[9] In Martinique, French missionary Father Jean Baptiste Du Tertre enjoyed mobbie and thought it tasted similar to claret.[10] Labat also described the widespread use of mobbie in the French islands.[11]

Mobbie was not typically associated with slaves until the eighteenth century. Oldmixon made a general reference to the use of mobbie by "Servants and Slaves" in Barbados and noted that slaves planted potatoes in their gardens.[12] As late as 1833, a variety of "mobee" mixed with sugar, ginger, and snakeroot was popular among slaves in St. Vincent.[13] However, some time in the nineteenth century, mobbie became the term for a non-alcoholic beverage in Barbados made not from potatoes but from tree bark. This updated usage is also found in Martinique and Guyana.[14]

The link between fermented sugarcane juice drinks and slaves is also strong. In the earliest New World reference to sugarcane-based alcohol, Spanish Dominican friar Bartolomé de Las Casas reported that slaves drank cane syrup concoctions [*guarapo*] and hinted that they were the primary consumers of these beverages.[15] In Martinique, Du Tertre wrote that slaves made their own variety of intoxicating drinks from the scum that came from the boiling sugar cauldrons.[16] Labat also wrote that slaves made *grappe*, which was the "ordinary" drink of slaves who worked on sugar estates.[17] In Barbados, the fact that Ligon, who tried a variety of local alcoholic drinks, never tried *grippo* suggests the drink may have been particularly associated with African slaves.[18] Similarly, Griffith Hughes, the rector of St. Lucy's parish church in Barbados, believed that *cowow*, a fermented sugarcane drink, was usually associated with the "poorer Sort."[19] In 1797, an anonymous writer in Jamaica observed that water was the common drink among slaves, "but they prefer *cool drink*, a fermented liquor made with chaw-stick, lignum vitae, brown sugar, and water."[20]

Distilled rum was universally consumed in the Caribbean, but in the seventeenth century its use seems to have been especially concentrated among slaves, servants, and Caribs. Du Tertre believed that rum was the ordinary drink of slaves in Martinique, and Labat considered tafia the drink of Caribs, slaves, poor whites, and tradespeople.[21] In 1690, Dalby Thomas, an advocate for British Caribbean planters, wrote that rum was "a Noble Intoxicating Liquor, which the Negroes as well as English Servants but too much delight in."[22] However, Oldmixon wrote that rum "is strong, but not very palatable, and seldom falls to the Servants Lot," suggesting its use was concentrated among slaves.[23]

Wealthy whites in the Caribbean drank a variety of alcoholic beverages. In Barbados in the late 1640s, Ligon attended a dinner at the estate of sugar planter James Drax. The alcoholic beverages available to guests included "Mobbie, Beveridge, Brandy, Kill-Devil, Drink of the Plantine, Claret-wine, White-wine, and Rhenish-wine, Sherry, Canary, Red sack, wine of Fiall, with all Spirits that come from *England*."[24] The wide variety of drinks was itself an expression of wealth. The heavy emphasis on imported alcoholic beverages also projected elite status.

Indeed, wine and brandy imported from France and Spain were reserved almost exclusively for Caribbean elites. According to Jamaican sugar planter Edward Long, in Cartagena, "Persons of distinction use Spanish brandy, but the lower sort a kind of rum distilled from sugar-cane."[25] Labat believed a good wine was "the soul of a meal" and always kept a good supply of wine imported from France, Madeira, and Canary.[26] The nationalistic sentiment surrounding the use of wine and brandy in southern European grape-growing nations, as well as the strong symbolic value of wine in Catholic religious practices, may have elevated the preference for wine and brandy by French and Spanish Caribbean elites.

British Caribbean elites similarly appreciated wine and brandy. Madeira and canary wines were so prevalent in Bridgetown, Barbados, that in the mid-seventeenth century, Madeira and Canary were adopted as the names for two major streets where merchants specialized in the importation and sale of wine from these two regions.[27] The consumption of Madeira was especially widespread among the elite in the British Caribbean. In part, this was due to the relatively open trade that existed between British America and Portugal after the Navigation Act of 1663 and the Methuen Treaty of 1703. In Barbados, Oldmixon considered Madeira "the chief Drink of the island that the Gentlemen make Use of."[28] In Jamaica, traveler Charles Leslie believed wine from Madeira was generally "used by the better Sort."[29] The island of Madeira was a critical supply station for ships traveling to the British Caribbean, which probably increased the availability of Madeira. Moreover, many believed that the hot climate of the Caribbean brought out a particularly pleasant taste in Madeira.

For example, Long wrote, "Madeira wine is in more esteem than claret, not only because it is cheaper, but as the greatest heat of the air only serves to improve its flavour."[30] Leslie also thought it was particularly well suited to the hot Caribbean climate: "*Madera* is a wholesome Wine, and agrees perfectly well with ones Constitution in this Place."[31] In Barbados, Hughes believed wine from Madeira could "invigorate the languid Spirits" of those who had fallen ill to a variety of tropical diseases.[32] Labat mentioned the frequent use of Madeira in the French islands and noted that it was the main ingredient in *sang-gris*, a fashionable drink among Caribbean elites.[33]

Imported European wine and brandy were, however, expensive and difficult to obtain, especially in the British Caribbean.[34] Wines often failed to survive the long sea voyage from Europe without becoming tainted or being consumed or lost at sea. As a result, rum became a more tolerable drink among the Caribbean elite. According to Ligon, rum was sold to wealthy planters who drank it "excessively," and he noted its presence at their dinner tables. On the other hand, a pattern of extensive planter rum use may be overstated. Rum was generally associated with poorer classes in the seventeenth century and even Ligon, usually an advocate of Barbadian produce, wrote, "it is common, and therefore the less esteem'd."[35] It is likely that, in the latter part of the seventeenth century, the growing wealth and stability of the Barbadian planter class increased its access to imported and expensive alcoholic beverages. Moreover, the large number of African slaves and poor whites may have inspired elites to use imported alcoholic beverages to widen social boundaries. In the early eighteenth century, Oldmixon wrote "no Planter of any Note will now deign to drink [rum]; his Cellars are better furnished."[36] In 1732, Reverend Robert Robertson estimated that Barbadians imported more than £40,000 worth of alcoholic beverages, including wine, brandy, beer, ale, and cider, which represented nearly 12 percent of the value of all imports.[37] Thus, despite being producers of rum, by the end of the seventeenth century Caribbean sugar planters regularly preferred to drink expensive and imported alcoholic beverages.

The only real exception to elite rum use was the consumption of rum punch, an elaborate concoction made with expensive and exotic Asian spices and other ingredients. According to Ligon, punch drinking was practiced in Barbados as early as the 1640s.[38] In 1661, shortly after Ligon, a Swiss medical doctor in Barbados named Felix Spoeri also described the production of punch: "one takes a basin of water and sweetens it with sugar, then lemon juice, and finally the above-mentioned Kill-Devil [rum] or Brandy."[39] Punch was a special variety of mixed drink made with spirits, lemon juice, spices, sugar, and water. In the seventeenth century, there were variations on ingredients. In Martinique, Labat wrote that punch was the "favorite drink" of the island and that it was made with two parts rum, one part water and contained sugar, cinnamon, powdered clove, nutmeg, a slice of toasted or slightly burnt bread, and egg yolks.[40] Although brandy was widely used in punch, rum became a more popular ingredient. Oldmixon wrote that, when making punch, "The good Husbands of Barbados use their own Manufacture Rum."[41] Thomas also noted that some British Caribbean planters preferred rum to brandy either for "Punch or other uses where Spirits are needed."[42] The base alcohol distinguished the punch and, thus, punch made with rum was specifically referred to as "rum punch."

In the late seventeenth and early eighteenth centuries, there is some confusion over the elite meaning of punch. Physician and traveler Hans Sloane wrote, "The common fuddling Liquor of the more ordinary sort is Rum-Punch," which was drunk by "Servants, and other of the poorer sort."[43] As late as 1740, Leslie failed to distinguish between rum punch and common unmixed rum or, as he still called it, kill-devil.[44] And, in 1750, Hughes also associated punch with the servants and slaves.[45] However, while ordinary rum may have been primarily considered the drink of poorer classes, rum punch, which was distinguished by careful preparation and addition of exotic ingredients, was an elite drink. In the eighteenth century, the distinction between rum punch and common kill-devil rum became slightly clearer. According to Long,

> Punch seems almost proscribed from the politer tables; though, when it is made with rum of due age, ripe fruit, and not too strong, it is a very pleasant, refreshing, and wholesome drink, and one of the best appropriated to a hot climate.[46]

The ready availability of rum and the occasional difficulty of procuring imported beverages meant that all classes in the Caribbean consumed rum. However, even though both wealthy and poor consumed rum, the upper classes still needed to distinguish their drinking patterns from the poor. As with the simple addition of a dash of sugar and bitters to turn common whiskey into a cocktail, the addition of exotic ingredients turned ordinary rum into an elite drink called punch.

The presentation of punch enhanced the elite value of punch drinking performances. Wealthy colonists, especially in the British Caribbean, prepared and distributed varieties of punch in punch bowls, hemispherical vessels typically made of refined earthenware and porcelain. Labat also mentioned the use of glass punch bowls.[47] Seventeenth-century punch bowls were smaller in size than ones produced in the Georgian period, which sometimes held as much as two gallons.[48] Archaeologists interpret the presence of punch bowls at domestic sites in North America and the Caribbean as indications of the elite status of residents.[49] Probate inventories also show the connection between punch drinking and wealth. For example, the 1722 probate inventory of John Pinney, a wealthy sugar planter in Nevis, included a porcelain punch bowl.[50] The presentation of punch in ornate bowls changed drinking from an ordinary activity into a social performance that allowed colonists to signal status on the colonial Caribbean frontier. In the British colonies, punch bowls created the appearance of refinement similar to that of English tea sets in the later eighteenth and nineteenth centuries.

The heavy emphasis on punch drinking reveals an important aspect of British Caribbean society—that British colonists were preoccupied with hospitality and the sociable art of drinking. British colonists in Barbados had an especially strong reputation for alcohol-based sociability. In 1654, Whistler wrote, "The peepell [of Barbados] have a very Generus fashon that if one come to a hous to inquier the way to any plase, they will macke him drinke."[51] Three years earlier, Giles Silvester, a Barbadian planter wrote, "For the merry planter, or freeman to give him a Caracter, I can call him noe otherwise then a German for his drinking, and a Welshman for his welcome."[52] And, according to Christopher Codrington, the governor of the Leeward Islands,

> The planters [of Barbados] think the best way to make their strangers welcome is to murther them with drinking; the tenth part of that strong liquor which will scarce warme the blood of our West Indians, who have bodies like Egyptian mummys, must certainly despatch a new-comer to the other world.[53]

The desire to engage in alcohol-based hospitality also existed in other parts of the Caribbean. For example, in 1688, Jamaican visitor John Taylor indicated that nearly every planter kept a bowl of rum punch at the ready to accommodate friends and visitors.[54] French Creole lawyer M. L. E. Moreau de St.-Méry believed that such hospitality was one of the "principal virtues" of white Creole men in St. Domingue.[55]

The constant flow of traders, mariners, and other visitors to the Caribbean increased the opportunity to engage in alcohol-based hospitality. In Barbados, for example, the capital Bridgetown was an active trading hub drawing hundreds of ships and thousands of transitory visitors each year. Many visitors to

Barbados were overwhelmed by the welcome they received. In 1695, Labat arrived in Bridgetown and was immediately treated to drinks. Labat wrote, "I was convinced by the kind manner in which I had been received that all I had been told about the country fell very short of the mark."[56] Alcohol was crucial to that hospitality and, upon departure, Labat wrote, "you may rest assured that we did not leave Bridgetown without having something to drink."[57]

Indeed, Barbadians seem to have developed a special lust for alcohol-based hospitality, which they considered a sign of wealth and gentility. The art of sociable drinking, usually within the context of punch drinking performances, was such an integral part of Barbadian hospitality that refusing to drink was considered disrespectful and an insult to gentlemanly honor. Whistler claimed "if the trafeller dose denie to stay to drinke they tacke it very unkindly of him."[58] Similarly, Silvester wrote,

> [The planter] takes it ill, if you pass by his doore, and not tast of Liquor. I shall breifely relate a story of a gentleman since my coming. Hee coming to have waited on my Lord, to make his way the shorter, crosses ones ground, that was newly sett over with Corne, and rydes by his house. The Planter meeting him, roughly demannds the reason of his preiudiciall Act, the Gentleman speaks him faire, promises to returne noe more that way. The Planter hee is pacified, and asked him what hee would drinke, hee answeared him nothing, soe denying severall drinkes which the man earnestly proposed. The angry planter after 2 or 3 curses Comannded him backe the same way he came for his uncivility (as hee tearmed it) in refusing his proferr.[59]

Refusing to drink challenged the legitimacy of gentlemanly status and was, as illustrated by Silvester, a serious affront to the honor-bound men of Barbados. To Barbadians, engaging in the art of sociable drinking was a way to acquire, express, and legitimate status.

Anxiety and Drunkenness

Alcohol use was widespread in the Caribbean and the enormous amounts of alcohol available contributed to a climate of excessive drinking. However, levels of alcohol consumption varied among different social groups, and those differences reflect more than simple access to spirits. As with the choice of alcoholic beverage, levels of drinking and drunken comportment helped express social group identities. The drinking patterns of particular social groups also conveyed messages about the underlying tensions that existed in the Caribbean, tensions driven by the coercive exploitation of labor and set within a highly contentious social hierarchy based on class, race, religion, and ethnic identity. Moreover, these tensions were magnified by epidemic disease, poor living conditions, natural disasters, international conflicts, and unstable food supplies. While nearly everyone in the Caribbean drank, the differing levels of alcohol use by different social groups highlight the ways in which drinking became a physical manifestation of, and a means to confront, anxiety.

Early writers paint a complicated picture of slave drinking. The lack of firsthand reporting by slaves forces us to rely heavily on white perceptions of slave alcohol use. In the 1830s, for example, Wesleyan missionaries in Antigua believed intemperance *"never had been one of the vices of the negroes."*[60] Others felt that slaves were "sober only when they cannot help themselves."[61] Whites made contrasting claims about slave drinking because they were ambivalent about how to treat it. On the one hand, whites feared slave drinking as liberating, a fomenter of insurrections that threatened the social order. On the other hand, alcohol was a tool of domination, a way to "humor" slaves and keep them in a daze about their bondage. Colonial legislatures enacted numerous laws meant to curb slave drinking, yet these laws were rarely enforced and planters continued to dole out huge amounts of rum to the slaves on their estates. In addition, Caribbean slave societies were based on the systematic extraction of labor. Concerns about the negative impact of excessive drinking on work performance, therefore, frequently tainted white discussions of slave drinking.

In their efforts to maximize plantation efficiency, planters established complex stereotypes about the constitutions of particular African ethnic groups. Often, these stereotypes made reference to drinking behaviors. For example, Moreau de St.-Méry believed that slaves from the Gold Coast were drunkards. In contrast, he considered slaves from Senegal, a region long influenced by Islam, very abstemious.[62] In Jamaica, Long embraced the reports of slave traders and believed that Gold Coast slaves were "much addicted to . . . drunkenness."[63] Long also described slaves from Angola and Benguela as "drunkards."[64] Planters knew that a temperate workforce was a more efficient workforce and, therefore, had practical economic reasons for observing the drinking of particular African ethnic groups.

Stereotypes about the drinking habits of particular African ethnic groups probably influenced the planters' decisions to assign slaves to specific alcohol-related tasks. For example, Long wrote,

Nothing can more plainly evince the fatal effects of [excessive rum drinking], than the general appearance and untimely end of most of the white men and Negroes employed in the distilling-houses, who, as they can supply themselves freely and without restraint, so they swill immoderate quantities of fresh distilled rum, piping hot from the worm.[65]

Slaves from ethnic groups with abstemious reputations were probably strong candidates for work in plantation distilleries. This may explain why, for example, Dr. Collins, a St. Vincent physician, believed that Mandingo slaves, coming from temperate Islamic backgrounds in Senegal, were well suited for employment in and around distilleries.[66]

Whites generally perceived slave drinking to be excessive. For example, in Dominica, sugar planter Thomas Atwood wrote, "Negros are in general much addicted to drunkenness, thievery, incontinency, and idleness. The first vice very few of them will refrain from when they can get liquor, and in their fits of this kind, many of them are very mischievous."[67] In Martinique, Du Tertre simply noted that slaves "drink to excess."[68] And, according to Collins, "It has been observed that all uncivilized nations, though reared in the habit of water drinking, soon acquire a relish for spirituous potations. . . . [and] This observation applies, with particular propriety, to negroes."[69] What Collins failed to understand, of course, was that most African slaves came from societies with strong traditions of alcohol use, and many were already familiar with rum and other alcoholic beverages long before they arrived in the Caribbean.

Slave drinking was considered especially strong among males. Long, for example, wrote that the male slaves of Jamaica have "no taste but for women; gormondizing, and drinking to excess."[70] In 1797, an anonymous writer in Jamaica also believed "Few strong liquors come amiss to the men [slaves], who frequently drink to excess."[71] One example was Plato, a habitual runaway from Jamaica for whom "rum was an article of first necessity."[72] Some in the French Caribbean thought that male slaves were generally abstemious, "with the exception of a few half-crazy old Africans called 'Papa Tafia' who neglected their gardens and preferred instead to cut firewood in exchange for tafia."[73] On the slave lists of York estate, Jamaica, appears Thomas, a cook. In 1779 and 1782, the plantation manager, recording the condition of the estate's slave population, wrote that Thomas "drinks as much as ever."[74] Male slaves' greater propensity for drinking may have helped shape the structure of sugar plantation work regimens. In the late seventeenth century, Labat advised French Caribbean planters to employ female rather than male slaves in distilleries, because "women are less subject to drink."[75] Apparently, they did not heed Labat's warning, as in 1768 the two slave distillers at both the Beaulieu and Galbaud du Fort estates in St. Domingue were men.[76]

However, excessive drinking was not confined to men. In 1778, Juba, a female domestic slave who worked in the great house at York estate, Jamaica, was also described in the slave lists as a "drunkard."[77] In 1796, George Pinckard, a visiting military physician in Barbados, wrote that both slave men and slave women "are very fond of rum."[78] In the late eighteenth century, one of the most popular satirical songs among slaves in Jamaica was about "a drunken Negro woman who used to get intoxicated very early in the morning."[79] Barbadian sugar planter Richard Hall noted, "most of the negroe women and many of their children drink rum."[80] Nor was rum drinking among children especially unusual. Jamaican sugar planter Thomas Roughley recommended that the slave children on his estate be given "a taste of good rum" each day as an "enlivener." Roughley believed it kept the children "cheerful."[81]

Drinking patterns expressed internal social divisions within the slave community. Collins, for example, argued that newly arrived African slaves "are not formed to habits of temperance, and have little inclination to learn them."[82] Moreau de St.-Méry also believed that African slaves were excessively fond of tafia.[83] In contrast, Creole slaves had a reputation for temperance in some places. Long argued that the sobriety of Creoles in Jamaica was a reaction against the excessive drinking of poorer classes of whites.

> The Creoles, in general, are more exempt from ebriety, that parent of many crimes! I have known several, who rejected every sort of spirituous liquor with loathing, and would drink nothing but water. If the Negroes could be restrained intirely from the use of spirits in their youth, they would probably never become very fond of dram-drinking afterwards. I have often thought, that the lower order of white servant on the plantations exhibit such detestable pictures of drunkenness, that the better sort of Creole Blacks have either conceived a disgust at a practice that occasions such odious effects, or have refrained from it out of a kind of pride, as if they would appear superior to, and more respectable than, such beastly white wretches.[84]

Long clearly believed that some Creoles actively abstained from alcohol as part of a broader social strategy to distinguish themselves from poorer classes of whites. Emma Carmichael, the wife of a planter in St. Vincent, wrote, "I have understood that the coloured men are by no means given to intoxication."[85] Moreau de St.-Méry also believed that drunkenness was more common among uneducated Europeans in St. Domingue than black Creoles.[86] Thus, temperance may have been a way for nonwhite Creoles throughout the Caribbean, free or enslaved, to define their identity, particularly in relationship to newly arrived Africans and poorer classes of whites. Although male Creole slaves were generally employed in specialized and skilled jobs, their temperance may also help explain why, in the late eighteenth century, the four slave distillers at Worthy Park estate in Jamaica were Creoles.[87] Not everyone, however, was convinced of the Creoles' abstemiousness, and some whites simply held that "New negroes, like old ones, are much addicted to the use of spirits."[88]

White fears about drunken slaves frequently led to legal restrictions against slave drinking. In 1692, the Barbados Assembly passed "An Act for prohibiting the selling of Rum or other Strong Liquors to any Negro or other Slave."[89] In 1692, whites in Barbados had discovered and thwarted a plot by slaves to revolt. The passage of this particular act was, no doubt, inspired by that aborted revolt. Colonial assemblies throughout the Caribbean passed similar laws during the slavery period, but, according to Collins, "it is to be lamented, that more effectual means have not been employed by our colonial legislatures, to prevent [the slaves'] easy access to rum."[90] Rum was abundant and its use such a requisite part of the slaves' social and spiritual world that these laws were "easily and often evaded."[91]

In reality, slave drinking was probably no more excessive than that found among most other social groups. Binge drinking among slaves appears to have been confined largely to ceremonial occasions, weekend events, and plantation holidays. Thomas and Juba were the only slaves noted at York estate for regularly overindulging in alcohol, and York had more than 450 slaves. This suggests that excessive drinking, or alcoholism, if we can call it that, was not widespread. However, as a cook and a domestic in the great house, Thomas and Juba were in more frequent contact with the planter than most of the other slaves on the lists who were, for the most part, field workers. In contrast to the field slaves, if the work performance of a cook and domestic suffered from excessive drinking, it was likely to have been noticed and recorded. Thus, excessive alcohol use may have been more widespread at York estate than can be gleaned from slave lists. Unfortunately, most plantation managers failed to record alcohol abuse in the slave lists.

Frequent contact in Caribbean towns between slaves and whites, particularly newly arrived whites, may help explain why some urban slaves were characterized as being prone to excessive drinking. For example, according to Atwood,

The negro porters are in general a very idle, insolent and thievish set of people, and are often guilty of much imposition, especially to strangers on their arrival in the islands. They are commonly the stoutest and worst disposed negros belonging to white people, or to free people of colour in the towns, and pay their owners a certain sum daily; but many of them will game away the whole of their earnings, or spend it in liquor, to the great injury of their masters.[92]

Urban domestics in Bridgetown also had a reputation for "fiddling, dancing, drinking, [and] gambling . . . which, every night, more or less, disturb the peace."[93] Urban slaves had more leisure time and increased access to alcohol in the many taverns that dominated Caribbean towns than plantation slaves in rural areas. However, the drinking of slave porters, like that of slave domestics, was conspicuous because of their public presence in areas heavily populated by whites.

Per capita rates of rum consumption among plantation slaves were not extreme. Labat estimated that plantation slaves annually received 3.4 gallons, and accounts from York estate, Jamaica, indicate an annual rate of 1.8 gallons per slave. However, in Barbados, Hall estimated an annual per capita consumption rate of seven gallons of rum. These rates are not excessive by contemporary North American standards. In the first decade of the eighteenth century, North Americans consumed an annual average of 2.7 gallons of absolute alcohol and, in 1770, an annual rate of 3.5 gallons.[94] Nor are these estimates especially remarkable when we consider the high proportion of adult male slaves—generally considered the heaviest alcohol consumers—in the Caribbean. Nonetheless, sugar plantation figures take into account the distribution of rum on estates and not necessarily that acquired through purchase, theft, reward, or allotted on special occasions. Moreover, these figures account only for the use of rum and not other alcoholic drinks, including fermented sugarcane drinks, which were frequently mentioned as being made by slaves.

The presence of green bottle glass fragments found by archaeologists at slave sites in the Caribbean attests to slave drinking.[95] However, glass bottles were not the only containers used for holding alcohol. Gourds also served as bottles.[96] According to one Jamaican writer,

When [slaves] travel, they have different ways of carrying their rum; the most common utensil is a calabash bottle, stopt with the stem on which the Indian corn grows. A cane is sometimes used for this purpose, to fit it for which they clear it of the membranes at the joints and cork the upper end: a large cane will hold a considerable quantity, and serves the double purpose of a bottle and a walking stick.[97]

The planter elite also had a reputation for excessive drinking. Descriptions of the various alcoholic beverages available to guests at the planters' tables reveal the extent to which alcohol permeated planter lifestyles. Drinking was a crucial facet of entertaining, hospitality, and social etiquette. As it is in accounts of slaves' drinking, our understanding of planter drinking is sometimes skewed by the bias of the writers, many of whom were members of the elite. They found little fault with what they perceived to be "noble" planters and expressed much pride in their comrades. Ligon, for instance, believed the planters of Barbados were "men of great abilities and parts." The fact that it was usually confined to relatively private events and more likely to occur in the great house than in public streets and taverns may also account for the perception of planter drinking as genteel. According to Oldmixon, "the Diversion of Gentlemen" in Barbados "are most within Doors."[98] A few writers, however, unmasked the drinking excesses of the elite.

> The Gallant People [of Barbados] delight most in Balls and Consorts; the good Fellows, in Drink and good Company; and though one would imagine, that Men should be afraid to drink such a hot Wine as Madeira, in such a hot Country, yet it has been known that some of them have drank their five and six Bottles a Day, and held it on for several Years.[99]

Boredom also fostered excessive drinking among the planter class. In 1721, slave trader John Atkins visited Barbados and wrote,

> The whole is a *Sweet* Spot of Earth, not a Span hardly uncultivated with Sugar-Canes; all sides bend with an easy Declivity to the Sea, and is ever green: This delight to the Planter has its Inconveniencies, that there is no Recreation out of Business, but in Drinking or Gaming.[100]

Similarly, Moreau de St.-Méry believed that wealthy white Creoles in St. Domingue engaged in alcohol-based hospitality with strangers to "inject some variety into an otherwise dull life."[101] The cartoon image of *A West India Sportsman* pokes fun at the notorious excesses of drink and idleness of the British Caribbean planter class. In the illustration, the planters' beverages include rum, brandy, several varieties of punch, and numerous unmarked and emptied bottles. One small jar of water amongst the jars of alcohol may have been meant to further emphasize planter intemperance.[102]

Figure 5.1. *A West India Sportsman* by Lieutenant Abraham James (1807). From the collection of the Barbados Museum and Historical Society.

In general, whites in the Caribbean had a reputation for heavy drinking. As early as 1631, Henry Colt, a visitor to Barbados, scolded the colonists: "You are all younge men, and of good desert, if you would but bridle ye excesse of drinkinge." Colt, imitating the intemperance of the Barbadians, was brought from drinking two drams of alcohol per meal to 30.[103] A century later, Thomas Walduck, a visitor to Barbados, wrote that the whites on the island brought copious amounts of rum punch to funeral ceremonies because "a funeral sermon makes them squeamish." According to Walduck, after the deceased was interred, the mourners sat on the porch of the church and drank until they were "drunk as Tinkers."[104]

Probably no other group in the Caribbean had a worse reputation for excessive drinking than indentured servants and other classes of poor whites. For example, Joseph West, the governor of South Carolina, complained about the intemperance of Barbadian servants and requested that no more be brought from the island. In the late seventeenth century, West wrote "we find that one of our Servants wee brought out of England is worth 2 of the Barbadians, for they are so addicted to Rum, that they will doe little but whilst the bottle is at their nose."[105] Some poor whites in Barbados were known to steal rum from sugar estates.[106] Excessive drinking among poor whites was not limited to Barbados, however, and Long argued that, in Jamaica, some servants were responsible for "bringing an *odium* upon the white people in general, by their drunkenness."[107]

Colonial assemblies occasionally attempted to curb the intemperance of poor whites. In Montserrat, the assembly prohibited planters from distilling all of their sugarcane juice into rum in order to reduce drunken violence in the island. The colonists, when drunk, apparently called one another derogatory names like "English dogg, Scots dogg, Tory, Irish dogg, Cavalier and Roundheade."[108] Planters in St. Vincent were prevented from distilling their entire crop for similar reasons.[109] In 1668, officials in Barbados believed that excessive drinking created such social and civil unrest that the assembly felt compelled to pass an act that greatly regulated and restricted the sale of spirits. The Barbados Assembly declared,

> Forasmuch as intolerable Hurts and Troubles to this Island, do continually grow and increase through the Multiplicity of such Abuses and Disorders as are daily had and used in Unlicens'd Tipling-Houses, commonly called Brandy, or Rum-Houses, which are for the most part situated and erected near to Broad-paths or High-ways; whereby the Keepers of such Houses take advantage to Trade and Deal with Servants and Negroes for Stolen Goods contrary to Law, and to the great Oppression and Damage of Honest and Industrious People. And Whereas on Sabbath Days, many Lewd, Loose and Idle People, do usually resort to such Tipling Houses, who by their Drunkenness, Swearing and other Miscarriages, do in a very high nature, blaspheme the Name of God, prophane the Sabbath, and bring a great Scandal upon true Christian Religion. For Prevention whereof for the future.[110]

In 1683, the Jamaica Assembly passed a similar act against blasphemy and for preventing disorders in alehouses, taverns, and victualing houses. Among the regulations was a fine for drinking and selling spirits during "the time of Divine Worship or Service."[111] In 1694, the colonial assembly of Curaçao also wrote, "We know that the Day of the Lord, in Curaçao, is the Day of Bacchus." The assembly instituted restrictive laws and mandated "no drinking-houses shall be open, or drinking-bouts take place" on Sundays.[112]

In contrast to the excessive drinking of white men, white women in the Caribbean were more temperate. Ligon, while trying to explain the current state and rapid spread of disease in Barbados, wrote,

Whether it were brought thither in shipping . . . or by the distempers of the people of the Island: who by the ill dyet they keep, and drinking strong waters, bring diseases upon themselves, was not certainly known. But I have this reason to believe the latter: because for one woman that dyed, there were ten men.[113]

William Dickson, a former secretary to Barbados's governor, wrote that the "œconomy, sobriety, fidelity" of white women in Barbados deserved "much praise."[114] According to Long, white Creole women in Jamaica were "temperate and abstemious in their diet, rarely drinking any other liquor than water."[115] Their good health, Long wrote, was due to their "less addiction to intemperance, and late hours."[116] In Dominica, Atwood wrote, "Withal, so very remarkable are the English Creole women for sobriety and chastity, that in the first instance very few of them drink any thing but water, or beverage of lime juice, water, and syrup."[117] In St. Domingue, Moreau de St.-Méry noted that French Creole women ordinarily drank pure water, though they occasionally indulged in lemonade mixed with molasses.[118]

Generalizations were also made concerning the drinking habits of freedmen and Jews. Long believed the Jews of Jamaica were abstemious and "may be supposed to owe their good health and longevity, as well as their fertility, to a very sparing use of strong liquors."[119] The Regenten, or communal leaders of the Sephardim, made similar claims about the Jews of Surinam.[120] Perhaps the overriding spiritual importance of alcohol in Judaism resulted in a healthy respect for alcohol and an abstemious Jewish drinking pattern.[121] Long also believed that freedmen "are not so averse [as Jews] to spirituous liquors; for both men and women are frequently intoxicated." Long wrote that, when compared to Jamaican Jews, the freedmen's intemperance shortened their lives. He added, "the native Whites in this island, I mean such of them as are not addicted to drunkenness, nor have any hereditary distemper, are equally healthy and long-lived [as Jews and abstemious freedmen]."[122] Yet not all whites saw freedmen as intemperate. Dickson, for example, described the freedmen of Barbados as "sober and industrious."[123]

The drinking habits of specific European cultures were also scrutinized. Long believed that artificers from northern Scotland were generally "sober" and "frugal," which may help explain why they were frequently employed as distillers on sugar estates.[124] According to Labat, the English in the Caribbean "invented two or three sorts of drinks whose use and abuse are attributed to the French, who are always very ardent imitators of the worst habits of their

Figure 5.2. *A Spanish Planter of Porto Rico, Luxuriating in His Hammock.* In John A. Waller, *A Voyage in the West Indies* (London, 1820). Courtesy of the John Carter Brown Library at Brown University.

neighbors."[125] Moreau de St.-Méry considered the Spanish Creoles in Santo Domingo remarkably temperate, noting that water was their usual drink.[126] Long also noted the temperance of Spanish Creoles. Long believed colonists in Jamaica would be as healthy as "Spaniards are found to be, if they would but depart a little more from a too plentiful flesh diet, and strong liquors."[127] Yet, Long also wrote,

> Among the Spaniards at Carthagena, the use of spirits is so common that the most regular and sober persons never omit drinking a small glass every forenoon about eleven o'clock, alledging that it strengthens the stomach, weakened by copious, constant perspiration, and sharpens the appetite. *Hacer las once, To do the eleven*; that is, to drink a glass of spirit, is the ordinary invitation. But this custom, which is not esteemed pernicious when used with *moderation*, has degenerated into vice; many being so fond of it, that they do nothing the whole day but *Hacer las once.*[128]

The Dutch reputation for excessive drinking was legendary and "The pipe and the bottle were the inseparable companions of the Dutch overseas as they were in the United Provinces."[129] In 1631, Colt described Jan Claezen Van Campen, the Dutch governor of St. Martin, as being the "only temperate Hollander" he had ever come across in the Caribbean.[130]

Soldiers in the Caribbean had a reputation for intemperance, and liberal attitudes toward drinking were granted to troops stationed in the numerous forts that dotted the landscape. Rum was considered a necessary ration, especially in the British army and navy. The growth of the British navy in the seventeenth century, due in large measure to the settlement of New World colonies, led to the structured implementation of rum rations. Rum benefited from maritime customs, beliefs about its salubrious qualities, and parliamentary incentives aimed at promoting the growth of the Caribbean colonies.

Drinking among the soldiers and sailors stationed in the Caribbean was legendary. Prior to its attack on the Spanish Caribbean colony of Hispaniola in 1654, the Penn and Venables expedition loaded up with rum in Barbados. However, troops and commanders from Barbados and St. Kitts drank so much that Venables blamed intemperance for their defeat at Hispaniola.[131] By the end of the eighteenth century, many British troops were receiving as much as a pint of rum each day.[132] Rum was so central to military life in the Caribbean that commanders often feared rebellion and mutiny if they failed to provide troops with their daily rations.[133] Archaeological investigations conducted at St. Anne's military garrison in Barbados have unearthed green glass wine

Figure 5.3. *A Surinam Planter in His Morning Dress.* In John Gabriel Stedman, *Expedition to Surinam* (London, 1796). Courtesy of the John Carter Brown Library at Brown University.

bottle shards, which attest to the widespread use of alcohol among British troops stationed there in the eighteenth century.[134]

Intemperance among soldiers stationed in the Caribbean became such an extreme social problem that troop commanders often placed restrictions on rum drinking and tried to substitute beer and wine because of their lower alcohol content.[135] In 1740, Captain Edward Vernon, who came to fame during the War of Jenkins' Ear, was so concerned about the excessive use of rum among his sailors in Jamaica that he ordered rum rations mixed equally with water. This drink, known as *grog*, was named after Vernon who was nicknamed "old grogram" for the waterproof boat cloak he wore. Although drinking was excessive in the military, an abstemious exception was found among those military men, usually British, who came to the Caribbean with their wives and children.[136]

Alcohol use was a central feature of maritime communities, and excessive drinking among Caribbean mariners and seamen was legendary. If new mariners and seamen were not already familiar with rum in Europe, they were quickly introduced to it on their voyage to the Caribbean. Upon crossing into the tropics, those who had not done so before were required to go through the long-standing tradition of "christening" or "baptism" to honor Neptune, the great god of the sea. The ceremony involved the consumption and offering of copious amounts of alcohol, usually rum, as well as a ritualistic shaving.[137] The first crew member or passenger to spot land also received a bottle of rum.[138] Public houses, especially in port towns, provided a venue for the seamen's drinking bouts. Jews in Surinam noted that their quiet community was often shattered by the noise of drunken seamen in neighborhood rum shops.[139] Colonial legislatures were sometimes forced to place restrictions on the activities of mariners and seamen at inns and taverns. For example, in 1715 the governor of Curaçao banned the sale of liquor to sailors in Willemstad after 9:00 p.m. The punishment for breaking this law included the loss of three months' pay and eight days in jail.[140] In Barbados, the seamen's excessive drinking and brawling led to such civil unrest that in 1652 the Barbados Assembly passed an act prohibiting seamen from drinking in taverns after 8:00 p.m.[141] The laws were ineffective, and only two years later, hundreds of drunken seamen in Bridgetown rioted soon after arriving on the island.[142] A century later, Hall estimated that transient seamen in Barbados consumed about 54,000 gallons of rum per year.[143]

Excessive drinking was typical of Caribbean port towns, which in the late seventeenth century were havens for pirates, buccaneers, and privateers—men who typically came from maritime backgrounds. Many were former merchant seamen and ex-servicemen in a national navy.[144] Before being razed by the earthquake of 1692, Port Royal, Jamaica, was a center of pirate activity. According to Long, "The town was inhabited by scarcely any other than merchants, warehouse-keepers, vintners, and retailers of punch; the latter were very numerous, and well supported by the buccaneers, who dissipated here whatever they got from the Spaniards."[145] Kill-Devil Hills, North Carolina, stands as a monument to infamous pirates like Blackbeard and Stede Bonnet, who sailed the inlets and sounds of the Outer Banks drinking kill-devil rum and attacking ships.

Pirate Robert Johnson drank so much that he often had to be hoisted into his ship with the aid of a block and tackle, and Blackbeard was said to have consumed a half gallon of rum per day.[146] Among the most famous Caribbean pirates was Captain Henry Morgan, who in the mid-seventeenth century challenged Spanish control of the Caribbean and helped consolidate British colonization. Morgan's reputation for excessive drinking was legendary, and it eventually led to his demise. The physician who treated Morgan during his last months of life described him as "Lean, sallow coloured, his Eyes a little yellowish, and Belly a little jetting out or prominent," symptoms typically associated with jaundice and liver cirrhosis.[147]

As early as the seventeenth century, pirate life was a romanticized part of Caribbean lore. Labat, for example, held a picnic, or buccaneer barbecue, in which the participants were required to follow buccaneer traditions and drink copious amounts of alcohol.[148] In the nineteenth century, popular culture continued to embellish the links between pirates and rum. This connection was most notably immortalized in Robert Louis Stevenson's *Treasure Island*.[149] The labels pasted on modern Caribbean rum bottles, including *Captain Morgan*, *Old Brigand*, and *Buccaneer,* highlight the continuing romanticism.

Beginning with the pioneering work of Donald Horton, anthropologists have stressed the links between anxiety and excessive drinking.[150] In the Caribbean, anxieties existed at the most basic levels of life. Epidemic diseases, natural disasters, inadequate food supplies, and unhealthy drinking water all contributed to uncertainty in the New World. In Barbados in the 1640s, Ligon wrote, "At the time of our arrival, and a month or two after, the sickness raign'd so extreamely, as the living could hardly bury the dead."[151] This epidemic is thought to have been the first epidemic in the Americas of yellow fever, a devastating disease for Europeans.[152]

Yellow fever begins with lassitude, a sudden headache, and burning fever. It can vary greatly in severity, but in "classic" cases the eyes become inflamed, nausea is experienced and pain in the muscles and back. The pulse is initially high but falls as compulsive vomiting sets in. Jaundice and delirium may appear, but its most characteristic symptoms are a falling pulse accompanied by continued high temperature, the vomiting of partly-digested blood, and, in the later stages, generalized haemorrhage.[153]

Symptoms of yellow fever were frequently registered in plantation slave lists as fevers and usually ranked among the most common causes of death for plantation slaves in the Caribbean.[154] However, whites were especially vulnerable to yellow fever.[155] Thousands of white colonists died during the Barbados yellow fever outbreak mentioned by Ligon. Yellow fever was a permanent part of Caribbean life until 1900. Famine and drought often compounded epidemic disasters. Earthquakes destroyed towns throughout the Caribbean, including Jamestown, Nevis, in 1680, Port Royal, Jamaica, in 1692, and Port-au-Prince, St. Domingue, in 1770. Between 1492 and 1800, 174 hurricanes were reported in the Caribbean, the worst being the hurricane of October 1780, which killed over 22,000 people, mostly in Barbados and Martinique.

The stress caused by poor working and living conditions, as well as the anomie felt by alienated workers, also spurred excessive drinking in the Caribbean. In particular, white indentured servants found a dehumanizing labor system. Contracted to work for three to seven years, they could be bought and resold for the duration of their contracts and their labor extracted through coercive means. Whereas farm workers in Europe could be assimilated into a family, in the Caribbean their labor was strictly a commodity. Servants had to contend with harsh work under the tropical sun and, often, the unpredictability of severe punishment from a cruel master. The goal of many servants was land-ownership and the opportunity to become planters, if they were able to survive their indenture. But large planters quickly swallowed up good lands making such dreams unattainable.[156] Such challenges and frustrations created an anxious climate in which alcohol provided a means of escape. William Gardner, a Congregationalist minister in Jamaica, summed up the uneasy lives of poor whites in the Caribbean.

> The old system of bond-servants was at an end, but large supplies of young men could be found as book-keepers. If coarse and uneducated, their mental suffering on reaching the colony would not be great, but to a young man accustomed to a cheerful, quiet home, the shock must have been very painful. He found he had no books to keep, but that his duty consisted in following the gangs of slaves to the field in all weathers, and superintending their labours there or in the boiling and still-house: he was thus exposed to the influence of heavy dews, sudden showers, and burning heat. No wonder that large numbers soon fell victim to the climate, or that, shut out from civilizing influences and virtuous female society, many lived a life of riotous debauchery night after night, and also on the Sabbath day. New rum and yellow fever hurried hundreds yearly to an untimely grave.[157]

The excessive drinking of planters in the Caribbean may also be related to their specific anxieties. Generally speaking, the planter's goal was to eventually return to Europe in luxury; but heavy debts and low returns from their plantations meant that, for many, return was unlikely. Planters also experienced contempt and resentment from their white servants and the masses of African slaves. The unpredictability of slave and servant uprisings and the risk of being poisoned forced many planters to seek drunken escape in the company of their peers.

African and Creole slaves also used alcohol to confront a hostile social climate, though many had other, less destructive, outlets for the release of frustrations. Anthropologist James Schaefer has argued that moderate drinking is common in highly structured societies characterized by paternalism and deference to hierarchical authority.[158] Paternalistic theories could certainly help explain the only moderate drinking that some colonists attributed to slaves. The slave community itself also provided a stable social setting that may have mitigated many anxieties. As with Caribbean Jews, African slaves came from societies with a healthy spiritual respect for alcohol. Except during holiday celebrations, the convivial aspects of drinking may have remained secondary to the ritualistic and community-strengthening uses of alcohol. The temperance Long and Moreau de St.-Méry ascribed to Creole slaves suggests that they may have developed an especially good coping strategy due to their greater familiarity with the disease environment and their ability to achieve upward social mobility. Moreover, Creoles were likely to perform less arduous types of work on the plantation. In addition, Creoles were born into preexisting kinship networks that probably served to lessen the effects of some of their anxieties. These factors made life more predictable and created a greater sense of stability, which would have reduced the need for alcoholic escape.

The temperance Long attributed to Creoles makes it difficult to explain the excessive drinking he ascribed to freedmen. Freedmen would have been as likely as Creole slaves to have developed strong family ties and kinship networks. Freedmen, however, occupied a liminal, socially unstable position, precariously situated between the worlds of free whites and enslaved blacks. Moreover, freedom did not necessarily result in better material conditions or economic independence. The dominant white power structures of the colonial Caribbean rarely offered such opportunities. Thus, as with white servants, disillusion and frustration may have contributed to intemperance among some freedmen. In addition, they were makers of their own time and had the freedom to get drunk.

Rum and Health

Rum and other alcoholic beverages had a major impact on the health of Caribbean peoples. Excessive drinking often compounded existing health problems and added to the anxieties already rampant in this unpredictable environment. Analysis of hard drinking also highlights contradictory beliefs about the meaning of alcohol. Some Caribbean writers saw rum as an elixir of life, while others warned about excessive rum drinking and saw intemperance as the cause of much illness. The Africans and Europeans who settled the Caribbean brought with them Old World notions about the benefits and perils of excessive alcohol use. Beliefs about the dual nature of alcohol were transferred to the Caribbean and, despite cultural traditions that warned about excessive drinking, intemperance was common.

European and African notions about the need to maintain inner body heat increased the demand for a "hot" spirit like rum. In Barbados, reasoned Ligon, "certainly strong drinks are very requisite, where so much heat is; for the spirits being exhausted with much sweating, the inner parts are left cold and faint, and shall need comforting, and reviving."[159] Rum also had external heat-restoring applications. In Jamaica, Long wrote,

> A traveler, caught in the rain . . . by the quick evaporation of his natural warmth, perceives his body chilled and aguish. It is usual here to strip, and rub all over with rum, and then put on dry cloaths; which prevents any ill consequence.[160]

After suffering a stroke, Henri Christophe, the black leader of Haiti, took a bath of hot peppers, rum, pepper, and tobacco. The combination of these ingredients was believed to generate heat that would "ease his pain" and "restore his vigor."[161]

Beliefs about the heat restoring qualities of rum led many planters to distribute it to servants and slaves during damp spells and bad weather. Du Tertre wrote, "slaves should be given some rum, especially when they do harsh work, like replanting tobacco in strong rain."[162] Labat similarly advised giving slaves rum when they were forced to "suffer in the rain."[163] Barbadian sugar planter Henry Drax wrote, "In wet Weather give Rum to each Negro every Morning; and at other Times as you shall see convenient, according to their early Rising, or the Work they are about."[164] Collins prescribed rum to slaves "during the wet weather, and while the negroes are engaged on very laborious work, such as holing."[165] In 1788, Governor Parry of Barbados told parliament that every plantation set aside a proportion of rum "for the occasional Use of the Slaves in damp Weather, and the more difficult Works."[166] In 1791, Atwood wrote that rum and water were given to slaves in Dominica "especially after [their] having been in the rain."[167] Roughley, describing the value of good management thirty years later, wrote, "In bad weather, a glass of good rum should be given to each [field slave]; and when making lime-kilns, roads, and digging cane-holes, a small proportion of rum and sugar likewise to each."[168] Jamaican plantation manager Thomas Thistlewood gave a pint of rum to his slaves during damp and wet weather, though children were exempt.[169]

Rum was considered something of a cure-all in plantation medicine. It was a central ingredient in the treatment of toothaches, fevers, obstructions [amenorrhea], dropsy, gonorrhea, postpartum fatigue, colic, bellyaches, and other disorders.[170] Some physicians used a "tormenting mixture" of rum and sea salt as an antiseptic to clean wounds and sores.[171] In 1771, managers at Turner's Hall estate, Barbados, set aside 645 gallons of rum specifically to "treat sick slaves."[172]

In Jamaica, Long was a champion of Robert Dossie's comparative research on the salubriousness of rum and even incorporated parts of Dossie's essay into his history of Jamaica. Long advocated moderate rum drinking and believed, because of Dossie's research, that well-made, aged rum "when used with due moderation, and not too frequently [was an] antiseptic, or antiputrescent."[173] This widely accepted view that rum had healthy qualities led officials to encourage rum contracts with the British army and navy. The preservative uses of rum even extended beyond death. For example, Moïse Gradis, a Martinican planter who wanted to be buried in France, had his body shipped home to Bordeaux in a barrel of rum after his death in 1826.[174] When Sir Ralph Woodford, governor of Trinidad, died on a voyage from Jamaica to England in 1828, the ship's captain placed Woodford's body in a cask of spirits for shipment back to Trinidad. However, "the extreme heat of the climate" caused an effluvium to rise from the cask, which made the crew members ill. The cask was subsequently deposited in the sea.[175] Legend has it that, after he was killed at Trafalgar, Admiral Horatio Nelson's body was shipped back to England in a cask of rum. In a ceremony reminiscent of the Eucharist, the sailors are said to have drunk from the cask to show respect for their fallen leader. Although brandy has also been credited as the preservative used, belief in the rum legend remained so strong that, even today, rum is often called "Nelson's blood."[176]

Many also held the opposite opinion about rum's salubrious qualities. In 1694, the governor of New Andalusia [Venezuela] argued that rum was harmful to the people.[177] In the eighteenth century, French wine and brandy interests used similar arguments to spur French officials to impose a ban on French imports of tafia. In the 1730s, the same concerns inspired James Oglethorpe, governor of the Georgia colony, to propose a ban on rum imports.[178] Colonial officials in North America noted the particularly negative impact of rum on the health of Native Americans and attempted to ban the use of rum in the North American fur trade.[179] Even Long, a strong advocate of Jamaican rum, warned that those who indulged too heavily must "be deemed guilty of self-murder."[180]

In the late eighteenth century, physicians also began to actively campaign against excessive alcohol use. In 1786, Philadelphia physician Benjamin Rush published *An Inquiry into the Effects of Ardent Spirits upon the Human Body and Mind*, which stressed the deleterious health consequences associated with the immoderate use of alcohol, especially distilled spirits.[181] The treatise was a crucial step for early temperance reformers in North America and Europe.[182] Rush challenged the conventional wisdom about alcohol, especially notions about its prophylactic qualities against excessive heat, extreme cold, and hard labor. Rush was especially critical of Caribbean rum, which is not unusual considering that it was the most available ardent spirit in eighteenth century North America. However, Rush's attack on rum may have also been fueled by his personal abolitionist sentiments.

Forty years earlier, rum had already come under tough medical scrutiny. In the 1740s, another Philadelphia physician, Dr. Thomas Cadwalader, identified rum as the source for the common and debilitating ailment known as the West Indian dry gripes.[183] Interestingly, Ligon had noted the connection between rum drinking and the West Indian dry gripes a century earlier, only shortly after the Barbadians began producing rum.

> We are seldom dry or thirsty, unless we overheat our bodies with extraordinary labour, or drinking strong drinks; as of our *English* spirits, which we carry over, of *French* Brandy, or the drink of the Island, which is made of the skimmings of the Coppers, that boyl the Sugar, which they call kill-Devil. And though some of these be needful if they be used with temper; yet the immoderate use of them, over-heats the body, which causes Costiveness, and Tortions in the bowels; which is a disease very frequent there; and hardly cur'd, and of which many have dyed.[184]

Cadwalader blamed excessive heat and the consumption of acidic spirits, and advised patients with this disorder to stay away from strong punch and rum, especially newly distilled rum that contained greater amounts of "hot fiery particles." What Cadwalader probably did not know, of course, was that those "hot fiery particles" were lead.

In the seventeenth and eighteenth centuries, rum and the ingredients used to make it came into contact with lead at just about every step of the production process.[185] This was true of nearly every distillery in the Caribbean. In the 1780s, Peter Marsden, a visitor to Jamaica wrote that so much lead was used about still houses "that the plumber and his gang of negroes have employment enough."[186] Much of the rum produced in the eighteenth century Caribbean did, in fact, contain lead. British army doctor John Hunter, while exploring the possible causes of colic among British troops stationed in the region, conducted chemical tests on freshly distilled Jamaican rum and found it to contain lead.[187] In a provocative study integrating historical, archaeological, and physical anthropological evidence, Jerome S. Handler and others discovered high lead levels in slave skeletal remains from Newton plantation, Barbados.[188] They attributed the high lead levels to the slaves' consumption of lead-contaminated rum.

Many early writers thought that the West India dry gripes and other terrible diseases were particularly common among those who consumed what colonial writers called *new rum*. Marsden observed, "Nothing is more destructive, particularly to our soldiers and seamen, than new rum."[189] In Barbados, Hughes wrote that slaves, servants, and distillers of rum suffered from several diseases "from immoderately drinking new hot rum." According to Hughes, the disease raged among those "much addicted to debauch in Spirits, and Punch made exceedingly strong with new Rum."[190] Those who drank new rum evidently lost the use of their limbs, a common symptom of lead toxicity.[191]

The term "new rum" is somewhat misleading, however. In order to avoid poor health consequences, many colonists recommended the use of aged rum. Long argued that no rum "should be issued [to troops] of less than a twelvemonth's age."[192] Aging was a corrective in wine and, therefore, it made sense to colonial rum makers that aging would correct the caustic qualities of rum. Hunter conducted follow-up tests on his rum samples and found that, after three or four months, lead levels in at least one sample had declined. Hunter believed that the "deposition of the lead from the spirits by keeping [aging] is most probably owing to the spirit attracting and uniting with the acid that dissolves the lead, and thereby precipitating the metal."[193] In fact, unless lead had somehow dissipated from the rum over time, aged rum made in lead-contaminated stills would have been equally as toxic as freshly made rum. However, since the solubility of precipitates is greater in water than in alcohol, the lead in rum containers would largely be insoluble. Many early writers assumed that the toxicity of new rum reflected its lack of age. In reality, being a heavy substance in its insoluble state, lead would have settled to the cask bottom over time, and its concentration when the rum was consumed would have been diminished.[194] Hunter may have even recognized this when he wrote, "In whatever manner the spirit becomes contaminated with lead, it is a fortunate circumstance, that by keeping it entirely deposits that material."

Lead toxicity was probably also the consequence of a particular distilling process. New rum appears to have been a type of moonshine produced on poorer estates or in small-scale distilling operations, usually in urban areas. Distillers of new rum either could not afford or did not care to heed the warnings of physicians such as Hunter and remove, or at least reduce, the amount of lead used in their distilling equipment, especially the critical worms and still heads. Poorer distillers, trying to cut fuel costs by distilling at low temperatures, probably also made less concentrated rum, which would have increased levels of soluble lead. Moreover, the addition of "signature" ingredients may have magnified the toxic qualities of new rum.

European soldiers and sailors experienced higher death rates than slaves in the Caribbean, and excessive drinking often contributed to their demise. Long wrote, "The greater mortality, observable here among the soldiers and transient Europeans, must be ascribed to their importing with them the English customs of eating and drinking in excess, but chiefly the latter."[195] The notoriously high death rate suffered by British troops during the Caribbean campaigns of the 1790s has usually been attributed to yellow fever epidemics. According to historian David Geggus, the mortality of British troops was highest among new arrivals who had no previous exposure to yellow fever and were, therefore, more vulnerable to the disease.[196] Death tolls among British troops increased in the wet season when mosquitoes, the vector for yellow fever, were most active. Death tolls were also highest in low-lying port towns crowded with new recruits. Geggus' research suggests that yellow fever, or a combination of maladies, was responsible for the great majority of deaths among British soldiers.

Alternately, historian Roger Buckley argues, "more British soldiers succumbed to diseases caused by chronic alcohol and lead poisoning than to malignant fevers."[197] While eighteenth-century doctors often blamed the intemperance of British troops for their high death rates, Buckley contends that the main cause was excessive consumption of lead-contaminated new rum. He explains that lead toxicity could have been responsible for the onset of diseases such as encephalitis, liver cirrhosis and necrosis, nephritis, anemia, and gout. In addition, yellow fever symptoms often mirrored those associated with alcohol poisoning, leading Buckley to conclude that "many of the deaths ascribed to yellow fever were in fact caused by a disorder resulting from rum intoxication."

While Geggus embraces eighteenth-century reports about the negative effects of alcohol on British troops, he disagrees with Buckley's emphasis on lead poisoning. Instead, Geggus argues that intemperance contributed to renal and hepatic failure, which compounded the already devastating effects of tropical diseases, especially yellow fever. Alcohol and lead poisoning damage the liver and kidneys, the organs most weakened by yellow fever. As did most Europeans in the eighteenth century, British soldiers and seamen stationed in the Caribbean believed that alcohol had salubrious qualities, and many felt that concentrated alcoholic beverages helped prevent the onset of disease. According to Geggus, "in the Windward Isles we find troops treating alcohol as a prophylactic, afraid that 'a sober hour might give the Disease an Opportunity to attack.'" Thus, "Heavy drinking can be seen as both a cause and effect of the high rate of mortality."[198]

In 1998, Buckley modified his earlier emphasis on alcohol and lead poisoning and focused, like Geggus, on the interplay between the British troops' excessive alcohol use and the effects of tropical diseases.[199] He nonetheless maintains that there was a significant link between high mortality and excessive rum consumption and that lead poisoning and liver cirrhosis greatly increased troop mortality. There is no clear evidence, however, that the consumption of lead-contaminated rum had such an immediate and devastating effect. Lead poisoning occurs over many years. The Handler team's analysis of slave skeletal remains from Newton plantation, Barbados, revealed that lead toxicity was most concentrated in adult slaves over the age of thirty who had accumulated lead in their bodies over years of constant exposure.[200] In fact, the analysis showed that even *after* years of exposure, only 6 percent of the sample had lead levels severe enough to be considered potentially deadly. Modern studies conducted by the United States Department of Health and Human Services also show lead poisoning as a degenerative disorder that results from long-term exposure.[201] Similarly, liver cirrhosis is a degenerative disease acquired from years of regular alcohol abuse. Only those troops stationed in the Caribbean who habitually imbibed rum over many years—especially lead-contaminated new rum—would have succumbed to such illnesses.

To support his position, Buckley cites cases of "hundreds of soldiers . . .

killed soon after binging on lethal moonshine rum."[202] In 1789, 26 soldiers from the 45th regiment stationed in Grenada died soon after an alcoholic binge, and in 1808, 200 members of the Royal Marine garrison stationed at Marie-Galante were hospitalized after binging on new rum. Mass alcohol poisoning cases are common even today, however. In Nairobi, Kenya, in November 2000, more than 137 people died after consuming illegally produced moonshine spirits, and scores more were sent to hospitals.[203] In such cases, toxins and contaminants in the brew or improper distilling methods are what actually poison consumers. Distilling at too low a temperature produces deadly methanol rather than ethanol. Such practice would probably be most common among marginal distillers seeking to economize on fuel. Additionally, illicit and small-scale distillers often establish their own "signature" by adding unique ingredients to a wash to give it a distinctive kick. Anthropologist Dwight Heath found that illicit distillers in Costa Rica add jungle vines, tree bark, and mushrooms to their brews with devastating effects on consumers.[204]

Such appears to have been the case in eighteenth-century Jamaica where, according to Long, British troops occasionally died from "their liberal indulgence in a vile sophisticated compound of *new rum*, pepper, and other ingredients, brewed here by Jew-retailers."[205] In 1750, Hughes also noted that some people added red peppers to their rum to "augment its Heat."[206] Based on best evidence, then, the most plausible explanation for the 1789 deaths of the 26 soldiers in Grenada is less their ingestion of lead-contaminated rum than of improperly distilled moonshine rum that may have also contained a toxic combination of "signature" ingredients.

British Caribbean planters had an economic interest in selling rum to the military and, therefore, avoided blaming their rum for high mortality among British troops. Instead, they argued that "excessive" drinking was the problem. Long argued that the general health of the troops could be greatly enhanced "by restraining them from the immoderate use of spirituous liquors."[207] He was also particularly critical of the poorer types of moonshine rum. According to Long, new rum consumed by soldiers and sailors stationed in the Caribbean was "so fiery, as to be no less unfit for human potation, than burning brimstone."[208] Newcomers were particularly vulnerable. Long warned,

> if 500 seamen or soldiers pass from England to the West Indies, setting out in very cold weather, and arriving there after a quick voyage, many of them will be seized with a diarrhoea, and with violent and mortal fevers, if they indulge, soon after their arrival, in *rum newly distilled*.[209]

Long accused Jews in Jamaica of producing and retailing new rum and advocated the sale of only high quality rum to troops:

> The common soldiers, employed in the West-India service, or at least the recruits sent over, have frequently been the very refuse of the British army: these men cannot be broke of their sottish habits; but since they must and will have spirituous liquor, care might be taken to provide them with such as, while it gratifies their inclination, may be the least detrimental to their health.[210]

Hunter made similar arguments.[211] The Jamaican legislature provided tax incentives to troops "that they might be enabled to buy [rum] of the best quality, instead of debauching with the balderdash liquor, sold under the name of rum by the keepers of retail shops."[212] Behind this caring sentiment, however, may have been the desire to push Jewish retailers out of the rum market and to encourage the sale of more expensive aged rum to British commissary agents.

Accepting Hunter's and Long's claims along with other evidence, Buckley's British soldiers were probably as much victims of their ignorance of rum's potency as of its inferiority or additives. From time to time, individuals, intentionally or not, simply drink themselves to death. Alcohol is a nervous system depressant that inhibits the respiratory center in the brain stem. Too much alcohol forces the body's respiratory system to shut down. Modern medical examiners report that hundreds of Americans die every year of acute ethanol poisoning, and the problem seems pandemic among university students unfamiliar with the dangers of an alcoholic binge.[213] What is most interesting about Buckley's case of 26 ill-fated British soldiers is that their binge and deaths occurred in Grenada. Grenada, like Jamaica, regularly produced highly concentrated rum. Rum from Grenada often contained 10 to 15 percent more alcohol than rum from the other British colonies. Some British troops, unfamiliar with the highly concentrated nature of rum from Grenada, may have simply overdosed. Fear about the excessive drinking of concentrated rum was apparently the basis for Admiral Vernon's practice of giving his troops watered-down grog.

One of the central debates informing discussions of Caribbean slavery is how to explain the high mortality and apparently low fertility of slaves. The negative health consequences of rum drinking deserve more emphasis in this vital debate. Rum, especially that contaminated with lead, contributed to a variety of diseases, accidents, and disorders that must have lowered slave fertility and hastened the demise of many slaves in the Caribbean.

Colonial writers recognized the connection between rum and slave health. At the parliamentary inquiries into the African slave trade in 1788, Governor Parry of Barbados stated that the many health problems he observed among Barbadian slaves were attributable to "the too free Use of Rum."[214] Modern scholars have also noted possible links between rum and the health of Caribbean slave populations. Historian Frank Wesley Pitman identified alcoholism as a major cause of slave health problems.[215] Kenneth Kiple argued that "excessive alcohol consumption over time may have damaged black livers and pancreata, just as it did among the Island whites."[216] Michael Craton also noted that liver, heart, and urinary conditions were often "exacerbated by excessive drinking."[217]

In an extensive study of slave registration records from the last decades before emancipation, historian Barry Higman has explored the numerous factors that influenced the natural increase of Caribbean slave populations, emphasizing high mortality. According to Higman, the arduous work and extreme hours of sugar plantation agriculture were a primary cause of high mortality among British Caribbean slaves.

> The crucial factor associated with sugar production was the importance of the manufacturing processes. . . . The demands of the manufacturing processes permitted the maximization of hours of work and physical exertion, while the standardization of cultivation permitted the development of gang labor and the driving system in the field.[218]

Other crops, such as coffee, indigo, and cotton, were physically less demanding, allowing slaves in nonsugar sectors to escape the arduous sugar-production regimen, especially its manufacturing toils.

The strong connection Higman has made between population growth and sugar-production work regimens is especially interesting because slaves in sugar-producing colonies also had greater access to rum. A comparison of British Caribbean rum exports figures and the natural increase of British Caribbean slave populations shows a possible link between rum consumption and mortality (Table 5.1). Presumably, colonies exporting the greatest quantities of rum also had the greatest quantities available for local consumption. Between the mid-1810s and 1830s, Tobago, Jamaica, Demerara, and Grenada exported the largest amount of rum and the most gallons of rum per cwt. of sugar. In 1820, these colonies produced 90 percent of all British Caribbean rum exported to Britain, more than 6 million gallons. They also had the lowest rates of slave population growth. As the table shows, four-fifths of colonies exporting more than one gallon of rum per cwt. of sugar had negative growth rates, and no colony exporting more than two gallons of rum per cwt. of sugar had a positive increase. In contrast, Barbados and Tortola were minor players in the rum market. In 1820, Barbados and Tortola exported a mere 2,611 gallons to Britain. They also had the highest rates of population increase. Most striking is the contrast between Barbados—which exported the least amount of rum per cwt. of sugar and had the highest rate of natural increase—and Tobago, which exported the highest amount of rum per cwt. of sugar and had the highest rate of decrease. Although Barbados still produced significant amounts of rum for local consumption, there was probably far less available than there had been in the eighteenth century. Records from Codrington and Turner's Hall estates, for example, show that in the 1820s, distillers at these plantations, among the two largest on the island, produced only a few thousand gallons of rum each year.[219]

Trinidad, St. Lucia, and St. Vincent show a trend toward high mortality and low rum exports, but, as Higman pointed out, these newer colonies, as well

Table 5.1. Ratio of Rum Exports to Britain to Slave Population Growth

Colony	Rum : sugar export ratio	Natural increase	Gallons of British rum imports	Gallons of rum exported per slave
Barbados 1817–1832	.02	+7.8	58,107	.144
Tortola 1818–1831	.08	+3.0	25,453	1.038
St. Lucia 1815–1831	.11	-4.8	167,803	2.438
Trinidad 1816–1831	.13	-8.8	466,248	3.805
Antigua 1817–1832	.34	-1.7	1,309,124	10.892
Dominica 1817–1832	.43	-1.9	405,733	5.283
Nevis 1817–1831	.54	-1.7	471,034	12.699
St. Vincent 1817–1831	.58	-6.5	2,821,512	29.216
St. Kitts 1817–1831	.96	-0.4	1,925,345	24.487
Montserrat 1817–1831	1.03	+3.5	511,359	21.248
Berbice 1817–1831	1.14	-6.4	1,499,597	14.050
Grenada 1817–1833	1.53	-6.1	5,495,867	12.652
Jamaica 1817–1832	2.18	-2.8	64,515,509	38.803
Demerara 1817–1832	2.20	-11.1	24,996,504	69.284
Tobago 1819–1833	3.45	-17.1	5,577,418	27.940

Sources: Higman, *Slave Populations*, 308–10; Ragatz, *Statistics*, 18.

as Demerara, Tobago, Grenada, Berbice, and Jamaica, had other obstacles to population increase, especially a large African-born slave population and a high male sex ratio.[220] Higman demonstrated that Creole slaves had lower age-specific death rates and, thus, colonies with large African-born slave populations had negative growth rates. By the same token, older colonies, such as Antigua, Nevis, and St. Kitts, which had more Creole slaves, still did not achieve positive population growth. These colonies also exported huge amounts of rum.

Alcohol use can increase mortality rates, and excessive drinking is known to compound existing health problems. Long-term exposure to alcohol triggers a variety of serious health conditions, including liver cirrhosis, heart disease, kidney disease, certain forms of cancer, and a depressed immune system.[221] It is possible to attribute many of the symptoms and causes of death detailed in plantation slave inventories to drinking. The link between the West India dry gripes and rum, for example, may reflect more than simple lead contamination. Alcoholic hepatitis appears to be a precursory condition to liver cirrhosis and includes symptoms very similar to the West India dry gripes, including fever, jaundice, and severe abdominal pain. While lead may have been a factor in the West India dry gripes, years of excessive drinking alone may also explain the symptoms.

Excessive drinking also increases the risk of accidental death. Runaway slave advertisements and plantation inventories mention numerous injuries that may have occurred as a result of drunkenness. In Dominica between 1829 and 1832, 7.5 percent of all slave deaths resulted from accidents, which were the fifth leading cause of death.[222] Between 1795 and 1838, accidents accounted for 4.3 percent of slave deaths at Worthy Park estate in Jamaica.[223] Other major causes of death included violence and suicide, often the indirect results of drunkenness.[224] Excessive drinking, which can spur risky sexual behavior, may have increased the transmission of venereal diseases and thereby shortened the lives of many in the Caribbean.[225]

Where slave women participated in the heavy drinking culture of the Caribbean, fetal alcohol syndrome may have elevated infant mortality rates. Higman found that in the early nineteenth century, less than half of slaves born in St. Lucia, Tobago, and Trinidad survived the first year.[226] Infant survival rates were not much better in the older sugar islands. In Barbados, there were about 420 infant deaths per 1,000 births. Most of these occurred during the first month of life. Fetal alcohol syndrome can lead to stillbirth, physical and mental retardation, and low birth weight that limits a child's chances of survival past

Table 5.2. Ratio of Rum Exports to Britain to Slave Fertility

Colony/year	Slave child to woman ratios	Gallons of rum exported per cwt. of sugar
Barbados/1817	0.597	0.010
St. Kitts/1817	0.469	0.687
Nevis/1817	0.468	0.116
Demerara/1820	0.431	2.850
St. Vincent/1817	0.402	0.688
Jamaica/1817	0.399	2.165
Tobago/1819	0.375	3.338
Grenada/1817	0.352	2.805

Sources: Higman, *Slave Populations,* 308–10, 356; Ragatz, *Statistics,* 18.

one year.[227] In addition, lead toxicity may have contributed to high infant mortality. Developing fetuses and infants are extremely vulnerable to lead poisoning, and colic and anemia are major symptoms of lead poisoning in children.[228] While the large percentage of African-born slaves, who were often weakened by the Middle Passage and lacked immunity to Caribbean diseases, is probably the best explanation for high slave mortality rates in the newer colonies, the evidence in Table 5.1 intimates a strong possibility that rum was also a factor.

Slave fertility also shaped population growth. Overwork, poor nutrition, disease, and the inability to find a partner all influenced fertility rates. A comparison of rum exports to Britain and the rate of natural increase among Caribbean slaves suggests another possible link (Table 5.2). Of the sugar-producing colonies in the late 1810s, Barbados had the highest slave child-to-woman ratio and the lowest level of rum exports. In contrast, the five largest rum exporters—Grenada, Tobago, Jamaica, Demerara, and St. Vincent—had the lowest child-to-woman ratios.[229] Once again, Trinidad, with its low fertility and low level of rum exports, did not fit the pattern. Higman showed that Creole slaves had higher age-specific fertility rates than African-born slaves, which is the most likely explanation for higher fertility rates in the older Caribbean colonies. However, the interplay between alcohol use and the hard work regimen of sugar plantations probably also had a major influence on slave fertility.

Colonial writers recognized the connection between alcohol use and low fertility. In 1788, Charles Spooner, a sugar planter from the British Leeward Islands, wrote,

The causes which impede the Natural Increase of Negroes are, the larger proportion of Males to Females on most Estates, the premature and promiscuous Commerce of the Sexes, the indiscriminate Prostitution of the Women in the younger part of their Lives, their frequent total Barrenness brought on by Debauchery, repeated abortions and Venereal Diseases, the immoderate use of *New Rum*, which brings on Debility and old Age long before Nature would otherwise give way.[230]

Governor Parry of Barbados also believed that the "Use of Rum," presumably by enslaved women, "impeded" the natural increase of the slave population.[231] Indeed, excessive drinking would have increased the likelihood of malnutrition among slave women, especially when combined with overwork and a generally poor diet. Malnutrition often leads to delayed menarche and the onset of amenorrhea, both of which inhibit a woman's ability to conceive a child. In 1811, Collins referred to amenorrhea as the "obstruction" and believed it was very common among slave women.[232] Obstructions were a frequent complaint and noted as the cause of death among female slaves at Worthy Park.[233] In men, excessive drinking can result in low sperm count and loss of libido. Moreover, conditions such as amenorrhea, miscarriage, stillbirths, reduced birth weights, and female/male infertility could have been exacerbated by the slaves' consumption of lead-contaminated rum.

Rum and Vulnerability

While drinking in the Caribbean was variously viewed as a means of physical release, emotional escape, spiritual performance, even prophylaxis against tropical disease, it was also a source of anxiety. The unpredictability of life on the Caribbean frontier, the coerced labor system, and the unbalanced power structures produced an atmosphere of individual vulnerability that was only heightened by excessive drinking. The result was a rich body of folklore that expresses a theme of drunken vulnerability.

Caribbean folklore is loaded with images of victims of drunken excess. Drinking reduced personal vigilance and exposed the drinker to deceit, capture, and death. This vulnerable-while-drunk theme can be found in the narratives of all Caribbean social groups. For Europeans, the immediate enemy was the new disease environment. Ligon wrote that the people of Barbados drink much rum, "indeed too much; for it often layes them asleep on the ground, and that is accounted a very unwholsome lodging."[234] Some British colonists got so drunk that they passed out in the open for an entire night, "which expos'd them to the injuries of the Air." Yet, the cool nighttime air was not the only danger. In the 1630s, Thomas Verney, a colonist in Barbados, wrote that land crabs sometimes bit off the fingers and toes of those who had gotten drunk and fallen asleep on the ground along the roadsides. In some instances, according to Verney, the land crabs were so voracious they killed their inebriated victims.[235] The threat was very serious for new arrivals to the Caribbean, especially those unfamiliar with the concentrated and sometimes toxic qualities of rum.

> Rum Punch is not improperly called *Kill Devil*, for Thousands lose their Lives by its Means: When new Comers use it to the least Excess, they expose themselves to imminent Peril; for it heats the Blood, and brings on Fevers which in a very few Hours send them to their Grave.[236]

Slave satires highlight the alcoholic dangers encountered by European seamen stationed in the Caribbean.

> Sanagree kill de captain,
> O dear, he must die;
> New rum kill de sailor,
> O dear, he must die;
> Hard work kill de negar,
> O dear, he must die.[237]

Drunken vulnerability was not limited to the interplay between the drinker and the natural hazards of the outdoors. Some servants were reported to get so drunk that they would "fall off their Horses in going home" at night.[238] Physicians treated colonists for a variety of injuries received during drinking binges. During his travels in the British Caribbean, Sloane, for example, treated a "Gentleman . . . very much given to Venery, and intemperance in Drinking." According to Sloane, "He had always after a debauch some bruised places about him, which were hurt by Accidents and Falls."[239]

In the early years of British and French Caribbean settlement, indentured servants made up the bulk of the labor force and kidnapping was one of the means of acquiring servants for New World plantations. As early as 1645, the British parliament passed an act to prevent the "spiriting" away of English citizens to the American colonies. The term "spirited away" was commonly applied to those who were kidnapped while drunk and taken to the Caribbean as indentured servants. To be "Barbadosed" was a real threat in seventeenth- and eighteenth-century England, and fear centered around the danger of drinking too much and being stolen.[240]

Caribbean folk heroes often fell victim to alcohol. For example, Makandal, the famous slave fugitive and poisoner in St. Domingue, was captured while drunk at a slave assembly. According to Moreau de St.-Méry's account,

> One day the negroes of Dufresne plantation in Limbé had arranged for a big dance there. Makandal, who had gone unpunished for a long time, came to join the dance. One young negro, perhaps because of the impression that the presence of this monster (Makandal) had produced on him, came to notify M. Duplessis, a surveyor, and M. Trevan, who were on the plantation. They distributed tafia so profusely that the negroes all became drunk, and Makandal, in spite of his [usual] caution, lost his good sense.[241]

Makandal was arrested that night and later executed. Jamaican planter Matthew Gregory Lewis recorded a similar story of a runaway slave named Plato who would only come out of hiding to satisfy his thirst for rum. According to Lewis, one night Plato found some rum, got drunk, and "sunk upon the ground."[242] In that drunken state Plato was captured and later executed.

Fear of poisoning was widespread in the Caribbean, and rum was often the vehicle through which poisons were administered. According to Labat, a dying slave confessed,

> He had allowed one of his fingernails to grow long, and said that when he intended to kill a man, he would scratch the stem of a plant, which grows on the Carbesterre, till his nail became full of the sap. He would then go home and ask his victim to have a drink with him. Having poured some of the rum into a *coui* he would first drink some himself and then hand it to his victim, taking care, however, to soak his nail in the rum as he did so. This was sufficient to poison the drink and kill the victim in less than two hours time.[243]

The highly combustible nature of rum meant that it was implicated in a number of deadly accidents. In the earliest recorded death-by-rum, Ligon wrote of a slave who, bringing a jar of rum, "from the Still-house, to the Drink-room, in the night," lit a candle to better see the transfer of rum from the jar to the puncheon. The rum caught fire and burned the slave to death.[244] In 1785, a slave revolt in Dominica ended when the rebels "in drawing off some rum by the light of their torches" set fire to the estate's buildings and "burnt them down to the ground." Ironically, the funds used for raising a militia against the rebels came heavily from the island's tavern licenses and rum duties.[245] Careless sailors, unfamiliar with the highly flammable nature of Caribbean rum, occasionally set fire to their ships. In 1781, scores of sailors were killed or injured when crew members aboard the *Intrépide* anchored at Cape François, St. Domingue, accidentally set fire to their spirituous cargo.[246]

Fire was not the only danger associated with rum. The process of rum making was also fraught with danger. In the 1680s, Barbadian planter Edward Lyttleton wrote, "If a Stiller slip into a Rum-Cistern, it is sudden death; for it stifles in a moment."[247] In 1743, Abel Allyne, manager of the Codrington estate for the Society for the Propagation of the Gospel in Foreign Parts, ordered his slaves to clean the estate's rum cistern, which had become thick with sediment. According to reports, "The first Negro Slave who attempted to clean it, was no sooner at the Bottom, than dead; the second and third met with the same Fate instantly."[248] Jamaican sugar planter Bryan Edwards also warned about the perils of cleaning "a foul cistern."[249] Residues in the fermenting cisterns emitted carbon monoxide and other poisonous gases that, if not properly ventilated, became trapped at the bottom of cisterns and suffocated slaves and servants who carelessly entered fermenting vats.

Drunken vulnerability was also a common theme in Carib society. European soldiers in the Caribbean were known for plying the Caribs with alcohol before killing them. In 1605, for example, the stranded members of the crew of the *Olive Branch*, abandoned in St. Lucia, gave the Caribs Spanish brandy in order to get them drunk so that they could more easily kill them.[250] Perhaps the most famous case of drunken vulnerability is that of Indian Warner, a Carib leader of mixed English and Carib descent, who in 1674 was murdered, along with his family, during a drinking party in Dominica. The commander of the military expedition that led the attack was Indian Warner's English half brother, Philip Warner.[251]

Alcohol, Resistance, Violence, and Accountability

As a social stimulant at weekend events and as a medium of spiritual experience, alcohol helped slaves transcend the physical bonds of slavery. Bacchanalian celebrations characterized the slaves' escapist performances, and the Caribbean planter found these symbolic expressions preferable to actual marronage, revolt, or other forms of resistance. Many planters even encouraged these temporary releases of pressure and supplied alcohol to their slaves. Planters overlooked excessive drinking and drunkenness at these events and became concerned only when drunkenness posed a genuine threat to the existing social order or when it interfered with labor productivity, the source of the planters' power.

Anthropologists Craig MacAndrew and Robert Edgerton have developed a model for understanding drunken comportment that challenges simple biological explanations. Biological models advance the principle that drinking suppresses the part of the brain that normally inhibits deviant social behavior. MacAndrew and Edgerton identified numerous cross-cultural examples in which drunken comportment remained inhibited and within the limits of acceptable social boundaries.[252] For example, although members of a society may get drunk, they are still aware that incest, murder, and the mistreatment of particular kin are deviant behaviors that transgress social limits. In the cases MacAndrew and Edgerton addressed, the absence of deviant drunken behavior supported their fundamental argument that drunken comportment is socially, rather than biologically, determined.

The argument has implications for understanding drinking patterns in the Caribbean. According to MacAndrew and Edgerton, drunkenness removes individual accountability, albeit temporarily, and helps circumvent certain social controls:

> the state of drunkenness is a state of societally sanctioned freedom from the otherwise enforceable demands that persons comply with the conventional proprieties. For a while—but just for a while—the rules (or, more accurately, *some* of the rules) are set aside, and the drunkard finds himself, if not beyond good and evil, at least partially removed from the accountability nexus in which he normally operates. In a word, drunkenness in these societies takes on the flavor of "time-out" from many of the otherwise imperative demands of everyday life.[253]

Thus, while drunken comportment remains within the boundaries of acceptable social behavior, alcohol can stretch those boundaries and do so without serious repercussions.

However, drunken comportment is more complicated in societies with diverse social classes. In these contexts, drunken comportment functions as a shield to safely challenge authority. In his study of the role of the drunk in the Oaxacan village, anthropologist Philip Dennis argued that the drunk is socially liberated and able to speak freely against those in positions of power.[254] In the case of Oaxaca, drunkenness provided a shield for less powerful individuals to verbally attack and embarrass public officials. The shield of drunkenness also allowed less powerful social groups to circumvent boundaries erected by colonial powers. For example, under British colonial rule in Kenya, young Kikuyu men often used the guise of drunkenness to hurl rude remarks and shoot blunt arrows at British soldiers.[255]

In the highly structured social organization of the Caribbean, the shield of drunken comportment was thin. Rigid boundaries between social classes and the planters' desire to maintain the status quo increased personal accountability and weakened the execution of time-out performances. As a result, slaves, Caribs, and poor whites rarely exhibited drunken aggression toward the planter class. They realized that verbal attacks or physical assaults against whites seriously transgressed social boundaries and would result in dangerous consequences.

Evidence that the shield of drunkenness was weaker than the need to defend social boundaries was most pronounced in the social interactions between slaves and whites. Colonial assemblies and metropolitan governments explicitly regulated the behavior of slaves. Informal rules also governed social interactions between slaves and whites. Because planters were so greatly outnumbered, metropolitan troops, colonial militias, and the plantation manager's whip helped sustain their power. Slaves' criticizing or insulting a member of white society was likely to result in physical punishment regardless of their lack of sobriety. "Flagrant insults to white men" wrote one Barbadian official "seldom escape either publick punishment, or private revenge."[256] The severity of the punishment was often magnified by the "intoxication, ill-nature, and revenge" of the slave owner.[257] Stills were sometimes employed as instruments of torture. In the 1770s, Anglo-Dutch mercenary John Stedman recorded the punishment of a slave in Surinam who had attempted to stab his plantation overseer. For this crime, the condemned was

> Chain'd to the Furnace that distils kildevil there to keep in a perpetual fire night and day, by the heat of which he was all over blistered till he should expire by Infirmity or old Age indeed of which last he but had little chance.[258]

While drunkenness did not shield slaves from punishment for immediate, physical challenges to whites, the guise of drunkenness may have helped them to sabotage the source of the planters' power.[259] In 1690, Thomas wrote, "as the Canes ripen they grow more and more Combustible, and are thereby Subject to the Malice and Drunken Rages of Angry and desperate run-a-way Negroes."[260]

The high level of slave accountability was most evident in the context of work relationships, the fundamental and least negotiable relationships between slaves and planters. In the early nineteenth century, Collins wrote,

> [Slaves] who have been dancing, or drinking, or otherwise engaged on some nocturnal excursion, either on the business of love, or depredation, will be found at the hospital the next morning. They may be detected by the lateness of the hour at which they come there, and the soundness of their sleep, much greater than indisposition would admit. You will order them to their work, and wink at their transgressions, unless too frequently repeated.[261]

Although planters may have winked at a few transgressions, they rarely tolerated frequent bouts of drunkenness, especially if it challenged their authority or reduced plantation productivity. In the Caribbean, slavery, more than anything else, shaped patterns of drunken comportment. To the planter, slaves were an investment in productive labor, and planters wanted sobriety from their slaves. In order to identify particularly hard-working and temperate slaves, planters even constructed stereotypes of African ethnic groups that included references to their drinking habits. For example, according to Moreau de St.-Méry, among the good qualities of Senegalese slaves was that they were "tres-sobre."[262] A temperate workforce was a more efficient workforce and, in 1812, a committee of British West Indian planters recommended a reward system for slaves who adhered to principles of sobriety.[263]

Like marronage, drunkenness was a form of escape that stole productive labor. Both forms of escape removed the planters' resources and were, thus, considered acts of theft. When drunkenness interfered with work, it was rarely tolerated and, like marronage, was severely punished. In 1792, Indian Will, a slave on William Young's St. Vincent estate, was "put into the stocks . . . for getting drunk and cutting a negroe lad's head open."[264] In 1823, Césaire, a slave on Pierre Dessalles's sugar estate in Martinique, was given 30 lashes for being drunk and, in 1844, Dessalles's cook Philippe received the same punishment for getting drunk and ruining dinner.[265] Slaves prone to frequent bouts of intoxication were sometimes forced to wear iron collars and masks or were chained to their beds. In 1778 and 1779, the slave lists from York estate, Jamaica, identified Juba and Thomas as excessive drinkers. Their excessive drinking was noted under the heading "conditions," a column usually reserved for information about a slave's illnesses and injuries. The fact that they remained heavy drinkers over the years suggests that their drinking did not

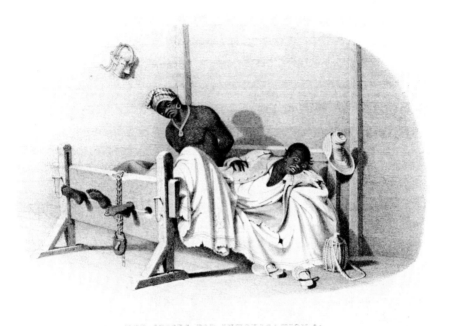

Figure 5.4. *Bed-Stocks for Intoxication, etc.* In Richard Bridgens, *West India Scenery . . . from sketches taken during a voyage to, and residence of seven years in . . . Trinidad* (London, 1836). Courtesy of the Virginia Historical Society, Richmond, Virginia.

become intolerable, but the potential danger was conspicuous enough to make it noteworthy as a disability.

There were times, however, when slave drunkenness was tolerated, and even encouraged, among the planter class. These occasions constituted rituals of rebellion, liminal periods when the planter class sanctioned the temporary reversal of social roles. The purpose of rebellion rituals is the release of pent-up tensions produced by routine and oppressive social inequity.[266] When Collins implied that winking at slaves' hangovers reduced their inclination to run away, he created an image of the tension-releasing function of provisionally permitted drunkenness.[267] In the Caribbean, rebellion rituals enacted in annual celebrations and festivals provided regular opportunities for slaves to temporarily reverse social roles and release aggressive impulses. The occasional release of tension, in turn, reaffirmed the normal social order. The physiological effects of alcohol drinking at these events helped make the change in status seem more convincing.

The tension-releasing function of alcohol was familiar to newly arrived African slaves in the Caribbean. Rituals of rebellion—such as the Akan *odwira* and the Igbo yam festivals, which have a long history in West and West Central Africa—were revived in modified form in the slave societies of the Caribbean. Bacchanalian celebrations occurred at Easter, crop-over, Christmas, and New Year. Mimicking the role of the Asantehene [king of the Asante] at the Akan odwira festival, the Caribbean planter encouraged rebellion rituals and often dispensed the alcohol. In 1791, Atwood wrote that the Christmas holiday was a time of "dancing, singing, and making merry."[268] Atwood added, "This they are enabled to do, by having also given them at this time four or five pounds of meat, the same quantity of flour or rice, with some rum and sugar to each negro." Plantation accounts frequently mention the distribution of rum to slaves for such celebrations.

It was only on these sanctioned occasions that alcohol provided a shield for slaves to stretch the limits of acceptable behavior. According to an anonymous writer in Jamaica, "The negroes ideas of pleasure [at the Christmas holiday] are rude and indistinct: They seem chiefly to consist in throwing off restraint and spending two or three days in rambling and drinking."[269] Of a New Year's celebration, Long wrote,

> The masquerader, carrying a wooden sword in his hand, is followed with a numerous croud of drunken women, who refresh him frequently with a sup of aniseed-water, whilst he dances at every door, bellowing out *John Connu!* with great vehemence; so that, what with the liquor and the exercise, most of them are thrown into dangerous fevers; and some examples have happened of their dying.[270]

It is generally thought that Akan slaves were the originators of the jonkonu [John Canoe] character and greatly influenced the nature of these ceremonies in the British Caribbean.[271]

Bacchanalian celebrations were not always limited to established holidays. In 1792, sugar planter William Young arrived at his plantation in Antigua and received a cheerful welcome from his slaves. Young then distributed rum to his slaves and "all was dance and song."[272] Lewis recorded a similar celebration at New Year's.

> The singing began about six o'clock, and lasted without a moment's pause till two in the morning; and such a noise never did I hear till then. The whole of the floor which was not taken up by the dancers was, through every

part of the house except the bed-rooms, occupied by men, women, and children, fast asleep. But although they were allowed rum and sugar by whole pailfuls, and were most of them *merry* in consequence, there was not one of them drunk; except indeed, one person, and that was an old woman, who sang, and shouted, and tossed herself about in an elbow chair, till she tumbled it over, and rolled about the room in a manner which shocked the delicacy of even the least prudish part of the company.[273]

While planters often promoted slaves' release of social pressure during established and impromptu celebrations, events did not always go according to expectations. The risk of slave revolts increased during holiday celebrations when huge allotments of rum were dispersed, social conventions were relaxed, plantation work was halted, and large numbers of slaves had greater opportunity to roam and assemble. The Barbados slave revolt of 1816 occurred during Easter, and the Jamaican slave revolt of 1831–1832 occurred at Christmas.[274] That more slaves were not involved in these revolts suggests that, despite the relaxation of rules and the shield of drunkenness, social inhibitions continued to exert force. Even so, revolts *did* increase during celebratory periods, demonstrating that some slaves exploited relaxed conventions and seized the rare opportunity to turn social reversal into real revolution. Alcohol became a powerful symbol in that cause.

Leaders of slave revolts often evoked African cultural traditions in order to mobilize and strengthen the resolve of the rebels. Within these traditions, alcohol exerted a powerful symbolism. Because alcohol was key to spiritual and physical escape, its centrality in slave uprisings and in the ritualistic manipulation of white victims is hardly surprising. Alcohol was the necessary medium for integrating ancestral spirits into revolts and for receiving ancestral guidance. For example, Jamaican maroons, after defeating British troops during an uprising in 1795, "returned to their town to recruit their spirits by the aid of rum."[275]

Oath drinks were an important feature of slave uprisings and conspiracies. In the British Caribbean, where they traced to Igbo and Akan origins, oath drinks strengthened alliances and reaffirmed individuals' community obligations, much as they had in Africa. During the organizational stages of the 1736 slave conspiracy in Antigua, the participants consumed oath drinks that consisted of rum, dirt from the graves of deceased slaves, and cock's blood.[276] During the Jamaica slave conspiracy of 1765, slaves consumed oath drinks that consisted of rum, gunpowder, grave dirt, and blood.[277] Prior to their uprising in 1795, slaves in Curaçao consumed an oath drink called *awa hoeramentoe*, consisting of rum and ground ox horns.[278] Similarly, the consumption of rum and gunpowder oath drinks preceded the slave uprising in St. Croix in 1848.[279] Even after emancipation, the oath drink continued to be an important facet of black resistance. During the peasant uprising at Morant Bay, Jamaica, in 1865, captured police officers were forced to consume oath drinks of rum and gunpowder in order to show loyalty to the rebels.[280]

The recurrence of key ingredients such as dirt and blood in oath drinks from different rebellions demonstrates the manipulation of basic signs to evoke shared beliefs among diverse African ethnic groups, especially Igbo and Akan. For example, grave dirt signaled the enduring, important role of ancestors in daily life and the need for their assistance in uprisings.[281] Gunpowder, the basis for white power in Africa and the Caribbean, may have signaled intensified commitment to the violent purpose of the oath and a symbolic appropriation of the white man's power. Ground horns in the Curaçao oath drink probably signaled identification with a potent, bull-like masculinity. An especially powerful symbol, blood was associated in many African cultures with ancestors and warfare. On the Gold Coast blood was offered to gods and ancestors to secure favors. In Akan society, blood offerings were usually reserved for war gods. Blood also symbolized military conquest, and the shared semiotic dimensions of blood and rum may explain the combination of blood, rum, and red color symbolism in slave oaths and uprisings. Ethnographies from the Gold Coast reveal that Akan war gods preferred the red color of rum, underscoring their particular desire for blood.[282]

The use of rum in oath drinks reflects shared beliefs about the spiritual force of alcohol and the loyalty-building role of oaths. Alcohol and blood were sacred fluids in both Igbo and Akan societies, and the widespread use of these ingredients in oath drinks suggests that Akan- and Igbo-styled oath customs remained particularly strong in the British Caribbean. Historian Barry Gaspar argues that the oath drinks consumed during the 1736 Antigua slave conspiracy were "deeply rooted in Akan religious tradition."[283] Alternately, there is evidence that oath-drink ingredients reflect an especially strong Igbo influence. Although oath drinks were common along the precolonial Gold Coast and blood was a symbol of warfare, the Akan did not integrate blood into their oath-drink potions. According to historian Robin Law, Igboland was one of the few places in West Africa where celebrants unquestionably used blood in their oath drinks. In addition, Law argues,

Despite the reputation of Igbo slaves in the Americas for docility (or more precisely for expressing their dissatisfaction through suicide rather than rebellion), it seems quite likely that it was the Igbo form of blood-oath which was utilized in some recorded slave insurrections.[284]

In fact, some sources indicate a strong Igbo component in the oath drinks consumed prior to the Antigua slave revolt.[285]

While the use of blood may have been characteristic of Igbo oath drinks, the use of alcohol, a substance for contacting spirits and receiving ancestral guidance, probably represents a braiding of Akan, Igbo, and other West and West Central African traditions. The widespread use of oath drinks in British Caribbean slave revolts reveals that slaves sought to mobilize all potential allies, including ancestral spirits, through the powerful symbolism of alcohol.

Oath taking was also evident in the French Caribbean where Kongo and Aja-Fon (Arada) influences appear to have been particularly strong. The Bois Caïman ceremony that preceded the 1791 St. Domingue slave uprising and, ultimately, the creation of Haiti, provides an excellent example. On the night of August 21, 1791, slaves gathered in the forest of Bois Caïman for a clandestine meeting.[286] At this meeting a black pig was slaughtered, and its blood was consumed as part of an oath ritual. Most scholars have argued that the Bois Caïman ceremony represents a Kongo-influenced petro ceremony, because petro is nowadays associated with black pigs. Petro, as Moreau de St.-Méry noted, appeared in the late eighteenth century and was distinguished by the consumption of rum and gunpowder.[287] The rum and gunpowder concoction imbibed by petro devotees was probably an oath drink used to bind participants to silence. Law has argued, however, that the Bois Caïman ceremony may have been a Dahomean-styled blood pact rather than a Kongo-influenced petro ceremony, because, he claims, the ritual sacrifice of pigs was common in Dahomean blood pacts.[288] According to Geggus, "one may doubt that the ceremony was narrowly identified with one particular ethnic group. It is more likely that the ceremony exhibited a blending of religious traditions."[289] The sketchy historical accounts of the Bois Caïman ceremony do not mention the use of alcohol. Nevertheless, Dahomean blood pacts included alcohol, and the use of rum was clearly a distinguishing feature of the Kongo-influenced petro cult.[290] As alcohol was a commonly used ingredient in both Arada- and Kongo-oriented oaths, it is likely that it also was used in the oath drink at the Bois Caïman ceremony.

In 1791, the slave uprising in St. Domingue erupted. One angry colonist would later complain, "The Africans against whom we fought are a cowardly people . . . and without rum there would never have been any fighting with those people."[291] As the uprising wore on, Toussaint-Louverture emerged as the revolutionary leader. Toussaint's leadership stemmed from his ability to communicate with and manipulate various social groups within St. Domingue including whites, freedmen, slave elite, Creole slaves, and especially, African slaves. According to Geggus,

> Toussaint did not lose touch with his African roots. He is said to have spoken fluently the language of his "Arada" father—apparently the son of a chief—and to have enjoyed speaking it with other slaves of his father's ethnic group. He seems also to have become skilled in the medicinal use of plants and herbs. Such slaves who lived at the interface between white and black society needed to know the ways of both worlds.[292]

Toussaint was personally abstemious, but appears to have understood the value of rum to the African slave when he stated "Give a negro a glass of rum and he'll do anything for you."[293]

Although this particular remark may have been meant disparagingly, it clearly shows Toussaint's recognition of rum's broad power—sacred or profane—to fuel political resistance. In fact, the rebels operated a distillery during the fighting to supply troops. The French Creole soldiers from St. Domingue probably also recognized the symbolic value of rum to the rebels, which is why they destroyed rebel rum supplies after their battlefield victories.[294] Seeing the negative consequences of excessive tafia drinking on the Haitian peasantry, especially in the south, Jean-Jacques Dessalines, Toussaint's successor, attempted to restrict rum making in Haiti in 1806. Although rum gave force to the revolutionary troops, excessive drinking appeared to be destabilizing the new nation. However, during the reign of Christophe, distilling was once again encouraged.[295]

As in the British Caribbean, a link existed between alcohol, blood symbolism, and warfare in Haiti. Anthropologist Melville Herskovits stressed the links between blood and the Haitian vodou war god Ogun. Herskovits pointed out that some of the Ogun loa preferred to drink red "Haitian rum," rather than the white clarin.[296] Aggressive spirits in Afro-Brazilian cults are also known to prefer rum for its powerful physiological effect and, perhaps, its blood-red color.[297]

The symbolic power of alcohol is also evident in the ritualistic treatment of white victims in Caribbean slave uprisings. For example, during Tacky's rebellion in Jamaica in 1760, slave rebels, after killing white servants at Ballard's Valley plantation, drank their victims' blood mixed with rum.[298] During a slave revolt at a plantation in St. Anne's parish, Jamaica, rebels cut off the head of the plantation owner and "made use of it as a punch-bowl."[299] According to reports of the 1701 slave uprising in Antigua, slaves cut off the head of a white victim and "washed it with rum and Triumphed Over it."[300]

Although rum was widely used in slave uprisings, its particular link to alliance building also made it an important symbol of peace. Disputes between slaves from neighboring plantations were sometimes resolved over shots of rum.[301] Even peace treaties between British colonial officials and maroon groups in Jamaica and Surinam were sealed by the pouring of libations and the drinking of rum mixed with the blood of both parties.[302]

Conclusion

Alcohol use was widespread in Caribbean slave societies. It provided a means of spiritual and physical escape from the many anxieties encountered in the Caribbean. In addition, many believed rum was a salubrious beverage that provided important health benefits. However, rum was also a cause of much anxiety and sent many to an early grave. Rum, especially lead-contaminated rum, probably increased rates of slave mortality and decreased rates of slave fertility. Drunkenness lowered usual defenses and made individuals vulnerable to a variety of dangers. Although rum was a symbol of slave rebelliousness, drinking provided an alcoholic marronage, a temporary relief from social inequities, which probably hindered organized efforts to resist slavery. Nevertheless, alcohol was instrumental in strengthening bonds between the living and ancestral worlds during times of war and peace.

In the nineteenth century, the social value and escapist function of drinking came under attack from Low Church Christian missionaries and temperance reformers from North America and Europe who flooded the Caribbean after slave emancipation and sought to reshape attitudes toward alcohol. Temperance challenged plantation traditions, as well as notions about rum's therapeutic qualities. Although reformers faced resistance from an aggressive planter class, they reinforced the long-standing temperance of black Creoles. They were, however, less successful at altering the drinking habits of poor whites and new immigrants from East Asia.

CHAPTER 6

Taming Rum in the Nineteenth and Twentieth Centuries

I N THE NINETEENTH CENTURY, alcohol continued to offer a route of physical and spiritual escape. Slave emancipation did not alleviate all the anxieties that confronted the majority of Caribbean peoples and, in many parts of the region, especially in the smaller and more densely populated islands, former slaves had few opportunities for economic independence. Colonial assemblies instituted vagrancy laws and other legal constraints that forced many former slaves back into grueling plantation labor. As with former indentured servants and the poorer classes of whites during the slavery period, those ex-slaves who were able to become independent farmers faced a precarious existence. Sugar planters also encountered heavy debts and declining sugar prices. Asian migrants, mainly from India and China, also found troubles, which, as with their European and African predecessors, fostered the pursuit of alcoholic escape.

On the other hand, social change and new attitudes about alcohol in this period began to challenge traditional Caribbean drinking patterns. Christian missionaries from Europe and North America arrived in the Caribbean in large numbers, converting emancipated slaves and advocating temperate lifestyles. Reformers confronted a tough and diverse set of alcohol-based traditions. Planters, who sought to maintain a stable and steady supply of labor after emancipation, offered rum-based work incentives as they had during slavery. Many former slaves remained anchored to African-oriented belief in the sacred dimensions of alcohol use, and folk customs positing alcohol's medicinal properties persisted in Caribbean society. Alternately, temperance fit well with the conventional attitudes of black Creoles, many of whom had rejected excessive drinking during the slavery period. Similarly, some Asian migrants embraced ascetic traditions, rather than alcohol, in order to cope with the anomie of their new American lives.

A Tropical Wave of Temperance

In the late eighteenth and early nineteenth centuries, Methodist, Baptist, and Moravian missionaries from Europe and North America began migrating to the Caribbean. They saw slaves as ripe for conversion and, often to the displeasure of the planter class, spread their versions of the gospel. Unlike Anglican ministers of the Church of England, these new missionaries actively encouraged slaves and freedmen to embrace the tenets of Christianity. In the early period, however, they had little success. In 1789, for example, Methodists erected a chapel in Bridgetown, Barbados, but the reverend was removed a decade later due to lack of interest. The Methodists made another attempt to establish themselves in Barbados in 1801, yet, by 1812, the congregation consisted of only 30 people, including 11 whites, 13 freedmen, and 6 slaves.[1]

A resurgence of Christian missionary activity occurred during the amelioration period just prior to slave emancipation, which breathed new life into the missionary movement. By the time of slave emancipation in 1834, Methodists, Moravians, and Baptists had put down deep roots. In the late 1830s, Moravian missionaries in Antigua had added about 15,000 members to their flock. Antigua also had about 6,000 Methodist congregants. Baptists were especially strong in Jamaica, and membership jumped dramatically after emancipation. In 1837, there were 16 Baptist missionaries and 31 chapels with a membership of 32,960.[2] By the mid-1840s, Methodists in Barbados had 8 chapels, 4 other preaching places, 3 missionaries, and 14 local preachers. They regularly attracted more than 5,000 people to their chapels and meetinghouses.[3]

In North America and Europe, these new Christian denominations, especially Methodists and Baptists, were leading advocates of temperance reform. The emancipation of British Caribbean slaves in 1834 occurred at the height of the temperance effort, and the passionate agitators carried their message of temperance to the former slaves. In 1837, Reverends James Thome and J. Horace Kimball, members of the American Anti-Slavery Society and temperance advocates, visited Antigua, Barbados, and Jamaica, and recorded the positive changes that had occurred since slave emancipation. Among the improvements they noted was the rise of temperance. They traveled to different estates in the islands and found that distilling had ceased on many plantations owned by Methodist, Moravian, and Baptist planters. Thome and Kimball expressed joy at the rise of Sunday churchgoing. Saturday, rather than Sunday, became the market day, and it was no longer an occasion of drunken excess. In 1843, Baptist minister James Phillippo visited Jamaica and also noted the changes.

> It is universally acknowledged that intemperance is not now the besetting sin of the lower classes in Jamaica. On the first introduction of the Gospel by black teachers, abstinence from intoxicating drinks was made a term of communion—and this previously to the existence of temperance and total-abstinence societies: so that even before the abolition of slavery intemperate habits had been abandoned by nearly one-third of the population.[4]

In 1861, a Moravian-based revival movement spread across Jamaica. According to Jamaican Congregational minister W. J. Gardner, the movement had a temperate effect. Jamaicans abandoned their "Evil habits" and "rum shops were forsaken by multitudes."[5]

In 1836, Antigua boasted the arrival of its first temperance society.[6] Within two years, temperance societies existed in the town of St. John's and on the estates of Wesleyan disciples. According to Joseph Sturge and Thomas Harvey, English Quaker abolitionists, the temperance societies in Antigua were very successful, and drunkenness was no longer an "overwhelming evil in this island, as in the United kingdom."[7] Thome and Kimball also celebrated the rise of temperance societies in Antigua.

> A large number of persons who once used spirituous liquors moderately, have entirely relinquished the use. Some who were once intemperate have been reclaimed, and in some instances an adoption of the principles of the temperance society, has been followed by the pursuit and enjoyment of vital religion. Domestic peace and quietness have superseded discord and strife, and a very general sense of astonishment at the gross delusion which these drinks have long produced on the human species is manifest.[8]

In Trinidad, wealthy white men and women, pursuing the philanthropic pastimes of the Victorian age, also started temperance societies. In 1873, Trinidad had a branch of the Independent Order of the Good Templars, one of the most powerful temperance societies in the world.[9] In 1888, the Good Templars challenged attempts by Trinidad's colonial council to extend rum shop hours. Other temperance societies in Trinidad included the Blue Ribbon Society, the Band of Hope, and the League of the Cross.[10] Total abstinence societies also operated in Jamaica.[11]

Many planters and plantation managers embraced temperance and encouraged their workers to do the same. Thome and Kimball recorded the impact of emancipation and temperance on James Howell's estates in Antigua.

> A great change in the use of *rum* had been effected on the estates under his management since emancipation. He formerly, in accordance with the prevalent custom, gave his people a weekly allowance of rum, and this was regarded as essential to their health and effectiveness. But he has lately discontinued this altogether, and his people had not suffered any inconvenience from it.[12]

Howell gave his workers molasses in lieu of rum, and set an example of teetotalism by abandoning his use of wine and malt liquor. Plantation managers at Wallen and Rose Hall estates in Jamaica also stopped dispensing weekly rations of rum.[13] In addition, many planters suspended the practice of allocating rum at Christmas and, as a result, Christmas celebrations became solemn events characterized by worship and prayer rather than "drunken riot."[14]

Even so, temperance defied plantation traditions. During the slavery period, planters liberally distributed rum to their slaves in weekly rations and as a work incentive. Despite protests from missionaries, as well as some colonial officials, rum rationing and incentives continued after emancipation in a modified form as planters doled out rum to free workers as a substitute for and supplement to wages. Weekly ledgers from Turner's Hall estate in Barbados, for example, indicate that plantation managers often paid workers in rum.[15] Planters in Barbados were known to supplement their workers' wages by a gill (four ounces) to half a pint of rum, which led to great social disorder in the colony. In 1845 the practice still prevailed in more than half of the parishes in Barbados, and "not only was all the rum made in the island consumed in it, but more was imported" to help fuel the system. In 1846, the use of rum to supplement wages was so necessary to retain plantation workers in St. Vincent that planters resisted any attempts by the colonial legislature to "interfere" with what reformers considered to be a "pernicious system."[16] Workers in Montserrat were also sometimes paid in rum.[17] In order to improve plantation productivity and reduce social decay, missionaries and colonial administrators forced planters in Trinidad and Demerara (British Guiana) to abandon the rum-based wage system in 1841.[18] Unlike the other British colonies in the Caribbean, Trinidad and Demerara were Crown colonies and, thus, more subject to the demands of metropolitan officials.

Planters found creative ways of circumventing colonial legislatures and the condemnation of temperance-minded missionaries. During the slavery period, some planters distributed food to their slaves in the middle of the week rather than at the end in order to prevent them from selling their rations for rum at weekend markets.[19] Planters feared, of course, that slaves who sold their rations would not have enough substantive food to get through the workweek and that they would either be required to provide additional rations or rely on underfed and less productive slaves. After emancipation, however, planters paid workers at the end of the week in the hope that their workers would spend extravagantly on rum on the weekend and, thus, be forced to return to work on Monday. The use of alcohol to supplement wages and create debt-ridden workers was mainly associated with itinerant work gangs, whose labor was especially needed during the intensive harvest season. Officials and missionaries condemned these rootless work gangs for their excessive drinking and immoral lifestyles.[20]

The establishment of plantation-owned stores and rum shops heightened the effectiveness of this system. Company stores and rum shops sold great amounts of rum to laborers, which created a large body of debt peons and ensured a stable workforce. Workers were compelled to return the next week or harvest in order to pay off their debts. Colonial officials in British Guiana complained, "'Nothing to do' is a deadly cry which lowers morale and stifles ambition, and it was no doubt the lack of opportunities for recreation after a day's work that helped to develop the habit of drinking at the estate rum-shop." Rum shops were present on nearly all estates, and they were usually located near pay offices. Some opened as early as 6:30 in the morning and remained open all night. Workers were sold rum on credit "whereby a man might drink away his wages before he had them." Officials in British Guiana denounced plantation rum shops and recommended "all rum shops upon estates should, by means of existing licensing regulations, be closed forthwith."[21] Yet, the company rum shop was such an integral part of the plantation economy that the institution prevailed well into the twentieth century.

Small farmers also received their share of rum. In some parts of the Caribbean, planters developed a system of sharecropping known as *métayer*. Under this system, sharecroppers worked small parcels of plantation land in exchange for a portion of the produce. In 1843, sharecroppers in Tobago received half of all the sugar as well as a bottle of rum for every barrel of sugar their plots produced.[22] In Grenada, rum was also shared between the plantation owner and *métayer*; the latter received a gallon of rum for every barrel of sugar.[23] The inclusion of rum in the métayer payment system was based on the supposition that the molasses that drained from the sugar and was sent to the distillery also belonged to the sharecropper.

Christian missionaries offered an alternative to rum-based wages and rum-laden company stores. During the period immediately following British Caribbean slave emancipation, Phillippo and other religious leaders instituted schemes to buy land for ex-slaves and establish "free villages." According to anthropologist Sidney Mintz, free villages in Jamaica involved as many as 100,000 people, and the social and economic importance of these settlements cannot be overstated.[24] The free village system provided land, education, and economic opportunities for many former slaves. Driven by the Protestant doctrine of hard work, free village members adopted principles of moderation and temperance in all forms of life, including drink. Mintz's study of Sturge Town, a free village in Jamaica, exemplifies the impact of the free village system. According to Mintz, free villagers "shared an ideology based on church membership and acceptance of its Christian tenets, particularly thrift, industry, and other doctrinal precepts associated with uprightness and humility."[25]

While the dedication of Methodist, Baptist, and Moravian missionaries in the Caribbean is indisputable, what was their actual impact on drinking patterns? Christian missionaries sought to relieve the many anxieties that confronted former slaves and to offer a constructive alternative to alcoholic escape. In Antigua, the rise of temperance societies and the entrenchment of missionaries fostered a spirit of teetotalism. In Jamaica, the missionary influence and free village systems may have been especially successful at reducing levels of alcohol consumption. In the 1890s, Jamaica was one of the world's largest rum producers, yet Jamaicans had one of the lowest rates of per capita rum consumption in the Caribbean. In the 1890s, Jamaicans consumed only about 660,000 gallons of rum annually for a per capita consumption rate of about one gallon per year.[26] Per capita rum consumption rates in Trinidad and British Guiana were also comparatively low (Table 6.1).

In contrast, the level of rum consumption in Barbados remained high. Although Barbados was a much smaller rum producer than Jamaica, its annual per capita rate of rum consumption in the 1890s was about 3.6 gallons, three and a half times greater than that of Jamaica. In large part, the higher per capita rum consumption rate reflects the more limited impact of missionary activity, which was resisted by the sizeable population of conservative whites in Barbados. For example, in 1789, white mobs frequently disrupted Methodist sermons and stoned the Methodist chapel in Bridgetown.[27] In 1823, whites in

Table 6.1. Estimated Annual Per Capita Rum Consumption in the
1890s in Gallons

Country	Consumed	Exported	Per capita consumption
Haiti	9,107,721	0	6.1
Dominican Republic	3,035,907	0	5.5
Guadeloupe	792,602	762,791	4.8
Martinique	792,602	4,533,748	4.5
French Guiana	105,680	0	4.1
Barbados	660,502	0	3.6
Trinidad	324,595	142,720	1.3
Jamaica	660,502	2,798,326	1.0
British Guiana	159,313	4,224,821	0.6

Sources: Volume of consumption based on Pairault, *Le rhum*, 14; population estimates for
French Guiana based on Pluchon, *Histoire des Antilles*, 427; population estimates for all
other countries based on Watts, *West Indies*, 459.

Barbados blamed Methodist reformers for inciting slave rebellion in Demerara. After learning of the unrest, a white mob in Bridgetown destroyed the
chapel of Methodist minister William Shrewsbury and ran him off the island.[28]
Local officials refused to help quell the riot. Other reform-minded religious
leaders in Barbados were publicly chastised and occasionally brought to
trial.[29] Although Methodism grew after emancipation, the Bishop of the Anglican Church in Barbados publicly denounced their teachings, and many planters refused to allow Methodists to preach on their estates. The negative impact
of Methodist teachings on plantation rum sales to workers and the local community probably strengthened their resolve. According to Thome and Kimball, resistance to Methodist preachers "greatly retarded the progress of religious instruction through their means."[30] In 1837, Methodists in the smaller
island of Antigua had six times as many converts and regular attendants at
Sunday sermons as Methodists in Barbados.[31] In addition, Moravians and
Baptists, the largest denominations in Jamaica and Antigua, all but failed to establish a foothold in the Barbados. Moreover, while organized temperance societies flourished in Antigua and Jamaica, historian Robert Schomburgk does
not record the presence of such organizations in his detailed list of Barbadian
societies in 1848. In the 1920s, Ernest Hurst Cherrington, a global temperance
advocate, wrote, "Generally speaking, both the men and the women of the is-

land [of Barbados] drink habitually. No temperance movement is known to have ever been promoted in the colony."[32] The suppression of missionary activity, the lack of an extensive free village system, and the absence of temperance societies largely explain the considerably high per capita rum consumption rate in Barbados in the 1890s.

However, the high per capita rum consumption rate in Barbados also reflects the larger number of white drinkers, especially poor whites. In the nineteenth century, as in earlier periods, visitors to Barbados condemned the excessive drinking of poor whites. Thome and Kimball wrote, "They live promiscuously, are drunken, licentious, and poverty-stricken,—a body of most squalid and miserable human beings."[33] In order for the per capita rum consumption rate of Barbados to equal that of Jamaica, poor whites in Barbados would have had to consume an almost deadly level of more than 48 gallons of rum per year, or more than a pint per day. Certainly many of the 10,000 or so poor whites in Barbados, especially adult males, achieved this enormous level. Yet, it is unlikely that they were solely responsible for the high per capita rum consumption rate in Barbados. While poor whites probably drank a disproportionate amount of rum, Barbados's relatively high per capita rum consumption rate also encompassed a large number of immoderate black drinkers. Of course, it is ironic that Barbados, which at present is considered the more conservative and law-abiding society with a sedate and stable image, consumed far more rum than "rude boy" Jamaica.

The substitution of rum for wages probably also contributed to the relatively high level of rum drinking in Barbados. After emancipation, the economically and politically powerful resident Barbadian planter class held onto their lands. In contrast to Jamaica, the small size and dense population of Barbados prevented the emergence of a large peasantry. In 1873, a visitor to Barbados wrote,

> since the island is so thickly inhabited, [the peasantry] are obliged to work; for though they generally own their own huts, and get a good deal out of the little patches of land attached to them, still it is not sufficient to keep them without working.[34]

Former slaves, therefore, were forced to work for Barbadian planters, who, unlike most of their counterparts in other parts of the British Caribbean, maintained the practice of paying former slaves with rum. Planters in British Guiana, for example, stopped using rum to supplement wages in 1841 and, as a result, colonial officials there believed "the young were less addicted to spirit-drinking than their elders."[35] In the 1890s, the annual rate of per capita rum consumption in British Guiana was one-sixth that of Barbados, which probably reflects both the impact of abandoning the rum-based wage system and its smaller poor white population.[36] Organized temperance societies may have also had an impact. In the 1840s, independent ministers, including Reverend Joseph Ketley, established the first temperance societies in British Guiana. In 1874, the capital Georgetown boasted a lodge of the Independent Order of the Good Templars. Bands of Hope and other temperance organizations also emerged. In 1917, per capita rum consumption in British Guiana was about .8 gallons. However, this figure does not account for the consumption of "bush rum," an often toxic rum made in small illegal stills in the marginal regions of the country, which probably represented a substantial proportion of rum consumed in the colony.[37]

Aboriginal groups in British Guiana, including Arawaks, Caribs, Wapisianas, and Warraws, maintained precolonial drinking patterns and primarily consumed cassava-based drinks. However, distilled rum also found its way into the "bush," often with devastating consequences. In an effort to curb alcohol abuse, the colonial legislature in 1909 forbade the sale of spirits to Indians and arrested and detained those found to be intoxicated.[38] Colonial officials were also concerned about excessive alcohol use by Caribs in the islands. By the end of the eighteenth century, European conquest of Carib lands was nearly complete. In 1763, British forces ousted the French from Dominica and took control of the island. They relegated local Caribs to a small settlement on a remote section of the northeastern coast of the island. In St. Vincent, thousands of Caribs were rounded up after the Carib War of 1795 and deported to Ruatán Island off the coast of Honduras. The remaining Black and Yellow Caribs in St. Vincent lost their fertile lands in the south and, as with their Dominican brethren, were relegated to a peripheral settlement. In 1880, Frederick Ober, an ornithologist working for the Smithsonian Institution, described the alcoholic malaise that characterized life on the Carib settlement in Dominica in the late nineteenth century.

> As I rode along, every house seemed deserted; no face appeared, and I met no one save the ancient king, old George, who was named for King George the Third, tottering toward the plantations, to spend for rum some money he had earned.[39]

In 1903, British colonial administrators turned the Carib settlement in Dominica into a reserve. Although alcoholic beverages were banned on the reserve, they continued to provide a temporary means of escape from the anomie of a subjugated life. In the early twentieth century, British colonial official Hesketh J. Bell described the ease with which Caribs were able to get rum.

> It is to be regretted that, generally speaking, any cash received by them invariably finds its way to the rum shop. No licensed dealer in spirits has been allowed to run a business in the Reserve, but, when on liquor bent, a trudge of many miles will not deter the Carib. Drink is his besetting sin, and unlike the negro inhabitants of Dominica, a small quantity of spirits rapidly shows an effect upon him.[40]

In 1930, police accusations that Caribs had stolen and smuggled rum into the Dominican reserve led to riots in which two Caribs were killed and several police seriously injured.[41] Like the Caribs of Dominica, those of St. Vincent and the interior regions of British Guiana also resorted to rum and oüicou to counter the effects of centuries of European colonialism on Carib reserves.[42]

Wealthy whites in the Caribbean drank heavily, but they tended to drink imported alcohols rather than rum. In 1917, the 6,000 or so whites in British Guiana drank almost all of the imported alcoholic beverages, including 29,099 gallons of spirits, 25,311 gallons of wine, and 192,765 gallons of malt liquor. One of the most popular drinks among wealthy whites was the *swizzle*. Swizzles are a combination of spirits, Angostura bitters, sugar, water, and ice shavings. The ingredients are mixed in a glass and stirred with a four- or six-pronged twig called a "swizzle stick." The pronged end of the swizzle stick, which looks similar to an azalea branch, is placed in the glass, while the smooth end is held between the palms of the hands and twirled rapidly back and forth until the mixture becomes frothy. The base spirits defined the type of swizzle and, thus, swizzles made with rum were specifically referred to as rum swizzles.[43] Whites had a reputation for excessive swizzle drinking and some considered British Guiana a place "where eight or nine gin zwizzles before breakfast" was almost an institution.[44]

Levels of rum consumption in both Jamaica and Barbados declined in the early twentieth century (Table 6.2). In the 1930s, Jamaica's annual per capita rate of only 0.5 gallons was considered "very weak."[45] The annual consumption rate in Barbados also declined, but still remained three times higher than Jamaica's. The decline probably reflects the ongoing success of missionary activity and the global attack on intemperance in the early twentieth century. Conversely, rum consumption in British Guiana increased and in the 1930s tripled to about 1.9 gallons. The increase may reflect the growing sophistication of the estate store and rum shop system. However, the increasing proportion of the population represented by Asians, who were generally less affected by missionary activity, may have also contributed to the increase.[46] Trinidad, which like British Guiana had a large influx of Asian migrants, also experienced a slight increase in per capita rum consumption between the 1890s and 1930s.

Temperance was a central canon of Protestant reformers in the British Caribbean, but Catholic priests and missionaries, based in the French and Spanish Caribbean, were much less aggressive in their proselytizing of former slaves or in their temperance crusades. While cost and availability certainly played a major role in dictating levels of rum consumption, a comparison of per capita rum consumption rates also suggests different attitudes toward drinking in the Protestant- and Catholic-oriented Caribbean. In the 1890s, Catholic regions of the Caribbean had a higher rate of per capita rum consumption than Protestant regions. Haitians, for example, annually consumed about six gallons of rum, tafia, and clarin per person, and Martinique and Guadeloupe had per capita consumption rates of over four gallons (Table 6.1).

Although we lack estimates for Cuba in the 1890s, rum consumption was probably not especially high. War and civil unrest in the 1890s had a devastat-

Table 6.2. Estimated Annual Per Capita Rum Consumption in the 1930s in Gallons

Country	Per capita consumption
Cuba	2.0
Haiti	1.1
Guadeloupe	4.0
Martinique	6.3
French Guiana	2.6
Barbados	1.5
Trinidad	1.5
Jamaica	0.5
British Guiana	1.9

Sources: Volume of consumption based on Kervégant, *Rhums*, 467–91; population estimates for French Guiana based on Pluchon, *Histoire des Antilles*, 427; population estimates for all other countries based on Watts, *West Indies*, 459.

ing impact on Cuban sugar production, which reduced the availability of rum. Moreover, Cuba had a high percentage of Spanish colonials, who, unlike their European counterparts in the Caribbean, generally had a reputation for temperance.[47] Former slaves in Cuba, however, probably consumed a great deal of rum. As in the British Caribbean, rum-based wages and rum-laden company stores increased the level of rum consumption. Ex-slaves in Cuba hired themselves to plantations or joined work gangs called *cuadrillas*. These roving workers received rations of aguardiente just as slaves had under slavery.[48] In 1892, the company store at Santa Lucia sugar factory in Gibara, Cuba, possessed a distillery and nine saloons.[49] Workers were paid with company tokens, which they spent on rum at the company stores and saloons. In the 1890s, the per capita rum consumption rate in the Dominican Republic was 5.5 gallons per year. Considering the temperate reputation of Spanish colonials, it is unlikely that Cuba reached that level, and the relatively high rate of rum consumption in the Dominican Republic may reflect rum consumed by the large number of seasonal migrants from Haiti.

Levels of rum consumption in the French Caribbean generally remained higher than in the British and Spanish Caribbean during the early twentieth century. In the 1930s, the annual rate of per capita rum consumption was about 2.6 gallons in French Guiana, about 4 gallons in Guadeloupe, and an incredible 6.3 gallons in Martinique (Table 6.2). Liberal Catholic attitudes toward drink, the growing popularity of rum drinking in France, and the substantial white [*béké*] population, especially in Martinique, probably had a positive impact on per capita rum consumption rates in the French Caribbean. Moreover, as some of the world's largest rum producers, colonists in the French Caribbean had easy access to rum.

The abstemious reputation of the Spanish in the Caribbean remained strong in the early twentieth century. In 1915, Albert Robinson, an American temperance advocate, traveled to Cuba and wrote,

> The Cubans are an exceedingly temperate people. Wine is used by all classes, and *aguadiente*, the native rum, is consumed in considerable quantity, but the Cuban rarely drinks to excess. . . . Beer is used, both imported and of local manufacture. Gin, brandy, and anisette, cordials and liqueurs are all used to some but moderate extent, but intoxication is quite rare.[50]

In the 1930s, Cubans produced an annual average of almost nine million gallons of aguardiente and exported only half a million gallons per year.[51] At this rate, per capita consumption was about two gallons—higher than that of the

British Caribbean, but still less than most of the other Catholic-oriented regions. Trade and production statistics also confirm Robinson's remarks that Cubans consumed a substantial amount of locally made beer and cider, as well as imported European and North American alcoholic beverages. For example, between 1920 and 1927, Cuba imported more than 3.5 million gallons of liquor, especially whiskey and gin. In this period, Cubans also imported more than 7.5 million gallons of white wine, 24 million gallons of red wine, 9 million gallons of beer, and 180,000 gallons of champagne.[52] Yet, much of this imported alcohol, as well as a great deal of the rum and aguardiente produced in the island, probably went down the throats of the millions of American tourists who traveled to Cuba during these years of Prohibition.

In the early twentieth century, Cuba became a destination for fantasy-seeking tourists. Robinson was already complaining in 1915 about the negative impact of North American visitors on temperate Cuban culture and wrote, "the temperance question in Cuba is only a question of how soon we [Americans] succeed in converting them into a nation of drunkards."[53] After 1919, Prohibition accelerated the growth of Cuba's tourist industry. Historian Louis Pérez wrote,

> Cuba entered the North American imagination in many forms, but principally as a place of pleasures unavailable at home—where one could do those "things" that usually were not done anywhere else. Access to alcoholic beverages during Prohibition was an early tourist attraction. "Never has so much beer, rum, and Daiquiri been consumed in so short a time," a tourist wrote home. Visitors availed themselves of the opportunity to drink immediately on arrival.[54]

Unemployed American saloonkeepers and bartenders migrated to Cuba and renewed operations during Prohibition, which helped magnify Cuba's image as an alcoholic retreat.[55] Ernest Hemingway and other popular writers celebrated Cuba's alcoholic freedoms and used rum to construct their romantic depictions of the tropics.

Puerto Rico, with its less developed tourist industry, pursued a more temperate path during Prohibition. As with their counterparts in Cuba, Spanish colonials in Puerto Rico had a temperate reputation. And, as in Cuba, they generally drank imported Spanish wine and brandy with meals. In the 1890s, William Dinwiddie, an American visitor to Puerto Rico, wrote, "the average Puertoriqueño is remarkably abstemious, drinking perhaps before dinner a brandy-and-water and before breakfast a little white wine." While the urban poor, both men and women, were known to get drunk more frequently, they did not, according to Dinwiddie, "get drunk as often as a vicious American." Moreover, the Puerto Rican rum industry was small until the mid-1930s. In 1898, during the Spanish-American War, U.S. troops occupied Puerto Rico and brought with them a penchant for heavy drinking, which some Puerto Ricans imitated. Though American-styled saloons also began to pop up during the occupation, Puerto Ricans largely rejected intemperance.[56]

After the Spanish-American War, U.S. social, political, and economic influence remained strong in Puerto Rico. Low Church missionaries, including Methodists, Congregationalists, and Presbyterians, saw Puerto Ricans as potential converts and descended upon the island. Missionaries were probably encouraged by the islanders' temperate reputation. By 1900, Puerto Rico boasted a branch of the Women's Christian Temperance Union, known as Liga de Temperancia de Puerto Rico. In 1917, the Jones Act made the people of Puerto Rico citizens of the United States. As a result of the efforts of some dry-minded prohibitionists in the U.S. congress, the act included a referendum on Prohibition. Surprisingly, two-thirds of Puerto Ricans voted in favor of Prohibition and, in 1918, Puerto Rico went dry. Although some claimed that Puerto Ricans simply misunderstood the ballot and mistakenly voted for Prohibition, historian Truman Clark argued that Puerto Ricans embraced the tenets of Prohibition out of a desire for civic improvement and a patriotic loyalty to the United States after the passage of the Jones Act.[57] Yet, Prohibition in Puerto Rico was difficult to enforce, and many believe that the consumption of alcohol, especially illicit moonshine rum, increased during the Prohibition era. In 1933, the Twenty-first Amendment repealed Prohibition in Puerto Rico, as it did in the United States. Shortly thereafter, Puerto Rico upgraded its distilling industry and emerged as the leading producer of rum for the U.S. market.

In the 1890s, Haiti had one of the highest rates of rum consumption in the Caribbean, but by the 1930s, rum drinking there experienced a sharp decline. Although the estimate in Table 6.2 probably does not account for the vast amount of rum, tafia, and clarin produced in the 2,000 or so small stills that operated in the rural areas, there appears to have been an actual decrease in rum consumption.[58] In the early twentieth century, the United States invaded Haiti and attempted to stabilize the country's politics. Between 1915 and 1934, U.S. marines occupied Haiti and instituted social, political, and economic reforms. The occupation of Haiti overlapped the height of temperance activity in the United States, and many U.S. marines and government officials considered excessive drinking inimical to Haiti's social stability. In 1928, U.S. officials imposed an excise tax on alcohol. Although the large number of small-scale rural distillers made it difficult to collect, one official considered the tax "a marked step toward the establishment of modern and productive internal taxes."[59] American officials probably also saw the tax as a way to curb excessive drinking.

Not everyone in Haiti shared this view. The following year, U.S. officials blamed anti-American agitators for supplying liquor to seasonal migrants from rural areas and inciting riots in Les Cayes. An American-owned distillery in Port-au-Prince generated substantial tax revenues and competed with a Haitian-owned distillery in Les Cayes. The local distillery in Les Cayes attempted to combat its American rival in Port-au-Prince by appealing to nationalism and convincing peasants to sell their cane at low prices. In 1930, U.S. officials began transferring power to local authorities and decided to impose martial law during the transition in order to quell internal unrest. The overabundance of cheap alcohol available to the "hoodlum fringe" helped the American high commissioner to Haiti justify his actions.[60]

Among the improvements that accompanied U.S. intervention was the implementation of protective tariffs. The tariffs increased U.S. capital investment and led to a revival in the Haitian sugar industry. Along with six other American agricultural firms, the Haitian American Sugar Company, which had operated in Haiti since before the U.S. intervention, greatly benefited from the surge in capital investment. The value of sugar exports jumped from an annual average of 3 percent in 1916–1926 to 20 percent in 1939.[61] The growing interest in sugar making apparently had a negative impact on rum production and therefore may help explain falling rum consumption rates.

The American occupation of Haiti also brought Protestant missionaries and strengthened the role of the Catholic Church. Among the objectives of some clerics was the eradication of African-oriented vodou practices, a project exemplified by the *campagne anti-superstitieuse* of the early 1940s.[62] Alcohol played a prominent role in vodou ceremonies and was, no doubt, a target of reformers. While temperance may not have been an explicit goal of the campaign, religious-based social movements generally embraced temperance ideals. However, political leaders continued to recognize the value of rum to the Haitian peasantry. In 1971, for example, François (Papa Doc) Duvalier plied the Haitian peasantry with rum and clarin in order to win the support of the electorate and guarantee that his son Jean-Claude Duvalier would succeed him as president.[63] The act was reminiscent of Toussaint-Louverture's disparaging comment that Haitians would follow the lead of anyone with rum.

New Migrants and Old Anxieties

In order to secure a steady and stable supply of labor after the emancipation of Caribbean slaves, contract workers, mainly from India, China, and the East Indies, were brought to the Caribbean as indentured servants. Between 1833 and 1917, more than 500,000 contract laborers from the East, as well as free migrants from Africa and the Atlantic islands, reached the Caribbean.[64] About 125,000 Chinese immigrants arrived in Cuba and 14,000 arrived in the mainland colony of British Guiana.[65] The majority of new migrants, however, came from India. Between 1845 and 1917, more than 230,000 East Indians entered British Guiana and, by 1911, they represented nearly half of the population.[66] Trinidad received about 140,000 East Indians and, by 1901, they made up 33 percent of the population. In the nineteenth and early twentieth centuries, Guadeloupe, Martinique, and Guyane received about 75,000 East Indian migrants.[67] Although many Asian laborers returned to their homelands after completing their indentures, most stayed, and their descendants now represent a large percentage of the modern Caribbean population. Today, for example, East Indians make up half of the population of Guyana (the former British Guiana) and about 40 percent of Trinidad's population.[68]

Asian migrants brought with them new attitudes about alcohol that added a fresh dimension to drinking in the Caribbean. East Indians came from societies with strong traditions of alcohol use that dated to ancient times. Moreover, in the mid-eighteenth century, British, Dutch, French, and Portuguese colonials erected distilleries in India, where they made sugarcane-based spirits popularly known as *arrack*. By the nineteenth century, rum making was a well-developed industry in many parts of colonial India, China, and Indonesia. Because indentured migrants departed from colonial centers in Asia, many were already familiar with rum before they arrived in the Caribbean.

Despite the ubiquity of alcoholic beverages in India, the ascetic Hindu philosophy of *dharma* placed tight restrictions on alcohol use. Proscriptions against drinking were most ardently embraced by higher castes, especially spiritually minded Brahmans. Brahmans saw alcoholic intoxication as harmful to religious life.[69] While Brahmans were models of Hindu asceticism and opposed the use of alcoholic beverages, drinking was tolerated, and even encouraged, in some segments of Indian society, especially among warrior castes.[70] The Sudras, members of low castes, also drank. In India, low-caste drinking was especially widespread at weddings and at the spring *Holi* festival. They also poured libations and made drink offerings to village deities.[71]

East Indian migrants entered a Caribbean social environment that held relatively liberal attitudes about drinking and where rum was cheap and readily available. Moreover, East Indians worked in the sugar sector of the economy and, therefore, frequently encountered rum and distilling activities. In the nineteenth century, Trinidad and British Guiana, the main destinations for East Indian migrants, were major rum producing colonies. In fact, by the end of the nineteenth century, British Guiana was among the world's leading rum producers.[72]

Poor living conditions, inadequate food supplies, an unbalanced sex ratio, the lack of safe medical care, hard labor, homesickness, and many other anxieties provided a favorable environment for social unrest. Between 1872 and 1898, East Indians in Trinidad committed 109 murders.[73] East Indian agitators also instigated numerous plantation strikes, riots, and work stoppages. In British Guiana, in 1869, plantation strikes and labor riots became so violent that military detachments were brought in to quell the unrest. In Trinidad, in 1884, one of the more spectacular riots occurred during the Muharram or Hosein religious celebration—originally a Shiite Muslim Tadjah festival that eventually became a syncretic popular event.[74] According to historian Walton Look Lai, religious celebrants defied restrictions on public celebration, which led to a clash between celebrants and police. The riots left 22 dead and hundreds seriously injured.[75] Unrest occurred even within some of the smaller East Indian migrant communities. For example, in the nineteenth century, arson became an especially common form of protest among East Indians in Guadeloupe.[76] Desertion from estates was also widespread.[77] Immoderate alcohol use provided a means of escape from the anomie.

Like white perceptions of slave drinking during the slavery period, white perceptions of East Indian drinking were also tainted by fears of social unrest and the desire to maintain a productive labor force. John Amphlett, an English visitor to British Guiana, expressed the usual complaint of planters.

> Coolies are very fond of rum, and their chief drink is rum-and-water; and rum of a very inferior description too, for they buy it from shops kept by Portuguese, as the managers are restrained from giving it to them by law. I was told by the manager of one of the largest estates in the colony, that nearly every coolie gets drunk when he receives his money on a Saturday, and remains drunk all Saturday, and lies about on the roadsides on Sunday, in the heat and glare of the sun, either drunk or incapable. I myself one Saturday, when calling at an estate some distance from Georgetown, found a

coolie man lying dead drunk in the middle of the drive to the manager's house, so that I had to turn aside the carriage to avoid him; and he had not moved an inch when I returned after a long call at the house. The consequence is, that on Monday the estate hospital is nearly full.[78]

Although British Guiana and Trinidad outlawed the rum-based wage system in 1841 and temperance societies flourished in the colonies, these reforms had little impact on East Indian drinking patterns. Few East Indians embraced the Christian denominations, especially the Methodists and Baptists who led the crusades against alcohol use in the Caribbean.[79] Moreover, many doubted the commitment of those East Indians who did convert.[80] In the 1930s, the Sanatan Dharma Association of Trinidad emerged, which had some success at reviving orthodox Hindu asceticism.[81] Nevertheless, alcohol abuse has remained a greater problem in modern East Indian communities than in Afro-Caribbean communities.[82]

Structural changes within the East Indian diaspora in the Caribbean helped liberalize attitudes toward alcohol. Migration weakened the traditional East Indian caste system: high-caste Brahmans, the arbiters of ascetic Hindu values, represented only a small percentage of East Indian migrants. In Trinidad, Brahmans made up only 14 percent of the East Indian migrants, while artisan, agricultural, and generally low castes represented more than 70 percent.[83] Moreover, British administrators sought to break Brahman control over the masses of East Indian migrants and, as a result, the ideology of Brahman asceticism diminished in overseas East Indian communities.[84] The caste organization ceased to function as it did in India. Instead, a progressive form of Hinduism emerged, which had a more egalitarian flavor.[85] The weakness of Brahmans and the large migration of low castes created a social climate that tolerated alcohol use.

The social and spiritual uses of alcohol among low-caste Hindus transferred to the Caribbean and enhanced the sense of alcoholic freedom. In the plantation villages, Hindus conducted religious ceremonies using makeshift platforms and shrines similar to those found in villages in India. Migrants practiced non-Brahmanic Hindu traditions, such as animal sacrifice, which frequently included the pouring of libations and the offering of alcohol to lesser deities and spirits. During pig sacrifices to the goddess Parmeshwari, which was conducted annually and at the birth or marriage of a son, offerings of rum were set before the dead animal.[86] Spirit possession followed the sacrifice, during which time participants ritualistically consumed rum.[87] In India, upper castes viewed these ceremonies as "impure" rites. The strength and persistence of these practices may be attributed to the fact that low-caste migrants represented the majority of East Indians in the Caribbean.

Among the more common Hindu blood sacrifice ceremonies, alcohol and cigarettes were annually offered to Dih, the tutelary demigod of lands.[88] Offerings to land gods may have been especially important to East Indian migrants starting a new life on new lands in the Caribbean. The offering, called a *totka*, required that the first few drops from a newly opened bottle of liquor be poured on the ground for the deity Dih.[89] The totka ensured successful harvests and a healthy household. While some religious ceremonies followed conventional Hindu traditions, others were modified to fit Christian rituals. For example, at Christmas celebrations in Trinidad in 1855, "a goat wearing garlands of red flowers and surrounded by pans of washed rice and bottles of molasses and rum was beheaded to the sound of drums."[90]

Chinese migrants also came from societies with strong traditions of alcohol use, and drinking became a way to confront anxiety. In 1873, a Chinese commission in Cuba recorded brutal assaults on Chinese laborers and noted their high rate of suicide.[91] According to historian Brian Moore, the absence of sufficient numbers of Chinese women provided little opportunity to re-create traditional Chinese family units.[92] The lack of traditional family structures tended to destabilize individuals, compounding existing anxieties within Chinese immigrant communities.[93] In the nineteenth century, opium use, which was widespread in China, also provided sanctuary for a number of Chinese migrants in the Caribbean. It was a major concern for colonial administrators. On the other hand, the difficulty of procuring opium in the Caribbean and the ready availability of rum meant that alcohol provided an alternative means of escape. In 1853, the Immigration Agent-General in Trinidad reported that some Chinese "had shown a stronger predilection for rum drinking 'than might have been predicted from tea drinkers.'"[94] In addition, Chinese laborers engaged in sporting events, such as climbing greased poles to retrieve bottles of rum.[95]

East Indians and Chinese were brought to the Caribbean as agricultural laborers, but many quickly became shopkeepers and entered the local alcohol trade. In 1891, more than 78 percent of East Indians in Trinidad were agricultural laborers, but prominent among the remainder were proprietors of rum shops.[96] In the 1890s, Indian government representative D.W.D. Comins reported "Some [East Indians] take out spirit licenses, and a few of the shops are of large size and do a thriving trade."[97] In 1913, 664 East Indians in Trinidad held rum shop licenses, which represented more than 11 percent of all licenses granted to East Indians.[98] Colonial officials in British Guiana were especially critical of the aggressive tactics of East Indian rum retailers who operated rum shops near pay offices on sugar estates.[99] Chinese were also strong in the local rum trade. In British Guiana, some Chinese laborers deserted the plantations and became involved in illicit rum-making and rum-smuggling operations. By the end of the nineteenth century, Chinese held a substantial number of the colony's liquor licenses.[100]

Yet, in Trinidad and British Guiana, the Portuguese initially dominated the alcohol trade. In the nineteenth century, Portuguese, mainly from the Atlantic island of Madeira, migrated to the British Caribbean in large numbers. Most went to British Guiana, which, between 1835 and 1881, received 32,216 Portuguese migrants. As with East Indians and Chinese, the Portuguese began as agricultural laborers, but many quickly opened retail shops and started selling rum. In British Guiana, Amphlett wrote that the Portuguese have "monopolised the liquor and the small shop-keeping trades; and there is hardly a village, however small, in the interior, without its Portuguese shop."[101] Whites in British Guiana may have encouraged the rise of the Portuguese shopkeepers in order to establish a "buffer class" between blacks and whites.[102] They instituted restrictive policies, such as high licensing fees, to drive black Creoles out of the retail trades. At the same time, supportive licensing boards, governed by white colonials, granted a disproportionate number of shop licenses to Portuguese retailers, while white-owned commercial houses offered Portuguese retailers easy credit. By 1852, nearly 79 percent of all rum shop licenses in British Guiana belonged to Portuguese.[103] Indeed, the 1841 ban on rum-based wages in British Guiana may have also been aimed at fostering the success of Portuguese rum retailers, because it forced blacks to purchase rum from them.

Whites in British Guiana designed a system whereby black Creoles usually found themselves in debt to Portuguese shopkeepers. The policies, therefore, stirred black Creole resentment toward the Portuguese rather than the local white elite. The success of Portuguese immigrants in the rum retail trade drove a wedge between Portuguese and black Creoles, which culminated in the anti-Portuguese riots of the 1840s and 1850s. Despite these conflicts, Portuguese retailers continued to control the lucrative rum shop trade, and by 1865, they held more than 90 percent of the licensed rum shops in the colony.[104]

In the twentieth century, Portuguese rum sellers continued to dominate the retail market and even integrated popular culture to bolster their trade. For example, in Trinidad, in the 1930s, Alphonso, a Portuguese rum seller, sponsored a calypso tent and hired calypsonians to write songs that would advertise his business. Lord Mentor, a popular calypsonian, wrote the lyrics:

> Drink your rum, and tumble down
> But don't make basa [be foolish] around the town
> For there is a man I know
> His name is Mr. Alphonso
> He is selling his rum so cheap and sweet
> It's bound to put you to sleep.[105]

Temperance and Alcohol-Based Spirituality

Africans, Europeans, Asians, and Caribs shared similar beliefs about the sacred nature of alcohol and its ability to strengthen connections to the spiritual world. The consumption of wine in the Christian communion rite, for example, has many parallels in traditional African religious practices. During the slavery period, slave owners found the use of alcohol in slave religious practice familiar and did not condemn it the way they did other African-oriented traditions, such as drumming. Moreover, Christian attitudes about alcohol may have enhanced its spiritual value among slaves, facilitating the widespread use of rum in slave religion. Alcohol became a universal substance for slave interactions with a spiritual world, particularly during funeral ceremonies and African-oriented religious rituals.

Temperance-minded missionaries faced the challenge of enticing former slaves away from African-oriented beliefs that embraced alcohol as a key to unlock the spiritual world. At the same time, nineteenth-century Christian temperance reformers struggled with their own contradictions. While the drinking of sacramental wine symbolically united Christians with their god, alcohol was also a profane substance that befuddled the mind and impeded the progress of Christian conversion. In the nineteenth century, Low Church leaders began to challenge the sanctity of wine. By the early twentieth century, Presbyterians, Methodists, Baptists, and Congregationalists affirmed their commitment to temperance by substituting grape juice for wine in Holy Communion. Their example, however, did not sway adherents to African-oriented traditions, and the belief in and use of alcohol as a sacred article has remained widespread in the Caribbean's diasporic religions.

Whites used the term *obeah* for a variety of African-oriented religious practices, and it was one of the most pervasive belief systems in the British Caribbean. Christian missionaries condemned obeah and saw it as an impediment to conversion. One French Roman Catholic priest in Grenada sought to stamp out obeah by refusing the sacraments to an entire family if a member of that family was known to be "dabbling in Obeah."[106] Bell reported,

> Of late years, with the progress of [Christian religious] education among the negroes [of Grenada], they have become a little ashamed of their belief in Obeah, but still cling tenaciously in secret to the mysteries they were taught in their youth to dread and venerate, and any man with the reputation of "working Obeah" is looked on by all with the greatest fear and treated with the utmost deference.[107]

Whites sometimes doubted the commitment of converts to the tenets of Christianity. Bell, for example, believed many were only "nominally Christians . . . [who] still clung to the old superstitions."[108] Rum remained a central ingredient of obeah practices and spells in Grenada.[109]

The use of rum was also strong in Jamaican obeah ceremonies. In the 1920s, folklorist Martha Beckwith explored obeah in rural Jamaica and described the prominence of rum in obeah rituals. Obeah largely involved the practice of catching shadows or spirits for personal use, and Beckwith recorded the many ways Jamaican peasants used rum to catch shadows and spirits.

> Get two wide-mouthed bottles of proof rum (alcohol) and a bunch of spirit-weed tied to a stick, and go naked to the grave at night. At twelve o'clock you go to the gravehead, put the rum at the head, strike one, two, three strokes with the spiritweed, and say: "So-and-so, come an' mek a tell you wha' fe do." Repeat this at the foot. Then "guard the head" and take up the bottle, guard the foot and take up the bottle, and tell the ghost what you want of it.[110]

As during the slavery period, grave dirt and rum were necessary ingredients for the production of an obeah guard.[111]

Myalists in Jamaica also used rum to invoke help from the spirit world, especially to counter the effects of obeah. Distinctions between *myal* and obeah are not entirely clear, and the two belief systems are not necessarily opposed.[112] Myal conjurers, for example, contacted spirits with rum offerings and libations when they needed protection from obeah magic. The "physical focus" of myalism is the cottonwood tree, around which congregate "the ghosts of the dead."[113] Myal men often received their power through interactions with spirits at cottonwood trees, and according to Beckwith, devotees will not cut a cottonwood tree without first making "propitiatory offerings of rum." Myal men poured rum around cottonwood trees because, according to Beckwith, "spirits love rum!"[114] During myal dances and events, which usually occurred around cottonwood trees, conjurers received charms and talismans from the spirits of the dead. These objects were given to devotees, who were expected to regularly pour rum over them.[115] Rum appeased angry spirits and helped myal followers receive spiritual guidance and protection.

In Jamaica, in the nineteenth century, African-oriented obeah and myalism merged with black Baptist beliefs to form a new Afro-Christianity. According to Caribbean researcher Richard Burton, one of the most significant changes to African-oriented religious beliefs was the integration of Christian elements into traditional obeah and myal practices.[116] Despite the influence of temperance-minded Christian missionaries, the role of alcohol remained a central feature of Afro-Christianity. Afro-Christian groups in Jamaica, such as Convince and Revivalist, continue to recognize the spiritual value of alcohol, and members make offerings of blood and rum to appease ancestral spirits.[117] Followers of Kumina—a sect originating among African indentured laborers who arrived in Jamaica after emancipation—also regularly employ rum in their ceremonies to worship ancestral spirits. In Trinidad, rum is a common ingredient in medicines used by Shango practitioners to treat the physically, emotionally, and spiritually ill.[118] In Montserrat, ancestral spirits, known as *jombees*, frequently receive offerings of rum during jombee dances and possession ceremonies.[119]

In contrast to other African-oriented religious groups in the British Caribbean, Rastafarians reject alcohol and see it as inimical to spiritual life. Instead, ganja smoking is considered the key to spiritual enlightenment. According to one Rastafarian poet,

> There is no comparison between ganja and rum
> The former keeps you "cool" the latter makes you glum
> Rum as we know is an agent of death
> With the using of ganja you draw new breath.[120]

The Rastafarians are shocked by the Jamaican government's reluctance to control the use of alcohol, despite the dangers associated with drinking. Moreover, some Rastafarians suspect "a plot exists on the part of the large distillers to keep ganja from being legalized so that it will not cut into their sales of rum."[121] While this is a possibility, alcohol and ganja, as the Rastafarian poem indicates, bring about two distinct feelings. While ganja is an appropriate drug for some spiritually minded groups, those who embrace materialistic and secular ideologies often feel uncomfortable with the sensation of being high.[122]

In the French and Spanish Caribbean, Catholic priests and missionaries also condemned African-oriented religious beliefs, but their objection to alcohol was relatively mild compared with that of Low Church Christian missionaries in the British Caribbean. Catholics upheld and continue to uphold the sacramental use of wine in the Holy Communion. Liberal attitudes toward alcohol in the Catholic Church and the integration of Catholic ideas into the ceremonial context of African diasporic religions probably combined to increase a certain reverence for alcohol in the French and Spanish Caribbean.

In the French Caribbean, the spiritual value of rum is most evident in Haitian vodou ceremonies.[123] Alfred Métraux's extensive study of Haitian vodou describes numerous instances in which devotees used alcohol to facilitate communication with the spirit world.[124] In fact, followers contact their particular *loa* [spirit] by making drink offerings. In Martinique, members of the African-oriented religion *quimboiserie* also employ alcohol in their transactions with the spirit world.[125] Alcohol offerings ensure the presence at vodou ceremonies of loa, who then offer spiritual guidance and grant requests. Followers make rum offerings to visitant loa and pour libations during animal sacrifices. Métraux recorded a sacrifice in which participants poured rum libations down the throat of a bull prior to slaughtering it.[126] Some loa, usually the more aggressive ones, prefer rum to other alcoholic beverages.[127] According to anthropologist Seth Leacock, aggressive spirits in the African diasporic cults of Brazil have a similar preference.[128] In Haiti, Ogun, the vodou god of war, has a special predilection for rum.[129] During the U.S. occupation of Haiti, Caco resistance fighters poured rum libations to enlist the help of Ogun and the spirits of past military leaders, including Dessalines, against American marines.[130]

In Cuba, followers of *santería* also pour rum libations and make offerings to *orishas* or spirits in public and private ceremonies. As with Kumina in Jamaica, santería originated from Yoruba immigrants who arrived in Cuba in the nineteenth century. Santería devotees maintain a commitment to a particular orisha, who guides them through life and protects them from harm. All orishas require "nourishment," including rum, which they receive from followers during regular ceremonies.[131] Like Ogun in Haitian vodou, Ogou, the aggressive warrior spirit in santería, typically prefers to drink rum.[132]

Spiritual possession also demands the extensive use of alcohol in Haitian vodou, Cuban santería, and other African-oriented religions. Followers of vodou and santería drink and make alcohol offerings to invoke spirits. Vodou devotees, for example, believe they will not be "mounted" by a loa unless they make the proper offerings.[133] Like other mind-altering activities such as fasting, meditating, and going without sleep, drinking enhances the potency of possession. However, spirit possession also has a more practical dimension. Drinking facilitates social interaction and integrates members into the group. Members receive spiritual guidance by making alcohol offerings and pouring libations, which may reduce their social anxiety. By liberating the participant's tongue, alcohol temporarily empowers the possessed. He or she can speak with authority and impunity, thereby identifying solutions to common, everyday problems.[134]

Anthropologist James Schaefer examined the Human Relations Area Files, a database collection of cultural ethnographies, and found drinking to be excessive in societies that fear unpredictable and malicious spirits.[135] Drinking provides drinkers with temporary feelings of power that allow them to confront spiritual and other dangers. If Schaefer is correct, then perhaps followers of obeah, vodou, and santería drink *more* than members of religious groups who have rejected such beliefs. This might explain the temperance ascribed during the slavery period to black Creoles, a group that was probably somewhat skeptical of African-oriented religious beliefs. Schaefer's argument might also help explain the relatively high per capita rum consumption rate in vodouist Haiti.

Despite the rapid pace of social change in the modern Caribbean, African-oriented belief systems and ceremonies involving alcohol persist among other conservative social groups. Members of modern-day maroon societies in Suriname and Jamaica continue to perform rites that rely heavily on the use of rum. Anthropologists Richard and Sally Price have recorded the extensive use of rum at the burial wakes of Saramaka maroons in Suriname.[136] Anthropologist Diane Vernon also describes, among the maroons of Suriname, the use of rum in concoctions that "wash" away evil spirits.[137] In Jamaica, Windward maroons routinely pour rum libations and make offerings of rum to their ancestors.[138]

The ritual use of rum is also found in generalized folk traditions that are not necessarily tied to particular religious rites. Describing a rural folk custom of Jamaica, Beckwith wrote,

> The momentous time in an infant's life arrives on the ninth day after birth, when for the first time he is taken out of doors. During the first nine days the

mother eats only soft food, like arrowroot, bread, and milk. On the ninth day, a bath is prepared for the child, a little rum thrown into it, and each member of the family must throw in a bit of silver "for the eyesight," or "for luck."[139]

Rum was also liberally distributed at Jamaican funerals and mourning ceremonies and, according to Beckwith, gravediggers received their usual allotments of rum.[140] Reverence for ancestors is also expressed in short, generalized rituals. In Barbados, for example, rum shop patrons often pour the first capful of a newly opened bottle of rum on the ground for ancestors. This practice is also widespread at rum shops and households in Guyana and in the western Caribbean island of Providencia.[141] In Montserrat, "the first capful of a new bottle of rum is poured out the window or on the floor, not so much as a sacrifice but as recognition of the jombees' presence and their potential for mischief."[142] Revivalists in Jamaica also pour libations before drinking and, in Haiti, similar practices are accompanied by the saying "pou mo yo" [for the dead].[143]

Conclusion

Since the nineteenth century, Christian missionaries have sought to reduce levels of alcohol use in the Caribbean. The missionary movement's greatest contribution, however, may have simply been to strengthen the resolve of temperate black Creoles. Jamaica, with its large Baptist following and sophisticated free village system, appears to have been the most affected by their work. The availability of land after slave emancipation led to the rise of an independent peasantry that escaped the rum-based-wage and company-store systems of other regions. Liberal attitudes toward alcohol in regions influenced by the Catholic Church, particularly the French Caribbean, fostered higher per capita rum consumption rates. Rum also found a home in the bodies of Asian migrants, who used it to cope with the many anxieties of life in the Caribbean.

Yet, while missionaries and temperance reformers were challenging the meaning and function of rum, rum making was becoming increasingly important to many Caribbean colonies. Slave emancipation raised the cost of sugar production, while competing beet sugar industries in Europe glutted sugar markets and reduced the value of Caribbean cane sugar. In order to survive economic hardship, many sugar planters in the Caribbean increased their production of rum.

CHAPTER 7

Rum and Economic Survival in the Nineteenth and Twentieth Centuries

ESPITE ATTACKS ON ALCOHOL by temperance crusaders and co-lonial administrators, rum making became increasingly important to Caribbean sugar planters in the nineteenth century as a means to escape debt. Competition from newcomers to the world's sugar markets and damage to European wine and brandy industries moved rum to center stage. The rise of free trade in the Atlantic world stimulated the expansion of French and Spanish Caribbean rum making, which, by the end of the nineteenth century, surpassed that of British Caribbean rivals. A growing number of working-class drinkers spurred demand for rum in Europe, Africa, and North America. And experimentation and scientific advances changed rum making from an art into a science. At the start of the twentieth century, metropolitan governments were sufficiently dependent upon colonial Caribbean rum revenues to institute protectionist quotas that brought greater security to rum makers.

However, rum also faced serious challenges. The nineteenth century began as a turbulent time for rum makers, especially in the older British Caribbean colonies. The emergence of new rum-making colonies in the Caribbean and Far East, the growth of North American whiskey drinking, and the rise of European sugar beet industries threatened the economic stability of the Caribbean. The abolition of the Atlantic slave trade and the emancipation of Caribbean slaves led to increasing labor costs and a general decline in production in much of the region. New sugar-making technology decreased the availability of scum and molasses for distilling. The spread of temperance philosophy reduced alcohol consumption throughout much of the western world and, in the early twentieth century, global conflict and state-sanctioned prohibitions against alcohol temporarily closed big markets to Caribbean rum.

The Nineteenth-Century Expansion of Rum Making

The high sucrose content of sugarcane makes it an ideal source for alcohol. As a result, rum making has emerged in nearly every region of the world where sugarcane grows. In the eighteenth century, sugar production began in the Indian Ocean colonies of Madagascar, the Seychelles, Mauritius, and Réunion, and rum distilling soon followed. These were at first small industries catering to local alcohol demands, but in the nineteenth century, these regions exported substantial amounts of rum to India, Australia, and East Africa.[1] In the mid-eighteenth century, Dutch and Chinese sugar planters produced rum, called *arrack*, in Jakarta, the largest city in Indonesia. The name *arrack* was originally used for alcohol made from rice and coconut palm, but it was eventually applied to spirits made from sugarcane juice and molasses.

Sugarcane-based arrack was also produced in colonial India, on the Dutch-controlled island of Ceylon, and in the Portuguese settlements of Goa and Coromandel on the southern coast. William Fitzmaurice, a Jamaican-trained sugar planter, established a sugar factory in Bengal and, in 1793, wrote a treatise on the manufacture of sugar and rum for the British East India Company. The treatise was meant to encourage Jamaican rum-making techniques in India, but Fitzmaurice also described the uniquely Indian production of flavored rum made by adding the juice and skins of peaches, pineapples, mangos, coconuts, and oranges to the fermenting cisterns.[2] Fitzmaurice was an advocate of East Indian rum making, but believed East Indian rum would have difficulty finding a good market because of its "nauseous taste." Apparently, East Indians were not attentive rum makers. Fitzmaurice blamed the poor quality of East Indian rum on the "bad treatment of the materials, neglect of the purity of the distilling utensils, and the great proportion of fermentable and putrid matter acquired in transporting the jaggery [molasses] from one place to the other."[3]

Rum making emerged in other parts of the globe. Sugarcane spread out from the South Pacific 8,000 years ago and returned as an alcoholic beverage in the ships of Captain Cook and other European explorers.[4] At the time of Cook's explorations in the 1770s, Hawaiian islanders used sugarcane only as a "vegetable plant."[5] By the early nineteenth century, however, American firms had built sugar estates in Hawaii that soon began distilling rum. Plantation-based agriculture introduced Pacific islanders, especially Hawaiians, to new work regimens that disrupted traditional social structures. The massive amounts of rum and other European-introduced alcoholic drinks created social problems, including alcoholism, which, as in Carib Indian society, hastened the demise of traditional Hawaiian culture.[6] In 1827, Hawaiian governor Boki sold his sugar factory to a syndicated company that abandoned sugar making for rum distilling. Christian missionaries objected to the distillery and persuaded Queen Kaahumanu to destroy the plantation.[7] In the 1880s, the French Pacific colonies of Tahiti and New Caledonia also produced rum and even managed to export some 20,000 gallons a year to France.[8]

The British settled Australia in 1788, and imported rum immediately became an item of trade with the Australian Aborigine. According to anthropologist Marcia Langton, plying the natives with rum helped British settlers to mask their own struggles and to "seduce" the Aborigines into compliance with British colonial agendas.[9] As in the Caribbean and North America, colonists overstated the drunken behaviors of native peoples and used these racist images to justify British rule. Yet, British military and criminal exiles in Australia also consumed rum excessively. During the early years of settlement, rum often supplemented military and settler wages, and per capita consumption rates sometimes reached more than seven gallons per year.[10] In 1807, the autocratic governor William Bligh, who had achieved fame as the captain of the mutiny-struck *Bounty*, took over command of the Australian colony. As governor of Australia, Bligh immediately placed restrictions on alcohol imports and attempted to ban the use of rum as a work incentive. He outlawed local alcohol production, closed rum shops, and seized distilling equipment. The following year, Bligh was deposed in a nonviolent overthrow of his authority known as the Rum Rebellion. In the mid-nineteenth century, sugar making began in Australia and rum distilling soon followed. By the late 1860s, there were 13 rum distilleries operating in Queensland and, in 1880, they produced nearly 300,000 gallons, mostly for local consumption.[11]

In the early eighteenth century, factors for the Royal African Company proposed the construction of a rum-making sugar plantation in West Africa to help feed the slave trade. However, the plan was never implemented, and little rum was ever produced in the region. Alcohol import revenues were so important to colonial governments in West Africa that officials generally restricted local alcohol production.[12] Even though rum making failed to take hold in West Africa, it flourished in other parts of the continent. In the eighteenth century, sugarcane-based arrack was produced in the Portuguese colony of Mozambique. In the nineteenth century, South Africa emerged as a major rum producer.[13]

Competition in the distilled spirits industries and the growing global demand for alcohol spurred technological advances in rum making. In 1801, Edward Adam introduced the first continuous still, which worked on the principle that, by closely regulating the temperature of the wash in a series of retorts, water and alcohol could be condensed separately, producing a concentrated spirit in a single distillation. In 1813, the Cellier-Blumenthal continuous still improved the continuous distilling process by making a more uniform spirit. The great advantage of the continuous still was that it used much less fuel (usually coal).[14] Fuel costs were always a major consideration for planters in the Caribbean sugar islands, which usually lacked sufficient fuel resources. Other design patents soon followed, and by the second decade of the nineteenth century, there were numerous types of continuous stills all working on the same basic principle. The introduction of the Coffey steam-heated still in the 1830s was a major advance in distilling. Steam heating was advantageous because it heated rapidly, reduced wear and tear of still bodies, and did not char organic matter in the still, which lessened the risk of spoiling the flavor of the spirits.[15]

While continuous stills were popular in Europe, colonial Caribbean distilling practices, particularly in the older Caribbean islands, remained technologically conservative. In 1848, Jamaican and Indian sugar planter Leonard Wray believed that the sugar colonies were not well suited for continuous-type stills.

> Stills of Blumenthal, Lougiers, and Coffey, though very excellent, and no doubt very efficient, are, notwithstanding, much better adapted to European distilleries than for sugar estates. I have seen many of them, as well as modifications of them, working on estates in India and the Straits; but I never knew them to afford satisfaction to their possessors: probably from not having such careful and skillful workmen to entrust them with, as are obtainable in Europe.[16]

Many Caribbean rum makers rejected the new technology and, instead, relied on the common pot still, which, although increasing in capacity, had been the basic distilling apparatus used in the Caribbean since the beginning of the rum industry. Some distillers, especially in the new rum-making colonies, modified their traditional pot stills by attaching the more fuel-efficient continuous patent still heads. These modified common stills were widely used in India and the East Indies. In the Caribbean, they were especially associated with Demerara. Distillers in Demerara simply adapted large common pot stills to the more fuel-efficient patent still head invented by Corty and improved by Shears and Sons. Jamaican distillers were more resistant to change. Wray wrote,

> I entertain a very good opinion of the [modified common stills], and con-
> sider them well adapted to the requirements of a sugar estate. But of all the
> different arrangements, I have never known any to surpass the common still
> and double retorts. As a distilling apparatus particularly suited by its sim-
> plicity, durability, economy, and efficiency to the wants of the planter, I
> consider that it stands unrivaled.[17]

In Jamaica, in 1888, sugar technologists also argued, "nothing is likely to su-
persede the common still and double retorts," and as late as 1944 the central factory at Frome estate produced over 450,000 gallons of rum from its five "pot stills."[18] Although common pot stills required a considerable expense in fuel, they produced an especially "fine" spirit. In fact, traditional pot stills continue to operate in parts of the Caribbean today, including at the River Antoine rum distillery in Grenada.

During the nineteenth century, other changes took place in rum making. Processed strains of yeast were introduced to help ensure proper and com-
plete fermentation. Once again, Jamaican distillers remained conservative. Wray argued vehemently against using processed strains of yeast, which he believed completely altered the character and taste of Jamaican rum.[19] As late as 1887, the director of public gardens and plantations in Jamaica complained that 40 percent of sucrose used in washes was lost due to the planters' resistance to adding commercial yeast strains.[20]

British Caribbean Rum in the Nineteenth Century

At the beginning of the nineteenth century, sugar making was still the domi-
nant economic activity in the British Caribbean. The Haitian Revolution had destroyed the world's leading sugar producer and opened new markets to British Caribbean sugar. War between Britain and France until 1815 also helped reinvigorate British Caribbean sugar production. In addition, new sugarcane-
growing regions emerged in the British Caribbean, which began to chal-
lenge the dominant position of Jamaica in the British sugar and rum markets (Table 7.1).

However, British Caribbean sugar making soon faced serious challenges. Historian Lowell Ragatz argued that, by the late eighteenth century, the profit-

Table 7.1. Annual Average Sugar and Rum Exports to Britain in the 1820s

Colony	Cwt. of sugar	Gallons of rum	Rum : Sugar
Antigua	1,603,239	607,112	0.379
Barbados	2,566,769	13,759	0.005
Berbice	707,845	959,633	1.356
Demerara	6,270,797	12,056,823	1.923
Dominica	452,481	179,784	0.397
Grenada	2,228,472	2,955,180	1.326
Jamaica	13,992,436	29,904,540	2.137
Montserrat	258,285	272,519	1.055
Nevis	490,659	219,718	0.448
St. Kitts	1,578,006	997,093	0.632
St. Lucia	788,988	110,712	0.140
St. Vincent	2,561,498	1,336,040	0.522
Tobago	1,057,477	3,637,709	3.440
Tortola	196,375	19,094	0.097
Trinidad	2,058,341	149,624	0.073

Source: Ragatz, *Statistics*, 18.

ability of British Caribbean sugar was on the decline. A key element of Ragatz's argument is that soil exhaustion had reduced the productivity of sugar estates, especially in older islands like Barbados.[21] By the early nineteenth century, competition from sugar producers in new and fertile cane-growing regions, such as Mauritius and Demerara, threatened to glut sugar markets. Moreover, poor management by corrupt plantation managers on absentee sugar estates led to chronic indebtedness. According to Ragatz, the British Caribbean sugar planters' insistence on one crop and their unwillingness to improve production methods using new technology were symptoms of this decline. Historian Eric Williams corroborates Ragatz' decline thesis, positing that the decreasing profitability of British Caribbean sugar estates led to the British abolition of the slave trade in 1807 and to the eventual emancipation of British Caribbean slaves in 1834.[22]

More recent analyses of the profitability of British Caribbean sugar estates have challenged many tenets of the decline thesis. Historian J. R. Ward argues that sugar estates were profitable throughout the slavery period and that decline theories are "pessimistic."[23] Ward shows that profits from British Caribbean sugar plantations hovered around 10 percent in the first two decades of the nineteenth century and around 7 percent for the last years of slavery. Historian Seymour Drescher argues that the abolition of the slave trade hastened the decline of British Caribbean sugar, not the other way around. According to Drescher, abolition and emancipation decreased the availability of a steady and stable labor force, which resulted in increased labor costs.[24] Jamaica fared especially badly due to the large amount of land available to peasants. After emancipation, the rate of Jamaican sugar production declined sharply, and by the 1840s, exports had dropped by two-thirds. Moreover, production costs in Jamaica nearly tripled after emancipation.[25] Similar increases in production costs occurred in much of the British Caribbean. In an effort to stabilize labor supplies, parliament encouraged the migration of indentured Asian workers, mainly from India and China, to the sugar plantations of the British Caribbean.

The only real exception to the decline was in some of the older sugar islands like Barbados, St. Kitts, and Antigua. The lack of available land in these colonies prohibited the rise of a peasantry. Sugar production in Barbados actually increased for several years after emancipation.[26] By the mid-nineteenth century, although the newer sugar colonies of Trinidad and Demerara managed to expand output, free trade and growing competition from new sugar-producing areas accelerated the decline of sugar's profitability.

In the early nineteenth century, the protected home market for British Caribbean sugar was under attack. In 1825, the import duty on sugar from the British Indian Ocean colony of Mauritius was lowered and essentially made equal to that of British Caribbean sugar. In 1835, Indian sugar was also admitted under equal conditions. While British Caribbean planters may have felt some pressure from the equal status accorded to British colonial sugar producers in the east, the admission of foreign sugar was a more serious threat. In 1844, foreign sugar produced in nonslaveholding colonies was admitted into the British market. In 1846, parliament passed the Sugar Duties Act, which began the process of admitting all foreign sugar on an equal basis. This process was completed in 1854. In an effort to protect British sugar refiners, the act equalized duties only on muscavado, but, by 1874, all sugars freely entered Britain.[27] In Jamaica, Christian missionary John Bigelow wrote,

> The abolition of slavery they aver, caused the price of labor to advance beyond the point of successful competition with countries where slavery

was tolerated. It became impossible, as they claimed, for a Jamaica planter, with free labor, to raise sugar for anything like the prices at which it was sold by the planters of Cuba, Brazil, and Porto Rico.[28]

However, the greatest challenge to Caribbean sugar producers in the nineteenth century was the rise of beet sugar industries in Europe. Germany, Austria, and France became major beet sugar producers, in part, to reduce their reliance on foreign imports of Caribbean cane sugar. Sugar beet industries in Europe, especially in France, were protected and received government subsidies. Until the mid-nineteenth century, sugarcane was the basis for world sugar. By 1860, 20 percent of world sugar production came from sugar beet and, in 1890, that figure had jumped to 59 percent: "From being a net importer of sugar, Europe became an exporter."[29] The Sugar Duties Act of 1846 allowed beet sugar to freely enter the British market, which was soon saturated. The United States and Canada became the only significant markets for Caribbean cane sugar.

Parliament attempted to compensate British Caribbean sugar producers for the loss of their protected home market. Previously prohibited, the use of sugar in British distilleries was now permitted.[30] Before this time, landed interests had proven to be so strong that the admission of sugar into British distilleries was allowed only in times of crisis, such as in the period 1799–1813 when war with France and poor harvests led to severe grain shortages.[31]

Duties on rum were also lowered. In the early nineteenth century, parliament imposed a series of taxes on rum to raise national revenues for its war against France. The customs and excise payable on rum consumed in Britain rose from 9s.3/4d. per gallon in 1803 to 13s.6 1/2d. per gallon in 1806. In Ireland, customs and excise duties jumped from 6s.11 1/4d. to 8s.6 1/4d. per gallon.[32] Although levied to help pay for the war effort, the oppressive taxes were only slightly reduced after the conflict. In 1825, parliament sought to help the British Caribbean sugar planters—and probably to compensate them for the equalization of import duties on sugar from Mauritius—by lowering the duties on rum. The plan lowered duties to 8s.6d. per gallon, but the duty on gin, which had been increased in the eighteenth century in order to curb drunkenness, was also reduced and made equal to that of rum. According to one frustrated planter, the reduction of the gin duty was counterintuitive because gin had been "more destructive to the morals of the lower class" in Britain "than all other causes combined." However, economic concerns, rather than the fear of moral decay, fueled the debate:

by these reductions in duty on rum and gin, the planter is placed in the situation of a general commanding an army in the presence of a much superior enemy and, who received enforcement of 10,000 men, at the very moment the enemy were reinforced with 15,000; for they are comparatively worse off with the reduced duty of 8s. 6d. than they were with the duty of 11s. 9d.[33]

The loss of the secure British sugar market led to the further reduction of rum duties "to put the colonial distiller, it was said, on a par with the home distiller."[34] Parliament, whether it intended to or not, was pushing the British Caribbean toward rum production. Export statistics from the mid-nineteenth century reveal that many sugar planters, in order to survive the economic damage caused by the loss of their protected home market for sugar, adopted production strategies that emphasized rum making.

In Jamaica, sugar production declined sharply after emancipation, and many planters switched to rum making, especially in the northwest region of the colony.[35] As early as the mid-eighteenth century, concentrated Jamaican rum had achieved a good reputation and sold well on the British market. While exports of Jamaican rum declined from 3.8 million gallons in 1830 to 1.5 million gallons a decade later, rum exports, unlike sugar, quickly stabilized and remained steady until the end of World War I.[36] Sugar planters simply varied the amount of sucrose used on the plantation to produce more rum than sugar. Jamaican missionary W. J. Gardner wrote,

> The produce of rum depends to a great extent on that of sugar, though far more puncheons have of late been made in proportion to hogsheads of sugar than was formerly the case. Years can be pointed out, as for example, 1797, 1802, 1822, and 1836, and some later ones, when only one puncheon was exported for every three hogsheads of sugar; but as a fair general statement, an average of two puncheons for five hogsheads may be taken. Since 1854, the average is as one to two.[37]

Jamaicans increased the ratio of rum to sugar exports throughout the nineteenth century in order to survive falling sugar prices and benefit from the improved rum duties. One of the great advantages of rum was that, unlike sugar, it could be stored for many years and sold when prices were high. Price determined the proportion of rum exported, and the relationship between price and export was fairly linear. During the 1830s, when a gallon of rum averaged 9 percent of the price of a cwt. of sugar, the export ratio was 2.7 gallons of rum per cwt. of sugar. In the 1890s, when the price of a gallon of rum averaged 18 percent of the price of a cwt. of sugar, the export ratio jumped to 5.3 gallons of rum per cwt. of sugar.[38] Sharp increases in rum exports in particular years correspond to high rum prices. In 1876, the price of a gallon of rum was 14 percent the price of a cwt. of sugar, and the export ratio was 7.5 gallons of rum per cwt. of sugar. In 1913, when the value of rum reached its peak relative to sugar, and a gallon of rum represented 37 percent the price of a cwt. of sugar, the rum to sugar export ratio was 11.7 gallons per cwt. The relationship between rum exports and price ratios reveals that Jamaican sugar planters were able to adapt quickly to changing price ratios. When sugar prices were low they channeled sucrose to their distilleries rather than their sugar cauldrons. They stockpiled rum and, when rum prices were high, released it in bulk on the British market. They were practical business managers who did not simply wait for a return to the glory days of sugar making.

In the first three decades of the nineteenth century, the value of rum represented 14 to 17 percent of Jamaican exports.[39] Rum revenues remained high throughout the nineteenth century. In the period 1878–1887, rum represented an average of 16 percent of the value of Jamaican exports. In 1887, Jamaican rum exports were worth 20 percent of the island's total export, and rum brought in more than sugar. By the early twentieth century, Jamaica had a more diversified economy and the increasing export of fruit, cocoa, and pimento, as well as coffee, which had been a valuable export commodity since the eighteenth century, reduced the relative value of rum. Between 1901 and 1910, rum represented an average of only about 7 percent of the value of Jamaica's total export trade. Yet, despite the relative decline in rum revenues, the value of rum exports usually exceeded those of sugar.[40]

In the nineteenth century, Trinidad, Demerara, Berbice, Tobago, and the ceded islands became strong competitors in the British rum market. By 1813, Demerara was exporting over one million gallons of rum annually to Britain, making it the world's second largest exporter of rum.[41] A decade later, Demeraran rum captured more than 20 percent of the British rum market.[42] In 1799, Trinidad exported 170,671 gallons of rum, and by 1819 exports reached more than 500,000 gallons.[43] Between 1827 and 1829, rum makers in St. Vincent produced an annual average of more than 700,000 gallons of rum. In these three years, even the small island of Bequia, in the St. Vincent Grenadines, managed to produce nearly 20,000 gallons per year. St. Vincent sugar planter Charles Shephard recorded the island's rum production and showed the variability of rum to sugar ratios on different estates.[44] Between 1827 and

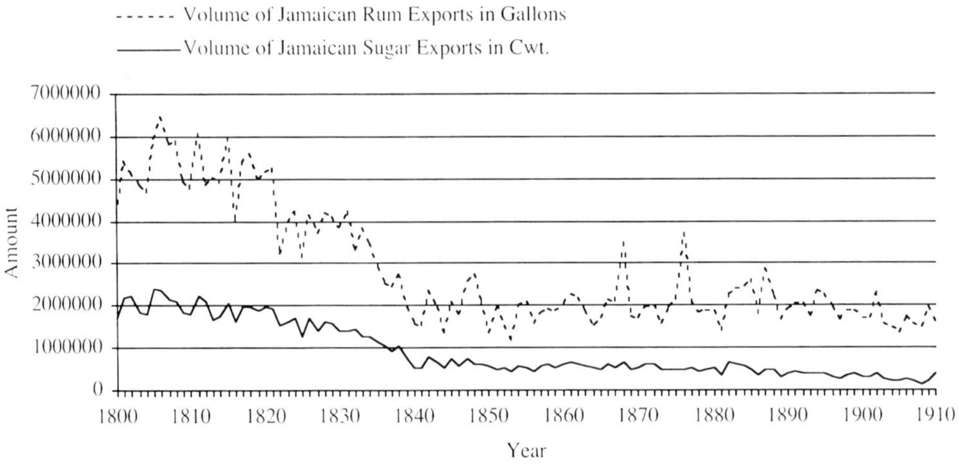

Figure 7.1. Rum and sugar exports from Jamaica. Graph by author. *Sources*: 1800–1833 from Ragatz, *Statistics*, 23; 1833–1887 from Eisner, *Jamaica*, 240–45; 1888–1910 from Jamaica, *Handbook* (1911).

1829, while a few estates produced no rum, others, like Rivulet plantation, St. George's parish, produced an enormous 9.5 gallons of rum per cwt. of sugar. In 1827, nearly every sugar estate produced some rum, and the average ratio for all rum-making plantations in St. Vincent was 2.7 gallons per cwt. of sugar.

In contrast to the success of rum making in Jamaica, Demerara, and some of the newer sugar colonies, rum makers in many of the older British Caribbean colonies suffered. British Caribbean rum began the nineteenth century largely excluded from the profitable U.S. market. The American Revolution and the reformed Navigation Acts that followed in 1783 greatly restricted the level of trade between the United States and the British Caribbean. Planters lost both an outlet for their rum and immediate access to plantation supplies. Although British Canada provided some relief, it could not supply enough plantation provisions or purchase enough rum. According to historian Selwyn Carrington, trade restrictions led colonial Caribbean governors to implement a policy of "emergency need proclamations," which temporarily lifted trade restrictions with the United States and helped reestablish some sense of trade security.[45] Rum was among the products admitted in the emergency trade.

However, British Caribbean rum also had to contend with the rise of U.S. nationalism. After the Revolution, Americans sought self-sufficiency and equated British Caribbean rum and molasses with colonial domination. According to historian William Rorabaugh, to buy rum from the British Carib-

bean "was foolish and unpatriotic because it was harmful to American distillers and their workmen."[46] Increasing access to cheap western grain provided
Americans with cheap American whiskey. In 1789, with strong support from
the rum-making New England states, the U.S. Congress approved an excise
tax on domestic whiskey. However, officials had difficulty collecting the tax
and faced widespread protest from western grain farmers. In 1794, dissent
from Pennsylvania farmers erupted in violent protests known as the Whiskey
Rebellion. The shift to whiskey drinking increased in 1802 when Congress repealed the whiskey tax, which lowered the cost of whiskey. Imported rum and
molasses still paid high import duties. Whiskey production also increased
considerably after 1815 when peace in Europe closed European markets to
American grain and generated a surplus of grain for distillation.[47] The high
cost of plantation goods, coupled with the Americans' increasing consumption
of whiskey, therefore, reduced the significance of British Caribbean rum in the
U.S. market. Jamaican sugar planter Bryan Edwards estimated that in 1774, Jamaica exported nearly one million gallons of rum to North America, primarily
to the thirteen continental colonies.[48] Yet, between 1808 and 1811, Jamaican
rum exports to the United States dropped to an annual average of only about
500,000 gallons.[49]

The American Revolution devastated Barbados rum making, which never
rebounded to its mid-eighteenth-century zenith. The trade restrictions that
followed the conflict and the growth of American whiskey drinking removed
the largest market for Barbados rum. Production accounts from Codrington
and Turner's Hall estates in Barbados show that the decline lasted well into the
nineteenth century (Figure 7.2). In fact, in the early nineteenth century, even
smaller sugar islands, like Montserrat and Nevis, frequently exported more
rum than Barbados. In the early 1820s, Britain usually imported less than one
thousand gallons of Barbados rum per year. Although trade between the
United States and Barbados resumed, the great American drinking binge was
on the decline after the 1830s.[50]

The decay of the Barbados rum industry is most evident in the rise of molasses exports, the basic ingredient in rum making. In the eighteenth century,
Barbados exported almost no molasses, and until the nineteenth century,
Codrington and Turner's Hall estates rarely mentioned molasses sales. However, between 1841 and 1845, while Barbados exported almost no rum, a large
amount of molasses was loaded onto U.S. ships and carried back to home distillers.[51] In those five years, Barbados molasses exports were worth £165,724,
while rum exports were worth a mere £860, one half of 1 percent the value of

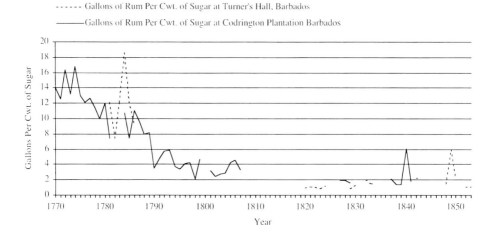

- - - - - - Gallons of Rum Per Cwt. of Sugar at Turner's Hall, Barbados

———— Gallons of Rum Per Cwt. of Sugar at Codrington Plantation Barbados

Figure 7.2. Rum production at the Codrington and Turner's Hall estates in Barbados. Graph by author. *Sources*: Barbados Department of Archives, Codrington plantation records and FitzHerbert Papers.

molasses. In 1843, the value of pickle exports was six times greater than that of rum exports. In the late nineteenth century, when rum exports increased throughout much of the British Caribbean, Barbadian rum continued to struggle. In 1864, Barbados exported 42,000 gallons; a decade later, only 20,000 gallons; and in 1876, less than 3,000 gallons.[52] At the height of the British Caribbean rum trade in the 1890s, Barbados produced an annual average of 550,000 gallons of rum, but all of it was consumed locally.[53]

Emancipation and the loss of a protected home market for sugar depressed the overall levels of British Caribbean rum production. Britain's efforts to bolster British Caribbean sugar plantations through the reduction of rum duties helped stabilize rum exports in the mid-nineteenth century, but despite favorable policy toward rum, nineteenth-century exports stagnated, and British Caribbean sugar estates that had once produced huge amounts of rum struggled to remain solvent. This trend occurred in many parts of the British Caribbean. For example, rum making in Tobago intensified at the end of the eighteenth century, and between 1805 and 1809, Tobago exported an average of more than 800,000 gallons of rum per year. In the early nineteenth century, Tobago became a major rum-making colony. After emancipation, Tobago's rum exports, like those of Jamaica, immediately fell and then stabilized (Figure 7.3).

While rum exports in most of the British Caribbean suffered, Demerara and

Jamaica emerged as major rum-making colonies. In 1876, an international exhibition in Philadelphia celebrated the high quality of Jamaican rum. Because of its distinctive taste, Jamaican rum was widely sought after in Germany, where it was used to adulterate spirits made from German beet sugar.[54] Rum exports from Demerara soon challenged the dominant position of Jamaica, however. In 1859, Britain imported about 8.4 million gallons of rum, 40 percent of which came from Demerara. Jamaica and the other British Caribbean colonies provided another 40 percent, while rum from Mauritius and the Spanish Caribbean represented the remaining 20 percent.[55] By the 1890s, Demerara annually exported an average of more than 4.2 million gallons of rum, a third more than Jamaica. Unlike Jamaican rum, Demerara's inferior product was made from poorer quality vacuum-pan molasses in modified pot stills.[56] What made it appealing was that it was cheap and exported in bulk. Moreover, Demerara, as a Crown colony, received favorable status in the British rum market. The British Indian Ocean colony of Mauritius also emerged as a major producer, surpassing rum makers in the older Caribbean islands. In the 1890s, Mauritius vied for a top spot in the world rum trade, exporting an average of nearly one million gallons per year.[57]

Britain was the main market for British Caribbean rum, but it also reexported much of its imports. In 1859, Britain imported about 8.4 million gallons of rum and reexported about 2.3 million gallons. Australia, Germany, Italy, and

Table 7.2. British Caribbean Rum Exports to Britain in 1776, 1826, and 1876 in Gallons

Colony	1776	1826	1876
Antigua	114,325	64,447	21,357
Barbados	196,419	2,064	2,638
Demerara	—	837,464	3,000,000
Dominica	74,955	7,007	18,912
Grenada	292,952	170,042	85,775
Jamaica	2,233,074	2,283,784	3,703,000
St. Kitts	151,254	73,029	117,467
St. Vincent	66,656	55,313	161,290
Trinidad	—	17,382	18,167

Sources: 1776 and 1826 from Ragatz, *Statistics*, 17–18; 1876 from Kervégant, *Rhums*, 24, 478; Jamaica 1876 from Eisner, *Jamaica*, 240–45.

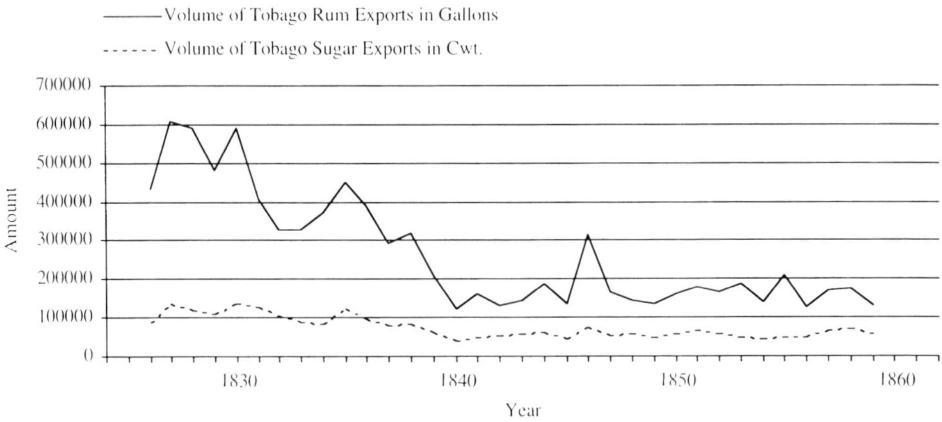

Figure 7.3. Rum and sugar exports from Tobago. Graph by author. *Source*: Woodcock, *History of Tobago*, appendix.

Africa were the primary destinations. In 1900, the per capita consumption of rum in Britain was only about one-tenth of a gallon.[58] Gin, whiskey, and brandy remained the most important spirits to British consumers.

The Rise of French Caribbean Rum in the Nineteenth Century

In the late eighteenth century, France lifted restrictions on French Caribbean rum imports, and French Caribbean rum makers were confident that they could penetrate the huge French alcohol market. In addition, the American Revolution legally opened a potentially large rum market. The increasing number of late-eighteenth-century treatises on French Caribbean rum making highlights their growing optimism.

French Caribbean planters, however, also faced serious challenges. The nineteenth century began with the loss of St. Domingue, the largest sugar-producing colony in the Caribbean. Efforts to revive the Haitian sugar industry after the revolution failed, and sugar production declined dramatically. Moreover, war with Britain interrupted French colonial trade. After the French abolition of slavery in 1848, many former slaves rejected plantation work and became peasant farmers, especially in Guadeloupe, which had plenty of uncultivated land.[59] The rise of subsidized beet sugar industries in France also hurt French Caribbean sugar producers. Overall, the profitability of French

Caribbean sugar making fell and, like their British Caribbean counterparts, many French planters turned to rum making to escape economic collapse.

Early French Caribbean rum making struggled. In 1786, an anonymous writer in St. Domingue wrote that the biggest problem facing French Caribbean rum was that it was "repugnant to foreigners."[60] Sugar planter J. F. Charpentier de Cossigny sought to explain the "disagreeable" taste of French Caribbean rum and, like other writers, blamed substandard distilling equipment and improper wash settings.[61] French Caribbean planters published detailed reports that advised how to rectify rum-making techniques and produce quality rum like that made in Jamaica.[62]

In 1803, Napoleon lifted the remaining restrictions on rum imports to bolster French Caribbean economies after years of war and economic instability. But due to its poor reputation, not much changed for French Caribbean rum makers. During the first half of the nineteenth century, Martinique and Guadeloupe produced about 250,000 gallons of rum per year, but exported very little. In 1819, for example, Martinique exported less than 100,000 gallons, and of that shipped to France, most was probably consumed in the port towns of Marseille, Nantes, Le Havre, and Bordeaux, the main ports for French Caribbean produce.[63] Some rum was reexported to Africa, but the loss of St. Domingue and Britain's determination after 1807 to abolish the slave trade meant a decrease in slave trafficking and, therefore, a fall in French Caribbean rum reexports to Africa. North Americans also thought French Caribbean rum had a particularly bad taste and preferred to import French Caribbean molasses for their own distilleries. The switch to whiskey drinking also reduced the demand for rum in North America.

In 1820, the French government imposed an import tax of 10 francs per hectoliter on French Caribbean rum, but tried to compensate for the tax by prohibiting the import of foreign rum.[64] In 1820, Martinique exported only 56,301 gallons of rum and, in 1824, Martinique sugar planter Pierre Dessalles complained that his rum sold poorly and that it would be "difficult to find anyone paying even 5 francs for tafia."[65] In 1826, Martinique had 84 distilleries, one-third the number that existed 40 years earlier.[66] In the mid-1830s, Martinique and Guadeloupe produced an average of about 400,000 to 500,000 gallons of rum per year, but almost all of it was consumed locally.[67] In 1833, France raised the import duty on rum to 20 francs per hectoliter, and in 1835 readmitted imports of foreign rum, but at a very high tax of 200 francs per hectoliter. Rum remained a marginal commodity and, in 1840, Martinique exported only about 130,000 gallons.[68]

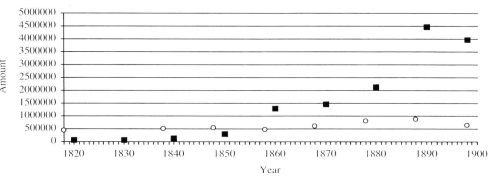

Figure 7.4. Rum and sugar exports from Martinique in the nineteenth century. Graph by author. *Source*: Josa, *Les industries*, 152–53.

Although sugar production virtually vanished in Haiti, cane cultivation did not, and the demise of Haitian sugar making was a boon for local rum makers and consumers. In the 1820s, Charles Mackenzie, British consul-general in Haiti, reported, "The quantity of rum exported has always been small, and was confined to Christophe's reign. At present, all that is made is consumed in the country."[69] Mackenzie did not list rum among the major exports, except at the port of Cape Haitian, where, between 1807 and 1820, exports averaged only 2,300 gallons per year.[70] Rum exports were still weak in the mid-nineteenth century. In 1862, for example, Spanish consul-general to Haiti Mariano Alvarez reported

> killings and woundings are generally the result of immoderate abuse of strong liquor, of which they [Haitians] consume a lot. Since the cessation of sugar making, that of syrup has increased, which they turn into tafia or rum. This drink and others imported by foreign merchants have considerably increased the vice of drunkenness that regrettably grows day by day throughout the whole of the Americas.[71]

Coincidentally, this report was written the same year that the world-famous Barbancourt distillery in Haiti began operations. In the 1890s, Haiti was one of the largest rum producers in the Caribbean. Sugar technologist M.E.-A. Pairault estimated that Haitians produced an annual average of more than nine million gallons of rum, tafia, and the low-alcohol-content clarin. However, Haiti exported no rum, and the entire production was consumed locally.[72]

In the mid-nineteenth century, several events helped thrust French Caribbean rum into the spotlight. Sugar planters in Martinique and Guadeloupe benefited from two devastating blights on the vineyards of France. In the 1850s, European vineyards faced a species of fungus known as *Oïdium tuckerii*. The *Oïdium*, which probably originated from the introduction of North American grapevines into Europe, severely damaged European viticulture. French wine production fell from an annual average of more than 1.1 billion gallons in the 1840s to only 290 million gallons in 1854. Because American grape vines were resistant to attack by *Oïdium*, many wine makers imported and cultivated American vines to save their operations. Although devastating, the *Oïdium* crisis was largely over in the early 1860s.[73]

Unfortunately however, the *Oïdium*-resistant American vines introduced an aphid known as the *phylloxera*. In the 1860s, the aphid *phylloxera* began destroying vineyards throughout Europe. It hit especially hard in France. French wine production fell from 2.2 billion gallons in 1875 to only 618 million gallons in 1889. The French government offered 300,000 francs to anyone who could discover a way to combat the pest. In the 1890s, viticulturists reluctantly decided to graft French vines onto more resistant American vines. This process continued well into the twentieth century, during which time French viticulture suffered.

The *Oïdium* and *phylloxera* attacks were turning points for French Caribbean rum makers. In 1854, Napoleon III suspended duties on French Caribbean rum imports in order to replenish alcohol supplies lost to the *Oïdium*. The move helped introduce rum to the French public on a wider scale. Between 1854 and 1857, France imported more than one million gallons of French colonial rum.[74] Following the military tradition of alcohol rationing, much of this rum was sent to French troops serving in the Crimea.[75] In the 1860s, the *Oïdium* crisis subsided, and rum imports fell to about 200,000 gallons per year as the availability of wine and brandy increased. The *phylloxera*, however, was much more destructive to French wine and brandy makers. In the 1880s, rum imports jumped to more than four million gallons. In 1896, at the height of the *phylloxera* crisis, France imported more than 6.3 million gallons of spirits, most of which was French colonial rum. Martinique provided the largest share, about 4.5 million gallons.[76]

Signs of the increasing importance of French Caribbean rum were evident in the decreasing exports of molasses. In 1819, Martinique exported 1.6 million gallons of molasses and only about 100,000 gallons of rum. Conversely, in 1884, Martinique exported only 15,423 gallons of molasses and 4.6 million gal-

Table 7.3. Rum and Molasses Exports from Martinique
in the Nineteenth Century in Gallons

Year	Rum	Molasses
1820	56,314	1,938,610
1830	64,629	1,226,833
1840	131,596	592,204
1846	341,739	704,046
1850	284,691	1,588
1860	1,305,877	19,069
1870	1,464,735	72,472
1880	2,125,324	7,581
1884	4,656,476	15,423
1890	4,467,507	402
1898	3,964,875	3,379

Source: Josa, *Les industries*, 152.

lons of rum.[77] In the 1890s, Martinique exported an annual average of more than 4.5 million gallons of rum. Martinican rum exports surpassed those of all other Caribbean colonies, including Demerara and Jamaica. Martinicans consumed another 800,000 gallons of rum per year, making it one of the top rum producers in the Caribbean. Needless to say, exports of raw molasses essentially ceased. French Caribbean rum's success was not confined to Martinique. In the 1890s, Guadeloupe annually produced 1.5 million gallons, more than half of which was consumed locally. The French Indian Ocean colony of Réunion also produced more than 600,000 gallons of rum per year and exported more than two-thirds of its produce. French Guiana supplied an additional 70,000 gallons per year.[78] In the 1890s, France was the main destination for French colonial rum.

In 1865, the rate of per capita alcohol consumption in Paris was 59 gallons of wine, 21 gallons of beer, and 3 gallons of spirits.[79] The decline in southern European viticulture benefited a variety of other alcohol producers. Wine makers in Algeria, less severely hit by the *phylloxera*, helped fill the void in European wine markets. Beer and cider production in Europe also increased.[80] *Absinthe*, made from wormwood, became especially popular among Parisian artists and the bourgeois elite. The distillation of beet sugar molasses in France also helped meet alcohol demands. By the end of the nineteenth century, rum was added to the list of alcoholic beverages typically found at cafés in France.[81] In the 1890s, France was importing more than five million gallons of rum per year from Martinique, Guadeloupe, and Réunion. Due to the ravages of the *phyllox-era*, rum from Jamaica, Demerara, and other British colonies occasionally contributed another two million gallons per year.[82] Some of it was reexported to northern Europe and Africa, but the majority remained in France.[83] At the end of the nineteenth century, France was importing as much, if not more, rum as Britain.

Revenues from rum helped stabilize the French Caribbean economy and save it from collapse after the drop in world sugar prices. Rum also kept many sugar estates solvent. The Martinican capital of St. Pierre was known as the rum capital of the world, and it was one of the wealthiest ports in the Caribbean. Between 1898 and 1900, revenues from rum exports were worth more than 25 million francs, and rum represented more than 40 percent of the value of rum and sugar exports.[84]

In the early nineteenth century, French Caribbean rum makers continued to rely on inferior distilling techniques, but, by the mid-nineteenth century, they were producing quality rum equal to that found in the British Caribbean. In

Table 7.4. Rum Exported and Produced in the 1890s in Gallons

Country	Production	Exportation
Haiti	9,107,722	0
Martinique	5,326,350	4,533,748
Demerara	4,384,134	4,224,821
Jamaica	3,458,828	2,798,326
Dominican Republic	3,035,907	0
Guadeloupe	1,555,393	762,791
Mauritius	1,159,975	856,132
Réunion	1,096,697	436,196
Barbados	554,822	0
Trinidad	467,315	142,720
St. Croix	241,383	96,553
St. Lucia	204,636	68,211
Suriname	179,232	139,602
French Guiana	38,309	0

Source: Pairault, *Le rhum*, 13–14.

1855, Martinican rum did exceptionally well at an international competition, which helped boost its reputation. The late start of French Caribbean rum making probably made French Caribbean distillers less prone to conservatism.[85] In the mid-nineteenth century, a wide variety of still types operated in Martinique, and although many plantations continued to use traditional pot stills—often referred to as "Père Labat–type stills" after the missionary who first described them at the end of the seventeenth century—some planters employed modified pot stills with continuous still heads.[86] Unlike their British Caribbean counterparts, the French also frequently employed continuous stills. Although pot stills were common on sugar plantations, the switch to centralized sugar factories in the mid-nineteenth century led to the rise of large industrial distilleries, especially in the Martinican port of St. Pierre.[87] French Caribbean rum makers also appear to have been more inclined than their Jamaican counterparts to experiment with processed strains of yeast.[88]

Planters and colonial officials distinguished between *rhum agricole*, made from pure sugarcane juice on sugar plantations, and *rhum industriel*, made from molasses in big urban distilleries. Plantation distilleries could produce about 130 gallons of rum per day, while large urban distilleries could produce ten times that amount. Many considered rhum agricole, such as that produced at Trois Rivières estate in Martinique, a particularly fine spirit due to the heavy use of pure cane juice and the care that went into its production.[89] The practice of aging the product in oak barrels may have also been a defining feature of rhum agricole.[90] However, by the 1890s, large urban distilleries in St. Pierre came to dominate rum making, and huge amounts of molasses were imported from other parts of the Caribbean, including Guadeloupe and French Guiana, to feed the distilleries.[91]

Aguardiente in the Nineteenth Century

In the seventeenth century, Spanish Caribbean rum making was outlawed. A few clandestine distillers produced rum for local consumption, and small farmers and slaves produced fermented guarapo. In the late eighteenth century, Spanish officials began lifting sanctions against Spanish Caribbean rum. Sugar planters in Cuba, Puerto Rico, Venezuela, and Santo Domingo benefited from a variety of global and regional events. The American Revolution and subsequent restrictions on trade between the United States and the British Caribbean opened new markets to Spanish Caribbean rum makers. In the 1790s, the Haitian Revolution devastated sugar making in France's largest colony and left a huge void in world markets for Spanish Caribbean sugar planters to fill. Cuba emerged as especially strong. Between 1789 and 1817, restrictions on Cuba's trade with foreigners were progressively eliminated, and the increase in Cuban sugar making provided more raw materials for distilling. By 1830, Cuba was the world's leading sugar producer, and by the end of the nineteenth century, Cuba was one of the largest rum producers.

However, Spanish Caribbean rum makers also faced serious challenges. Early sanctions against rum making meant that *criollos* had little experience with advanced distilling techniques and, as a result, Spanish Caribbean rum making remained an immature industry. In the 1790s, a large number of St. Domingue planters fled to Cuba bringing with them slaves, rum-making equipment, and capital. In light of the poor reputation of French Caribbean rum in this period, migrants from St. Domingue probably did little to improve Cuban rum-making practices. French colonial migrants from Trinidad and Louisiana, as well as those from metropolitan France, probably also sparked interest in Cuban rum making, but, in order to compete on the world market, Cuban rum makers would be forced to rectify their product. In the first decade of the nineteenth century, Cubans began to make distinctions between *ag-uardiente de caña* and *ron*. Aguardiente appears to have been equivalent to French Caribbean rhum industriel, while ron was equal to French Caribbean rhum agricole. However, Spanish Caribbean distillers seem to have placed greater emphasis on the aging process, rather than, like the French, on the in-gredients. Ron was aged in oak barrels, while aguardiente was not. In addition, while rhum agricole was produced on sugar estates in the French Caribbean, ron was typically produced in large urban distilleries, suggesting a greater use of molasses than pure cane juice. Cuban rum makers made significant progress in the nineteenth century, but the war for Cuban independence (1895–1898), and the American occupation that followed, disrupted further gains in Cuban rum making.

Despite the initial gains made during the American and Haitian revolu-tions, Cuban rum exports fell dramatically after 1815. Peace in Europe closed an important outlet for American grain, and the surplus was made into cheap whiskey, which glutted the American market.[92] Also, better trade relations be-tween the United States and Britain opened American ports to British Carib-bean produce, including rum. Although there was a slow and steady increase, Cuban rum exports hovered around 500,000 gallons per year for the next three decades.

Cuban rum exports jumped in 1854, the year that Britain opened its ports to

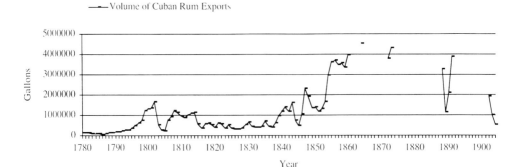

Figure 7.5. Rum exports from Cuba. Graph by author. *Sources*: 1780–1891 from Moreno Fraginals, *El ingenio*, III:43–46; 1902–1904 from Cuba, *Resumenes estadisticos selecciona-dos*, 56.

foreign produce, including commodities made in slave-holding regions. This was also the worst year of the *Oïdium* crisis, which devastated European vine-yards, including those in Spain. In the 1850s, Cuban rum exports averaged nearly three million gallons per year. In 1860, Britain equalized foreign rum import duties putting Cuban rum makers on par with those in the British Car-ibbean.[93] The following year, France also reduced import duties on foreign rum to help ease the effects of the *Oïdium* blight.[94] The growth of U.S. sugar syndicates in Cuba had a positive impact on the level of rum production, which became especially important during the U.S. Civil War. In 1864, Cuban rum exports reached record levels of more than 4.5 million gallons. The Franco-Prussian War (1870–1871) may have also contributed to the rise in exports.[95] Although export statistics are incomplete for the second half of the nineteenth century, it appears that Cuban rum exports remained high during the *phyllox-era* epidemic, which was as ruinous to Spanish vineyards as it was to those in France. By the end of the nineteenth century, Cuba exported rum to the United States, Spain, Germany, and Britain, challenging Demerara for second place, behind Martinique, in the world rum market.[96]

Sugar, however, was still the dominant industry in Cuba. By 1829, Cuban sugar makers outproduced all of the British Caribbean colonies combined. The rise of European sugar beet industries had less of an impact on Cuban sugar planters than on their British and French counterparts. Beet sugar re-duced the European market to Caribbean cane sugar, but the U.S. market, which lacked substantial cane or beet sugar industries, remained open. By the 1860s, 60 percent of sugar consumed in the United States came from Cuba.

Much of the remaining 40 percent came from Puerto Rico and the Dominican Republic.[97]

In the mid-nineteenth century, technological change propelled Cuban sugar making forward. Railways, steamships, and telegraphs improved the infrastructure for sugar planters. New central factories emerged on fertile lands. Entrepreneurial criollos installed new machinery, such as steam-driven grinders, vacuum pans, and centrifuges, which extracted twice as much sugar as the traditional muscavado method. In 1860, 70 percent of Cuban sugar mills were steam powered, and there were 66 large mills using the vacuum pan process. That number continued to grow in the late nineteenth century.[98]

As a result, rum in Cuba never achieved the dominant economic position that it did in Martinique, Demerara, and Jamaica, and Cuban sugar planters relied less on rum revenues than their British and French Caribbean counterparts. Throughout the nineteenth century, Cuban rum exports remained well below one gallon per cwt. of sugar. In 1837, rum exports from Cuba were valued at less than .05 percent of major exports and, in 1852, rum exports from Cuba were worth only 1 percent of revenues from sugar, molasses, and rum.[99] According to Caribbean traveler Alexander Humboldt, some large estates with distilleries produced two gallons of rum per cwt. of sugar, and rum sales brought in as much as 26 percent of revenues from sugar and rum. Yet, by the late 1850s, sugar yields began to increase, reducing the value of rum to these large estates.[100] Moreover, while planters in Jamaica and Martinique distilled their molasses, Cubans were still exporting huge amounts of raw molasses. In 1864, Cuba exported more than 35 million gallons of molasses and only 4.5 million gallons of rum. In the last quarter of the nineteenth century, sugar, molasses, and tobacco represented 95 percent of the value of all Cuban exports to the United States, the largest market for Cuban goods. Rum and other goods accounted for the remaining 5 percent.[101]

One reason for the relatively low level of rum exports may have been the advanced methods of sugar production in Cuba. The high-tech vacuum pans and the centrifugal process of extracting sugar left less sucrose for distillation. American traveler William Henry Hurlbert wrote, "The molasses, which on the old-fashioned estates eventually distils into diamond drops of aguardiente is converted by this process into sugar."[102] Vacuum pans and centrifuges produced a drier and lighter sugar and converted more of the sucrose obtained from the cane juice into sugar than into molasses and scum for distillation. In the late nineteenth and early twentieth centuries, some of the older British Caribbean colonies, like Barbados, still preferred the traditional and less efficient muscavado method, which produced a rich blackstrap molasses that found a good market in Europe and North America.[103] The negative impact of vacuum pan and centrifugal processes on rum-making levels is indicated in the detailed Colonial Office reports from Jamaica. For the period 1886–1887, the reports revealed that on plantations where the method of sugar production was identified as "ordinary open battery of boilers," the ratio was 6.5 gallons of rum per cwt. of sugar. However, on plantations where the method of sugar making was listed as "vacuum pan and centrifugal," the ratio was only 3.1 gallons per cwt. of sugar.

The slow transition to free labor also reduced levels of Cuban rum making. In part, rum making in Jamaica, Demerara, and Martinique expanded to offset the high cost of labor that followed slave emancipation. Yet, the strong U.S. market and the high productivity of mechanized sugar factories reduced the impact of slave emancipation on Cuban sugar producers. In 1870, the Moret Law began the gradual emancipation of Cuban slaves. By 1881, an apprenticeship system known as the *patronato* was created to smooth the transition to free labor. Cuban officials and *patrones*, former slave owners, maintained tight legal control over former slaves through vagrancy laws, state sanctioned wage controls, and rural policing.[104] As in some parts of the British and French Caribbean, Asian workers, including 125,000 Chinese, were brought in to bolster labor ranks.[105] As a result, sugar production continued to increase until the war for Cuban independence.[106]

In 1830, Facundo Bacardí, a Catalonian immigrant, arrived in Cuba and settled in Santiago de Cuba. Within a decade of his arrival, he began selling rum for John Nunes, an Englishman who had established a small distillery in Santiago to compete with rum makers in Jamaica and Martinique. In 1862, Facundo, with financial backing from his brother José, purchased Nunes' distillery and started what was to become a rum empire. In 1876, at the International Centennial Exposition in Philadelphia, Bacardi rum won its first international award, beating out Jamaican contenders who at the time were considered the world's best rum producers. During the Ten Years War (1868–1878), Facundo supported the crown while his son Emilio, a criollo, supported the nationalist cause. After the war, Emilio was exiled to North Africa, but returned in 1883 to take over the distillery. During the war for Cuban independence, Emilio was an officer under the command of José Maceo, brother of the revolutionary hero Antonio. In 1897, Emilio was captured and exiled to Jamaica. The Bacardi rum distillery fell into ruin. In 1898, after American intervention, Emilio returned and was appointed mayor of Santiago de Cuba by the American commander Leonard Wood. In an effort to rejuvenate the economy after the revolution, Wood encouraged the United States to increase trade with Cuba, including trade in Bacardi rum.[107]

In the nineteenth century, rum makers in Puerto Rico, Venezuela, and the Dominican Republic produced rum for local consumption. Puerto Rican sugar making was less mechanized than that of Cuba and lacked the infrastructural support. After slave emancipation in 1873, Puerto Rican sugar production declined and little rum was exported. In 1873, Puerto Rico exported about 38,000 gallons of rum and a large amount of molasses, much of it to distillers in the Danish Virgin Islands. Rum making there, in St. Thomas and St. Croix, emerged after the American Revolution. Between 1777 and 1807, the two islands exported nearly one million gallons of rum per year, although much of this rum was probably produced in the French and British Caribbean and reexported to the United States. By 1863, rum exports from the Danish Virgin Islands were about 250,000 gallons and, for the rest of the century, averaged just below 100,000 per year.[108]

Venezuelan rum making also emerged in the nineteenth century. John Alderson, an English distiller and migrant who arrived in Venezuela in 1811, and the Gosslings, a powerful Dutch merchant family, are credited with sparking Venezuelan rum making. The arrival of Corsican migrants in the mid-nineteenth century also contributed to the rise of Venezuelan rum making, especially in the eastern provinces of Carúpano and Cumaná. The Corsicans introduced French rum-making techniques, which had greatly improved by the mid-nineteenth century. Low taxes on rum distilling and high taxes on brandy imports helped fuel the local demand for Venezuelan rum. Most of the rum and aguardiente made in Venezuela was consumed locally and, by the 1880s, annual per capita consumption reached nearly two gallons.[109] In 1889, rum from Carúpano did exceptionally well at a Paris exhibition and enhanced the reputation of Venezuelan rum. Yet, in the nineteenth century, little Venezuelan rum was exported. According to historian José Rodriguez, Le Havre and Bordeaux were primary destinations for Venezuelan rum, which probably reflect the influence of Corsican merchants in the Venezuelan rum trade.[110]

In the 1890s, the Dominican Republic produced more than three million gallons of rum, but exported none, despite being one of the largest rum makers in the Caribbean. Like Haitians, Dominicans consumed all of the rum they produced. In addition, Dominicans drank large amounts of the low-alcohol-content clarin, which was usually made in small crude stills.[111] Rum making emerged in other sugarcane-growing regions of Latin America. In Ecuador,

Guatemala, Honduras, El Salvador, and Paraguay, rum drinkers especially preferred a variety of rum made with aniseed. Central and South American rum primarily fed local demand, but it also found its way to Mexico and Brazil.[112]

The Expanding African Rum Trade

After the abolition of the Atlantic slave trade, alcoholic beverages, including Caribbean rum, continued to saturate the West and West Central African coasts. The African trade had shifted from slaves to the commodities needed to fuel the industrial revolutions of Europe and North America. According to historians David Eltis and Lawrence Jennings,

> It is probable that at some point between 1840 and 1850 the traffic in African goods surpassed the slave trade in value. Taken as a whole, the 1840s were probably similar to the 1680s in that the slave and commodities trades were roughly balanced, with the commodities trade perhaps worth slightly more.[113]

In the mid-nineteenth century, gum, peanuts, rubber, cocoa, palm oil and other palm products were major African exports. Alcohol remained a crucial part of the African trade. Eltis and Jennings estimate that African alcohol imports annually averaged 750,000 gallons in the 1780s and 6.1 million gallons in the 1860s—an almost tenfold increase in just 80 years.[114] The rise of a wealthy entrepreneurial African bourgeoisie probably increased the desire for western alcoholic beverages. Migratory workers in the coastal regions, who confronted loneliness and alienation in their rootless labors, also demanded alcoholic beverages with high alcohol contents, such as rum. Anomie also penetrated the lives of colonial administrators and European soldiers stationed in West and West Central Africa, who found solace in excessive rum drinking.

In the mid-nineteenth century, the value of British alcohol exports to West Africa steadily increased. Historian Joseph Inikori has shown that in the 1820s, the value of alcohol exports represented an annual average of 14 percent of British exports to West Africa.[115] In the last years of the 1840s, the value of alcohol exports jumped to an annual average of 21 percent. The alcohol trade was especially strong in the Gold Coast. In 1891, over 1.2 million gallons of alcohol were imported, the majority of which was rum. In 1914, the Gold Coast imported 1.7 million gallons of alcohol, about two-thirds of it rum.[116] French West Africa also imported huge amounts of rum. In 1879, Dahomey imported almost 700,000 gallons, and in 1894, rum accounted for 42 percent of the value of Dahomean imports.[117]

Colonial administrators in Africa complained that excessive alcohol use created serious social problems. In 1889, an international convention gathered in Brussels to discuss the African liquor trade. At the convention, officials representing the major colonial powers agreed to ban liquor from parts of Africa with no prior history of spirit use. However, the need for import revenues blocked tighter restrictions, particularly in the Gold Coast where, between 1910 and 1913, liquor taxes represented almost 40 percent of colonial revenues.[118] Growing fears about social disorder, as well as protests from temperance-minded missionaries and African chiefs, led British officials at the 1919 international liquor convention in St.-Germain-en-Laye, France, to support greater controls. British administrators on the Gold Coast experimented with prohibition and tighter alcohol regulations in the 1920s and 1930s, but these efforts largely failed due to the need for colonial import revenues.

Rum Making in the Twentieth Century

At the beginning of the twentieth century, Caribbean sugar continued to suffer from a glutted market, and rum making remained a crucial alternative. Despite the 1902 Brussels convention, which abolished the bounties favoring beet sugar, world overproduction led to an almost complete collapse of Caribbean sugar industries. In 1909, Britain imported 1.6 million tons of sugar, of which only 129,000 tons were from cane.[119] In 1913, Jamaica exported less than 100,000 cwt. of sugar, the lowest rate of production since the seventeenth century. Central factories replaced more and more independent sugar estates. Cuba, which benefited from technologically advanced sugar-making methods and a strong U.S. market, was the exception to the rule. The rise of U.S. interests in Cuba, especially after the war for Cuban independence, resulted in preferential trade deals that helped make Cuba and other former Spanish colonies, including Puerto Rico, the main suppliers of the U.S. sugar market. This restriction of the U.S. market was another major setback for British and French Caribbean sugar producers.[120]

The continuing demise of sugar production in the British and French Caribbean fostered the ongoing expansion of rum making. In the twentieth century, Britain and France implemented protectionist rum quotas to help stabilize their colonies. Cuba also produced a huge amount of rum, much of which was consumed locally or exported to the friendly U.S. market. Two world wars and smaller conflicts throughout the century also spurred Caribbean rum making as the number of servicemen, who have often been the driving force behind alcohol trends, increased. Industrial sugarcane-based alcohol also found a place in the war efforts. Rum making emerged in a few new sugarcane-growing regions, including parts of Southeast Asia and East Africa.

However, twentieth-century rum makers also confronted new social changes. Well-organized and well-funded temperance organizations emerged throughout the world winning the hearts and minds of many in Europe and North America. New attitudes about drinking led to the eventual abandonment of rum rations in the British Royal Navy in 1970. Missionary-based temperance movements arose in Africa, the Caribbean, and the Pacific. Occasionally, reformers won state-sanctioned support. Metropolitan officials and colonial administrators in Africa, for example, greatly curtailed the liquor traffic.[121] But reformers were most successful in the United States, one of the main markets for Caribbean rum. Per capita consumption of absolute alcohol in the United States fell from a high of 3.9 gallons in 1830 to 1 gallon in 1850.[122] In the late nineteenth and early twentieth centuries, the Women's Christian Temperance Union and the Anti-Saloon League continued the fight against alcohol.[123] By 1914, 33 states in the United States had gone "dry," and in 1919, the U.S. Congress enacted the Eighteenth Amendment, which prohibited the use of alcohol in the United States except for industrial, religious, and medicinal purposes. Canada, another important market for Caribbean rum, upheld wartime restrictions on alcohol use after World War I and, like the United States, experimented with prohibition.[124]

British Caribbean Rum in the Twentieth Century

The shrinking market for British Caribbean cane sugar meant that rum continued to play a critical role in bolstering British Caribbean economies and keeping British Caribbean sugar estates solvent. In 1913, Jamaica exported 9.7 gallons of rum per cwt. of sugar. The low level of sugar production, however, also meant less scum and molasses available for rum making. Thus, while the rum-to-sugar ratio was high, the amount of rum actually exported fell below one million gallons. World War I reignited Jamaican rum making, and between 1913 and 1916, Jamaican rum exports averaged more than 1.5 million gallons per year. Jamaican rum helped fuel the war effort. Rum met the alcohol needs of the British armed forces, especially the navy, which still maintained its tradition of rum rations. Alcohol was also an ingredient in the preparation of powder explosives, and Jamaican spirits may have been used for that purpose.[125]

Before the end of World War I, Jamaican rum exports temporarily collapsed. The conflict disrupted European sugar beet industries, which led to a resurgence of Jamaican sugar making. Moreover, German submarines, a constant threat in the Caribbean, reduced shipping. In 1918, despite relatively good rum prices, Jamaica exported less than 250,000 gallons.

After World War I, Jamaican rum exports rebounded. In 1919, Jamaica exported more than three million gallons—more than it had exported in four decades. Part of this huge rise may reflect the export of rum stockpiled between 1917 and 1918 because of unsafe shipping. The destruction of European sugar beet industries during World War I increased sugar prices and rejuvenated Jamaican interest in sugar production. Jamaican sugar exports jumped from a low of 98,000 cwt. in 1913 to more than one million cwt. in 1922. The growing mechanization of Jamaican sugar making left less scum and molasses for rum making and reduced the level of rum exports. After World War I, Jamaican rum exports typically remained below one million gallons per year for the next two decades.

In the early twentieth century, rum makers in Demerara continued to outproduce and outexport those in Jamaica. Between 1897 and 1901, Demerara exported an average of more than 4.8 million gallons of rum per year. Yet, as with Jamaica, rum production dropped after World War I. Postwar fears about unsteady sugar markets led to the creation of an "Imperial Preference" system. The system included the Commonwealth Sugar Agreement, which implemented sugar and rum quotas that brought greater stability to the British Caribbean.[126] Between 1931 and 1939, Demerara produced an annual average of about 1.8 million gallons of rum and exported an average of about 1.1 million gallons per year.[127] In the 1920s and 1930s, South Africa also emerged as a major player in the British rum trade. In 1922, a quarter of the rum imported into Britain came from South Africa, and in 1931, South Africa exported more rum to Britain than Demerara. In the 1930s, about a quarter of the rum imported into Britain was reexported, mainly to Canada, Newfoundland, Germany, and Ireland.[128]

After World War II, a lack of grain in Britain reduced British gin production and led to a temporary resurgence in British Caribbean rum exports.[129] Both Demeraran and Jamaican rum exports jumped to two million gallons, although some of this may represent rum stockpiled during the war. Sugar planters also began to distill their molasses into industrial forms of alcohol, which were

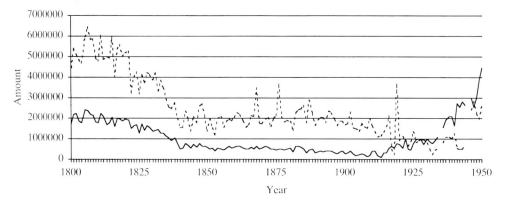

Figure 7.6. Rum and sugar exports from Jamaica. Graph by author. *Sources*: 1800–1833 from Ragatz, *Statistics*, 18; 1833–1887 from Eisner, *Jamaica*, 240–45; 1888–1946 from Jamaica, *Handbook* (1888/1889; 1903; 1911; 1946); 1947–1950 from Colonial Office, *Report on Jamaica*.

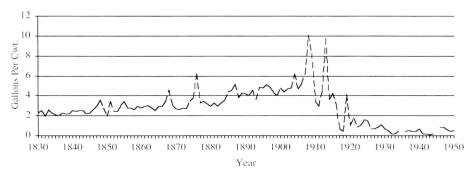

Figure 7.7. Jamaican rum exports per cwt. of sugar. Graph by author. *Sources*: 1830–1833 from Ragatz, *Statistics*, 18; 1833–1887 from Eisner, *Jamaica*, 245–50; 1888–1946 from Jamaica, *Handbook* (1888/1889; 1903; 1911; 1946); 1947–1950 from Colonial Office, *Report on Jamaica*.

used to adulterate motor fuel. In 1951, the Jamaican Assembly approved legislation requiring that anhydrous alcohol made from sugar by-products be mixed with petrol for use as a "motor spirit."[130] Barbadian rum exports, which were all but dead in the late nineteenth century, also rebounded. In the 1930s, Barbados rum exports averaged almost 100,000 gallons per year, and after World War II, rum exports represented 5 to 7 percent of the value of all exports until the early 1970s. While rum exports remained steady, their relative value declined as Barbados began to diversify its economy and export a greater variety of light industrial goods.

French Caribbean Rum Making in the Twentieth Century

At the beginning of the twentieth century, rum represented about 10 percent of all the spirits consumed in France, and Martinique was the major supplier of rum to the French market. In the 1890s, it exported four times more rum than its French colonial neighbor, Guadeloupe. In the shadow of Mount Pelée, the port town of St. Pierre was the hub of the Martinican rum industry. It was the primary destination for molasses from Martinican sugar estates that had no distilleries, as well as for imported molasses from Guadeloupe, St. Kitts, and Demerara. On May 8, 1902, Mount Pelée erupted killing more than 40,000 St. Pierre residents and destroying that commercial rum-making center. From 1899 to 1901, Martinique exported an annual average of almost four million gallons of rum. For the three years following the eruption (1902–1904), rum exports were cut in half. The eruption destroyed the large urban distilleries. Many Martinican sugar planters took advantage of St. Pierre's demise and upgraded their plantation distilleries in order to produce high quality rhum agricole on a larger scale.

World War I had a positive effect on French Caribbean rum production. The conflict depressed wine and brandy making throughout Europe. Rum fed large numbers of soldiers, who had historically provided an important outlet for rum. The French also used rum in the preparation of powder explosives. The war effort fostered a boom in rum industry speculation. The number of distilleries in Martinique grew from 86 in 1913 to 96 in 1917. In the period 1913–1917, Martinique exported over 30 million gallons of rum. Between 1917 and 1919, rum represented 75 percent of the total value of Martinican exports.[131]

But speculation led to overproduction and declining rum prices. In 1922 and 1923, despite complaints from national wine and brandy interests, the French government was forced to intervene and implement a quota system for

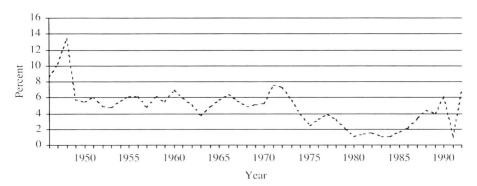

Figure 7.8. Barbados rum exports. Graph by author. *Sources*: Worrell, *Economy of Barbados*, 72–73; United States International Trade Commission, *Rum: Annual Report* (Washington, D.C., 1984–1992).

the French rum-producing colonies. The annual French import quota was set at 160,000 hectoliters (4.2 million gallons). Martinique was given the largest share: 80,000 hectoliters (2.1 million gallons). Guadeloupe received 60,000 hectoliters (1.6 million gallons), and Réunion received 18,000 (500,000 gallons). The remainder was to come from other French colonies in the east. Between 1920 and 1923, rum still represented a considerable 60 percent of Martinican exports. In 1923, France established the Office National de l'Alcool to help track Caribbean rum affairs and make adjustments to the quota system. In 1924, the annual rum quota was increased to 185,000 hectoliters (4.9 million gallons) and eventually extended until 1939.[132] In Martinique, the number of distilleries reached 150. However, the decline in rum prices and the rise of sugar and banana exports decreased the overall value of rum to the Martinican economy. Between 1933 and 1937, rum represented only about 31 percent of the value of exports. By the end of the 1930s, rum represented between 20 percent and 25 percent of all spirits consumed in France.[133] Ernest Hemingway and other great writers sat in Parisian cafés and contemplated life behind glasses of Martinican rum.[134]

After World War II, protectionism continued, and rum making rebounded. In 1949, rum represented nearly half the value of Martinican exports.[135] The quota system eliminated small distillers in Martinique. Those distilleries that survived were usually associated with reputable estates, like St. James, which produced rhum agricole, as well as with big urban operations that produced rhum industriel on a large scale.[136] In 1958, however, rum as a value of total exports dropped to only 14 percent due to the increasing value of banana exports.

In the 1980s, Martinicans essentially abandoned sugar making and channeled nearly all of their sugarcane juice to their distilleries. In 1983, Martinique produced 2.7 million gallons of pure alcohol and only 77,589 cwt. of sugar. In contrast, Guadeloupe continued to rely more heavily on sugar. In 1983, Guadeloupe produced more than 1.1 million cwt. of sugar and only 1.8 million gallons of pure alcohol. A small number of distillers dominated rum making in Martinique and Guadeloupe. In 1989, annual quotas were revised and fixed at about 5.4 million gallons of pure alcohol. Martinique received the biggest share, about 44 percent, while Guadeloupe received 33 percent, Réunion 18 percent, French Guiana 1 percent, and the Republic of Madagascar 3 percent.[137] In 1982, in Martinique, there were 11 distilleries operating, less than one-fifth the number that existed in 1952.[138] Protectionism extended to the particular plantations and brands of rhum agricole, including Trois-Rivières, St. James, and Maniba.[139] In the late 1980s and early 1990s, production of rhum agricole was four to five times greater than rhum industriel.

Spanish Caribbean Rum Making in the Twentieth Century

In the early twentieth century, rum makers in Cuba, Puerto Rico, Venezuela, and the Dominican Republic produced rum on about the same scale as their French and British Caribbean counterparts. Bounty-fed beet sugar and preferential trade agreements during the period of U.S. interventionism ensured that the United States was the main market for Spanish Caribbean goods. Cuba began the century as the leading Spanish Caribbean rum maker, but rum makers in Puerto Rico soon surpassed their Cuban rivals.

In the late nineteenth century, Cuba challenged Martinique, Demerara, and Jamaica for top spot in the Caribbean rum industry. Cuban rum exports varied greatly from year to year. In 1891, rum exports reached 3.8 millions gallons, almost double the exports of the year before. In the 1890s, the war for Cuban independence curtailed the progress of Cuban rum makers. Although we lack complete statistics for the late nineteenth century, Cuban rum exports were probably weak. During the war, thousands of acres of cane fields were set ablaze.[140] Cuban sugar production fell to 271,505 metric tons, less than one-quarter of its prewar level.[141] Molasses exports also crumbled, and in 1897, Cuba exported less than 100,000 gallons.

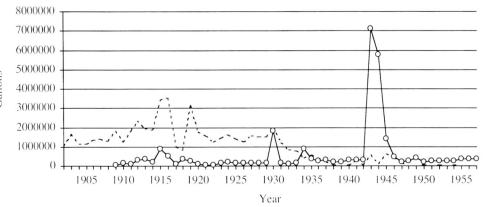

Figure 7.9. Cuban rum and aguardiente exports. Graph by author. *Sources*: Cuba, *Resumenes estadisticos seleccionados*, 56–57; American Chamber of Commerce, *Cuba: Facts and Figures*, 127; Maspons Franco, *La reorganización*, 127–32.

In the early twentieth century, Cubans distilled a great deal of sugarcane juice, molasses, and scum. They produced high quality rum, less esteemed aguardiente, and industrial forms of alcohol. Between 1902 and 1908, exports of rum, aguardiente, and industrial alcohol averaged nearly 1.4 million gallons per year.

Cuban aguardiente production increased during the U.S. occupation, but dropped in 1908 as U.S. servicemen returned home. Yet, as usual in the history of alcohol, the returning troops brought back a taste for Cuban rum, including the specialty rum-based drink known as the Daiquiri, which they had been introduced to while stationed in the southern port town of the same name.[142] Although aguardiente production declined after the U.S. occupation, exports rose steadily in the early 1910s. Aguardiente probably fed a variety of markets, including Spain, Italy, parts of South America, and the United States. Higher quality rum, on the other hand, was probably reserved exclusively for the U.S. market.[143] In 1915, Cuba exported more than 4.2 million gallons of aguardiente and rum, four times what it had exported only six years earlier. Initially, World War I was a boon for Cuban rum makers, but the lack of safe shipping in 1917 led to a collapse in exports. In 1919 and 1920, Cuba exported an annual average of more than 2.6 million gallons of aguardiente and rum, much of which was probably stockpiled during the war.

Cuban aguardiente and rum exports fell in the 1920s, and the drop coincides with the passage of the Eighteenth Amendment. The sharper drop in rum exports, rather than aguardiente exports, supports the claim that rum was primarily made for the U.S. market. Between 1921 and 1925, rum and aguardiente exports fell to 1.5 million gallons per year. Despite Prohibition, rumrunners used the island of Nassau in the Bahamas as a base to smuggle Cuban rum to the coast of Florida.

The loss of the U.S. alcohol market during Prohibition was especially hard on Cuban rum makers. On the other hand, beverages were not the only use for alcohol. In the 1930s, Cuban distilleries produced alcohol for a variety of industrial purposes. Distillers distilled sugarcane juice, molasses, and scum to make the natural and denatured alcohol used in perfumeries and hospitals. Alcohol was also used to make gunpowder and lubricating oil. More importantly, the Cuban government required that motor fuel contain 25 percent ethanol produced from molasses.[144]

During Prohibition, thousands of American tourists flocked to Cuba where they were introduced to Cuban rum, especially that made by the Bacardi distilleries. Like the U.S. soldiers two decades earlier, American tourists brought back a taste for Cuban rum. In 1933, Congress passed the Twenty-first Amendment, which repealed Prohibition. The following year, Cuban rum exports reached 900,000 gallons. In 1930, Bacardi, now the largest distillery in Cuba, produced over 500,000 gallons of rum. In 1929 and 1930, Bacardi paid more than $400,000 in taxes, more than half of all taxes collected from Cuban distilleries.[145] It was one of the most valuable companies in Cuba.

Rum making also expanded in Puerto Rico. In the 1890s, William Dinwiddie traveled to Puerto Rico and noted that rum was produced at nearly every big sugar factory: "The consumption of this fiery liquor is almost entirely confined to the native population, though some thousands of gallons are exported each year to Spain." In 1894 and 1895, rum exports were less than 20,000 gallons. After the Spanish-American War, things changed. In 1904, the Foraker Act ensured that all internal taxes collected on articles manufactured in Puerto Rico were reverted to the island's treasury. Those tax revenues came mainly from tobacco and rum. As tobacco production and cigar manufacturing declined, rum, which was on the increase, became the primary source of excise taxes and, thus, the source of treasury funds. In 1917, the United States implemented the Jones Act, which made Puerto Ricans citizens of the United States. Included in the Jones Act was a referendum on Prohibition, which Puerto Ricans adopted the following year. The Puerto Ricans' embrace of Prohibition was astonishing. The rum industry was central to the Puerto Rican economy, and tax revenues from rum reached 60 to 70 million dollars some years. Between 1918 and 1933, rum making in Puerto Rico ceased, though illicit stills operated in the rural sugarcane-growing regions of the country that produced a type of moonshine called *canita*.[146]

In 1934, the year after the U.S. government passed the Twenty-first Amendment, the United States imported about 10,000 gallons of rum from Puerto Rico, while Cuban rum imports were 211,000 gallons. Yet, as a territory of the United States, Puerto Rican goods, including rum, received especially favorable duties. The U.S. government may have also felt the need to compensate Puerto Rico for adopting Prohibition. Puerto Rico modernized its rum industry and took advantage of the preferential U.S. trade policies. In 1936, the United States imported 350,000 gallons of Puerto Rican rum, which represented more than a third of all U.S. rum imports. After 1936, U.S. imports of Puerto Rican rum regularly surpassed those from Cuba. In 1940, more than half of the rum imported into the United States came from Puerto Rico. In that year, the United States imported more than 1.4 million gallons of Puerto Rican rum and a mere 162,130 gallons of rum from Cuba. In 1941, Puerto Rican rum exports to the United States reached 2.4 million gallons. Rum making also expanded in the Virgin Islands, which the United States purchased from Denmark in 1917. In 1940, the United States imported nearly 400,000 gallons of rum from the Virgin Islands, an amount second only to that from Puerto Rico.[147]

World War II accelerated the expansion of rum making in Puerto Rico, the Virgin Islands, and Cuba. Rum exports from these islands skyrocketed as the conflict cut European alcohol supplies and reduced the availability of brandy, gin, and vodka. In addition, the fear of bread shortages curtailed the distillation of grain in Britain and North America. Whiskey distilleries modified their operations and produced industrial forms of alcohol—often from imported Caribbean molasses—for the war effort. However, German submarine forays in the Caribbean greatly reduced U.S. molasses imports.[148] Even so, the increasing volume of U.S. imports of Caribbean rum suggests that the decline in molasses exports, especially from Puerto Rico, Cuba, and the Virgin Islands, was dictated less by German submarine attacks than by the Caribbean distillers' desire to produce rum for the profitable American alcohol market that had been opened by the war. Rum makers in Puerto Rico, the Virgin Islands, and Cuba, like their Jamaican and Martinican counterparts during World War I, took advantage of the unstable alcohol market and flooded it with rum. In 1943, for example, Puerto Rico exported 6.3 million gallons of rum to the United

States. That year, Cuba exported well over 7 million gallons of rum, more than 4.1 million gallons of which went to the United States. Another 1.7 million gallons of rum came from the Virgin Islands.[149] Rum from these islands also met the alcohol demands of soldiers and sailors in Europe, the Pacific, and Africa.[150] In the 1930s, whiskey, gin, and brandy were the primary distilled spirits consumed in the United States, and rum represented only about 0.5 percent of spirits consumed. By the end of World War II, U.S. imports of Caribbean rum surpassed all other categories of imported distilled spirits, including Scotch and Irish whiskies.

In 1959, Fidel Castro came to power, and in 1961 the United States imposed economic sanctions against Cuba. The revolution devastated Cuban rum exports. The Union of Soviet Socialist Republics became the main destination for Cuban rum, but the Soviet government's monopoly on liquor and the Russian demand for vodka limited the export market for Cuban rum. The decline in exports was partially offset by an increase in local rum consumption in Cuba. Perhaps under the influence of American tourism that began in the early twentieth century, per capita rum consumption in Cuba was increasing. As early as 1915, an American visitor, recognizing the negative consequences of American influence, had wondered how long it would take for U.S. tourists to turn Cuba "into a nation of drunkards."[151] The system of government rum rations implemented during the Castro regime probably also spurred rum consumption rates. Between 1986 and 1987, Cuba produced more than 22 million gallons of rum and exported less than 4 percent of its total produce. Cuba's production of ethanol for industrial purposes, including motor fuel, was even more impressive. Between 1970 and 1987, Cuba produced 230 million gallons of industrial ethanol.[152] In the 1980s, the revolutionary government's interest in cattle diverted molasses from distilleries to cattle feed. According to historian Jorge Pérez-López, the policy "eroded" Cuba's alcohol industry.[153]

In the 1980s, Cold War insecurities and concerns about the rise of socialist governments in the Caribbean led to American interventionist policies, which included economic incentives for the rum trade. On April 13, 1983, the U.S. government began public hearings on the Caribbean Basin Economic Recovery Act, part of the Ronald Reagan administration's Caribbean Basin Initiative (CBI). CBI sought to bolster the friendly economies of the Caribbean through tariff reductions. The act offered discretionary tariff reductions and tax incentives to Caribbean rum makers. The act also transferred all revenues from rum excise taxes to Puerto Rico and the Virgin Islands, which were the biggest beneficiaries of CBI. The Cold War and CBI were especially helpful to Puerto

Rico. In 1959, the Bacardi family fled Cuba and reestablished operations in Puerto Rico. Since then, Bacardi has become a multinational corporation and a major player in the world spirits market. In 1992, Puerto Rico and the Virgin Islands exported more than 21 million gallons of rum to the United States. Puerto Rico contributed 90 percent of this total. In contrast, Jamaica, the next largest supplier under CBI, exported only about 600,000 gallons to the U.S. market. Yet, rum makers in many islands have benefited from CBI. In Barbados, the value of rum as a percentage of total exports returned to pre-1970 levels. In 1992, rum represented almost 7 percent of the total value of Barbadian exports, reflecting the growth of the U.S. rum market—a goal of CBI.

Conclusion

In the nineteenth and twentieth centuries, rum making took on increasing economic importance. The abolition of the slave trade, slave emancipation, and falling sugar prices reduced the profitability of sugar making and spurred Caribbean planters to produce greater quantities of rum. Rum makers in the French Caribbean benefited from the devastation of European vineyards in the nineteenth century and the rise of protectionist policies in the twentieth century. In the Spanish Caribbean, expansion of sugar making and the rise of a protected U.S. market fueled the growth of Spanish Caribbean rum industries. At the beginning of the twenty-first century, rum continues to provide a means of social escape and an economic safety net in the Caribbean.

CHAPTER 8

Conclusion

SINCE THE SEVENTEENTH CENTURY rum has provided multiple social outlets and temporary escape from the worries of Caribbean life. As a result, rum has been elevated to the level of a cultural symbol, and it has helped define the identities of the Caribbean people, as well as overseas Caribbean migrants in Europe and North America. The diversity of the Caribbean has led to different drinking patterns. Yet, despite the ready availability of rum in the Caribbean, alcoholism and alcohol-related problems have been relatively mild when compared with the European and North American powers that once dominated the region. Moreover, rum production has continued to offer relief from debt. Although globalization has restructured the form of that debt, rum continues to bolster many Caribbean economies.

Marketing Rum

At the end of the twentieth and the beginning of the twenty-first century, rum is one of the most widely used spirits. In 1992, world consumption of rum was more than 264 million gallons of proof spirit. Rum accounted for 11.4 percent of the world distilled spirits market and was the third most widely consumed distilled spirit. Whiskey had the largest share of the world market with 28 percent, and brandy was in second place with 14 percent.[1] Multinational corporations, marketing particular brand names, now dominate the rum industry.

The United States is one of the largest consumers of Caribbean rum. Spurred in part by the policies implemented under CBI, U. S. rum consumption is also increasing at a faster rate than for any other distilled spirit. In the

1950s, the United States imported an annual average of about 2.3 million gallons of rum. In the 1990s, that figure jumped to an annual average of more than 31 million gallons.[2] In 2001, rum imports reached 42.5 million gallons, and rum represented about 12 percent of all distilled spirits consumed in the United States. Maintaining a trend that began in the early nineteenth century, whiskies had the largest share of the U.S. market with 29 percent. Vodka took 25 percent, while brandy, cognac, tequila, gin, and various cordials and liqueurs made up the remainder of the U.S. alcohol market.[3] In Europe, rum is the fifth most popular distilled beverage, and Europeans consume about 20 percent of the world's rum.[4]

Most Caribbean rum sold today is produced on a massive scale for large multinational corporations that own the rights to various brand names. In 2001, Americans consumed more than 18 million gallons of Bacardi rum, which controlled 43 percent of the U.S. rum market. Bacardi-Martini USA is a two billion–dollar company and a dominant force in the world's spirits industry. Although Bacardi rum is the flagship spirit of Bacardi-Martini USA, the company also controls a variety of other brands, including the popular British spirit, Dewar's Scotch whiskey.

Caribbean rum is still subject to broad political and economic forces. Recently, the Bacardi organization has clashed with the Cuban government and the European Union over trademark rights to the Havana Club brand name. In 1976, the Cuban government registered Havana Club with the U.S. Patent and Trademark Office, though Bacardi claims to have purchased the name from a Cuban family whose business was expropriated by the Cuban government in 1960. In 1995, Bacardi sued Pernod Ricard, a French spirits company, and the Cuban government, which jointly market the Havana Club brand in Europe. The U.S. Congress even enacted legislation to support Bacardi's claims to the patent rights of Havana Club. However, in 2000, the European Union filed a complaint with the World Trade Organization, which ruled in favor of Pernod Ricard the following year. The United States currently faces World Trade Organization sanctions if it does not recognize the Cuban-French rights to Havana Club.

While Bacardi dominates the U.S. rum market, the remainder of the U.S. rum market is divided among a variety of smaller brands managed by other multinational corporations. Rémy-Amérique, for example, owns a variety of distilled spirits, including Mount Gay rum from Barbados. Seagram's oversees other popular American brands, including Myers's and Captain Morgan. Bacardi has recently faced tough competition from Seagram's brand Captain

Morgan, which now accounts for 20 percent of the U.S. rum market. Seagram's exemplifies the structure of the modern rum industry. Rum is distilled in Jamaica to 150 proof (75 percent alcohol) and arrives at Seagram's blending facility in the United States in tankers and railcars where it is adulterated to 90 proof (45 percent alcohol). It is stored in 10,000- to 40,000-gallon tanks until it is ready to be barreled and aged for three years.[5] After aging, it is bottled and released on the market.

Bottle labels and the advertising campaigns for Caribbean rum shed light on the marketing strategies of Caribbean rum producers, as well as on the alcoholic fantasies of western rum consumers. Rum bottle labels are loaded with information about the country of origin; taxes; volume of the bottle; percentage of alcohol per volume (proof); name of the distilling, blending, and bottling facilities; trademark; and whether the contents are intended for export markets. In the United States, rum labels include health warnings to pregnant women about the dangers of alcohol to a fetus. The labels also often tell how long the rum has been aged. For example, Cruzan markets a two-year-old rum; Barbancourt, a four- and a twelve-year-old rum; and Havana Club, a three-, a five-, and a seven-year-old rum. Some rum is simply identified as "très vieux" or "extra old." Mount Gay Extra Old is actually a blend of seven-, eight-, and ten-year-old varieties of Mount Gay rum. Rum is also identified as white, dark, light, réserve, dry, agricole, industriel, traditionnel, spécial, spiced, and premium.

Rum bottle labels overflow with nationalism. Among the most common images are the countries of origin. For example, Grenada is depicted on varieties of Westerhall, Clarke's Court, and Jack Iron. Barbados is depicted on Mount Gay and Old Brigand. Twin Island rum labels depict St. Kitts and Nevis; Bielle depicts Marie-Galante; and varieties of Trois Rivières depict Martinique. National flags, state seals, and symbols of national identity are also displayed. The seal on Barbados's Mount Gay dark rum displays two national flags. Antigua's English Harbour rum label includes an image of St. John's Harbour. Havana Club's trademark is the bronze Giraldilla statue that sits atop Havana's Castillo de la Real Fuerza. Fort St. Louis, overlooking Marigot Bay, is illustrated on St. Martin Spiced Rhum.

Caribbean rum bottle labels also express a sense of plantationalism. Trois Rivières, Dillon, Depaz, Busco, and Dunfermline all include images of their plantations of origin and of their distilleries. This pattern is most pronounced on labels of agricole rums from the French Caribbean. Rhum agricole, unlike rhum industriel, is distinguished by its plantation of origin. Thus, like French wine and brandy bottle labels, which venerate estate vineyards and châteaux, rhum agricole honors its particular estate. For similar reasons, Appleton estate rum is one of the few British Caribbean rum makers to highlight the plantation complex. Rum makers often place an additional label on the backs of their bottles to honor the distillery's history. "The Legend of Mount Gay," for example, can be found on the back of some Mount Gay bottles.

Generalized images of sugar plantation life are also common rum bottle label themes. For example, one brand of Cruzan Virgin Island rum and one brand of Doorly's Barbados rum highlight the windmill. The rum puncheon is celebrated on nearly every label, including varieties of Old Oak, Myers's, Barbados Gold, Damoiseau, and Castillo. Sugarcane is also a popular image on labels. Some rum makers prefer symbols that seem to hark back to the old glory days of simple plantation life. For example, cane cutters are depicted on varieties of Ferdi's, La Mauny, Fajou, and Charles Simonnet. One brand of Doorly's rum illustrates people filling a lighter boat with rum casks.

Rum labels embrace symbols of masculinity. Pirates adorn Old Brigand, Captain Morgan, Buccaneer, and Tortola Spiced rums. Some labels portray maritime images that highlight the rugged and independent seafaring life. Sailing ships, for example, grace varieties of Nelson, Montebello, El Dorado, and Bounty. Two sailors lean on a cask of rum on the label of Cruzan 151. Pusser's rum romanticizes the tradition of rum rations in the British Royal Navy. Bounty and Captain Bligh honor the career of the mutiny-struck ship's captain. Don Q, Grand Corsaire, and Cavalier labels are adorned with images of independent swashbuckling gentlemen from a more adventurous age. Some masculine images are less explicit. The cock on varieties of Cockspur rum, for example, expresses strength and arrogance. Attractive women seem especially common on French Caribbean rum labels, including varieties of St. Martin Spiced Rhum, La Mauny, St. Etienne, and Maniba. Rum advertisement posters of the early twentieth century venerate the "exotic" Caribbean woman. Modern advertising campaigns continue to hawk sexual images and, for example, the Internet website of Captain Morgan features a new "Morganette" each month.

Since the beginning of Caribbean rum industries, rum has provided a means of escape from the anxieties and anomie of plantation labor. Today, Caribbean rum bottle labels indulge the escapist fantasies of European and North American consumers who feel unfulfilled in their regimented lives. Through the tropical scenes that dominate many rum labels, companies market their product as passages to fun, adventure, and paradisiacal solace. Sunset, El Dorado, and Malibu celebrate palm trees, warm weather, and sandy beaches. Rum companies offer "get away" Caribbean vacations and sponsor sailing races, volleyball tournaments, and windsurfing competitions.

Some rum label images are more difficult to explain. The label on bottles of Captain Bligh rum depicts breadfruit. Although Bligh carried the breadfruit to the Caribbean, it seems odd that the breadfruit would be celebrated on a bottle of alcohol made from sugarcane. Varieties of Doorly's rum highlight the macaw, not native to Barbados. The Bacardi bat emblematizes the story of the colony of fruit bats that occupied the rafters of the original Bacardi distillery in Santiago de Cuba. Although there are no seals in Bermuda, the label for Gosling's Black Seal rum illustrates a seal balancing a cask of rum on its nose.

Some brands have adopted more pretentious labels similar to those found on fine European cognac and brandy bottles. Family crests are especially common on varieties of Spanish Caribbean rum, including Ron Llave and Ronrico. Bacardi and Barbancourt rum bottle labels exemplify a more classical model. Neither displays nationalistic images, plantation work, women, or tropical exoticism. Instead Bacardi and Barbancourt display international awards, 8 and 22 respectively. Perhaps they wish to conceal their Caribbean origins in order to promote themselves as more universal spirits.

In the past decade, new varieties of rum have been introduced. Consumers can now purchase rums blended with the juice of oranges, limes, and coconuts. Rum-flavored malt beverages have also emerged. In part, major rum companies market brand-name malt beverages to skirt television-advertising restrictions against distilled spirits.

Alcoholism and Alcohol-Related Problems in the Caribbean

Although modern per capita alcohol consumption rates in the Caribbean are generally below those of the United States, Britain, and France, alcoholism and alcohol-related problems are a concern in the Caribbean. A 1988 drug and alcohol survey sponsored by the Pan American Health Organization identified alcohol as the most frequently abused drug in the Caribbean.[6] In 1999, the World Health Organization published its *Global Status Report on Alcohol*, which included comparative statistics for many Caribbean countries. While irregular recording and external variables, such as the level of per capita alcohol consumption by foreign tourists, obscure conclusions about per capita alcohol consumption rates, the report provides some insights into drinking patterns in the modern Caribbean (Table 8.1).

Table 8.1. Per Capita Consumption of Pure Alcohol in Gallons for Adults 15 Years of Age and Older

Country	1970–1972	1994–1996	1996
Guyana	1.0	3.8	4.0
Bahamas	4.6	3.2	3.2
Venezuela	1.9	2.5	2.5
Netherlands Antilles	2.6	2.2	2.3
Barbados	2.0	2.4	2.2
Haiti	1.8	1.5	1.7
Dominican Republic	0.7	1.5	1.6
Trinidad and Tobago	1.2	1.3	1.0
Jamaica	1.1	1.1	1.0
Cuba	0.7	1.0	0.9

Source: World Health Organization, *Global Status Report*, 9–19.

Although North American visitors tested the abstemious reputation of Cubans in the first half of the twentieth century, Cubans remained temperate. In 1959, the socialist government of Fidel Castro came to power and the revolutionary movement had an even more tempering effect on Cuban society. In 1961, the per capita alcohol consumption rate in Cuba was 0.3 gallons of pure alcohol. This level held steady for almost a decade, dropping slightly to 0.2 gallons of pure alcohol in 1969. Economic crises, and perhaps the erosion of revolutionary ideals, have brought about a gradual increase in alcohol use. In the early 1980s, Cuba's annual per capita rate of alcohol consumption for adults over 15 was about one gallon of pure alcohol. With the dissolution of the Soviet Union in the late 1980s and early 1990s, Cuba lost the main market for its goods. The negative impact on Cuba's economy had a positive impact on alcohol use. In the early 1990s, the per capita alcohol consumption rate for Cubans over the age of 15 was almost 1.3 gallons of pure alcohol.[7]

Despite its abstemious past, including the adoption of Prohibition between 1918 and 1933, Puerto Rico currently ranks among the top ten countries in the world in per capita alcohol consumption.[8] Poverty, unemployment, industrialization, urbanization, and the fact that Puerto Rico is one of the largest rum producers, making rum cheap and readily available, have contributed to the increasing levels of alcohol abuse. Standard death rates from chronic liver disease and cirrhosis are three to four times higher in Puerto Rico than in Cuba.

The rate of alcohol dependency is eight times greater than in Cuba, and standard death rates from alcohol dependency are five to six times greater. The situation is much the same in Venezuela, where per capita alcohol consumption for adults over 15 years of age has increased in the past three decades. The declining prosperity of Venezuela's oil industry since the 1970s may be to blame for this increase. In addition to high rates of chronic liver disease and cirrhosis, alcohol use in Venezuela is implicated in half of all road accidents, as well as homicides, purposeful injuries, and other violent crimes.[9]

Following trends that existed in the late nineteenth century, alcohol consumption in the Dominican Republic has remained relatively high for the Spanish Caribbean. In the early 1990s, the per capita consumption rate of pure alcohol for adults over 15 was more than 1.5 gallons. Moreover, per capita alcohol use among adults over 15 years of age has more than doubled in the past three decades. Anthropologist Gerald Murray has investigated the increasing use of alcohol in the Dominican Republic and argues that alcohol's growing importance in daily life is most evident in the "dramatic invasion of alcohol," especially rum, into grocery stores [colmados].[10] One shop, for example, sold 23 brands and sizes of rum but only four beer products. Murray also found that modern corner grocery stores had in stock three times as much alcohol by value as soft drinks and milk.[11] In fact, alcohol represented 20 percent of their total inventory, 28 percent of sales, and more than a third of profits. Once-simple colmados have evolved into places of alcohol consumption, and store-owners attract drinkers with music, dominoes, and dances, even while retaining their basic grocery function. According to Murray, this change reflects, in part, the increasing cost of living, which makes colmados cheaper sources of alcohol than bars and restaurants. In turn, there are fewer bars and restaurants because this new competition has forced their decline. A lack of licensing restrictions has also brought about the alteration in the colmados. Murray points out that patrons buy four bottles of rum for every bottle of milk, suggesting that household income is not being used to meet family needs.[12] While some believe the Dominican Republic's growing economic woes are fueling the rise in alcohol use, Murray also stresses the impact of advertising campaigns that glorify drinking.

Jamaica continues to have one of the lowest rates of alcohol consumption in the British Caribbean. The ongoing influence of temperance reform in Low Church religions and, perhaps, according to some researchers, a more permissive attitude toward alcohol in Jamaican families appears to have sustained a temperate ideology.[13] In contrast, Barbados and Guyana continue to jockey for first place in levels of per capita alcohol consumption. Young urban males of no particular religious affiliation are the heaviest drinkers. Elderly women, married or widowed, who belong to sectarian religious faiths—especially the Methodist, Pentecostal, and Seventh Day Adventist—are the most abstemious. In the 1950s, Raymond Smith investigated family life in British Guiana and showed that men tended to spend a good percentage of extra household income on rum for entertaining. These men purchased rum at rum shops rather than in grocery stores as in the Dominican Republic today.[14] In Barbados, in the 1970s, sociologist Graham Dann conducted a survey on alcohol use and found that Barbadians over the age of 18 consumed an average of about 1.9 gallons of alcohol per year. Rum, by far, represented the greater amount of this alcohol. Dann concluded that "heavy drinkers" represented about 6 percent of the adult population and that they consumed an incredible 22 gallons of pure alcohol per year, the equivalent of a pint of rum per day.[15]

In the nineteenth century, missionaries assumed that poor whites in Barbados were responsible for the incredibly high level of rum consumption. As noted in an earlier chapter, those poor whites would have had to consume nearly the same amount of rum Dann has identified for heavy drinkers in modern Barbados. In contrast to the statements of nineteenth century missionaries, Dann's survey reveals that heavy drinkers in modern Barbados tend to have above-average incomes. Although, Dann's study does not account for race, it does show that a small segment of Barbados's population, such as poor whites, could significantly shape overall per capita consumption rates.

Adolescent drinking has been a central focus of alcohol research in the Caribbean. In the Bahamas in the mid-1990s, a Pan American Health Organization survey found that 66 percent of students under the age of 18 had used alcohol. In 1985, a similar study conducted in Trinidad revealed that 91 percent of students there had used alcohol.[16] The higher per capita consumption rate identified by the World Health Organization in the Bahamas largely reflects the alcohol consumption of foreign tourists, which researchers were apparently unable to differentiate from local Bahamian consumption.[17] The lower incidence of drinking among Bahamian adolescents in the Pan American Health Organization survey probably offers an accurate picture of a moderate Bahamian drinking pattern. The different rates of adolescent exposure to alcohol in Trinidad and the Bahamas may, on one hand, reflect the reduced availability of locally made rum in the latter. On the other, compared to Trinidad, the Bahamas is home to fewer East Indians, a group that comprises a large proportion of Trinidad's population and that appears to have a greater propensity to drink than the Afro-Trinidadian population.

Indeed, despite proscriptions against alcohol use in the three major religions of East Indians in Trinidad (Hindu, Muslim, and Presbyterian), alcoholism has been especially pronounced among East Indian men. While the agricultural work regimen creates downtime that may encourage excessive drinking, anthropologist Carole Yawney also stresses the influence of antagonistic social relationships within the East Indian community. According to Yawney, the higher incidence of alcoholism among East Indian men in Trinidad is the result of the East Indian male's desire to escape intense personal conflicts with wives, parents, children, and in-laws. These conflicts, including intergenerational tensions between young men and their fathers, stem from rigid Hindu attitudes about proper male roles, which force young East Indian men to seek sanctuary in all-male drinking clubs. Hindu taboos against men drinking with their parents magnify these tensions. According to Yawney,

> The East Indian son should never drink with [his father] or in his presence even after marriage. This value is particularly frustrating for those men who are married, raising their own families, successfully employed, and in many cases supporting their parents to some extent, for it means that the son is never fully recognized as an adult male by his parents.[18]

Abstaining from drinking with parents is one of the strongest Hindu principles of familial respect in the East Indian diaspora.[19] Yawney argues that antagonistic relationships have led to the rise of a "utilitarian" form of drinking among East Indian men, which is superficially convivial and attaches a positive value to drunkenness.[20] The high rates of alcohol use in Guyana, and to a lesser extant Trinidad, may therefore reflect a disproportionate number of East Indian drinkers.

Alcohol abuse has led to health and social problems in parts of the Caribbean. For example, as with lead-contaminated new rum in the eighteenth century, numerous health problems in Trinidad have been attributed to the consumption of illicitly produced "bush rum."[21] In addition, crime, motor vehicle accidents, homicide, suicide, domestic abuse, and risky sexual behavior are all provoked by immoderate alcohol use.[22] Excessive drinking has also exacerbated existing health problems. In the early 1990s, for example, a devastating epidemic struck Cuba and incapacitated more than 50,000 residents. Symptoms included vision loss and nerve damage. The epidemic coincided with

Cuba's economic decline, which followed the breakup of the Soviet Union. Some doctors attributed the epidemic to malnutrition and vitamin B deficiency, because the outbreak was most pronounced in alcohol users—a group that often lacks sufficient levels of vitamin B. In 1987, the rate of per capita rum consumption in Cuba was about 1.2 gallons, suggesting that alcoholism was neither widespread nor the primary cause of the epidemic. However, alcohol use within the context of malnutrition apparently compounded existing health problems and hastened the spread of the epidemic.[23]

In the early nineteenth century, British Caribbean physician Dr. Collins wrote, "A man drunk is at least a fool, if not a madman."[24] The belief that alcoholism is a mental health issue shapes treatment programs in the modern Caribbean. For example, in 1986, 85 percent of people admitted to St. Vincent's psychiatric hospital were drug and alcohol abusers.[25] Alcoholics in Barbados also receive treatment at the psychiatric hospital. Between 1980 and 1984, 12 to 18 percent of admissions to the Barbados psychiatric hospital were for the treatment of alcoholism.[26] These figures represent only inpatient admissions, but numerous other cases were seen in outpatient clinics. In 1982, an Alcoholics Anonymous group was "restarted," and by the 1990s, a separate rehabilitation program was organized to deal specifically with substance abuse. Males were consistently more likely to abuse alcohol.[27] In 1983, 139 people were referred to the Barbados treatment program, and the male-to-female ratio was about 5 to 1 (Table 8.2). Dann's survey of alcohol use in Barbados also found that women were less likely to become heavy drinkers.[28]

In Barbados, madness and drunkenness often overlap, and both are treated as mental health disorders. In fact, the "madman" figure, according to anthropologist Lawrence Fisher, is typically a heavy drinker.[29] The connection between drunkenness and madness reveals the particularly negative attitude to-

Table 8.2. Treatment for Alcoholism at the Barbados Psychiatric Hospital

Year	Number of admissions	Percentage of total	Male : Female
1980	114	12	7 : 1
1981	188	18	5 : 1
1982	163	17	4 : 1
1983	139	13	5 : 1

Source: Barbados Ministry of Health, *Annual Report* (1984).

ward uninhibited and drunken comportment in Barbadian society and a strong overriding cultural concern with physical and emotional control. The ability to hold one's liquor is an admired masculine quality, so there is a general intolerance for drunkenness. The serious tone of drinking found in rum shops in Barbados, as well as in other parts of the Caribbean, underscores this preoccupation with personal control.[30]

Rum Shops and Popular Culture

In 1949, officials in British Guiana wrote that rum shops "are a source of evil from every angle" and that they encouraged "quarrels and fights."[31] Rum shops are arenas for male drinking, and they have become symbols of Caribbean identity. Popular artists, musicians, and writers in the Caribbean and abroad have romanticized the atmosphere of Caribbean rum shop life. In Barbados, foreign tourists can take rum shop tours. In Cuba, tourists can visit the rum shops frequented by Ernest Hemingway, including La Bodeguita del Medio in Havana.

In the late 1990s, during my archaeological investigations on Suttle Street in Bridgetown, Barbados, I was introduced to the world of Barbadian rum shops. Informants told me that, in the 1950s, just before independence, Suttle Street was the center of popular culture, and rum shops provided a stage for the expression of Barbadian nationalism. Unlike other parts of Bridgetown, however, the neighborhood around Suttle Street did not benefit from Barbados's strong economy in later years. Today, many Barbadians associate the neighborhood with drugs, prostitution, and crime.

There were six rum shops in the Suttle Street neighborhood. Some were little more than open-faced, one-room tenements covered by steel burglar bars. Others were brightly painted structures that possessed various amenities. The Robin Hood rum shop, for example, had a jukebox and television. Cida's rum shop had a long saloon-style bar and a large, framed mirror. The Something For Nothing rum shop boasted a karaoke machine. Rum shops on Suttle Street sold various goods and provided a wide array of services. One 80-year-old shop owner sold fruits and vegetables, which he had acquired from local dockworkers who lived in the neighborhood. Others offered sandwiches, snacks, and a place to watch televised cricket matches.

Drinking, however, is the mainstay of a Barbadian rum shop's existence. From what I observed, the most common alcoholic beverages served there were Barbadian-made drinks, including Mount Gay, Cockspur, and E.S.A.

Field rum, as well as Banks beer. Alcohol fanned the flames of sociability at the shops, which enhanced interaction and helped integrate members into the community. Each rum shop had a crew that regularly met, a small group of usually four or five men. Upon their arrival, a server—usually a member of the shop owner's family—brought a bottle of rum, a pitcher of water, and a tray of ice cubes to the crew's table. Drinking was a group activity, and alcohol was purchased communally. Less wealthy patrons drank white rum mixed with water. Wealthier patrons drank beer and, occasionally, dark rum mixed with soft drinks. A few patrons, especially returning nationals, or "Bajan Yankees," preferred imported British gin and American whiskey. Class distinctions were evident at the rum shops on Suttle Street, and patrons often expressed social rank through their choice of alcoholic beverage.

Caribbean rum shops are places for male social interaction. Anthropologist Peter Wilson, who examined rum shop life in the western Caribbean island of Providencia in the 1970s, emphasizes the rum shops' role as refuges of male fellowship and as places for the development and display of male identity.[32] Similarly, Yawney argues that the desire to reinforce male peer relationships motivates drinking among Afro- and Indo-Trinidadian men at rum shops.[33] In general, rum shop crews consist of men of the same age who share similar occupations and life experiences.[34]

Anthropologist Gary Brana-Shute also investigated the role of Caribbean rum shops as sites for the construction of masculine values.[35] According to Brana-Shute, rum shops in Paramaribo, Suriname, express the public nature of the male-dominated "outside" world, which complements the private female-dominated "inside" world of the household. Brana-Shute describes rum shops as liminal spaces, where male camaraderie acts as a "shock absorber" for those who have fallen on hard times largely because of the high unemployment rates in the region. According to Brana-Shute, rum shops are sanctuaries where men can resolve the conflicts they encounter at work and home. The shops also function as social welfare centers where unemployed men can receive small loans and snacks. Men also use rum shops to advertise their sexual availability.[36]

The rum shops I got to know on Suttle Street in Bridgetown were also centers of male activity. Rum shop crews sat around tables and discussed political events, economic woes, and neighborhood gossip. A few women patronized the rum shops, but most women directly involved in rum shop life were the wives and daughters of rum shop owners, and they were responsible for serving food and drink. Women hucksters, mainly from rural areas, occasionally stopped in to the shops to sell their wares, including locally grown fruits, vegetables, and spices. Some sold handmade goods, such as straw brooms. Urban hucksters sold lottery tickets. Women also participated at the margins of the rum shop. Women passersby, for example, often called out to men in the rum shops from the street, while others watched from doorways. At the tables in the rum shops, men slapped dominoes, played cards, or simply "limed." The language of rum shop life inflated the masculine atmosphere. "Come, let we fire one," is the usual invitation to drink rum. The militaristic connotation of such sayings underscores the prevailing masculine approach to drinking. The masculine connotations of rum drinking are also apparent in the metaphorical connection between rum and women, such as when male rum shop patrons refer to rum as a "white missy" or a "sweet girl."

Drinking releases inhibitions and gives men the opportunity to imitate the language and actions of the highly masculine and powerful.[37] As a result, drinking at rum shops confers upon men a special status and a momentary sense of power.[38] The rum shop provides a stage for men to express power through dramatic speech and actions. Men speak with authority and slam dominoes without reservation or inhibition. Rum shops, therefore, provide an important context for the socialization, construction, and performance of powerful male roles, and alcohol magnifies changes in status.[39]

At the start of the twenty-first century, rum is embedded in the fabric of Caribbean popular culture. In Cuba, rum drinking is widespread at rumba events and competitions.[40] In Grenada, rum ensures a successful Calenda dance.[41] In Jamaica, rum is a fundamental ingredient of reggae festivals. Participants in the Big Drum Dance of Carriacou and jombee dancers in Montserrat also expend large sums of money on rum. The centrality of rum in Caribbean popular culture is most evident, however, during Trinidad Carnival.

The origin of Carnival is the Catholic tradition of Lent. In the late eighteenth century, Trinidad Carnival began as a private affair dominated by French Creoles who used it to imitate Afro-Caribbean culture. After emancipation, the celebration was co-opted by black Creoles who celebrated publicly.[42] During Carnival, blacks in Trinidad turned the social order on its head by imitating the white Creole class. As with jonkonu celebrations in Jamaica, Trinidad Carnival was a Bacchanalian ritual of rebellion replete with excessive rum drinking. In the late nineteenth century, Carnival celebrations in Trinidad provided a venue for challenging colonial authority, and drunkenness provided a shield during these confrontations. Several Carnival celebrations ended in violent clashes, which led officials to impose tight restrictions on Carnival events.

According to Caribbean researcher Richard Burton, by the mid-twentieth century, Carnival had been "purged" of its rebellious content.[43] Though rum drinking remains a central element of Carnival, it has been "exoticized and modified for foreign consumption" as the need for tourist dollars has partially dulled the expression of Caribbean identity typically celebrated at Carnival time.

Other parts of the Caribbean have cashed in on tourist dollars by sponsoring their own national cultural celebrations. Barbados crop-over is just such an event. First organized in 1971, Barbados crop-over adopted the Carnival flavor and reaped profits from foreign tourists and returning nationals. As with Trinidad Carnival, alcohol retailers in Barbados sponsor calypso tents, musicians, and crop-over fêtes. In Barbados, rum manufacturers Mount Gay, Malibu, Cockspur, and E.S.A. Field, as well as the Banks beer company, organize crop-over events and advertise their products along the parade route.

Calypso music and rum drinking are among the most prominent symbols of Caribbean identity, and they merge at Carnival and crop-over time. Although the lyrics of many calypso songs address political, social, and economic issues, rum drinking is a common theme in many of the lighter pieces. Perhaps the best-known celebration of rum's place in Caribbean identity is the calypso tune "Rum and Coca-Cola." According to musicologist Donald Hill, the song emerged in the 1940s and combined the melody of the late-nineteenth-century Martinican folk song "L'Année Passée" with the lyrics of the famous Trinidadian calypso artist Lord Invader (Rupert Grant). The song was brought to the United States, where it was sanitized for American audiences and recorded by the Andrews Sisters. Hill documented Lord Invader's rendition of the song's chorus as it was played in Trinidad in the 1950s:

> Rum and Coca-Cola
> Go down point Cumana
> Both mothers and daughters
> Working for the Yankee dollar[44]

"Rum and Coca Cola" expressed the mixing of Caribbean and American cultures within the context of prostitution and the heavy U.S. military presence in Trinidad during World War II. Tourism, globalization, and the continuing foreign military presence in the Caribbean have strengthened the construction of a pan-Caribbean identity and elevated rum to the status of cultural symbol.

Caribbean migrant and exile communities overseas have continued to embrace the symbolic meanings of rum. The use of alcohol in Haitian vodou and

Cuban santería ceremonies, for example, has followed many migrants and exiles overseas. Anthropologists Karen McCarthy Brown and Joan Dayan have explored Haitian vodou practices in Brooklyn, New York. While many vodou rites, dances, and temples (*humfo*) had to be modified in Brooklyn's densely populated urban environment, alcohol has continued to play a key role in vodou ceremonies.[45] Santería, and the spiritual role of alcohol in santería rites, can also be found among Cuban exile communities around the world.[46] In fact, in the same way that African slaves in the Caribbean used alcohol to strengthen their symbolic attachment to their brethren in Africa, overseas followers of Haitian vodou and Cuban santería pour libations and make offerings to loa and orishas, which enables them to bridge the gap to family, friends, and community at home.

In his autobiography, former U.S. secretary of state Colin Powell highlighted the way Caribbean migrants used rum to maintain links to the Caribbean. Powell, the son of Jamaican-born parents who migrated to New York in the early twentieth century, recounted that, as a young man, Appleton estate rum from Jamaica flowed at New Year's Day celebrations.[47] Powell wrote, "In my family, to serve anything else was considered an affront." Powell's family, like many other Caribbean migrants around the world, embraced the symbolic meaning of rum and used it to strengthen cultural and national identity abroad.

Notes

Chapter 1. Introduction

1. True rum is made in sugarcane-growing regions of the world, but the name has also been applied to sugarcane-based alcoholic beverages made in non-sugarcane-growing regions. For example, New Englanders, who distilled molasses purchased from the Caribbean sugar islands, also called their spirits rum. To a lesser extent, Europeans who distilled syrup, the waste product of metropolitan sugar refineries, also applied the name rum to their product.

2. Mintz, *Sweetness and Power*.

3. McCusker, *Rum and the American Revolution*.

4. Barrows and Room, *Drinking: Behavior and Belief*; Blocker and Warsh, *Changing Face of Drink*; Garine and Garine, *Drinking: Anthropological Approaches*; M. Douglas, *Constructive Drinking*; Everett, Waddell, and Heath, *Cross-Cultural Approaches*; Gefou-Madianou, *Alcohol, Gender, and Culture*; M. Marshall, *Beliefs, Behaviors, and Alcoholic Beverages*.

Chapter 2. At the Margins of the Atlantic World: Caribbean Rum in the Seventeenth Century

1. Ligon, *True and Exact History*, 31.

2. Hodge and Taylor, *Ethnobotany*, 597; D. Taylor, *Caribs of Dominica*, 154.

3. Scott, cited in Campbell, *Some Early Barbadian History*, 247; see also Handler, "Amerindian Slave Population," 42.

4. Ligon, *True and Exact History*, 31.

5. Spoeri, cited in Gunkel and Handler, "Swiss Medical Doctor's Description," 10; Hughes, *Natural History*, 228.

6. Labat, *Nouveau voyage*, 1:133; see also Du Tertre, *Histoire generale*, 2:120.

7. The Taino Indians of the Greater Antilles probably did not produce or consume alcohol prior to the arrival of Europeans. See, for example, Rouse, *Tainos*, 12, 158; Sauer, *Early Spanish Main*, 51. Mobbie was apparently absent in Taino centers of the Greater Antilles.

8. See Du Tertre, *Histoire generale*, 2:117.

9. In the French Caribbean, cassava-based drinks were sometimes mixed with other ingredients, including potatoes, sugarcane juice, and bananas. See Breton, *Relations de l'ile de la Guadeloupe*, 46; Labat, *Nouveau voyage*, 1:133; La Borde, *Relation de l'origine*, 23.

10. Ligon, *True and Exact History*, 32; Silvester, "Breife Discription of the Ilande," 46. In 1595, Sir Walter Raleigh led an expedition up the Orinoco River, not far from the Essequibo, and identified the province of Parino. Perhaps the Caribs that migrated to Barbados were from the Parino province, and the Barbadians simply applied the name of their homeland to the cassava-based alcoholic drink they made. See Whitehead, *Discoverie of . . . Guiana by Sir Walter Ralegh*, 187.

11. Ligon, *True and Exact History*, 32.

12. In 1596, Dr. Layfield, a chaplain on George Clifford's expedition to the Caribbean, identified the use of fermented cassava-based alcoholic drinks among the Spanish colonists of Puerto Rico. Although Puerto Rico was not a Carib center, Caribs probably occupied the eastern tip of the island at the time of European contact (see *Large Relation*, 97). In the late seventeenth century, Caribbean traveler Hans Sloane described the production of perino in Jamaica, an area far removed from Carib culture. Perhaps, migrants from Barbados introduced perino to Jamaica in the early years of Jamaican settlement. Sloane also noted that the use of perino was concentrated in the Guianas, the ancient homeland of the Island Carib (*Voyage to the Islands*, 1:xviii, xxix).

13. Breton, *Relations de l'ile de la Guadeloupe*, 45–46; Du Tertre, *Histoire generale*, 2:117; Hodge and Taylor, *Ethnobotany*, 574–75; Labat, *Nouveau voyage*, 1:133; Rochefort, *Histoire naturelle*, 501; D. Taylor, *Caribs of Dominica*, 137.

14. Ligon, *True and Exact History*, 32.

15. Du Tertre, *Histoire generale*, 2:117; Labat, *Nouveau voyage*, 1:133; La Borde, *Relation de l'origine*, 23; Rochefort, *Histoire naturelle*, 501.

16. Ligon, *True and Exact History*, 32.

17. Ibid.

18. Ibid., 33.

19. Labat, *Nouveau voyage*, 1:134.

20. Du Tertre, *Histoire generale*, 2:112–21; Labat, *Nouveau voyage*, 1:133–38; Ligon, *True and Exact History*, 32–33, 69, 80; Oldmixon, *British Empire*, 2:132; Rochefort, *Histoire naturelle*, 339; Sloane, *Voyage to the Islands*, 1:xxix, lxix.

21. Ligon, *True and Exact History*, 31–32; Ligon also believed that mobbie made from red potatoes looked like claret, while mobbie made from white potatoes looked like white wine.

22. Spoeri, cited in Gunkel and Handler, "Swiss Medical Doctor's Description," 10.

23. Du Tertre, *Histoire generale*, 2:117; Labat, *Nouveau voyage*, 1:133.

24. Ratekin, "Early Sugar Industry."

25. Oviedo cited in Craton, Walvin, and Wright, *Slavery, Abolition, and Emancipation*, 8.

26. See, for example, Herrero, "La estructura comercial del Caribe"; Ratekin, "Early Sugar Industry."

27. Unwin, *Wine and the Vine*, 236. The commercial expansion of distilling began in England a century later when Charles I granted the Worshipful Company of Distillers a distilling monopoly for a 21-mile radius around London and Westminster. See Berlin, *Worshipful Company of Distillers.*

28. Underwood, "Historical Development of Distilling," 42.

29. Brunschwig, *Liber de arte distillandi*; Andrew, *The Vertuose Boke*; Gesner, *Treasure of Euonymus;* Baker, *Practise of the New and Old Phisicke.*

30. Historian John McCusker argued that the high cost of distilled spirits hindered the early growth of European distilling industries. In particular, early stills were small and could not achieve economies of scale. Moreover, the high cost of base materials, such as wine and grain, greatly limited the growth of early distillation in Europe. According to McCusker, the success of European distilling industries had to wait until the 1650s, when the rise of New World sugar making, and subsequent rise of sugar refining in Europe, provided distillers with cheap and abundant syrup, the molasses-like by-product of sugar refining (see "Distilling and Its Implications" and "The Business of Distilling"). In addition, technological stagnation slowed the geographical spread of alcohol distillation in northern Europe. For example, early alembics lacked an effective cooling apparatus for generating the quick and efficient condensation of alcohol. See Underwood, "Historical Development of Distilling," 46.

31. Fermented sugarcane-based drinks were known in the Old World in ancient times. In his search for the origins of sugar making, anthropologist Sidney W. Mintz argued that the earliest datable mention of sugarcane came from Alexander the Great's general, Nearchus, during his conquest of the Indus river region in 327 B.C. Nearchus wrote, "a reed in India brings forth honey without the help of bees, from which an intoxicating drink is made though the plant bears no fruit." Ironically, the statement refers not to sugar, but to an alcoholic drink made from sugarcane. See Mintz, *Sweetness and Power*, 20; see also Deerr, *History of Sugar*, 1:15.

32. Las Casas cited in Craton, Walvin, and Wright, *Slavery, Abolition, and Emancipation*, 10; see also Las Casas, *History of the Indies*, 258.

33. Fermented sugarcane-based drinks are found throughout the sugarcane-growing regions of the Americas in the late sixteenth and early seventeenth century. In 1600, for example, a request was made to the mayor of the mining district of Taxco that the sale of wine made from sugarcane juice be prohibited because it caused "death, illness and other harm" to the Indians. See Zavala, *Fuentes para la historia*, 6:163–67. In 1625, English Dominican monk Thomas Gage reported that the Indians of Guatemala made drinks that they "confection in such great Jarrs as come from *Spain;* wherein they put some little quantity of water, and fill up the Jar with some Melasso's,

or juice of the Sugar Cane" (see *New Survey*, 323). See also Sandoval, *La industria del azúcar*, 64–65.

34. Layfield, *Large Relation*, 98.

35. The term *guarapo* probably derives from the Italian word *grappa*, a cheap wine made from the dregs of earlier wine fermentations. Grappa was a popular drink among peasants in the winemaking regions of Europe as early as the twelfth century. In the New World, grappa was a fitting model for an alcohol made from the unwanted skimmings, or dregs, of sugar production.

36. For garapa in Brazil, see Àntonil, *Cúltura é ópulencia*, 252–53, n. 132. See also Moreau cited in Thornton, *Africa and Africans*, 174. For grappe in the French Caribbean see Labat, *Nouveau voyage*, 1:134. Grappe later became the name for the fermenting wash compound made prior to distilling in the French Caribbean.

37. Ligon, *True and Exact History*, 32. Ligon made the only reference to grippo, and the term is not found again in the British Caribbean. Subsequently, fermented sugarcane-based alcoholic drinks in the British Caribbean were called the cool drink and cowow. See, for example, Sloane, *Voyage to the Islands*, 1:xxix, lxii; Hughes, *Natural History*, 34.

38. Rochefort, *Histoire naturelle*, 502.

39. Du Tertre, *Histoire generale*, 2:124–25.

40. Ligon, *True and Exact History*, 85.

41. Dunn, *Sugar and Slaves*, 62; Ligon, *True and Exact History*, 34, 85–86.

42. Du Tertre, *Histoire generale*, 2:471.

43. Ibid., 1:457–61; Emmanuel, "New Light on Early American Jewry"; Emmanuel and Emmanuel, *History of the Jews*, 37–90; Ligon, *True and Exact History*, 85–86; Rochefort, *Histoire naturelle*, 332.

44. The Dutch were so central in the distilling industry that the word for brandy derives from the Dutch, meaning literally "burnt-wine" (see Unwin, *Wine and the Vine*, 236–37).

45. Emmanuel, "New Light on Early American Jewry," 22; Labat, *Nouveau voyage*, 1:31; Peytraud, *L'esclavage aux antilles française*, 214.

46. Cited by Jacques Breton, "Relation de l'establissement des Francois depuis l'an 1635 en l'isle de la Martinique," *Généalogie et histoire de la Caribe* 88 (Dec. 1996):1814. I wish to thank David Geggus for the English translation.

47. For brusle ventre, see also Du Tertre, *Histoire generale*, 2:359.

48. Ibid., 2:124–25.

49. Ibid., fold-out plate following page 122 in vol. 2.

50. Rochefort, *Histoire naturelle*, 502.

51. Colt, "Voyage of Sir Henry Colt," 65. Colt's use of the term "good distillers" was meant to convey the heavy drinking of Barbadian colonists. It is synonymous with good topers.

52. Thomas, *Historical Account*, 13.

53. Archaeologist Ivor Noel-Hume recovered a locally made ceramic still head from a 1620s deposit at the Martin's Hundred site in Virginia. Although the still may have been used to concoct medicines from local plants rather than alcohol for commercial purposes, its presence indicates that at least some early British colonists in the Americas were familiar with the art of distillation. See Noel-Hume, *Martin's Hundred*, 101–2.

54. Ligon, *True and Exact History*, 32.

55. Lucas, "Lucas Manuscript Volumes," 115.

56. Silvester, "Breife Discription of the Ilande," 46. Although identified as anonymous, the author is clearly Giles Silvester (see F. H. Smith, "Disturbing the Peace").

57. Davis, "Etymology of the Word Rum."

58. Ligon, *True and Exact History*, 113.

59. Ibid., 92–93.

60. Rochefort, *Histoire naturelle*, 334.

61. Du Tertre, *Histoire generale*, 2:124.

62. Ibid., 2:514–15.

63. Labat, *Nouveau voyage*, 1:135; Sloane, *Voyage to the Islands*, 1:xxx.

64. McCusker, "Business of Distilling," 221.

65. Belgrove, *Treatise Upon Husbandry*, 22.

66. Lucas, "Lucas Manuscript Volumes," 115.

67. Du Tertre, *Histoire generale*, fold-out plate following page 122 in vol. 2.

68. See, for example, Gesner, *Treasure of Euonymus*. See also Holme, *Academy of Armory*, 423; Underwood, "Historical Development of Distilling," 44–46.

69. See Braudel, *Structures of Everyday Life*, 244; Underwood, "Historical Development of Distilling," 53–54.

70. Puckrein, *Little England*, 57–60.

71. Eltis, "New Estimates of Exports."

72. In contrast, rum exports from Jamaica were minor. In 1672, for example, governor Thomas Lynch did not list rum among Jamaica's major exports (see Blome, *Description of the Island*). In the period 1698–1700, Jamaican rum exports averaged only a little more than 5,000 gallons per year and rum represented only 1 percent of the total value of Jamaica's export trade (see Eltis, "New Estimates of Exports").

73. Ligon, *True and Exact History*, 112.

74. Ibid., 93.

75. Eltis, "New Estimates of Exports." Puckrein, *Little England*, 57–60.

76. Due to a settlement with Charles II in 1663, Barbados paid an additional 4.5 percent tax on all exported goods. The tax was a burden to Barbadian planters for nearly two centuries.

77. Ligon, *True and Exact History*, 93.

78. Ibid., 112.

79. Labat, *Nouveau voyage*, 1:321–24.

80. Ibid., 1:317, 323; see also Josa, *Les industries du sucre*, 54, 60; Pairault, *Le rhum et sa fabrication*, 6; Stein, *French Sugar Business*, 43.

81. Labat believed that the sale of tafia defrayed about 50 percent of plantation expenses. See Labat, *Nouveau voyage*, 1:321–34. See also Josa, *Les industries du sucre*, 58–60; Kervégant, *Rhums et eaux-de-vie*, 21.

82. Josa, *Les industries du sucre*, 54, 60; Kervégant, *Rhums et eaux-de-vie*, 21.

83. Josa, *Les industries du sucre*, 60.

84. Rawlin, *Laws of Barbados*, 71–72.

85. Cited in Eltis, *Rise of African Slavery*, 202.

86. Berleant-Schiller, "Free Labor and the Economy," 551, 560.

87. Eltis, "Total Product of Barbados" and *Rise of African Slavery*, 202.

88. Eltis, "New Estimates of Exports."

89. Campbell, *Some Early Barbadian History*, 145.

90. Dunn, *Sugar and Slaves*, 96.

91. Ligon, *True and Exact History*, 93.

92. For discussions about alcohol and concerns about tainted water in Jamaica, see Long, *History of Jamaica*, 1:228, 253–54; Sloane, *Voyage to the Islands*, 1:x. Similar fears increased the demand for alcohol in other historical settings. See, for example, Rorabaugh, *Alcoholic Republic*, 95–97.

93. Colt, "Voyage of Sir Henry Colt," 67.

94. Ligon, *True and Exact History*, 28.

95. Ibid., 25.

96. Handler, "Plantation Slave Settlements in Barbados, 1650s–1834."

97. Labat, *Nouveau voyage*, 2:274.

98. Colt, "Voyage of Sir Henry Colt," 66.

99. Ligon, *True and Exact History*, 93.

100. Laudan, "Birth of the Modern Diet"; Rorabaugh, *Alcoholic Republic*, 136.

101. Geggus, *Slavery, War, and Revolution*, 368–69.

102. Ewing and Rouse, "Drinks, Drinkers, and Drinking," 15–16.

103. Labat, *Nouveau voyage*, 1:323; Peytraud, *L'esclavage aux antilles française*, 196.

104. Rorabaugh, *Alcoholic Republic*, 117.

105. Ligon, *True and Exact History*, 29–38.

106. Ibid., 94.

107. Ibid., 93.

108. Berlin, *Worshipful Company of Distillers*, 3.

109. Ligon, *True and Exact History*, 93.

110. Gibb and King, "Gender, Activity Areas, and Homelots"; McCusker, *Rum and the American Revolution*, 430; Moussette, "Site of the Intendant's Palace in Québec City"; Rorabaugh, *Alcoholic Republic*, 9–10, 110–13, 229.

111. See Unwin, *Wine and the Vine*, 248–49.

112. Cotter, *Archaeological Excavations*, 67; Noel-Hume, *Martin's Hundred*, 102. For discussion of the problems faced by early distillers in North America, see McCusker, *Rum and the American Revolution*, 441–43.

113. Eltis, "New Estimates of Exports," 641–46.

114. Schumpeter, *English Overseas Trade Statistics*, 52–59.

115. Sloane, *Voyage to the Islands*, 1:xxx.

116. Rorabaugh, *Alcoholic Republic*, 63–64.

117. Colonial Williamsburg Foundation Library, Williamsburg, Virginia: Robert Carter papers, 1772–1794, Nomini Hall (Westmoreland County), Virginia; also Richmond, Northumberland, Loudoun, Prince William, and Frederick counties, Virginia, and Baltimore, Maryland, microform.

118. F. H. Smith, "Disturbing the Peace."

119. Bailyn, *New England Merchants*, 88–89.

120. Ibid., 84.

121. Ibid., 130; Emmanuel and Emmanuel, *History of the Jews*, 71–72.

122. Mancall, *Deadly Medicine*, 82–83.

123. Gould, "Trade Between the Windward Islands and the Continental Colonies," 474–76.

124. Dailey, "Role of Alcohol Among North American Indian Tribes," 117.

125. Mancall, *Deadly Medicine*, 137.

126. Cited in Bridenbaugh and Bridenbaugh, *No Peace*, 92. See also Bailyn, *New England Merchants*, 130; Pope, "Fish into Wine."

127. Mather, *Sober Considerations*.

128. See Herd, "Paradox of Temperance," 355.

129. Rorabaugh, *Alcoholic Republic*, 64.

130. Conroy, "Puritans in Taverns," 30.

131. Bailyn, *New England Merchants*, 129.

132. Conroy, "Puritans in Taverns," 51.

133. It is not entirely clear whether Downing was distilling rum from imported molasses or whiskey from local grain. See Bailyn, *New England Merchants*, 129; Coughtry, *Notorious Triangle*, 81; McCusker, *Rum and the American Revolution*, 434.

134. In 1697, the last year of King William's War, England and Wales imported less than 100 gallons of rum, and none of it came from North America. In fact, the first New England rum exports did not reach England until 1704 and even this shipment was a mere 20 gallons. See McCusker, *Rum and the American Revolution*, 434–36, 945.

135. Bailyn, *New England Merchants*, 129–30; McCusker, *Rum and the American Revolution*, 435.

136. W. Taylor, *Drinking, Homicide, and Rebellion*, 54–55.

137. Jamieson, *Domestic Architecture and Power*, 95–96.

138. Rice, "Peru's Colonial Wine Industry" and "Wine and Brandy Production in Colonial Peru."

139. W. Taylor, *Drinking, Homicide, and Rebellion*, 47.

140. Gage, *New Survey*, 62; W. Taylor, *Drinking, Homicide, and Rebellion*, 45–49.

141. Las Casas, *History of the Indies*, 59.

142. Sandoval, *La industria del azúcar*, 165; Chez Checo, *El ron en la historia*, 50.

143. Mora de Tovar, *Aguardiente y conflictos sociales*, 17, n. 1. As early as 1635, prohibitions against distilling in New Spain stressed the harmful effects of distilled spirits on Indian peasants, though it is not clear whether colonists in the region were distilling rum. See also Zavala, *Fuentes para la historia*, 6:163–67, 400–401.

144. Huetz de Lemps, *Histoire du rhum*, 65.

145. Mora de Tovar, *Aguardiente y conflictos sociales*, 17, n. 2.

146. Archivo General de la Nación, Caracas, Venezuela, sección Reales Cédulas, primera parte, vol. 10, Real Cédula number 37, folios 168–77v. I wish to thank Jeremy Cohen for this reference.

147. Ligon, *True and Exact History*, 93.

148. Chez Checo, *El ron en la historia*, 51.

149. Labat, *Nouveau voyage*, 1:135.

150. Emmanuel, "New Light on Early American Jewry."

151. Gage, *New Survey*, 37.

152. Labat, *Nouveau voyage*, 1:29.

153. Du Tertre, *Histoire generale*, 2:467.

154. Ibid., 1:428.

155. Akyeampong, *Drink, Power, and Cultural Change*, 42–43; Mancall, *Deadly Medicine*, 47; Thornton, *Africa and Africans*, 66–67.

156. Labat, *Nouveau voyage*, 1:29, 2:101.

157. Braithwaite cited in Southey, *Chronological History*, 2:233.

158. Breton, *Relations de l'île de la Guadeloupe*, 56–57; La Borde, *Relation de l'origine*, 13–14; Rochefort, *Histoire naturelle,* 472.

159. Breton, *Relations de l'île de la Guadeloupe*, 56–57; La Borde, *Relation de l'origine*, 13; Rochefort, *Histoire naturelle,* 468–72.

160. La Borde, *Relation de l'origine*, 7; see also translation in Hulme and Whitehead, *Wild Majesty*, 142.

161. Anthropologist Douglas Taylor argued that the Caribs did not make offerings to evil spirits [Mápoya], but only to "spirit helpers" (see "Interpretation of Some Documentary Evidence on Carib Culture," 389–90). However, Neil Whitehead showed that Carib shamans [Boyéz], at least in parts of the Guianas, made alcohol offerings to call down the more aggressive "evil spirits," which they used to attack their enemies (see *Dark Shamans*, 48–49).

162. Breton, *Relations de l'île de la Guadeloupe*, 66. See also translation in Hulme and Whitehead, *Wild Majesty*, 112; La Borde, *Relation de l'origine*, 32–33.

163. Du Tertre, *Histoire generale*, 2:373; Rochefort, *Histoire naturelle*, 550–51; D.

Taylor, "Meaning of Dietary and Occupational Restrictions Among the Island Carib." La Borde reported that women undergo a similar fast when they reach marriageable age, during which time they eat cassava and oüicou (see *Relation de l'origine*, 34–35).

164. Breton, *Relations de l'île de la Guadeloupe*, 66–67; Du Tertre, *Histoire generale*, 2:374–75; La Borde, *Relation de l'origine*, 35; Rochefort, *Histoire naturelle*, 554–55.

165. Breton, *Relations de l'île de la Guadeloupe*, 65–67; Du Tertre, *Histoire generale*, 2:372–80; La Borde, *Relation de l'origine*, 32–38; Rochefort, *Histoire naturelle*, 553–54; D. Taylor, "Kinship and Social Structure," 185–86.

166. Breton, *Relations de l'île de la Guadeloupe*, 79–80; La Borde, *Relation de l'origine*, 37; D. Taylor, "Kinship and Social Structure," 187.

167. Breton, *Relations de l'île de la Guadeloupe*, 80.

168. La Borde, *Relation de l'origine*, 37–38.

169. Ibid., 7.

170. Labat, *Nouveau voyage*, 1:30.

171. Layfield, *Large Relation*, 56.

172. Young cited in Edwards, *History, Civil and Commercial*, 3:255.

173. Braithwaite cited in Southey, *Chronological History*, 2:234.

174. Hulme and Whitehead, *Wild Majesty*, 172.

175. Du Tertre, *Histoire generale*, 2:386.

176. La Borde, *Relation de l'origine*, 26.

177. Ibid., 14.

178. Ibid., 24.

179. Ibid., 19. Ironically, despite the French missionaries' condemnation of Carib drunkenness, some missionaries had no problem dispensing shots of brandy to entice Caribs into Christian Baptism. See, for example, Labat, *Nouveau voyage*, 1:31; Rochefort, *Histoire naturelle*, 481.

180. Du Tertre, *Histoire generale*, 2:386.

181. Anthropologist Seth Leacock has argued that alcohol-induced spirit possession in Afro-Brazilian cults enhanced one's ability to play a godlike role (see "Ceremonial Drinking"). In Carib society, shamans invoked spirits who possessed the bodies of women (see Rochefort, *Histoire naturelle*, 473).

182. Staden, "Veritable History," 106.

183. La Borde, *Relation de l'origine*, 24.

184. Schaefer, "Drunkenness."

185. La Borde, *Relation de l'origine*, 5–6, 14–15; Rochefort, *Histoire naturelle*, 474–75.

186. Rochefort, *Histoire naturelle*, 558.

187. According to sociologist Mark Keller (see "Great Jewish Drink Mystery"), the overriding ritual importance of alcohol in Judaism is responsible for the infrequency of alcoholism among American Jews.

188. Rochefort, *Histoire naturelle*, 462.

Chapter 3. Rum's Threat to Competing Alcohol Industries in the Eighteenth Century

1. Mintz, *Sweetness and Power*, 47–51.

2. Martin, *Essay Upon Plantership*, 53.

3. Long, *History of Jamaica*, 1:441–42, 2:75.

4. Beckford, *Descriptive Account*, 1:154–55.

5. Baikow, *Manufacture and Refining*, 223; Barnes, *Sugar Cane*, 119; Wray, *Practical Sugar Planter*, 391.

6. Charpentier de Cossigny, *Mémoire sur la fabrication*, 5.

7. Long, *History of Jamaica*, 1:457, 2:79, 179.

8. Wray, *Practical Sugar Planter*, 399–400. See also Young, *West India Commonplace Book*, 63.

9. Belgrove, *Treatise Upon Husbandry*, 35.

10. Anonymous, cited in *Affiches Américaines*, December 7, 1786; Charpentier de Cossigny also believed fermentation was best in the summer months (see *Mémoire sur la fabrication*, 4).

11. Lock, Newlands, and Newlands, *Sugar: A Handbook*, 751–52.

12. Wray, *Practical Sugar Planter*, 400–403.

13. Roughley, *Jamaica Planter's Guide*, 385.

14. Belgrove, *Treatise Upon Husbandry*, 29; Stein, *French Sugar Business*, 66–67, 123.

15. See, for example, Edwards, *History, Civil and Commercial*, 2:285, note.

16. Long, *History of Jamaica*, 2:565; see also Oldmixon, *British Empire*, 2:128.

17. *Affiches Américaines*, March 2, 1768; *Affiches Américaines*, March 16, 1768; Clement, "Settlement Patterning on the British Caribbean Island of Tobago."

18. Sloane, *Voyage to the Islands*, 1:xxx.

19. Beckford, *Descriptive Account*, 1:55. See also Long, *History of Jamaica*, 3:901.

20. Anonymous, "Some Observations," 2:245; Thistlewood cited in D. Hall, *Miserable Slavery*, 46.

21. Taylor cited in Dunn, *Sugar and Slaves*, 197.

22. Edwards, *History, Civil and Commercial*, 2:279–80.

23. In 1774, Long noted that distillers in Jamaica practiced the same equal three parts method (see *History of Jamaica*, 2:560–61). See also Martin, *Essay Upon Plantership*, 55.

24. Barbadian distillers appear to have developed advanced wash compounds earlier than distillers in Jamaica. For example, the wash recipe consisting of three equal parts scum, dunder, and water was an average wash proportion typically used among early rum distillers in the British Caribbean. Yet, in 1755, Belgrove referred to this method as an "ancient Practice" in Barbados and proceeded to describe a variety of complex local wash recipes (see *Treatise Upon Husbandry*, 26). In 1774, two decades after Belgrove's observation, Long noted that Jamaican distillers continued to practice

that "ancient" method (see *History of Jamaica*, 2:560–61). It was not until 1794, nearly 40 years after Belgrove's initial reference to the "ancient practice," that Edwards argued that the average wash recipe in Jamaica had "improved."

25. Wray, *Practical Sugar Planter*, 398.

26. Belgrove, *Treatise Upon Husbandry*, 26; Edwards, *History, Civil and Commercial*, 2:283; Roughley, *Jamaica Planter's Guide*, 387; Wray, *Practical Sugar Planter*, 398–99.

27. Wray, *Practical Sugar Planter*, 395–97.

28. Ibid., 400.

29. Martin, *Essay Upon Plantership*, 57.

30. Ibid., 56; see also Wray, *Practical Sugar Planter*, 403.

31. Gibbons, "Alcohol: The Legal Drug," 7.

32. Roughley, *Jamaica Planter's Guide*, 391; Martin, *Essay Upon Plantership*, 56.

33. Belgrove, *Treatise Upon Husbandry*, 21–22.

34. Edwards, *History, Civil and Commercial*, 2:276–77.

35. *Affiches Américaines*, March 2, 1768.

36. *Affiches Américaines*, December 7, 1786.

37. Wray, *Practical Sugar Planter*, 400. See also Charpentier de Cossigny, *Mémoire sur la fabrication*, 6.

38. Martin, *Essay Upon Plantership*, 54.

39. *Affiches Américaines*, December 7, 1786.

40. Martin, *Essay Upon Plantership*, 53.

41. McCusker, *Rum and the American Revolution*, 821.

42. Martin, *Essay Upon Plantership*, 53.

43. Barbados Department of Archives, Codrington plantation records.

44. McCusker, *Rum and the American Revolution*, 151–52; Ragatz, *Fall of the Planter Class*, 16, 167–69.

45. McCusker, *Rum and the American Revolution*, 138–42; Wray, *Practical Sugar Planter*, 385–86.

46. McCusker, *Rum and the American Revolution*, 139.

47. Ibid., 93–94; see also Drescher, *Econocide*, 193.

48. Anonymous, "Some Observations," 2:242.

49. Anonymous, *Art of Making Sugar*, 27.

50. Anonymous, "Some Observations," 2:244; Roughley, *Jamaica Planter's Guide*, 352–53.

51. Martin, *Essay Upon Plantership*, 54, n. *.

52. Edwards, *History, Civil and Commercial*, 2:285, note.

53. McCusker, *Rum and the American Revolution*, 216.

54. Anonymous, "Some Observations," 2:244.

55. McCusker, *Rum and the American Revolution*, 156–57, 258, n. 86.

56. Anonymous, "Some Observations," 2:245.

57. Martin, *Essay Upon Plantership*, 60.

58. Roughley, *Jamaica Planter's Guide*, 393–94.

59. Ligon, *True and Exact History*, 92–93.

60. Bridenbaugh and Bridenbaugh, *No Peace*, 297.

61. Anonymous, "Some Observations," 2:242.

62. Belgrove, *Treatise Upon Husbandry*, 21–22.

63. Long, *History of Jamaica*, 2:565.

64. Edwards, *History, Civil and Commercial*, 2:283–84. According to Edwards, the rum obtained through the double-distilling method in Jamaica weighed 7 pounds 12 ounces per gallon, or 8.62 drams avoirdupois per cubic inch, making it slightly more than 50 percent absolute alcohol.

65. Edwards, *History, Civil and Commercial*, 2:285–86, note.

66. Roughley, *Jamaica Planter's Guide*, 393.

67. Wray, *Practical Sugar Planter*, 386, 398, 403.

68. Pairault, *Le rhum et sa fabrication*, 109.

69. Martin, *Essay Upon Plantership*, 60.

70. Charpentier de Cossigny, *Mémoire sur la fabrication*, 1–2.

71. Ibid., 5.

72. Pairault, *Le rhum et sa fabrication*, 2 n. 1, 114–15.

73. Unwin, *Wine and the Vine*, 246.

74. Deagan, "Fig Springs" and *Spanish St. Augustine*; Fairbanks, "Spaniards, Planters, Ships, and Slaves"; Goggin, *Spanish Olive Jar*.

75. Ligon, *True and Exact History*, 39.

76. Deagan, "Fig Springs"; Gage, *New Survey*, 37; Las Casas, *History of the Indies*, 188.

77. Gage, *New Survey*, 62.

78. Chez Checo, *El ron en la historia*, 62–63; Gage, *New Survey*, 62; Mora de Tovar, *Aguardiente y conflictos sociales*; Sandoval, *La industria del azúcar*, 167; W. Taylor, *Drinking, Homicide, and Rebellion*.

79. Schumpeter, *English Overseas Trade Statistics*, 52–59.

80. Archivo General de la Nación, Caracas, Venezuela, sección Reales Cédulas, primera parte, vol. 10, real cédula number 37, folios 168–77v.

81. Schumpeter, *English Overseas Trade Statistics*, 52–59.

82. Rice, "Peru's Colonial Wine Industry" and "Wine and Brandy Production in Colonial Peru."

83. Chez Checo, *El ron en la historia*, 62–63.

84. Ibid., 61. Illicit distilling was also common in New Spain and New Granada. See W. Taylor, *Drinking, Homicide, and Rebellion*, 55; Mora de Tovar, *Aguardiente y conflictos sociales*.

85. Tarrade, *Le commerce colonial*, 174–78. See also Tarrade, "Le commerce entre les Antilles françaises."

86. Chez Checo, *El ron en la historia*, 62, 156.

87. Sandoval, *La industria del azúcar*, 167.

88. Moreno Fraginals, *El ingenio*, 3:43–46. Spanish officials gradually removed restrictions on rum making in the Spanish colonial world. In 1796, restrictions were lifted in New Spain. See also Hernandez Palomo, *El aguardiente de caña*; W. Taylor, *Drinking, Homicide, and Rebellion*, 55.

89. Bruman, *Alcohol in Ancient Mexico*; Jamieson, *Domestic Architecture and Power*, 184–85; Mora de Tovar, *Aguardiente y conflictos sociales*; W. Taylor, *Drinking, Homicide, and Rebellion*, 30, 55–59.

90. Josa, *Les industries du sucre*, 112–13.

91. Ibid., 110–14; Nardin, *La mise en valeur de l'île de Tobago*, 231–32; Tarrade, "Le commerce entre les Antilles françaises," 35–37.

92. Moreau de St.-Méry, *Topographical and Political Description*, 1:50.

93. Long, *History of Jamaica*, 1:499.

94. Ragatz, *Fall of the Planter Class*, 121–23, 138–39.

95. Edwards, *History, Civil and Commercial*, 1:297.

96. Moreno Fraginals, *El ingenio*, 3:43–46.

97. Gardner, *History of Jamaica*, 324.

98. Moreno Fraginals, *El ingenio*, 3:43–46.

99. Unwin, *Wine and the Vine*, 221, 235–36.

100. Hancock, "Commerce and Conversation"; Unwin, *Wine and the Vine*, 247–48.

101. Schumpeter, *English Overseas Trade Statistics*, 52–59.

102. Leslie, *New and Exact Account of Jamaica*, 32.

103. Robertson, *Detection of the State*, 8–11.

104. Labat, *Nouveau voyage*, 1:135–36.

105. Kervégant, *Rhums et eaux-de-vie*, 12–13.

106. Josa, *Les industries du sucre*, 92.

107. Schumpeter, *English Overseas Trade Statistics*, 52–59.

108. Bosman, *New and Accurate Description of the Coast of Guinea*; Robertson, *Detection of the State*, 8–11; Sheridan, "Molasses Act."

109. Kervégant, *Rhums et eaux-de-vie*, 468. Between 1743 and 1745, Martinique exported an annual average of 4,261 barriques of tafia to French and foreign American colonies. Labat estimated that a barrique contained 120 pots or 67.3 gallons (see *Nouveau voyage*, 1:323). Thus, annual exports were about 286,000 gallons. See also Josa, *Les industries du sucre*, 54; Pairault, *Le rhum et sa fabrication*. However, by the mid-eighteenth century, if not earlier, a barrique was equal in capacity to the British puncheon (110–120 gallons). The larger barrique size is more appropriate for determining mid- to late-eighteenth-century exports. See Nardin, *La mise en valeur de l'île de Tobago*, 231–32.

110. Josa, *Les industries du sucre*, 112–13.

111. Goebel, "New England Trade"; Gould, "Trade Between the Windward Islands and the Continental Colonies"; Pope, "Fish into Wine."

112. Josa, *Les industries du sucre*, 110–14; *Affiches Américaines*, December 7, 1786; Tarrade, *Le commerce colonial*, 175, 365.

113. Goebel, "New England Trade," 352.

114. Stein, *French Sugar Business*, 60–67.

115. Poyer, *History of Barbados*, 267.

116. Butel-Dumont, *Histoire et commerce*, 131.

117. Oldmixon, *British Empire*, 2:88–89.

118. Sheridan, "Molasses Act."

119. Goebel, "New England Trade," 344.

120. Martin, *Essay Upon Plantership*, 5, n. *.

121. Quoted in Goebel, "New England Trade," 371.

122. Josa, *Les industries du sucre*, 112–13.

123. Tarrade, "Le commerce entre les Antilles françaises," 35–37. A *boucaut* probably held 110 gallons. See Nardin, *La mise en valeur de l'île de Tobago*, 231–32.

124. Meyer et al., *Histoire de la France coloniale*; Tarrade, *Le commerce colonial*, 173–74, 329–31.

125. Kervégant, *Rhums et eaux-de-vie*, 485; Meyer et al., *Histoire de la France coloniale*, 249; Saugera, *Bordeaux, port négrier*, 76–80.

126. Quoted in Stein, *French Sugar Business*, 73.

127. Josa, *Les industries du sucre*, 101–2.

128. *Affiches Américaines*, July 6, 1768; Josa, *Les industries du sucre*, 103; Meyer et al., *Histoire de la France coloniale*, 247–54; E. Williams, *From Columbus to Castro*, 175.

129. Meyer et al., *Histoire de la France coloniale*, 255.

130. *Affiches Américaines*, December 7, 1786; Charpentier de Cossigny, *Mémoire sur la fabrication*; Dutrône de la Couture, *Précis sur la canne*.

131. *Affiches Américaines*, November 16, 1768.

132. Carrington, *British West Indies*, 178.

133. Hilliard d'Auberteuil, *Considérations sur l'état présent*, 1:65–73.

134. Edwards, *History, Civil and Commercial*, 3:144.

135. Ibid., 3:214; Lepelletier de St.-Remy, *Saint Domingue*, 52–53; Moreau de St.-Méry, *Description topographique*, 1:100.

136. Frémond de la Merveillère, "L'habitation sucrière."

137. Schnakenbourg, "Statistiques pour l'histoire," 87, 110.

138. Moreau de St.-Méry, *Description topographique*, 1:100.

139. *Affiches Américaines*, November 23, 1768.

140. Tarrade, "Le commerce entre les Antilles françaises," 35–37.

141. *Affiches Américaines*, November 16, 1768; Josa, *Les industries du sucre*, 112; Tarrade, *Le commerce colonial*, 329–31.

142. Josa, *Les industries du sucre*, 113.

143. Cauna, *Au temps des isles à sucre*, 187, 259.

144. Josa, *Les industries du sucre*, 112–14.

145. Rorabaugh, *Alcoholic Republic*, 67.

146. Ibid., 53–55, 69.

147. *Affiches Américaines*, December 7, 1786.

148. Arthur, "Roman Amphorae"; Galliou, "Days of Wine and Roses?"; D. Williams, "Impact of the Roman Amphorae Trade."

149. Unwin, *Wine and the Vine*, 157–59.

150. Ibid., 197–204.

151. Hariot, "A Brief and True Report," 111–12.

152. Unwin, *Wine and the Vine*, 249.

153. Hancock, "Commerce and Conversation," 197; Unwin, *Wine and the Vine*, 264.

154. Schumpeter, *English Overseas Trade Statistics*, 52–59.

155. Dossie, *Essay on Spirituous Liquors*, 5.

156. French, *Art of Distillation*; Gesner, *Treasure of Euonymus*; Underwood, "Historical Development of Distilling."

157. McCusker, "Distilling and Its Implications" and "Business of Distilling."

158. P. Clark, "'Mother Gin' Controversy"; George, *London Life*, 28–29; Kinross, "Prohibition in Britain"; Maples, "Gin and Georgian London."

159. Berlin, *Worshipful Company of Distillers*, 47.

160. P. Clark, "'Mother Gin' Controversy," 64, 67.

161. Schumpeter, *English Overseas Trade Statistics*, 52–59.

162. Anonymous, *Short Animadversions*, 19.

163. George, *London Life*, 27.

164. P. Clark, "'Mother Gin' Controversy"; Warner and Ivis, "'Damn you, you informing Bitch'"; Rudé, "Mother Gin and the London Riots."

165. Schumpeter, *English Overseas Trade Statistics*, 52–59.

166. Warner and Ivis, "'Damn you, you informing Bitch,'" 304.

167. P. Clark, "'Mother Gin' Controversy," 83.

168. Pares, *War and Trade*, 484–85.

169. Mintz, *Sweetness and Power*, 170.

170. Pack, *Nelson's Blood*, 7.

171. Buckley, *British Army*, 286.

172. Barty-King and Massel, *Rum: Yesterday and Today*; Hamshere, *British in the Caribbean*, 188; Pack, *Nelson's Blood*, 12, 107.

173. Kopperman, "'The Cheapest Pay,'" 447–48.

174. Buckley, *British Army*, 284.

175. Long, *History of Jamaica*, 2:304. See also Young, *West India Common-Place Book*, 228.

176. Thistlewood in D. Hall, *Miserable Slavery*, 98.

177. Young, *West India Common-Place Book*, 64–65.

178. Anonymous, *Short Animadversions*, 8.

179. Ibid., 9.

180. P. Clark, "'Mother Gin' Controversy," 74.

181. Fielding, *Enquiry into the Causes.*

182. Rush, *Inquiry into the Effects.*

183. Fox, *Address to the People.*

184. Burns, *A Second Address to the People of Great Britain*, 12.

185. Mintz, *Sweetness and Power.*

186. Thomas, *Historical Account*, 9.

187. Dossie, *Essay on Spirituous Liquors*, 5.

188. Ibid., 29, 31.

189. Connell, "Punch Drinking."

190. Long, *History of Jamaica*, 1:496–99; McCusker, *Rum and the American Revolution*, 961.

191. Martin, *Essay Upon Plantership*, 60; McCusker, *Rum and the American Revolution*, 403–405; Young, *West India Common-Place Book*, 68.

192. McCusker, *Rum and the American Revolution*, 974–75.

193. Oldmixon, *British Empire*, 2:88–89.

194. Sheridan, "Molasses Act," 72–75.

195. Sheridan, *Sugar and Slavery*, 350–51.

196. Frere, *Short History of Barbados*, 114.

197. Sheridan, "Molasses Act," 76.

198. Nash, "Irish Atlantic Trade," 338.

199. R. Hall, *General Account*, 12.

200. Frere, *Short History of Barbados*, 114.

201. Eltis, "Total Product of Barbados."

202. Young, *West India Common-Place Book*, 67.

203. Ragatz, *Fall of the Planter Class*, 121–23.

204. Edwards, *History, Civil and Commercial*, 1:303–4; Long, *History of Jamaica*, 1:498.

205. Colonial Williamsburg Foundation library, Robert Carter Papers, acquisition no. 007900014, Williamsburg, Virginia.

206. Fitzmaurice, *Treatise*, 58.

207. Sheridan, "Molasses Act," 78.

208. Pope, "Fish into Wine," 51.

209. McCusker, *Rum and the American Revolution*, 528–30.

210. Edwards, *History, Civil and Commercial*, 2:297; Long, *History of Jamaica*, 1:496.

211. University of Florida, Gale-Morant Papers.

212. Barbados Department of Archives, Codrington plantation records, FitzHerbert Papers.

213. Long, *History of Jamaica*, 1:496–97.

214. Edwards, *History, Civil and Commercial*, 2:297; *Affiches Américaines*, December 7, 1786, n.68.

215. University of Florida, Gale-Morant Papers. See also Craton and Walvin, *Jamaican Plantation*, 88–89.

216. Higman, *Slave Population and Economy in Jamaica*, 21.

217. Barbados Department of Archives, Codrington plantation records; see also Klingberg, *Codrington Chronicle*, 72.

218. University of Florida, Gale-Morant Papers.

219. Edwards, *History, Civil and Commercial*, 2:297.

220. Labat, *Nouveau voyage*, 1:323.

221. Barbados Department of Archives, Codrington plantation records; Klingberg, *Codrington Chronicle*, 46.

222. Barbados Department of Archives, FitzHerbert Papers.

223. For 1770–1787, see Carrington, *British West Indies*, 179. For 1793–1800, see Young, *West India Common-Place Book*, 30.

224. Carrington, *British West Indies*, 56, 59–64.

225. McCusker, *Rum and the American Revolution*, 346–55.

226. Kervégant, *Rhums et eaux-de-vie*, 475.

227. E. Williams, *From Columbus to Castro*, 225.

228. Carrington, *British West Indies*, 179.

229. Ibid., 59; See also Ragatz, *Fall of the Planter Class*, 165–66; Schumpeter, *English Overseas Trade Statistics*, 52–59.

230. Barbados Department of Archives, Codrington plantation records.

231. Barbados Department of Archives, FitzHerbert Papers.

232. Edwards, *History, Civil and Commercial*, 1:347; Poyer, *History of Barbados*, 446–56; Schomburgk, *History of Barbados*, 48–51, 149.

233. Carrington, *British West Indies*, 164; Edwards, *History, Civil and Commercial*, 2:495–509; Keith, "Relaxations in British Restrictions."

234. Edwards, *History, Civil and Commercial*, 1:286, 304.

235. Ibid., 1:350.

236. Quoted in Carrington, *British West Indies*, 178.

237. Keith, "Relaxations in British Restrictions"; Ragatz, *Fall of the Planter Class*, 188.

238. Young, *West India Common-Place Book*, 30, 67.

239. Ibid., 64–65.

240. Schomburgk, *History of Barbados*, 153.

241. Edwards, *History, Civil and Commercial*, 1:350; Young, *West India Common-Place Book*, 28, 68.

242. Cited in Carrington, *British West Indies*, 178.

Chapter 4. Ancestors and Alcohol in Africa and the Caribbean

1. Atkins, *Voyage to Guinea*, 159.
2. Pan, *Alcohol in Colonial Africa*, 7.
3. Fernandes, *Description de la côte occidentale d'Afrique*, 17.
4. Barbot, *Description of the Coasts*, 260.
5. Atkins, *Voyage to Guinea*, 159, 168; Barbot, *Description of the Coasts*, 142; Bosman, *New and Accurate Description of the Coast of Guinea*, 487.
6. Atkins, *Voyage to Guinea*, 170–71.
7. Bosman, *New and Accurate Description of the Coast of Guinea*, 404.
8. Thornton, *Africa and Africans*, 66–67.
9. Eltis and Jennings, "Trade," 948.
10. Law, *Slave Coast of West Africa*, 202; Postma, *Dutch in the Atlantic Slave Trade*, 104; Saugera, *Bordeaux, port négrier*, 247; Atkins, *Voyage to Guinea*, 164.
11. Curto, "Alcohol and Slaves," 160–82; McCusker, *Rum and the American Revolution*, 492–97.
12. Ortiz, *Cuban Counterpoint*, 25.
13. E. Williams, *Capitalism and Slavery*, 78.
14. Langton, "Rum, Seduction, and Death," 195–206; Mancall, *Deadly Medicine*.
15. Cited in Pan, *Alcohol in Colonial Africa*, 20–21.
16. Akyeampong, *Drink, Power, and Cultural Change*, 27.
17. Welsh, "Voyage to Benin," 297.
18. Cited in Curto, "Alcohol and Slaves," 57–59.
19. Pigafetta, *Report of the Kingdom of Congo*, 123.
20. Barbot, *Description of the Coasts*, 328; Isert, *Reise nach Guinea*, 127.
21. Bosman, *New and Accurate Description of the Coast of Guinea*, 391.
22. Barbot, *Description of the Coasts*, 331, 333; Bosman, *New and Accurate Description of the Coast of Guinea*, 392.
23. Ruiters cited in de Marees, *Description and Historical Account*, 227.
24. Bosman, *New and Accurate Description of the Coast of Guinea*, 438.
25. Ibid., 403.
26. Eltis, *Rise of African Slavery*, 301.
27. Thornton, *Africa and Africans*, 105.
28. Akyeampong, *Drink, Power, and Cultural Change*, 40–41; Bosman, *New and Accurate Description of the Coast of Guinea*, 158–59; Dumett, "Social Impact"; Field, *Religion and Medicine*, 22–24, 47–56; Isert, *Reise nach Guinea*, 47.
29. Thornton, *Africa and Africans*, 235–53.
30. Akyeampong, *Drink, Power, and Cultural Change*, 21.
31. Ibid., 30.
32. Barbot, *Description of the Coasts*, 314; Bosman, *New and Accurate Description of the Coast of Guinea*, 151.
33. de Marees, *Description and Historical Account*, 42–43.

34. Atkins, *Voyage to Guinea*, 100–101; Barbot, *Description of the Coasts*, 255.

35. Akyeampong, *Drink, Power, and Cultural Change*, 40; Barbot, *Description of the Coasts*, 308.

36. Barbot, *Description of the Coasts*, 392.

37. Equiano, *Life of Olaudah Equiano*, 13, 21.

38. Arinze, *Sacrifice in Ibo Religion*, 16–20; Parrinder, *West African Religion*, 124.

39. Bosman, *New and Accurate Description of the Coast of Guinea*, 369.

40. R. F. Burton, *Mission to Gelele*, 76.

41. Herskovits, *Dahomey*, 2:173.

42. Balandier challenges in this passage the 1705 judgment of Portuguese missionary Laurent de Lucques that the inhabitants of Soyo "do nothing but drink" (*Daily Life*, 160).

43. Laman, *Kongo*, 1:83.

44. de Marees, *Description and Historical Account*, 184.

45. Barbot, *Description of the Coasts*, 283.

46. Basden, *Niger Ibos*, 269–88.

47. Arinze, *Sacrifice in Ibo Religion*, 87–88.

48. A. B. Ellis, *Land of Fetish*, 134; Equiano, *Life of Olaudah Equiano*, 21.

49. Balandier, *Daily Life*, 251.

50. Miller, *Kings and Kinsmen*, 177, n. 6.

51. Forbes, *Dahomey and the Dahomans*, 1:49.

52. Herskovits, *Dahomey*, 1:352–86. See also R. F. Burton, *Mission to Gelele*, 305.

53. For the pacifying and anxiety-reducing effects of drinking, see Horton, "Functions of Alcohol in Primitive Societies," and Schaefer, "Drunkenness."

54. de Marees, *Description and Historical Account*, 23.

55. Anthropologist Seth Leacock explored alcohol use in Afro-Brazilian cults and argued that one of the primary functions of drinking was to integrate members into the community ("Ceremonial Drinking").

56. Herskovits, *Dahomey*, 2:65.

57. Equiano, *Life of Olaudah Equiano*, 44.

58. Collins, *Practical Rules*, 59.

59. Ligon, *True and Exact History*, 93; Long, *History of Jamaica*, 2:490, n. *t*.

60. York Estate plantation accounts in the University of Florida, Gale-Morant Papers.

61. Craton, *Searching for the Invisible Man*, 60–84; Craton and Walvin, *Jamaican Plantation*, 136; Phillips, "Jamaica Slave Plantation."

62. Gardner, *History of Jamaica*, 389–390.

63. Labat, *Nouveau voyage*, 1:323. Josa, *Les industries du sucre*, 54; Pairault, *Le rhum et sa fabrication*, 6.

64. Cited in Long, *History of Jamaica*, 3:926; Peytraud, *L'esclavage aux antilles française*, 196.

65. Debien, *Les esclaves*, 136, 152; Labat, *Nouveau voyage*, 1:331–32.

66. Anonymous, "Characteristic Traits," 14.

67. Leslie, *New and Exact Account of Jamaica*, 35. See also Long, *History of Jamaica*, 3:901–2.

68. Roughley, *Jamaica Planter's Guide*, 90–91.

69. For an in-depth discussion of the rewards-incentives system in Barbados, see Handler and Lange, *Plantation Slavery*, 78–81.

70. Labat, *Nouveau voyage*, 1:331.

71. N. Hall, *Slave Society*, 72.

72. Atwood, *History of the Island*, 257–58.

73. Dickson, *Letters on Slavery*, 13; Labat, *Nouveau voyage*, 1:331; Roughley, *Jamaica Planter's Guide*, 101, 122.

74. Lewis, *Journal*, 128–29.

75. Ibid., 83.

76. Collins, *Practical Rules*, 80, 65–66.

77. Thistlewood cited in D. Hall, *Miserable Slavery*, 18.

78. Lewis, *Journal*, 73.

79. Young cited in Edwards, *History, Civil and Commercial*, 3:264.

80. Stedman, *Narrative of a Five Years Expedition*, 94; Thistlewood cited in D. Hall, *Miserable Slavery*, 47.

81. Anonymous, *Letter to the Most Honourable*, 54; Marsden, *Account of the Island*, 33; Barbados Department of Archives, Codrington plantation records, annual reports.

82. Du Tertre, *Histoire generale*, 2:527–28.

83. Parry cited in Craton, Walvin, and Wright, *Slavery, Abolition, and Emancipation*, 91.

84. Drax cited in Belgrove, *Treatise Upon Husbandry*, 57.

85. Cited in Handler and Lange, *Plantation Slavery*, 90.

86. Long, *History of Jamaica*, 1:499.

87. Labat, *Nouveau voyage*, 1:332.

88. Collins, *Practical Rules*, 101.

89. Rawlin, *Laws of Barbados*, 189.

90. N. Hall, *Slave Society*, 121.

91. Anonymous, "Characteristic Traits," 15.

92. Armstrong, *Old Village*, 101–8, 158–60.

93. N. Hall, *Slave Society*, 121.

94. Handler, "Joseph Rachell and Rachael Pringle Polgreen."

95. Pinckard, *Notes on the West Indies*, 1:249.

96. Marsden, *Account of the Island*, 7.

97. Long, *History of Jamaica*, 2:314.

98. Fraser, *History of Trinidad*, 2:289.

99. Du Tertre, *Histoire generale*, 2:124.

100. Dessalles cited in Forster and Forster, *Sugar and Slavery*, 20.

101. Ibid., 55.

102. Geggus, "On the Eve of the Haitian Revolution," 125–26.

103. Herskovits, *Myth of the Negro Past*.

104. Herskovits, *Life in a Haitian Valley*; Herskovits and Herskovits, *Trinidad Village*.

105. Mintz and Price, *Birth of African-American Culture*.

106. Ibid., 44–46.

107. Eltis, "Slave Economies"; Eltis and Richardson, "West Africa and the Transatlantic Slave Trade" and "'Numbers Game' and Routes to Slavery."

108. Law, "On the African Background."

109. Chambers, "'My own nation.'"

110. Thornton, *Africa and Africans*.

111. Ibid., 235.

112. Chambers, "'My own nation,'" 77.

113. Herskovits, *New World Negro*, 96–98; Mintz and Price, *Birth of African-American Culture*, 42–51.

114. Eltis and Richardson, "West Africa and the Transatlantic Slave Trade"; Law, "On the African Background."

115. Stein, *The French Sugar Business*, 18–19.

116. Geggus, "Demographic Composition" and "French Slave Trade."

117. Geggus, "Sex Ratio, Age and Ethnicity."

118. Moreau de St.-Méry, *Description topographique*, 1:39.

119. Chambers, "'My own nation,'" 88. For claims of the Akan background of obeah, see J. Williams, *Voodoos and Obeahs*, 108–41. See also Long, *History of Jamaica*, 2:473.

120. Handler, "Slave Medicine and Obeah in Barbados," 80.

121. Equiano, *Life of Olaudah Equiano*, 24.

122. Cited in J. Williams, *Voodoos and Obeahs*, 191.

123. Edwards, *History, Civil and Commercial*, 2:111–12.

124. Moreau de St.-Méry, *Description topographique*, 1:36.

125. Herskovits, *Life in a Haitian Valley*, 139.

126. Geggus, "Haitian Voodoo," 41–42.

127. J. Williams, *Voodoos and Obeahs*, 57.

128. Geggus, "Haitian Voodoo," 35.

129. Moreau de St.-Méry, *Description topographique*, 1:49. See also translation in J. Williams, *Voodoos and Obeahs*, 66.

130. Moreau de St.-Méry, *Description topographique*, 1:49–51.

131. Herskovits, *Dahomey*, 2:173.

132. Geggus, "Haitian Voodoo," 33–35.

133. Métraux, *Voodoo in Haiti*.

134. Herskovits, *Life in a Haitian Valley*, 181.

135. Bourguignon, "Comments on Leacock's Ceremonial Drinking."

136. Métraux, *Voodoo in Haiti*, 121.

137. Leacock, "Ceremonial Drinking," 344–54.

138. Herskovits, *Life in a Haitian Valley*, 226.

139. Long, *History of Jamaica*, 2:421–22.

140. Taylor cited in Handler and Lange, *Plantation Slavery*, 199, 202–3.

141. Sloane, *Voyage to the Islands*, 1:xlviii.

142. Leslie, *New and Exact Account of Jamaica*, 325–26.

143. Atwood, *History of the Island*, 268.

144. Handler and Lange, *Plantation Slavery*; Corruccini, Brandon, and Handler, "Inferring Fertility."

145. Crain, Farmer, Smith, and Watson, "Human Skeletal Remains." At the eighteenth-century Harney slave cemetery in Montserrat, archaeologist David Watters recovered a bottle from the cemetery that may have once contained rum and been a grave good buried with one of the deceased. However, the recovery of a single glass bottle from the numerous slave burials excavated in the Caribbean suggests that the practice of interring the dead with glass bottles was not widespread. See Watters, "Mortuary Patterns."

146. Atwood, *History of the Island*, 261–63.

147. Peytraud, *L'esclavage aux antilles française*, 208.

148. Herskovits, *Life in a Haitian Valley*, 209.

149. For an interesting discussion of the way in which chiefs and elders in what is today Ghana used alcohol to maintain their power, see Akyeampong, *Drink, Power, and Cultural Change*, 15.

150. See, for example, Moreau de St.-Méry, *Description topographique*, 1:63–64.

151. Anonymous, "Characteristic Traits," 15.

Chapter 5. Alcoholic Marronage: Identity, Danger, and Escape in Caribbean Slave Societies

1. Ligon, *True and Exact History*, 32. Labat also believed that oüicou was the "favorite" drink of the Caribs (see *Nouveau voyage*, 1:133).

2. Oldmixon, *British Empire*, 2:132.

3. Rochefort, *Histoire naturelle*, 501.

4. Labat, *Nouveau voyage*, 1:331.

5. In 1710, Thomas Walduck visited Barbados and made a general reference to the use of perino by white colonists. There were few, if any, Amerindian women in Barbados at this time, suggesting that whites had begun to produce it. See "T. Walduck's Letters," 44.

6. Ligon, *True and Exact History*, 37–38, 44.

7. Whistler, "Account of Barbados in 1654," 184.

8. Uchteritz cited in Gunkel and Handler, "German Indentured Servant," 93; Biet cited in Handler, "Father Antoine Biet's Visit," 62.

9. Rochefort, *Histoire naturelle*, 501.

10. Du Tertre, *Histoire generale*, 2:120.

11. Labat, *Nouveau voyage*, 1:133–34.

12. Oldmixon, *British Empire*, 2:132. As late as 1750, mobbie was one of the most popular drinks in Barbados (see Hughes, *Natural History*, 34).

13. Carmichael, *Domestic Manners*, 1:288.

14. David Geggus and Jerome Handler, personal communication.

15. Las Casas, *History of the Indies*, 258. See also Craton, Walvin, and Wright, *Slavery, Abolition, and Emancipation*, 10.

16. Du Tertre, *Histoire generale*, 2:124, 514–15.

17. Labat, *Nouveau voyage*, 1:134, 331.

18. Ligon, *True and Exact History,* 32.

19. Hughes, *Natural History*, 34.

20. Anonymous, "Characteristic Traits," 15. Fermented sugarcane juice drinks were also associated with Indians, especially in Spanish and Portuguese America. For example, in 1600, the mayor of Taxco, New Spain, attempted to curb the sale of fermented sugarcane drinks to Indians (see Zavala, *Fuentes para la historia*, 6:400–401). In the early eighteenth century, André João Àntonil described garapa as a sour drink that the Brazilian slaves used to get drunk and which found a good market among the slaves and Indians along the rivers (see *Cúltura é ópulencia*, 133).

21. Du Tertre, *Histoire generale*, 2:514–15; Labat, *Nouveau voyage*, 1:135.

22. Thomas, *Historical Account*, 17.

23. Oldmixon, *British Empire*, 2:132.

24. Ligon, *True and Exact History*, 38–39.

25. Long, *History of Jamaica*, 2:562.

26. Labat, *Nouveau voyage*, 2:74.

27. Alleyne, *Historic Bridgetown*, 50.

28. Oldmixon, *British Empire*, 2:164.

29. Leslie, *New and Exact Account of Jamaica*, 32.

30. Long, *History of Jamaica*, 2:266.

31. Leslie, *New and Exact Account of Jamaica*, 32.

32. Hughes, *Natural History*, 37.

33. Labat, *Nouveau voyage*, 1:135–36.

34. See, for example, Uchteritz cited in Gunkel and Handler, "German Indentured Servant," 93.

35. Ligon, *True and Exact History*, 32.

36. Oldmixon, *British Empire*, 2:133.

37. Robertson, *Detection of the State*, 8–11.

38. Ligon wrote, "*Punch* . . . is made of water and sugar put together, which in ten dayes standing will be very strong, and fit for labourers." Ligon's description of punch is typical of the fermented sugarcane-based alcoholic beverage known as *grappe* in the French Caribbean and *guarapo* in the Spanish Caribbean. Ligon never tasted punch and appears to have mistaken it for what he called *grippo* (*True and Exact History*, 32).

39. Spoeri cited in Gunkel and Handler, "Swiss Medical Doctor's Description," 10.

40. Labat, *Nouveau voyage*, 1:136.

41. Oldmixon, *British Empire*, 2:128.

42. Thomas, *Historical Account*, 17.

43. Sloane, *Voyage to the Islands*, 1:xxix.

44. Leslie, *New and Exact Account of Jamaica*, 32.

45. Hughes, *Natural History*, 36.

46. Long, *History of Jamaica*, 2:266.

47. Labat, *Nouveau voyage*, 1:135.

48. Connell, "Punch Drinking."

49. Leath, "'After the Chinese Taste'"; Watters and Nicholson, "Highland House," 226.

50. Connell, "Punch Drinking," 10.

51. Whistler "Account of Barbados in 1654," 185.

52. Silvester, "Breife Discription of the Ilande," 44.

53. Codrington cited in McCusker, *Rum and the American Revolution*, 219.

54. Taylor cited in Dunn, *Sugar and Slaves*, 277.

55. Moreau de St.-Méry, *Description topographique*, 1:16.

56. Labat, *Nouveau voyage*, 2:131.

57. Ibid., 2:139.

58. Whistler "Account of Barbados in 1654," 185.

59. Silvester, "Breife Discription of the Ilande," 44.

60. Thome and Kimball, *Emancipation*, 26.

61. Jefferys, *Natural and Civil History*, 2:191.

62. Moreau de St.-Méry, *Description topographique*, 1:27.

63. Long, *History of Jamaica*, 2:473.

64. Ibid., 2:373.

65. Ibid., 2:569–70, n. *a*.

66. Collins, *Practical Rules*, 37.

67. Atwood, *History of the Island*, 272.

68. Du Tertre, *Histoire generale*, 2:497–98.

69. Collins, *Practical Rules*, 101.

70. Long, *History of Jamaica*, 2:353.

71. Anonymous, "Characteristic Traits," 15.

72. Lewis, *Journal*, 91.

73. Malenfant, *Des colonies*, 203.

74. University of Florida, Gale-Morant Papers.

75. Labat, *Nouveau voyage*, 1:324.

76. Debien, *Les esclaves*, 137–38.

77. University of Florida, Gale-Morant Papers.

78. Pinckard, *Notes on the West Indies*, 1: 205.

79. Anonymous, "Characteristic Traits," 19.

80. R. Hall, *General Account*, 13.

81. Roughley, *Jamaica Planter's Guide*, 122.

82. Collins, *Practical Rules*, 51.

83. Moreau de St.-Méry, *Description topographique*, 1:39.

84. Long, *History of Jamaica*, 2:409–10.

85. Carmichael, *Domestic Manners*, 1:76.

86. Moreau de St.-Méry, *Description topographique*, 1:43. See also 1:90.

87. Craton, *Empire, Enslavement, and Freedom*, 183.

88. Collins, *Practical Rules*, 59.

89. Those convicted of selling rum to slaves paid a fine of twenty shillings. See Rawlin, *Laws of Barbados*, 189.

90. Collins, *Practical Rules*, 101.

91. Oldmixon, *British Empire*, 2:52.

92. Atwood, *History of the Island*, 265.

93. Dickson, *Letters on Slavery*, 39.

94. Rorabaugh, *Alcoholic Republic*, 232; University of Florida, Gale-Morant Papers; *Papers Relating to York Plantation and Gale's Valley Plantation*; Labat, *Nouveau voyage*, 1:323; R. Hall, *General Account*, 13.

95. See, for example, Armstrong, *Old Village*, 135; Farnsworth, "Influence of Trade on Bahamian Slave Culture." Mouer and Smith, "Revisiting Mapps Cave."

96. Sloane, *Voyage to the Islands*, 1:lxxi.

97. Anonymous, "Characteristic Traits," 16.

98. Oldmixon, *British Empire*, 2:137; Ligon, *True and Exact History*, 55.

99. Oldmixon, *British Empire*, 2:137.

100. Atkins, *Voyage to Guinea*, 206.

101. Moreau de St.-Méry, *Description topographique*, 1:16.

102. The print is titled "A West-India Sportsman," and is signed J. F., 1807. It is a hand-colored engraving located in the Barbados Museum and Historical Society collection.

103. Colt, "Voyage of Sir Henry Colt," 65–66.

104. "T. Walduck's Letters," 45.

105. West cited in Bridenbaugh and Bridenbaugh, *No Peace*, 393.

106. Dickson, *Letters on Slavery*, 42.

107. Long, *History of Jamaica*, 2:289.

108. Cited in Dunn, *Sugar and Slaves*, 125.

109. Collins, *Practical Rules*, 103.

110. Rawlin, *Laws of Barbados*, 71–72.

111. Anonymous, *Laws of Jamaica*, 33–36.

112. Cited in Goslinga, *Dutch in the Caribbean . . . 1680–1791*, 252.

113. Ligon, *True and Exact History*, 21.

114. Dickson, *Letters on Slavery*, 38.

115. Long, *History of Jamaica*, 2:280.

116. Ibid., 2:534.

117. Atwood, *History of the Island*, 212.

118. Moreau de St.-Méry, *Description topographique*, 1:20.

119. Long, *History of Jamaica*, 2:29.

120. Regenten of Surinam, *Essai historique*, 154.

121. See Keller, "Great Jewish Drink Mystery."

122. Long, *History of Jamaica*, 2:29.

123. Dickson, *Letters on Slavery*, 92.

124. Long, *History of Jamaica*, 2:288.

125. Labat, *Nouveau voyage*, 1:135.

126. Moreau de St.-Méry, *Topographical and Political Description*, 1:50. In 1596, Dr. Layfield also noted that water was the usual drink of the Spanish in the Caribbean (*Large Relation*, 98).

127. Long, *History of Jamaica*, 2:557.

128. Ibid., 2:561–62.

129. Boxer, *Dutch Seaborne Empire*, 234.

130. Colt, "Voyage of Sir Henry Colt," 94.

131. Deerr, *History of Sugar*, 1:151; Long, *History of Jamaica*, 1:286, 617–19.

132. Buckley, *British Army*, 240; Kopperman, "'The Cheapest Pay,'" 449.

133. Buckley, *British Army*, 285; Kopperman, "'The Cheapest Pay,'" 466.

134. Agbe-Davies et al., *Architectural and Archaeological Analysis*.

135. Buckley, *Slaves in Red Coats*, 103; Buckley, *British Army*, 286–87; Geggus, "Yellow Fever," 56.

136. Long, *History of Jamaica*, 2:304. See also Long, *History of Jamaica*, 2:569–70, n. *a*.

137. Pinckard, *Notes on the West Indies*, 1:205–8. See also Labat, *Nouveau voyage*, 1:12.

138. Pinckard, *Notes on the West Indies*, 1:192.

139. Regenten of Surinam, *Essai historique*, 166.

140. Goslinga, *Dutch in the Caribbean . . 1680–1791*, 526.

141. Rawlin, *Laws of Barbados*, 7.

142. Bowden, "Three Centuries of Bridgetown," 23.

143. R. Hall, *General Account*, 13.

144. See Cordingly, *Under the Black Flag*, 10.

145. Long, *History of Jamaica*, 2:140; Hamilton and Woodward, "Sunken Seventeenth-Century City"; Marx, *Wine Glasses Recovered*.

146. Cordingly, *Under the Black Flag*, 93.

147. Sloane, *Voyage to the Islands*, 1: xcviii. See also Cordingly, *Under the Black Flag*, 43.

148. Labat, *Nouveau voyage*, 2:72–74.

149. Stevenson's pirates in *Treasure Island* sing, "Fifteen men on the dead man's chest / Yo-ho-ho, and the bottle of rum! / Drink and the devil had done for the rest / Yo-ho-ho, and a bottle of rum!"

150. Horton, "Functions of Alcohol in Primitive Societies"; Schaefer, "Drunkenness."

151. Ligon, *True and Exact History*, 25.

152. Watts, *West Indies*, 215–16.

153. Geggus, *Slavery, War, and Revolution*, 347.

154. Higman, *Slave Populations of the British Caribbean*, 339–47.

155. Collins, *Practical Rules*, 260–61; Higman, *Slave Populations of the British Caribbean*, 331; Schomburgk, *History of Barbados*, 80.

156. Ligon, *True and Exact History*, 43–46.

157. Gardner, *History of Jamaica*, 378–79.

158. Schaefer, "Drunkenness."

159. Ligon, *True and Exact History*, 27.

160. Long, *History of Jamaica*, 2:524.

161. La Selve, *La république d'Haïti*, 170.

162. Du Tertre, *Histoire generale*, 2:514–15.

163. Labat, *Nouveau voyage*, 1:331.

164. Drax cited in Belgrove, *Treatise Upon Husbandry*, 67.

165. Collins, *Practical Rules*, 101.

166. Parry cited in Craton, Walvin, and Wright, *Slavery, Abolition, and Emancipation*, 88.

167. Atwood, *History of the Island*, 258.

168. Roughley, *Jamaica Planter's Guide*, 101.

169. Thistlewood cited in D. Hall, *Miserable Slavery*, 37.

170. Collins, *Practical Rules*; Marsden, *Account of the Island*, 44.

171. Bourgeois, *Voyages intéressans*, 497; Debien, *Les esclaves*, 323; Dickson, *Letters on Slavery*, 35.

172. Barbados Department of Archives, FitzHerbert Papers.

173. Long, *History of Jamaica*, 2:537.

174. Huetz de Lemps, *Histoire du rhum*, 37.

175. Fraser, *History of Trinidad*, 2:203–4.

176. Pack, *Nelson's Blood*, 190.

177. Huetz de Lemps, *Histoire du rhum*, 65.

178. Rorabaugh, *Alcoholic Republic*, 38.

179. Mancall, *Deadly Medicine*, 91–93.

180. Long, *History of Jamaica*, 2:538.

181. Rush, *Inquiry into the Effects*.

182. Rorabaugh, *Alcoholic Republic*, 39–41.

183. Cadwalader, *Essay on the West India Dry-Gripes*.

184. Ligon, *True and Exact History*, 27.

185. Handler et al., "Lead Contact and Poisoning"; Hunter, *Some Experiments*, 5.

186. Marsden, *Account of the Island*, 27.

187. Hunter, *Some Experiments*.

188. Handler et al., "Lead Contact and Poisoning."

189. Marsden, *Account of the Island*, 43–44.

190. Hughes, *Natural History*, 34–36.

191. Greeley, "Getting the Lead Out"; United States Department of Health and Human Services, "Toxic Hypoglycemic Syndrome."

192. Long, *History of Jamaica*, 2:30.

193. Hunter, *Some Experiments*, 6.

194. I wish to thank Dr. James Winefordner of the chemistry department at the University of Florida for his insights into lead contamination.

195. Long, *History of Jamaica*, 2:30.

196. Geggus, "Yellow Fever" and *Slavery, War, and Revolution*, 347–72.

197. Buckley, *Slaves in Red Coats*, 100–104.

198. Geggus, *Slavery, War, and Revolution*, 368.

199. Buckley, *British Army*, 293.

200. Handler et al., "Lead Contact and Poisoning."

201. Greeley, "Getting the Lead Out."

202. Buckley, *British Army*, 292.

203. Reuters, "Kenyan brew death toll 137," November 19, 2000 <http://archives.cnn.com/2000/WORLD/africa/11/19/kenya.brew.reut/ index.html>, accessed February 2005.

204. Heath, *Drinking Occasions*, 149–50.

205. Long, *History of Jamaica*, 2:30.

206. Hughes, *Natural History*, 34.

207. Long, *History of Jamaica*, 2:305.

208. Ibid., 2:30.

209. Ibid., 2:518.

210. Ibid., 2:30.

211. Hunter, *Some Experiments*, 6.

212. Long, *History of Jamaica*, 2:304.

213. Hudson, "Medical Examiner Looks at Drinking."

214. Parry cited in Craton, Walvin, and Wright, *Slavery, Abolition, and Emancipation*, 91.

215. Pitman, "Slavery on British West India Plantations," 642–43.

216. Kiple, *Caribbean Slave*, 153.

217. Craton, "Death, Disease, and Medicine," 190; See also Fogel, *Without Consent or Contract*, 153.

218. Higman, *Slave Populations of the British Caribbean*, 375.

219. Barbados Department of Archives, FitzHerbert Papers and Codrington plantation records.

220. Higman, *Slave Populations of the British Caribbean*, 308–10, 355, 467.

221. Lieber, "Hepatic and Other Medical Disorders of Alcoholism."

222. Higman, *Slave Populations of the British Caribbean*, 340.

223. Craton, "Death, Disease, and Medicine," 187.

224. Higman, *Slave Populations of the British Caribbean*, 340.

225. Craton, "Death, Disease, and Medicine," 187; Higman, *Slave Populations of the British Caribbean*, 340; Wolfgan, "Charting Recent Progress."

226. Higman, *Slave Populations of the British Caribbean*, 25–33, 317–22.

227. Wolfgan, "Charting Recent Progress."

228. Greeley, "Getting the Lead Out."

229. Higman, *Slave Populations of the British Caribbean*, 356.

230. Spooner cited in Pitman, "Slavery on British West India Plantations," 638.

231. Parry cited in Craton, Walvin, and Wright, *Slavery, Abolition, and Emancipation*, 93.

232. Collins, *Practical Rules*, 325–26. See also Dunn, "Sugar Production and Slave Women in Jamaica."

233. Craton, "Death, Disease, and Medicine," 184.

234. Ligon, *True and Exact History*, 33.

235. Sloane, *Voyage to the Islands*, 1:xxix–xxxx; Verney cited in Gragg, "Puritans in Paradise," 161.

236. Leslie, *New and Exact Account of Jamaica*, 32–33.

237. Phillippo, *Jamaica*, 189.

238. Sloane, *Voyage to the Islands*, 1:xxix–xxxx.

239. Ibid., 1:cxlix.

240. Horn, "Servant Emigration," 55 n. 17. See also Long, *History of Jamaica*, 2:287–88.

241. Moreau de St.-Méry, *Description topographique*, 1:651–53.

242. Lewis, *Journal*, 93–94.

243. Labat, *Nouveau voyage*, 2:66–67.

244. Ligon, *True and Exact History*, 93.

245. Atwood, *History of the Island*, 237–42.

246. Moreau de St.-Méry, *Description topographique*, 1:482.

247. Lyttleton, *Groans of the Plantations*, 19–20.

248. Hughes, *Natural History*, 251–52.

249. Edwards, *History, Civil and Commercial*, 2:283 note.

250. Cited in Hulme and Whitehead, *Wild Majesty*, 72–73.

251. For a full account of the incident, see Hulme and Whitehead, *Wild Majesty*, 89–106.

252. MacAndrew and Edgerton, *Drunken Comportment*, 72–73.

253. Ibid., 89–90.

254. Dennis, "Role of the Drunk."

255. MacAndrew and Edgerton, *Drunken Comportment*, 75.

256. Dickson, *Letters on Slavery*, 15.

257. Ibid.

258. Stedman, *Narrative of a Five Years Expedition*, 95–96.

259. Lyttleton provides examples of slaves destroying sugarcane fields in *Groans of the Plantations*.

260. Thomas, *Historical Account*, 20.

261. Collins, *Practical Rules*, 224.

262. Moreau de St.-Méry, *Description topographique*, 1:27.

263. Cited in Handler and Lange, *Plantation Slavery*, 78.

264. Young cited in Edwards, *History, Civil and Commercial*, 3:263.

265. Forster and Forster, *Sugar and Slavery*, 58, 189.

266. V. Turner, *Ritual Process*, 94–130.

267. Collins, *Practical Rules*, 224.

268. Atwood, *History of the Island*, 260.

269. Anonymous, "Characteristic Traits," 23.

270. Long, *History of Jamaica*, 2:424.

271. For an overview of the African origins of John Canoe, see Chambers, "'My own nation,'" 87.

272. Young cited in Edwards, *History, Civil and Commercial*, 3:264.

273. Lewis, *Journal*, 80–81.

274. Craton, *Testing the Chains*, 254–321; Dirks, *Black Saturnalia*.

275. Dallas, *History of the Maroons*, 1:191.

276. Craton, *Testing the Chains*, 122. See also Gaspar, *Bondmen and Rebels*, 244.

277. J. Williams, *Voodoos and Obeahs*, 163. For Barbados, see Alleyne, *Historic Bridgetown*, 18.

278. Goslinga, *Dutch in the Caribbean . . . 1791/5–1942*, 9.

279. N. Hall, *Slave Society*, 223.

280. Heuman, "*Killing Time*," 6.

281. Gaspar, *Bondmen and Rebels*, 245.

282. Akyeampong, *Drink, Power, and Cultural Change*, 28.

283. Gaspar, *Bondmen and Rebels*, 245.

284. Law, "On the African Background."

285. Gaspar, *Bondmen and Rebels*, 244.

286. Geggus, "Haitian Voodoo"; "Marronage"; "The Bois Caiman Ceremony." Also see Law, "On the African Background."

287. Moreau de St.-Méry, *Description topographique*, 1:51.

288. Law, "On the African Background."

289. Geggus, "The Bois Caiman Ceremony," 50.

290. Hazoume, *Le pacte de sang*, 47, 70; Argyle, *Fon of Dahomey*, 156–61; Law, "On the African Background."

291. Dorigny, *Léger-Félicité Sonthonax*, 58.

292. Geggus, "Haitian Revolution," 34.

293. Toussaint cited in Jean Price-Mars, "Toussaint-Louverture," 14.

294. Creole of St. Domingue, *My Odyssey*, 62.

295. Mackenzie, *Notes on Haiti*, 2:169; Madiou, *Histoire d'Haïti*, 3: 339–40, 512.

296. Herskovits, *Life in a Haitian Valley*, 316–17.

297. Leacock, "Ceremonial Drinking."

298. Edwards, *History, Civil and Commercial*, 2:78.

299. Long, *History of Jamaica*, 2:447.

300. Craton, *Testing the Chains*, 118.

301. Labat, *Nouveau voyage*, 2:66.

302. de Groot, "Comparison," 180.

Chapter 6. Taming Rum in the Nineteenth and Twentieth Centuries

1. Schomburgk, *History of Barbados*, 96.

2. Thome and Kimball, *Emancipation*, 25, 86.

3. Schomburgk, *History of Barbados*, 96–97.

4. Phillippo, *Jamaica*, 264.

5. Gardner, *History of Jamaica*, 466.

6. Thome and Kimball, *Emancipation*, 28.

7. Sturge and Harvey, *West Indies in 1837*, appendix A, vi.

8. Thome and Kimball, *Emancipation*, 28.

9. Fahey, "Blacks, Good Templars."

10. Brereton, *Race Relations*, 56–57.

11. Phillippo, *Jamaica*, 264.

12. Thome and Kimball, *Emancipation*, 12.

13. Sturge and Harvey, *West Indies in 1837*, appendix F, xxxviii.

14. Thome and Kimball, *Emancipation*, 12.

15. Barbados Department of Archives, FitzHerbert Papers.

16. Mathieson, *British Slave Emancipation*, 133 n. 1.

17. Berleant-Schiller, "From Labour to Peasantry," 58.

18. Mathieson, *British Slave Emancipation*, 133, 139.

19. Collins, *Practical Rules*, 65–66, 80.

20. Mathieson, *British Slave Emancipation*, 138–39.

21. Colonial Office, *Report of a Commission*, 136.

22. Woodcock, *History of Tobago*, 190.

23. W. Marshall, "Metayage," 67.

24. Mintz, *Caribbean Transformations*, 160.

25. Ibid., 173.

26. For consumption figures for each region, see Pairault, *Le rhum et sa fabrication*, 13–14. For population estimates for each region, see Watts, *West Indies*, 459.

27. Schomburgk, *History of Barbados*, 96.

28. Bisnauth, *History of Religions*, 133; Schomburgk, *History of Barbados*, 96–97; Thome and Kimball, *Emancipation*, 71–72.

29. Bisnauth, *History of Religions*, 137.

30. Thome and Kimball, *Emancipation*, 72.

31. Ibid., 25, 71.

32. Cherrington, *Standard Encyclopedia*, 1:273.

33. Thome and Kimball, *Emancipation*, 57.

34. Amphlett, *Under a Tropical Sky*, 57.

35. Mathieson, *British Slave Emancipation*, 139.

36. Pairault, *Le rhum et sa fabrication*, 14. For population estimates for British Guiana, see Newman, *British Guiana*, 43.

37. Cherrington, *Standard Encyclopedia*, 1: 425–26.

38. Ibid.

39. Ober, *Camps in the Caribbees*, 79–80.

40. H. Bell, "Report on the Caribs," 28–29.

41. For a summary of reports about this event, see Hulme and Whitehead, *Wild Majesty*, 283–98.

42. Amphlett, *Under a Tropical Sky*, 92. See also Hulme and Whitehead, *Wild Majesty*, 312–13.

43. Cherrington, *Standard Encyclopedia*, 1:425.

44. H. Bell, *Obeah*, 190.

45. Kervégant, *Rhums et eaux-de-vie*, 472–73.

46. Bisnauth, *History of Religions*, 140–64; Colonial Office, *Report of a Commission*, 136; Kervégant, *Rhums et eaux-de-vie*, 478; Newman, *British Guiana*, 43.

47. Layfield, *Large Relation*, 98; Long, *History of Jamaica*, 2:557; Moreau de St.-Méry, *Topographical and Political Description*, 1:50.

48. Scott, *Slave Emancipation*, 230.

49. Moreno Fraginals, "Plantations in the Caribbean," 332.

50. Robinson, *Cuba, Old and New*, 76–77.

51. Cuba, Dirección General de Estadística, *Resúmenes estadísticos seleccionados*, 56–57; American Chamber of Commerce of Cuba, *Cuba: Facts and Figures*, 127. See also Maspons Franco, *La reorganización*, 127–32.

52. Maspons Franco, *La reorganización*, 115–32; Robinson, *Cuba, Old and New*, 76–77.

53. Robinson, *Cuba, Old and New*, 77.

54. Pérez, *On Becoming Cuban*, 183.

55. Ibid., 168–69.

56. Dinwiddie, *Puerto Rico*, 152, 165; Cherrington, *Standard Encyclopedia*, 5:2186–188.

57. T. Clark, "Prohibition in Puerto Rico."

58. Millspaugh, *Haiti*, 129.

59. Ibid.

60. Ibid., 178–80.

61. E. Williams, *From Columbus to Castro*, 440.

62. Nicholls, *From Dessalines to Duvalier*, 161, 181–83.

63. Heinl and Heinl, *Written in Blood*, 660–61.

64. Knight, *Caribbean*, 186–87; Parry, Sherlock, and Maingot, *Short History*, 174–75; Watts, *West Indies*, 483.

65. Newman, *British Guiana*, 25–26; Scott, *Slave Emancipation*, 29; M. Turner, "Chinese Contract Labour," 135–136.

66. Moore, *Cultural Power*, 8; Newman, *British Guiana*, 26, 43.

67. Pluchon, *Histoire des Antilles*, 427; Renard, "Immigration and Indentureship," 166.

68. Newman, *British Guiana*, 43; Malik, *East Indians in Trinidad*.

69. Carstairs, "Daru and Bhang," 298. See also Dorschner, *Alcohol Consumption*, 63–70.

70. Carstairs, "Daru and Bhang"; Dorschner, *Alcohol Consumption*, 20; Malik, *East Indians in Trinidad*, 31.

71. Dorschner, *Alcohol Consumption*, 59–60. See also Srinivas and Shah cited in Vertovec, *Hindu Trinidad*, 51.

72. Pairault, *Le rhum et sa fabrication*, 13–14.

73. Look Lai, *Indentured Labor*, 144.

74. Bisnauth, *History of Religions*, 159.

75. Look Lai, *Indentured Labor*, 145.

76. Renard, "Immigration and Indentureship," 165.

77. Laurence, *Question of Labour*, 147; M. Turner, "Chinese Contract Labour," 135.

78. Amphlett, *Under a Tropical Sky*, 109.

79. Malik, *East Indians in Trinidad*, 31, 38.

80. H. Bell, *Obeah*, 128.

81. Malik, *East Indians in Trinidad*, 33–34; Vertovec, *Hindu Trinidad*, 119.
82. Yawney, "Drinking Patterns and Alcoholism."
83. Vertovec, *Hindu Trinidad*, 96.
84. Singh, *Race and Class Struggles*.
85. Bisnauth, *History of Religions*, 150; Vertovec, *Hindu Trinidad*, 55, 111.
86. Vertovec, *Hindu Trinidad*, 214–15.
87. Bisnauth, *History of Religions*, 151.
88. Vertovec, *Hindu Trinidad*, 215, 114.
89. Ibid., 217.
90. Ibid., 109.
91. Scott, *Slave Emancipation*, 33.
92. Moore, *Cultural Power*, 287–89.
93. Scott, *Slave Emancipation*, 271.
94. Look Lai, *Indentured Labor*, 92.
95. Moore, *Cultural Power*, 291.
96. Look Lai, *Indentured Labor*, 236.
97. Cited in ibid., 234.
98. Ibid., 250.
99. Colonial Office, *Report of a Commission*, 136.
100. Look Lai, *Indentured Labor*, 197–200.
101. Amphlett, *Under a Tropical Sky*, 70.
102. Look Lai, *Indentured Labor*, 17; Wagner, "Rum, Policy, and the Portuguese."
103. Wagner, "Rum, Policy, and the Portuguese."
104. Ibid.
105. Cited in Hill, *Calypso Calaloo*, 80.
106. H. Bell, *Obeah*, 14.
107. Ibid., 8.
108. Ibid., 28.
109. Ibid., 16.
110. Beckwith, *Black Roadways*, 137.
111. Ibid., 109. See also Edwards, *History, Civil and Commercial*, 2:111–12.
112. R. D. E. Burton, *Afro-Creole*, 101.
113. Beckwith, *Black Roadways*, 145; R. D. E. Burton, *Afro-Creole*, 99.
114. Beckwith, *Black Roadways*, 145–46.
115. Ibid., 144.
116. R. D. E. Burton, *Afro-Creole*, 97–103.
117. Ibid., 97–122. See also Chevannes, "New Approach," 22–23; Hurston, *Voodoo Gods*; Simpson, *Religious Cults*, 171.
118. Simpson, *Religious Cults*, 61–62.
119. Dobbin, *Jombee Dance*, 47.
120. Cited in Barrett, *Rastafarians*, 132.

121. Owens, *Dread*, 164.

122. Carstairs, "Daru and Bhang."

123. Bourguignon, "Comments on Leacock's Ceremonial Drinking"; Herskovits, *Life in a Haitian Valley*; Hurston, *Voodoo Gods*; Métraux, *Voodoo in Haiti*; J. Williams, *Voodoos and Obeahs*.

124. Métraux, *Voodoo in Haiti*.

125. Alexis, *Vodou et quimbois*.

126. Métraux, *Voodoo in Haiti*, 174.

127. Ibid., 85–86, 176.

128. Leacock, "Ceremonial Drinking."

129. Herskovits, *Life in a Haitian Valley*, 317.

130. Ibid., 216, 316–17.

131. Brown, *Mama Lola*, 44.

132. Ibid., 119. See also González-Wippler, *Santería Experience*, 158–61; Métraux, *Voodoo in Haiti*, 130, 176.

133. Métraux, *Voodoo in Haiti*, 121.

134. Leacock, "Ceremonial Drinking."

135. Schaefer, "Drunkenness."

136. Price and Price, *Two Evenings in Saramaka*, 41–61.

137. Vernon, "Bakuu: Possessing Spirits," 19.

138. Bilby, "Kromanti Dance," 67–74.

139. Beckwith, *Black Roadways*, 57–58. See also R. Smith, *Negro Family*, 130–31.

140. Ibid., 75. See Chevannes, "New Approach," 24; Hurston, *Voodoo Gods*, 45.

141. Wilson, *Crab Antics*; R. Smith, *Negro Family*, 52.

142. Dobbin, *Jombee Dance*, 47.

143. Chevannes, "New Approach," 23; David Geggus, personal communication.

Chapter 7. Rum and Economic Survival in the Nineteenth and Twentieth Centuries

1. Huetz de Lemps, *Histoire du rhum*, 100–105.

2. Fitzmaurice, *Treatise*, 59–60.

3. Ibid., 58.

4. Marshall and Marshall, "Opening Pandora's Bottle."

5. W. Ellis, *Authentic Narrative*, 2:135.

6. Lemert, "Forms and Pathology of Drinking."

7. Deerr, *History of Sugar*, 1:252.

8. Kervégant, *Rhums et eaux-de-vie*, 481.

9. Langton, "Rum, Seduction, and Death."

10. Crowley, *New History of Australia*, 34.

11. Kervégant, *Rhums et eaux-de-vie*, 481.

12. Akyeampong, *Drink, Power, and Cultural Change*; Pan, *Alcohol in Colonial Africa*.

13. Charpentier de Cossigny, *Mémoire sur la fabrication*, 70–71.

14. Lock, Newlands, and Newlands, *Sugar: A Handbook*, 766–67.

15. Underwood, "Historical Development of Distilling," 58.

16. Wray, *Practical Sugar Planter*, 407, 324–27, 404–8.

17. Ibid., 407–8.

18. Lock, Newlands, and Newlands, *Sugar: A Handbook*, 777; Jamaica, *Handbook of Jamaica* (1946), 326.

19. Wray, *Practical Sugar Planter*, 401.

20. *Handbook of Jamaica* (1888/89), 460.

21. Ragatz, *Fall of the Planter Class*. See also E. Williams, *Capitalism and Slavery*, 113.

22. E. Williams, *Capitalism and Slavery*.

23. Ward, *British West Indian Slavery* and "Profitability," 207–8.

24. Drescher, *Econocide*.

25. Lobdell, "Patterns of Investments," 319.

26. Curtin, "British Sugar Duties," 162.

27. Ibid., 159.

28. Bigelow, *Jamaica in 1850*, 71.

29. Moreno Fraginals, "Plantations in the Caribbean," 333.

30. Davy, *West Indies*, 19–20, n. *.

31. Ragatz, *Fall of the Planter Class*, 290–91, 318–19.

32. Ibid., 295.

33. Anonymous, *Letter to the Most Honourable*, 89.

34. Davy, *West Indies*, 19–20, n. *.

35. Beachey, *British West Indies Sugar*, 44.

36. All British imperial gallons have been converted to U.S. gallons of 3.785 liters.

37. Gardner, *History of Jamaica*, 322.

38. Eisner, *Jamaica, 1830–1930*, 240–45.

39. Higman, *Slave Population and Economy in Jamaica*, 213; Ragatz, *Statistics*, 23.

40. Eisner, *Jamaica, 1830–1930*, 240–45; *Handbook of Jamaica* (1903 and 1911).

41. Ragatz, *Statistics*, 18.

42. Kervégant, *Rhums et eaux-de-vie*, 478; Ragatz, *Statistics*, 18.

43. Fraser, *History of Trinidad*, 2:211–12.

44. Shephard, *Historical Account*, appendix, vi–xxvi.

45. Carrington, "United States and the British West Indian Trade."

46. Rorabaugh, *Alcoholic Republic*, 67.

47. Ibid., 80.

48. Edwards, *History, Civil and Commercial*, 1:304.

49. Gardner, *History of Jamaica*, 324.

50. Rorabaugh, *Alcoholic Republic.*

51. Schomburgk, *History of Barbados*, 160–61.

52. Kervégant, *Rhums et eaux-de-vie*, 24, 474.

53. Pairault, *Le rhum et sa fabrication*, 14.

54. Beachey, *British West Indies Sugar*, 76.

55. Kervégant, *Rhums et eaux-de-vie*, 489.

56. Beachey, *British West Indies Sugar*, 76–77.

57. Pairault, *Le rhum et sa fabrication*, 13.

58. Kervégant, *Rhums et eaux-de-vie*, 489.

59. Renard, "Labour Relations in Post-Slavery Martinique and Guadeloupe," 81.

60. *Affiches Américaines*, December 7, 1786.

61. Charpentier de Cossigny, *Mémoire sur la fabrication* and *Moyens d'amélioration.*

62. *Affiches Américaines*, December 7, 1786; Charpentier de Cossigny, *Mémoire sur la fabrication*, 23 and *Moyens d'amélioration*; Dutrône de la Couture, *Précis sur la canne*, 304–16.

63. Kervégant, *Rhums et eaux-de-vie*, 485.

64. Ibid.

65. Dessalles cited in Forster and Forster, *Sugar and Slavery*, 66.

66. Schnakenbourg, "Statistiques pour l'histoire," 110.

67. Blerald, *Histoire économique*, 60–61; Josa, *Les industries du sucre*, 127–28.

68. Huetz de Lemps, *Histoire du rhum*, 118; Josa, *Les industries du sucre*, 151–52; Kervégant, *Rhums et eaux-de-vie*, 484–85.

69. Mackenzie, *Notes on Haiti*, 2:169.

70. Ibid., 2:302.

71. I wish to thank David Geggus for this reference, which he found at the Archivo General de la Nación, Santo Domingo, Dominican Republic, Anexion a España, leg. 1 exp 10.

72. Kervégant, *Rhums et eaux-de-vie*, 467; Pairault, *Le rhum et sa fabrication*, 14.

73. Kervégant, *Rhums et eaux-de-vie*, 24–25, 485; Unwin, *Wine and the Vine*, 282–84.

74. Kervégant, *Rhums et eaux-de-vie*, 24, 485.

75. Huetz de Lemps, *Histoire du rhum*, 119.

76. Kervégant, *Rhums et eaux-de-vie*, 485–88.

77. Blerald, *Histoire économique*, 60; Josa, *Les industries du sucre*, 146.

78. Kervégant, *Rhums et eaux-de-vie*, 467; Pairault, *Le rhum et sa fabrication*, 13–14.

79. Haine, *World of the Paris Café*, 91.

80. Unwin, *Wine and the Vine*, 294.

81. Haine, *World of the Paris Café*, 95–97.

82. Kervégant, *Rhums et eaux-de-vie*, 486; Pairault, *Le rhum et sa fabrication*, 17.

83. Huetz de Lemps, *Histoire du rhum*, 122.

84. Josa, *Les industries*, 147–49.

85. Huetz de Lemps, *Histoire du rhum*, 119.

86. Pairault, *Le rhum et sa fabrication*, 64.

87. Kervégant, *Rhums et eaux-de-vie*, 25.

88. Kervégant, *Rhums et eaux-de-vie*, 94–125, 162; Pairault, *Le rhum et sa fabrication*, 197–200.

89. Rose-Rosette, *Essai d'approche du punch martiniquais*.

90. Rodriguez, "Venezuelan Rums," 57.

91. Pairault, *Le rhum et sa fabrication*, 50–77.

92. Rorabaugh, *Alcoholic Republic*, 80.

93. Beachey, *British West Indies Sugar*, 74–75.

94. Kervégant, *Rhums et eaux-de-vie*, 485.

95. Moreno Fraginals, "Plantations in the Caribbean."

96. Kervégant, *Rhums et eaux-de-vie*, 476.

97. Moreno Fraginals, "Plantations in the Caribbean."

98. Ibid. See also Scott, *Slave Emancipation*, 22.

99. Turnbull, *Travels in the West. Cuba*, 115; Humboldt, *Island of Cuba*, 301–2.

100. Humboldt, *Island of Cuba*, 260–61. See also 259, n. 2.

101. Moreno Fraginals, *El ingenio*, 3:88–89.

102. Hurlbert cited in Pérez, *Slaves, Sugar, and Colonial Society*, 58.

103. Beachey, *British West Indies Sugar*, 74.

104. Scott, *Slave Emancipation*, 221–26.

105. Ibid., 120.

106. Moreno Fraginals, *El ingenio*, 3:35–40.

107. Foster, *Family Spirits*, 17–20.

108. Kervégant, *Rhums et eaux-de-vie*, 474–75; Pairault, *Le rhum et sa fabrication*, 13–14.

109. Huetz de Lemps, *Histoire du rhum*, 127–28; Rodriguez, "Venezuelan Rums," 63.

110. Rodriguez, "Venezuelan Rums," 64.

111. Pairault, *Le rhum et sa fabrication*, 14, 114–17.

112. Kervégant, *Rhums et eaux-de-vie*, 480–81.

113. Eltis and Jennings, "Trade," 945.

114. Ibid., 955.

115. Inikori, "West Africa's Seaborne Trade."

116. Akyeampong, *Drink, Power, and Cultural Change*, 84–85; Dumett, "Social Impact," 76–81.

117. Manning, *Slavery, Colonialism, and Economic Growth*, 348, 356.

118. Akyeampong, *Drink, Power, and Cultural Change*, 81–82; Pan, *Alcohol in Colonial Africa*, 8.

119. Newman, *British Guiana*, 30.

120. Eisner, *Jamaica, 1830–1930*, 250.

121. Akyeampong, *Drink, Power, and Cultural Change*; Pan, *Alcohol in Colonial Africa*.

122. Rorabaugh, *Alcoholic Republic*, 232.

123. Pegram, *Battling Demon Rum*.

124. Heron, *Booze*, 145–85.

125. Josa, *Les industries du sucre*, 155.

126. Newman, *British Guiana*, 27–32.

127. Colonial Office, *Report of a Commission*.

128. Kervégant, *Rhums et eaux-de-vie*, 489–90.

129. Colonial Office, *Report of a Commission*, 48.

130. Barnes, *Sugar Cane*, 378; Colonial Office, *Report on Jamaica*, 33.

131. Josa, *Les industries du sucre*, 154–55.

132. Blerald, *Histoire économique*, 64; Laurens, *La législation économique*, 57–94.

133. Kervégant, *Rhums et eaux-de-vie*, 488.

134. Hemingway, *A Moveable Feast*, 5.

135. Blerald, *Histoire économique*, 189.

136. Ibid., 137. See also Pairault, *Le rhum et sa fabrication*, 55–75.

137. Institut d'émission des départements d'outre-mer, *La filière canne-sucre-rhum*, 23.

138. Blerald, *Histoire économique*, 217.

139. Institut d'émission des départements d'outre-mer, *La filière canne-sucre-rhum*, 60.

140. Moreno Fraginals, "Plantations in the Caribbean," 339.

141. Moreno Fraginals, *El ingenio*, 3:35–40.

142. Foster, *Family Spirits*, 16; Ortiz, *Cuban Counterpoint*, 25.

143. American Chamber of Commerce of Cuba, *Cuba: Facts and Figures*, 99–102.

144. Ibid., 175. See also Maspons Franco, *La reorganización*, 33–35; Pérez-López, *Economics of Cuban Sugar*, 107–108.

145. Maspons Franco, *La reorganización*, 132–33.

146. Dinwiddie, *Puerto Rico*, 105–6, 257; T. Clark, "Prohibition in Puerto Rico."

147. Licensed Beverage Industries, *Beverage Distilling Industry*, 79.

148. Ibid., 125–26.

149. Ibid., 79. See also J. Bell, *Conditions in Puerto Rico*, 1–6.

150. Cuba, Dirección General de Estadística, *Resúmenes estadísticos seleccionados*, 57.

151. Robinson, *Cuba, Old and New*, 77.

152. Pérez-López, *Economics of Cuban Sugar*, 104–8. See also Hagelberg, *Caribbean Sugar Industries*, 131.

153. Pérez-López, *Economics of Cuban Sugar*, 108.

Chapter 8. Conclusion

1. Institut d'émission des départements d'outre-mer, *La filière canne-sucre-rhum*, 21.

2. Adams Business Media, *Adams Liquor Handbook*, 216–17.

3. Ibid., 17.

4. Institut d'émission des départements d'outre-mer, *La filière canne-sucre-rhum*, 21.

5. Demetrakakes, "Mixing Drinks."

6. Mahy and Barnett, "Mental Health," 206.

7. World Health Organization, *Global Status Report*, 135–36. See also International Beverage Consumption and Production Trends, *World Drink Trends*, 44–45.

8. Mahy and Barnett, "Mental Health"; Canino et al., "Prevalence"; Rivera, "David Defeats Goliath."

9. World Health Organization, *Global Status Report*, 169–71.

10. Murray, *El colmado*, 209, 234.

11. Ibid., 217.

12. Ibid., 226–29.

13. Smith and Pike, "Relationship." For permissive attitudes toward drinking in Afro-Caribbean populations in general, see Yawney, "Drinking Patterns and Alcoholism."

14. R. Smith, *Negro Family*, 40, 92.

15. Dann, *Patterns of Drinking*, 116–17.

16. Mahy and Barnett, "Mental Health," 206.

17. World Health Organization, *Global Status Report*, 116.

18. Yawney, "Drinking Patterns and Alcoholism," 98.

19. Vertovec, *Hindu Trinidad*, 105.

20. Yawney, "Drinking Patterns and Alcoholism," 99.

21. Gray, *Comprehensive Study of Bush Rum*.

22. Mahy and Barnett, "Mental Health," 206.

23. Tucker and Hedges, "Food Shortages and an Epidemic."

24. Collins, *Practical Rules*, 169.

25. Mahy and Barnett, "Mental Health," 205.

26. Barbados Ministry of Health, *Annual Report* (1984).

27. Dann, *Patterns of Drinking*, 119; Mahy and Barnett, "Mental Health," 206.

28. Dann, *Patterns of Drinking*, 119.

29. Fisher, *Colonial Madness*, 59.

30. Brana-Shute, "Drinking Shops," 59; Price, *Behind the Planter's Back*, 154; Wilson, *Crab Antics*, 164, 166–68; Yawney, "Drinking Patterns and Alcoholism," 102.

31. Colonial Office, *Report of a Commission*, 136.

32. Wilson, *Crab Antics*.

33. Yawney, "Drinking Patterns and Alcoholism." See also R. D. E. Burton, *Afro-Creole*, 160–61.

34. Wilson, *Crab Antics*, 168.

35. Brana-Shute, "Drinking Shops" and "Some Aspects."

36. Brana-Shute, "Drinking Shops," 56, 61.

37. See Leacock, "Ceremonial Drinking," 92.

38. McClelland et al., "Cross-Cultural Study"; Schaefer, "Drunkenness."

39. For an alternative view, see sociologist Neil Price, who stresses the declining emphasis on "machismo" among rum shop peer groups in Bequia (*Behind the Planter's Back*, 154).

40. Daniel, *Rumba*, 10, 61.

41. H. Bell, *Obeah*, 33.

42. R. D. E. Burton, *Afro-Creole*, 198–220.

43. Ibid., 203, 208.

44. Cited in Hill, *Calypso Calaloo*, 239, 234–40.

45. Brown, *Mama Lola*, 41; Dayan, "Vodoun, or the Voice of the Gods," 18. See also Métraux, *Voodoo in Haiti*, 77.

46. González-Wippler, *Santería Experience*, 95–96.

47. Powell, *My American Journey*, 14.

References

Adams Business Media

2002   *Adams Liquor Handbook*. New York.

Agbe-Davies, Anna, Carrie Alblinger, Marley R. Brown, Edward Chappell, Willie Graham, and Kelly Ladd

2000   *The Architectural and Archaeological Analysis of Bush Hill, the Garrison, St. Michael, Barbados*. Report of the Colonial Williamsburg Foundation, Department of Archaeological Research, Williamsburg, Virginia.

Akyeampong, Emmanuel

1996   *Drink, Power, and Cultural Change: A Social History of Alcohol in Ghana, c. 1800 to Recent Times*. Portsmouth, New Hampshire: Heinemann.

Alexis, Gerson

1976   *Vodou et quimbois: Essai sur les avatars du vodou à la Martinique*. Port-au-Prince: Les Editions Fardin.

Alleyne, Warren

1978   *Historic Bridgetown*. Published by the Barbados National Trust. Bridgetown, Barbados: Letchworth Press.

American Chamber of Commerce of Cuba

1955   *Cuba: Facts and Figures*. Havana.

Amphlett, John

1873   *Under a Tropical Sky: A Journal of First Impressions of the West Indies*. London.

Andrew, L.

1527   *The Vertuose Boke of Distyllacyon of the Waters of all Maner of Herbes, with the Fygures of the Styllatoryes*. London.

Anonymous

1683   *The Laws of Jamaica Passed by the Assembly and Confirmed by His Majesty in Council, Feb. 23 1683, to Which is Added, a Short Account of the Island and Government Thereof*. London.

1737   "Some Observations, Occasioned by the Improvements in the Late Art of Distilling, by One Mr. Moe, of Barbados." Reprinted 1978 in *Caribbeana: Containing letters and dissertations, together with poetical essays on various subjects and occasions*, 2:242–45. Millwood, New York: Kraus.

1752   *The Art of Making Sugar . . . With an Appendix Containing the Art of Fermenting and Distilling Melasses, Scums, Etc. For Rum*. London.

1760   *Short Animadversions on the Difference Now Set Up Between Gin and Rum and our Mother Country and Colonies*. London.

1797   "Characteristic Traits of the Creolian and African Negroes in Jamaica, &c. &c." In *Columbian Magazine* Kingston, Jamaica, April–October. Reprinted 1976, ed. B. Higman. Jamaica: Caldwell Press.

1830   *A Letter to the Most Honorable the Marquis of Chandos by a West India Planter*. London.

Àntonil, André João

1711   *Cúltura é ópulencia dó Brazil por suas drogas e minas*. Reprinted 1968, ed. A. Mansuy. Saint-Guillaume, Paris: Institut des Hautes Études de l'Amérique Latine.

Argyle, William J.

1966   *The Fon of Dahomey: A History and Ethnography of the Old Kingdom*. Oxford: Clarendon Press.

Arinze, Francis

1970   *Sacrifice in Ibo Religion*. Nigeria: Ibadan University Press.

Armstrong, Douglas

1990   *The Old Village and the Great House: An Archaeological and Historical Examination of Drax Hall Plantation, St. Ann's Bay, Jamaica*. Urbana, Illinois: University of Illinois Press.

Arthur, Paul

1986   "Roman Amphorae from Canterbury." *Britannia* 17: 139–258.

Atkins, John

1735   *A Voyage to Guinea, Brasil, and the West Indies; In His Majesty's Ships, the Swallow and Weymouth*. London.

Atwood, Thomas

1791   *The History of the Island of Dominica*. London.

Baikow, V. E.

1967   *Manufacture and Refining of Raw Cane Sugar*. Amsterdam: Elsevier.

Bailyn, Bernard

1955   *The New England Merchants in the Seventeenth Century*. New York: Harper and Row.

Baker, George

1599   *The Practise of the New and Old Phisicke, Wherein is Contained the Most Excellent Secrets of Phisicke and Philosophie, by Gesner*. London.

Balandier, Georges

1968   *Daily Life in the Kingdom of the Kongo from the Sixteenth to the Eighteenth Century*. Trans. H. Weaver. New York: Pantheon Books.

Barbados Department of Archives

1711–1841   Society for the Propagation of the Gospel in Foreign Parts. Codrington plantation records, annual reports. Black Rock, Barbados.

1758–1853   William FitzHerbert Papers. Turner's Hall: letters and correspondences, abstracts and accounts. Black Rock, Barbados.

Barbados Ministry of Health

1984   *Annual Report of the Chief Medical Officer*. Bridgetown, Barbados.

Barbot, John

1746   *A Description of the Coasts of North and South Guinea*. London.

Barnes, A. C.

1964   *The Sugar Cane*. London: Leonard Hill.

Barrett, Leonard

1988   *The Rastafarians: Sounds of Cultural Dissonance*. Boston: Beacon Press.

Barrows, Susanna, and Robin Room, eds.

1991   *Drinking: Behavior and Belief in Modern History*. Berkeley: University of California Press.

Barty-King, Hugh, and Anton Massel

1983   *Rum: Yesterday and Today*. London: Heinemann.

Basden, George

1938   *Niger Ibos: A Description of the Primitive Life, Customs and Animistic Beliefs, etc., of the Ibo People of Nigeria*. London: Frank Cass.

Beachey, R. W.

1957   *The British West Indies Sugar Industry in the Late 19th Century*. Oxford: Basil Blackwell.

Beckford, William

1790   *A Descriptive Account of the Island of Jamaica: With Remarks Upon the Cultivation of the Sugar Cane*. 2 vols. London.

Beckwith, Martha Warren

1929   *Black Roadways: A Study of Jamaican Folklife*. Chapel Hill: University of North Carolina Press.

Belgrove, William

1755   *A Treatise Upon Husbandry or Planting*. London.

Bell, Hesketh J.

1889   *Obeah; Witchcraft in the West Indies*. Reprinted 1970, Westport, Connecticut: Negro Universities Press.

1937   "Report on the Caribs of Dominica in 1903." *Journal of the Barbados Museum and Historical Society* 5(1): 18–31.

Bell, Jasper

1944   *Conditions in Puerto Rico*. Report to the U.S. Congress of the Committee of Insular Affairs, Washington, D.C.: U.S. Government Printing Office.

Berleant-Schiller, Riva

1989   "Free Labor and the Economy in Seventeenth-Century Montserrat." *William and Mary Quarterly* 46(3): 539–64.

1995   "From Labour to Peasantry in Montserrat after the End of Slavery." In *Small Islands, Large Questions*, ed. K. Olwig, 53–72. London: Frank Cass.

Berlin, Michael

1996   *The Worshipful Company of Distillers: A Short History*. West Sussex: Phillimore.

Bigelow, John

1851   *Jamaica in 1850. Or, the Effects of Sixteen Years of Freedom on a Slave Colony*. London.

Bilby, Kenneth

1981   "The Kromanti Dance of the Windward Maroons of Jamaica." *New West Indian Guide* 55: 52–101.

Bisnauth, Dale

1996   *History of Religions in the Caribbean*. Trenton, New Jersey: Africa World Press.

Blerald, Alain-Philippe

1986   *Histoire économique de la Guadeloupe et de la Martinique du XVII siècle à nos jours*. Paris: Karthala.

Blocker, Jack S., and Cheryl Krasnick Warsh, eds.

1997   *The Changing Face of Drink: Substance, Imagery, and Behaviour*. Ottawa, Canada: Les Publications Histoire Sociale.

Blome, Richard

1672   *A Description of the Island of Jamaica; with Other Isles and Territories in America*. London.

Bosman, William

1705   *A New and Accurate Description of the Coast of Guinea, Divided Into the Gold, the Slave, and the Ivory Coasts*. London.

Bourgeois, Nicolas Louis

1788   *Voyages intéressans dans différentes colonies françaises, espagnoles, anglaises, &c*. London.

Bourguignon, Erika E.

1964   "Comments on Leacock's Ceremonial Drinking in an Afro-Brazilian Cult." *American Anthropologist* 66: 1393–394.

Bowden, Martyn

2003   "Three Centuries of Bridgetown: An Historical Geography." *Journal of the Barbados Museum and Historical Society* 49: 3–137.

Boxer, C. R.

1990   *The Dutch Seaborne Empire, 1600–1800.* Harmondsworth: Penguin Books.

Brana-Shute, Gary

1976   "Drinking Shops and Social Structure: Some Ideas on Lower-Class West Indian Male Behavior." *Urban Anthropology* 5(1): 53–68.

1978   "Some Aspects of Youthful Identity Management in a Paramaribo Creole Neighborhood." *New West Indian Guide* 52(1): 1–20.

Braudel, Fernand

1982   *The Structures of Everyday Life: The Limits of the Possible.* Trans. S. Reynolds. New York: Harper and Row.

Brereton, Bridget

1979   *Race Relations in Colonial Trinidad, 1870–1900.* Cambridge: Cambridge University Press.

Breton, Raymond

1978   *Relations de l'ile de la Guadeloupe.* Basse-Terre: Société d'Histoire de la Guadeloupe.

Bridenbaugh, Carl, and Roberta Bridenbaugh

1972   *No Peace beyond the Line: The English in the Caribbean 1624–1690.* New York: Oxford University Press.

Brown, Karen McCarthy

1991   *Mama Lola: A Vodou Priestess in Brooklyn.* Berkeley: University of California Press.

Bruman, Henry

2000   *Alcohol in Ancient Mexico.* Salt Lake City: University of Utah Press.

Brunschwig, Hieronymus

1500–1507   *Liber de arte distillandi de simplicibus. Das buch der rechten kunst zu distilieren die eintzige ding.* 2 vols. Strasburg.

Buckley, Roger

1979   *Slaves in Red Coats: The British West India Regiments, 1795–1815.* New Haven: Yale University Press.

1998   *The British Army in the West Indies: Society and the Military in the Revolutionary Age.* Gainesville: University Press of Florida.

Burns, Andrew

1792   *A Second Address to the People of Great Britain; Containing a New and Most Powerful Argument to Abstain from the Use of West India Sugar.* London.

Burton, R. F.

1864   *A Mission to Gelele, King of Dahome.* Reprinted 1966, C. Newbury, ed. London: Routledge and Kegan Paul.

Burton, Richard D. E.

1997   *Afro-Creole: Power, Opposition, and Play in the Caribbean.* Ithaca, New York: Cornell University Press.

Butel-Dumont, Georges Marie

1755   *Histoire et commerce des colonies angloises, dan l'Amérique septentrionale.* London.

Cadwalader, Thomas

1745   *An Essay on the West India Dry-Gripes; with the Method of Preventing and Curing that Cruel Distemper.* Philadelphia.

Campbell, P. F.

1993   *Some Early Barbadian History.* Bridgetown, Barbados: Caribbean Graphics and Letchworth Press.

Canino, G. J., H. Bird, P. Shrout, M. Rubio-Stipec, K. Geil, and M. Bravo

1987   "The Prevalence of Alcohol Abuse and/or Dependence in Puerto Rico." In *Health and Behavior: Research Agenda for Hispanics,* ed. M. Gaviria and J. Arana, 127–44. Research Monograph series no. 1. Chicago: University of Illinois at Chicago.

Carmichael, A. C.

1833   *Domestic Manners and Social Condition of the White, Coloured, and Negro Population of the West Indies.* 2 vols. Reprinted 1969, New York: Negro Universities Press.

Carrington, Selwyn

1988   *The British West Indies during the American Revolution.* Providence: Foris Publications.

1996   "The United States and the British West Indian Trade, 1783–1807." In *West Indies Accounts: Essays on the History of the British Caribbean and the Atlantic Economy in Honour of Richard Sheridan,* ed. R. McDonald, 149–68. Barbados: Press University of the West Indies.

Carstairs, G. M.

1979   "Daru and Bhang: Cultural Factors in the Choice of Intoxicant." In *Beliefs, Behaviors, and Alcoholic Beverages: A Cross-Cultural Survey,* ed. M. Marshall, 297–312. Ann Arbor: University of Michigan Press.

Cauna, Jacques

1987   *Au temps des isles à sucre: Histoire d'une plantation de Saint Domingue au XVIIIe siècle.* Paris: Karthala.

Chambers, Douglas B.

1997   "'My own nation': Igbo Exiles in the Diaspora." In *Routes to Slavery: Direction, Ethnicity, and Mortality in the Transatlantic Slave Trade,* ed. D. Eltis and D. Richardson, 72–97. London: Frank Cass.

Charpentier de Cossigny, J. F.

1781   *Mémoire sur la fabrication des eaux-de-vie de sucre et particulièrement sur celle de la guildive et du tafia; avec une appendice sur le vin de cannes et des observations sur la fabrication du sucre.* L'isle de France.

1803 *Moyens d'amélioration et de restauration, proposés au gouvernement et aux habitans des colonies.* Paris.

Cherrington, Ernest Hurst, ed.

1924–30 *Standard Encyclopedia of the Alcohol Problem.* 6 vols. Westerville, Ohio: American Issue Publishing.

Chevannes, Barry

1998 "New Approach to Rastafari." In *Rastafari and Other African Caribbean Worldviews*, ed. B. Chevannes, 20–42. New Brunswick: Rutgers University Press.

Chez Checo, José

1988 *El ron en la historia Dominicana.* Santo Domingo: Centenario de Brugal y Compania.

Clark, Peter

1988 "The 'Mother Gin' Controversy in the Early Eighteenth Century." *Transactions of the Royal Historical Society* 38: 63–84.

Clark, Truman

1995 "Prohibition in Puerto Rico, 1917–1933." *Journal of Latin American Studies* 27(1): 77–97.

Clement, Christopher

1997 "Settlement Patterning on the British Caribbean Island of Tobago." *Historical Archaeology* 31(2): 93–106.

Collins, Dr.

1811 *Practical Rules for the Management and Medical Treatment of Negro Slaves, in the Sugar Colonies.* London.

Colonial Office

1949 *Report of a Commission of Inquiry into the Sugar Industry of British Guiana.* London: His Majesty's Stationery Office.

1951 *Report on Jamaica for the Year 1950.* London: His Majesty's Stationery Office.

Colt, Sir Henry

1631 "The Voyage of Sir Henry Colt." Reprinted 1967 in *Colonising Expeditions to the West Indies and Guiana, 1623–1667*, ed. V. T. Harlow. Nendeln, Liechtenstein: Kraus.

Connell, Neville

1957 "Punch Drinking and Its Accessories." *Journal of the Barbados Museum and Historical Society* 25(1): 1–17.

Conroy, David W.

1991 "Puritans in Taverns: Law and Popular Culture in Colonial Massachusetts, 1630–1720." In *Drinking: Behavior and Belief in Modern History*, ed. S. Barrows and R. Room, 29–60. Berkeley: University of California Press.

Cordingly, David
1997   *Under the Black Flag: The Romance and the Reality of Life among Pirates.* San Diego: Harcourt Brace.
Corruccini, Robert S., Elizabeth M. Brandon, and Jerome S. Handler
1989   "Inferring Fertility from Relative Mortality in Historically Controlled Cemetery Remains from Barbados." *American Antiquity* 54(3): 609–14.
Cotter, John
1958   *Archaeological Excavations at Jamestown, Virginia.* National Park Service Archaeological Research Series, no. 4. Washington, D.C.
Coughtry, Jay
1981   *The Notorious Triangle: Rhode Island and the African Slave Trade 1700–1807.* Philadelphia: Temple University Press.
Crain, Christopher, Kevin Farmer, Frederick H. Smith, and Karl Watson
2004   "Human Skeletal Remains from an Unmarked African Burial Ground in the Pierhead Section of Bridgetown, Barbados." *Journal of the Barbados Museum and Historical Society* 50:66–83.
Craton, Michael
1978   *Searching for the Invisible Man: Slaves and Plantation Life in Jamaica.* Cambridge, Mass.: Harvard University Press.
1982   *Testing the Chains: Resistance to Slavery in the British West Indies.* Ithaca: Cornell University Press.
1991   "Death, Disease, and Medicine on the Jamaican Slave Plantations; the Example of Worthy Park, 1767–1838." In *Caribbean Slave Society and Economy: a Student Reader*, ed. H. Beckles and V. Shepherd, 183–96. New York: New Press.
1997   *Empire, Enslavement, and Freedom in the Caribbean.* Kingston: Ian Randle.
Craton, Michael, and James Walvin
1970   *A Jamaican Plantation: The History of Worthy Park 1670–1970.* Toronto: University of Toronto Press.
Craton, Michael, James Walvin, and David Wright, eds.
1976   *Slavery, Abolition, and Emancipation: Black Slaves and the British Empire, a0 Thematic Documentary.* London: Longman Group.
Creole of St. Domingue
1959   *My Odyssey: Experiences of a Young Refugee from Two Revolutions,* ed. Althéa de Puech Parham. Baton Rouge: Louisiana State University Press.
Crowley, F. K.
1974   *A New History of Australia.* Melbourne: Heinemann.
Cuba, Dirección General de Estadística
1959   *Resúmenes estadísticos seleccionados.* Havana, Cuba.

Curtin, Philip

1954 "The British Sugar Duties and West Indian Prosperity." *Journal of Economic History* 14(2):157–64.

Curto, José Carlos

1996 "Alcohol and Slaves: The Luso-Brazilian Alcohol Commerce at Mpinda, Luanda, and Benguela during the Atlantic Slave Trade c. 1480–1830 and Its Impact on the Societies of West Central Africa." Ph.D. diss., University of California, Los Angeles.

Dailey, R. C.

1979 "The Role of Alcohol among North American Indian Tribes as Reported in the Jesuit Relations." In *Beliefs, Behaviors, and Alcoholic Beverages: A Cross-Cultural Survey*, ed. M. Marshall, 116–27. Ann Arbor: University of Michigan Press.

Dallas, Robert Charles

1803 *The History of the Maroons, from Their Origin to the Establishment of their Chief Tribe at Sierra Leone.* 2 vols. London.

Daniel, Yvonne

1995 *Rumba: Dance and Social Change in Contemporary Cuba.* Bloomington: Indiana University Press.

Dann, Graham

1980 *Patterns of Drinking in Barbados: The Findings of a Sample Survey of Adult Residents.* Bridgetown: CEDAR Press.

Davis, N. Darnell

1885 "The Etymology of the Word Rum." *Journal of the Royal Agricultural and Commercial Society of British Guiana* 4: 76–81.

Davy, John

1854 *The West Indies, Before and Since Slave Emancipation, Comprising the Windward and Leeward Islands' Military Command.* London.

Dayan, Joan

1997 "Vodoun, or the Voice of the Gods." In *Sacred Possessions: Vodou, Santería, Obeah, and the Caribbean*, ed. M. Fernandez Olmos and L. Paravisini-Gebert, 13–36. New Brunswick: Rutgers University Press.

Deagan, Kathleen

1972 "Fig Springs: The Mid-Seventeenth Century in North Central Florida." *Historical Archaeology* 6: 23–46.

1983 *Spanish St. Augustine: The Archaeology of a Colonial Creole Community.* New York: Academic Press.

Debien, Gabriel

1974 *Les esclaves aux antilles françaises, XVIIe-XVIIIe siècles.* Basse-Terre: Société d'Histoire de la Guadeloupe.

Deerr, Noel

1949–50   *The History of Sugar*. 2 vols. London: Chapman and Hall.

de Groot, Silvia

1986   "A Comparison between the History of Maroon Communities in Surinam and Jamaica." In *Out of the House of Bondage: Runaways, Resistance, and Marronage in Africa and the New World*, ed. G. Heuman, 173–84. London: Frank Cass.

de Marees, Pieter

1602   *Description and Historical Account of the Gold Kingdom on Guinea*. Trans. and ed. A. van Dantzig and A. Jones, 1987. Oxford: Oxford University Press.

Demetrakakes, Pan

1999   "Mixing Drinks (Management and Production at Seagrams Americas' Relay, Md. Facility)." *Food Processing* 60(1): 47–50.

Dennis, Philip

1975   "The Role of the Drunk in a Oaxacan Village." *American Anthropologist* 77: 856–63.

Dickson, William

1789   *Letters on Slavery: To Which are Added, Addresses to the Whites, and to the Free Negroes of Barbadoes*. London.

Dinwiddie, William

1899   *Puerto Rico: Its Conditions and Possibilities*. New York: Harper and Brothers.

Dirks, Robert

1987   *The Black Saturnalia: Conflict and Its Ritual Expression on British West Indian Slave Plantations*. Gainesville: University Press of Florida.

Dobbin, Jay

1986   *The Jombee Dance of Montserrat: A Study of Trance Ritual in the West Indies*. Columbus: Ohio State University Press.

Dorigny, Marcel

1997   *Léger-Félicité Sonthonax: La première abolition de l'esclavage: La révolution française et la révolution de Saint Domingue*. Texts réunis et présentés par M. Dorigny. Saint-Denis: Société Française d'Histoire d'Outre-Mer; Paris: Association pour l'Étude de la Colonization Européenne.

Dorschner, Jon Peter

1983   *Alcohol Consumption in a Village in North India*. Ann Arbor: UMI Research Press.

Dossie, Robert

1770   *An Essay on Spirituous Liquors with Regard to Their Effects on Health, in Which the Comparative Wholesomeness of Rum and Brandy are Particularly Considered*. London.

Douglas, Mary, ed.

1987   *Constructive Drinking: Perspectives on Drink from Anthropology*. Cambridge: Cambridge University Press.

Drescher, Seymour

1977   *Econocide: British Slavery in the Era of Abolition.* Pittsburgh: University of Pittsburgh Press.

Dumett, Raymond

1974   "The Social Impact of the European Liquor Trade on the Akan of Ghana (Gold Coast and Asante), 1875-1910." *Journal of Interdisciplinary History* 5(1): 69-101.

Dunn, Richard S.

1973   *Sugar and Slaves: The Rise of the Planter Class in the English West Indies, 1624-1713.* New York: W.W. Norton.

1993   "Sugar Production and Slave Women in Jamaica." In *Culture and Cultivation: Labor and the Shaping of Slave Life in the Americas*, ed. I. Berlin and P. D. Morgan, 49-72. Charlottesville: University Press of Virginia.

Du Tertre, Jean Baptiste

1667-71   *Histoire generale des Antilles habitées par les françois.* 4 vols. Paris.

Dutrône de la Couture, Jacques-François

1791   *Précis sur la canne et sur les moyens d'en extraire le sel essentiel.* Paris.

Edwards, Bryan

1819   *The History, Civil and Commercial, of the British West Indies.* 5th ed. 5 vols. London.

Eisner, Gisela

1961   *Jamaica, 1830-1930; A Study in Economic Growth.* Manchester: Manchester University Press.

Ellis, A. B.

1883   *The Land of Fetish.* Reprinted 1970, Westport, Conn.: Negro Universities Press.

Ellis, William

1782   *An Authentic Narrative of a Voyage Performed by Captain Cook and Captain Clerke . . .* Reprinted 1969 in 2 vols. New York: Da Capo Press.

Eltis, David

1995   "The Total Product of Barbados, 1664-1701." *Journal of Economic History* 55(2): 321-38.

1995   "New Estimates of Exports from Barbados and Jamaica, 1665-1701." *William and Mary Quarterly* 52(4): 631-48.

1997   "The Slave Economies of the Caribbean: Structure, Performance, Evolution and Significance." *General History of the Caribbean.* Vol. 3, *The Slave Societies of the Caribbean*, ed. F. Knight, 105-37. London: UNESCO.

2000   *The Rise of African Slavery in the Americas.* Cambridge: Cambridge University Press.

Eltis, David, and Lawrence Jennings

1988   "Trade between Western Africa and the Atlantic World in the Pre-Colonial Era." *American Historical Review* 93(4): 936–59.

Eltis, David, and David Richardson

1997   "The 'Numbers Game' and Routes to Slavery." In *Routes to Slavery: Direction, Ethnicity, and Mortality in the Transatlantic Slave Trade*, ed. D. Eltis and D. Richardson, 1–15. London: Frank Cass.

1997   "West Africa and the Transatlantic Slave Trade: New Evidence of Long-Run Trends." In *Routes to Slavery: Direction, Ethnicity, and Mortality in the Transatlantic Slave Trade*, ed. D. Eltis and D. Richardson, 16–35. London: Frank Cass.

Emmanuel, Isaac

1955   "New Light on Early American Jewry." *American Jewish Archives* 7(1): 3–63.

Emmanuel, Isaac, and Suzanne Emmanuel

1970   *History of the Jews of the Netherlands Antilles*. 2 vols. Cincinnati: American Jewish Archives.

Equiano, Olaudah

1837   *The Life of Olaudah Equiano, or Gustavus Vassa the African*. Reprinted 1969, New York: Negro Universities Press.

Everett, Michael W., Jack O. Waddell, and Dwight B. Heath, eds.

1976   *Cross-Cultural Approaches to the Study of Alcohol: An Interdisciplinary Perspective*. The Hague: Mouton Publishers.

Ewing, John, and Beatrice Rouse

1978   "Drinks, Drinkers, and Drinking." In *Drinking: Alcohol in American Society—Issues and Current Research*, ed. J. Ewing and B. Rouse, 5–30. Chicago: Nelson Hall.

Fahey, David

1997   "Blacks, Good Templars, and Universal Membership." In *The Changing Face of Drink: Substance, Imagery, and Behaviour*, ed. J. Blocker and C. K. Warsh, 133–62. Ottawa: Les Publications Histoire Sociale.

Fairbanks, Charles

1976   "Spaniards, Planters, Ships, and Slaves: Historical Archaeology in Florida and Georgia." *Archaeology* 29: 164–72.

Farnsworth, Paul

1996   "The Influence of Trade on Bahamian Slave Culture." *Historical Archaeology* 30(4): 1–23.

Fernandes, Valentim

1510   *Description de la côte occidentale d'Afrique, 1506–1510*. Reprinted 1951, ed. T. Monod and R. Mauny. Bissau: Centro de Estudos da Guiné Portuguesa, no. 11.

Field, M. J.

1937   *Religion and Medicine of the Gã People*. London: Oxford University Press.

Fielding, Henry

1751   *An Enquiry into the Causes of the Late Increase of Robbers.* London.

Fisher, Lawrence

1985   *Colonial Madness: Mental Health in the Barbadian Social Order.* New Brunswick: Rutgers University Press.

Fitzmaurice, W.

1793   *A Treatise on the Cultivation of Sugar Cane and the Manufacture of Sugar.* Calcutta: World Press.

Fogel, Robert William

1989   *Without Consent or Contract: The Rise and Fall of American Slavery.* New York: W. W. Norton.

Forbes, Frederick E.

1851   *Dahomey and the Dahomans: Being the Journals of Two Missions to the King of Dahomey, and Residence at His Capital, in the Years 1849 and 1851.* 2 vols. London.

Ford, Richard

ca. 1674   *A New Map of the Island of Barbadoes.* London.

Forster, Elborg, and Robert Forster

1996   *Sugar and Slavery, Family and Race: The Letters and Diary of Pierre Dessalles, Planter in Martinique, 1808–1856.* Baltimore: Johns Hopkins University Press.

Foster, Peter

1990   *Family Spirits: The Bacardi Saga.* Toronto: MacFarlane Walter and Ross.

Fox, William

1792   *An Address to the People of Great Britain, on the Propriety of Abstaining from West India Sugar and Rum.* 9th ed. Philadelphia.

Fraser, Lionel Mordaunt

1891–96   *History of Trinidad.* 2 vols. Port-of-Spain: Government Printing Office.

Frémond de la Merveillère, Olivier

1935   "L'habitation sucrière d'une habitation nantaise à Saint Domingue, 1742–1762." *Fontenay-Le-Comte: Imprimerie Modern.*

French, John

1664   *The Art of Distillation, Or a Treatise of the Choicest Spagyrical Preparations, Experiments, and Curiosities, Performed by Way of Distillation.* London.

Frere, George

1768   *A Short History of Barbados, from its First Discovery and Settlement, to the End of the Year 1767.* London.

Gage, Thomas

1677   *A New Survey of the West Indies: Or, The English American His Travel by Sea and Land: Containing a Journal of Three Thousand and Three Hundred Miles Within the Main Land of America.* 3rd ed. London.

Galliou, Patrick

1984 "Days of Wine and Roses? Early Armorica and the Atlantic Wine Trade." In *Cross-Channel Trade between Gaul and Britain in the Pre-Roman Iron Age*, ed. S. Macready and F. Thompson, 24–36. London: Society of Antiquaries.

Gardner, W. J.

1873 *A History of Jamaica from its Discovery by Christopher Columbus to the Year 1872.* Reprinted 1971, London: Frank Cass.

Garine, Igor de, and Valerie de Garine, eds.

2001 *Drinking: Anthropological Approaches.* New York: Berghahn Press.

Gaspar, David Barry

1978 "The Antigua Slave Conspiracy of 1736: A Case Study of the Origin of Collective Resistance." *William and Mary Quarterly* 35(2): 308–23.

1993 *Bondmen and Rebels: A Study of Master-Slave Relations in Antigua.* Durham: Duke University Press.

Gefou-Madianou, Dimitra, ed.

1992 *Alcohol, Gender, and Culture.* London: Routledge.

Geggus, David Patrick

1979 "Yellow Fever in the 1790s: The British Army in Occupied Saint Domingue." *Medical History* 23(1): 38–58.

1982 *Slavery, War, and Revolution: The British Occupation of Saint Domingue, 1793–1798.* Oxford: Clarendon Press.

1986 "On the Eve of the Haitian Revolution: Slave Runaways in Saint Domingue in the Year 1790." In *Out of the House of Bondage: Runaways, Resistance, and Marronage in Africa and the New World*, ed. G. Heuman, 112–28. London: Frank Cass.

1989 "The Haitian Revolution." In *The Modern Caribbean*, ed. F. Knight and C. Palmer, 21–50. Chapel Hill: University of North Carolina Press.

1989 "Sex Ratio, Age and Ethnicity in the Atlantic Slave Trade: Data from French Shipping and Plantation Records." *Journal of African History* 30: 23–44.

1990 "The Demographic Composition of the French Caribbean Slave Trade." *Proceedings of the 13th and 14th Meetings of the French Colonial Historical Society*, ed. P. Boucher, 14–30. Lanham, Maryland: University Press of America.

1991 "The Bois Caiman Ceremony." *Journal of Caribbean History* 25(3):41–57.

1991 "Haitian Voodoo in the Eighteenth Century: Language, Culture, Resistance." *Jahrbuch für geschichte von staat, wirtschaft und gesellschaft Lateinamerikas* 28: 21–51.

1992 "Marronage, Voodoo, and the Saint Domingue Slave Revolt of 1791." *Proceedings of the 15th Meeting of the French Colonial Historical Society*, 22–35. Lanham, Maryland: University Press of America.

1998 "The French Slave Trade: An Overview." Paper presented at the W.E.B. Du Bois slave trade database conference, Williamsburg, Virginia.

George, M. Dorothy

1951   *London Life in the Eighteenth Century*. Reprinted by the London School of Economics and Political Science, University of London.

Gesner, Conrad

1559   *The Treasure of Euonymus*. Reprinted 1969, London: Da Capo Press.

Gibb, James, and Julia King

1991   "Gender, Activity Areas, and Homelots in the Seventeenth Century Chesapeake Region." *Historical Archaeology* 25(4): 109–31.

Gibbons, Boyd

1992   "Alcohol: The Legal Drug." *National Geographic* 181(2): 3–35.

Goebel, Dorothy

1963   "The 'New England Trade' and the French West Indies, 1763–1774: A Study in Trade Policies." *William and Mary Quarterly* 20(3): 331–72.

Goggin, John

1960   *The Spanish Olive Jar: An Introductory Study*. Yale University Publications in Anthropology, no. 62. New Haven: Yale University Press.

González-Wippler, Migene

1982   *The Santería Experience*. Englewood Cliffs, New Jersey: Prentice-Hall.

Goslinga, Cornelis

1985   *The Dutch in the Caribbean and in the Guianas 1680–1791*. Assen: Van Gorcum Press.

1990   *The Dutch in the Caribbean and in Surinam 1791/5–1942*. Assen: Van Gorcum Press.

Gould, Clarence

1939   "Trade between the Windward Islands and the Continental Colonies of the French Empire, 1683–1763." *Mississippi Valley Historical Review* 25(4): 473–90.

Gragg, Larry D.

1988   "Puritans in Paradise: The New England Migration to Barbadoes, 1640–1660." *Journal of Caribbean History* 21 (2):154–67.

Gray, Christopher

1988   *A Comprehensive Study of Bush Rum in Trinidad and Tobago*. Diego Martin, Trinidad, and Tobago: Aware Publications.

Greeley, Alexandra

1991   "Getting the Lead Out of Just About Everything." *FDA Consumer* 25(6): 26–32.

Gunkel, Alexander, and Jerome S. Handler

1969   "A Swiss Medical Doctor's Description of Barbados in 1661: The Account of Felix Christian Spoeri." *Journal of the Barbados Museum and Historical Society* 33(1): 3–13.

1970 "A German Indentured Servant in Barbados in 1652: The Account of Heinrich von Uchteritz." *Journal of the Barbados Museum and Historical Society* 33(3): 91–100.

Hagelberg, G. B.

1974 *The Caribbean Sugar Industries: Constraints and Opportunities.* New Haven, Connecticut: Yale University Press.

Haine, W. Scott

1996 *The World of the Paris Café: Sociability among the French Working Class, 1789–1914.* Baltimore: Johns Hopkins University Press.

Hall, Douglas

1989 *In Miserable Slavery: Thomas Thistlewood in Jamaica, 1750–1786.* London: Macmillan.

Hall, Neville A. T.

1992 *Slave Society in the Danish West Indies: Saint Thomas, Saint John and Saint Croix.* Ed. B. Higman. Mona, Jamaica: University of the West Indies Press.

Hall, Richard

1755 *A General Account of the First Settlement and of the Trade and Constitution of the Island of Barbados.* Transcribed with a foreword by E. M. Shilstone, Barbados, 1924.

Hamilton D. L., and Robyn Woodward

1984 "A Sunken Seventeenth-Century City: Port Royal, Jamaica." *Archaeology* 37(1): 38–45.

Hamshere, Cyril

1972 *The British in the Caribbean.* Cambridge, Mass.: Harvard University Press.

Hancock, David

1998 "Commerce and Conversation in the Eighteenth Century Atlantic: The Invention of Madeira Wine." *Journal of Interdisciplinary History* 29(2): 197–219.

Handler, Jerome S.

1967 "Father Antoine Biet's Visit to Barbados in 1654." *Journal of the Barbados Museum and Historical Society* 32: 56–76.

1969 "Amerindian Slave Population of Barbados in the Seventeenth and Early Eighteenth Centuries." *Caribbean Studies* 8(4): 38–64.

1981 "Joseph Rachell and Rachael Pringle Polgreen: Petty Entrepreneurs." In *Struggle and Survival in Colonial Latin America*, ed. D. Nash and G. Nash, 376–91. Berkeley: University of California Press.

2000 "Slave Medicine and Obeah in Barbados, Circa 1650 to 1834." *New West Indian Guide* 74(1&2): 57–90.

2002 "Plantation Slave Settlements in Barbados, 1650s–1834." In *In the Shadow of the Plantation: Caribbean History and Legacy. In Honour of Professor Emeritus Woodville K. Marshall*, ed. A. Thompson, 121–61. Kingston: Ian Randle.

Handler, Jerome S., Arthur C. Aufderheide, Robert S. Corruccini, Elizabeth M. Brandon, and Lorentz E. Wittmers Jr.

1986   "Lead Contact and Poisoning in Barbados Slaves: Historical, Chemical, and Biological Evidence." *Social Science History* 10(4): 399–425.

Handler, Jerome S., and Frederick W. Lange

1978   *Plantation Slavery in Barbados: An Archaeological and Historical Investigation.* Cambridge, Mass.: Harvard University Press.

Hariot, Thomas

1587   "A Brief and True Report of the New Found Land of Virginia." Reprinted 1986 in *Richard Hakluyt, Voyages to the Virginia Colonies.* London: Folio Society.

Hazoume, Paul

1956   *Le pacte de sang au Dahomey.* Paris: Institut d'ethnologie.

Heath, Dwight B.

2000   *Drinking Occasions: Comparative Perspectives on Alcohol and Culture.* Philadelphia: Brunner/Mazel.

Heinl, Robert, and Nancy Heinl

1978   *Written in Blood: The Story of the Haitian People, 1492–1971.* Boston: Houghton-Mifflin.

Hemingway, Ernest

1987   *A Moveable Feast.* New York: Collier Books.

Herd, Denise

1991   "The Paradox of Temperance: Blacks and the Alcohol Question in Nineteenth Century America." In *Drinking: Behavior and Belief in Modern History*, ed. S. Barrows and R. Room, 354–75. Berkeley: University of California Press.

Hernandez Palomo, Jose Jesus

1974   *El aguardiente de caña en Mexico, 1724–1810.* Sevilla: Escuela de Estudios Hispano-Americanos de Sevilla.

Heron, Craig,

2004   *Booze: A Distilled History.* Toronto: Between the Lines Books.

Herrero, Pedro Pérez

1987   "La estructura comercial del Caribe en la segunda mitad del siglo XVI." Paper presented at the España, Florida y el Caribe: Exploraciones y asentamientos en el siglo XVI conference, University of Florida, Gainesville, Florida.

Herskovits, Melville J.

1937   *Life in a Haitian Valley.* New York: Alfred A. Knopf.

1941   *The Myth of the Negro Past.* New York: Harper and Brothers.

1966   *The New World Negro: Selected Papers in Afro-American Studies.* Ed. F. Herskovits. Bloomington: Indiana University Press.

1967   *Dahomey: An Ancient West African Kingdom.* 2 vols. Evanston, Ill.: Northwestern University Press.

Herskovits, Melville J., and Frances S. Herskovits

1947   *Trinidad Village*. New York: Alfred A. Knopf.

Heuman, Gad

1994   *"The Killing Time": The Morant Bay Rebellion in Jamaica*. Knoxville: University of Tennessee Press.

Higman, Barry W.

1976   *Slave Population and Economy in Jamaica, 1807–1834*. Cambridge: Cambridge University Press.

1984   *Slave Populations of the British Caribbean, 1807–1834*. Baltimore: Johns Hopkins University Press.

Hill, Donald R.

1993   *Calypso Calaloo: Early Carnival Music in Trinidad*. Gainesville: University Press of Florida.

Hilliard d'Auberteuil, Michel René

1776   *Considérations sur l'état présent de la colonie française de Saint Domingue*. 2 vols. Paris.

Hodge, Walter, and Douglas Taylor

1957   *The Ethnobotany of the Island Caribs of Dominica*. Firenze: Instituto Botanico dell'Universita.

Holme, Randle

1688   *The Academy of Armory*. London.

Honychurch, Lennox

1997   "Crossroads in the Caribbean: A Site of Encounter and Exchange on Dominica." *World Archaeology* 28(3): 291–304.

Horn, James

1979   "Servant Emigration to the Chesapeake in the Seventeenth Century." In *The Chesapeake in the Seventeenth Century: Essays on Anglo-American Society*, ed. T. Tate and D. Ammerman, 51–95. New York: W.W. Norton.

Horton, Donald

1943   "The Functions of Alcohol in Primitive Societies: A Cross-Cultural Study." *Quarterly Journal of Studies on Alcohol* 4: 199–320.

Hudson, Page

1978   "The Medical Examiner Looks at Drinking." In *Drinking: Alcohol in American Society—Issues and Current Research*, ed. J. Ewing and B. Rouse, 71–92. Chicago: Nelson Hall.

Huetz de Lemps, Alain

1997   *Histoire du rhum*. Paris: Editions Desjonquéres.

Hughes, Griffith

1750   *The Natural History of Barbados*. London.

Hulme, Peter, and Neil Whitehead, eds.

1992   *Wild Majesty: Encounters with Caribs from Columbus to the Present Day, an Anthology.* Oxford: Clarendon Press.

Humboldt, Alexander

1856   *The Island of Cuba.* Trans. J. S. Thrasher. Reprinted 1969, New York: Negro Universities Press.

Hunter, John

1785   *Some Experiments Made upon Rum in Order to Ascertain the Cause of the Colic Frequent Among the Soldiers in the Island of Jamaica in the Years 1781 and 1782.* London.

Hurston, Zora

1939   *Voodoo Gods: An Inquiry into Native Myths and Magic in Jamaica and Haiti.* London: J. M. Dent and Sons.

Inikori, Joseph

1998   "West Africa's Seaborne Trade." Paper presented at W.E.B. Du Bois slave trade database conference, Williamsburg, Virginia.

Institut d'émission des départements d'outre-mer

1992   *La filière canne-sucre-rhum dans les départements d'outre-mer.* Paris.

International Beverage Consumption and Production Trends

1997   *World Drink Trends, 1997.* Henley-on-Thames, Oxfordshire, England: Productschap Voor Gedistilleerde Dranken and NTC Publications.

Isert, Paul Erdman

1788   *Reise nach Guinea. Letters on West Africa and the Slave Trade: Paul Erdmann Isert's Journey to Guinea and the Caribbean Islands in Colombia.* Trans. S. A. Winsnes and reprinted 1992. Oxford: Oxford University Press.

Jamaica

1888–89   *The Handbook of Jamaica: Comprising Historical, Statistical and General Information.* Issue 8. London; Kingston, Jamaica.

1903   *The Handbook of Jamaica.* Issue 23. London; Kingston, Jamaica.

1911   *The Handbook of Jamaica.* Issue 31. London; Kingston, Jamaica.

1946   *The Handbook of Jamaica.* Issue 58. London; Kingston, Jamaica.

Jamieson, Ross

2000   *Domestic Architecture and Power: The Historical Archaeology of Colonial Ecuador.* New York: Kluwer Academic/Plenum.

Jefferys, Thomas

1760   *The Natural and Civil History of the French Dominions in North and South America.* 2 vols. London.

Josa, Guy

1931   *Les industries du sucre et du rhum à la Martinique, 1639–1931.* Paris: Presses Modernes.

Keith, Alice

1948   "Relaxations in British Restrictions on the American Trade with the British West Indies, 1783–1802." *Journal of Modern History*: (20)1:1–18.

Keller, Mark

1979   "The Great Jewish Drink Mystery." In *Beliefs, Behaviors, and Alcoholic Beverages: A Cross-Cultural Survey*, ed. M. Marshall, 404–14. Ann Arbor: University of Michigan Press.

Kervégant, D.

1946   *Rhums et eaux-de-vie de canne*. Vannes: Editions du Golfe.

Kinross, Lord

1959   "Prohibition in Britain." *History Today* 9: 493–99.

Kiple, Kenneth

1984   *The Caribbean Slave: A Biological History*. New York: Cambridge University Press.

Klingberg, Frank

1949   *Codrington Chronicle: An Experiment in Anglican Altruism on a Barbados Plantation, 1710–1834*. University of California Publications in History, vol. 37. Berkeley: University of California Press.

Knight, Franklin W.

1990   *The Caribbean: The Genesis of a Fragmented Nationalism*. 2nd edition, New York: Oxford University Press.

Kopperman, Paul

1996   "'The Cheapest Pay': Alcohol Abuse in the Eighteenth-Century British Army." *Journal of Military History* 60: 445–70.

Labat, Jean Baptiste Père

1724   *Nouveau voyage aux isles de l'Amérique*. 2 vols. La Haye, France.

La Borde, Sieur de

1674   *Relation de l'origine, moeurs, coustumes, religion, guerres et voyages des Caraibes, sauvages des isles Antilles de l'Amérique*. In *Recueil de divers voyages faits en Afrique et en l'Amérique*, ed. L. Billaine. Paris.

Laman, Karl

1953   *The Kongo*. 2 vols. Studia ethnographica Upsaliensia.

Langton, Marcia.

1993   "Rum, Seduction, and Death: Aboriginality and Alcohol." *Oceania* 63: 195–206.

Las Casas, Bartolomé de

1971   *History of the Indies*. Trans. A. Collard. New York: Harper and Row.

La Selve, Edgar

1871   *La république d'Haiti: Ancienne partie française de Saint Domingue*. Port-au-Prince.

Laudan, Rachel

2000   "Birth of the Modern Diet." *Scientific American* 283(2): 76–81.

Laurence, K. O.

1994   *A Question of Labour: Indentured Immigration into Trinidad and British Guiana, 1875–1917.* New York: Saint Martin's Press.

Laurens, André

1939   *La législation économique et fiscale du rhum en France.* Bordeaux: Imprimerie-Libraire Delmas.

Law, Robin

1991   *The Slave Coast of West Africa 1550–1750: The Impact of the Atlantic Slave Trade on an African Society.* Oxford: Clarendon Press.

1999   "On the African Background to the Slave Insurrection in Saint-Domingue (Haïti) in 1791: The Bois Caiman Ceremony and the Dahomian 'Blood Pact.'" Paper presented at the Harriet Tubman seminar, Department of History, York University.

Layfield, Dr.

1906   "A Large Relation of the Port Ricco Voiage; Written, as is Reported, by that Learned Man and Reverend Divine Doctor Layfield, his Lordships Chaplaine and Attendant in that Expedition; Very Much Abbreviated." Vol. 16, *Hakluytus Postumus or Purchas his Pilgrimes*, ed. S. Purchas, 44–106, Glasgow.

Leacock, Seth

1964   "Ceremonial Drinking in an Afro-Brazilian Cult." *American Anthropologist* 66: 344–54.

Leath, Robert

1999   " 'After the Chinese Taste': Chinese Export Porcelain and Chinoiserie Decoration in Eighteenth-Century Charleston." *Historical Archaeology* 33(3): 48–61.

Lemert, Edwin M.

1964   "Forms and Pathology of Drinking in Three Polynesian Societies." *American Anthropologist* 66(2): 361–74.

Lepelletier de St.-Remy, M. R.

1846   *Saint Domingue: Étude et solution nouvelle de la question Haïtienne.* Paris.

Leslie, Charles

1740   *A New and Exact Account of Jamaica.* 3rd edition, Edinburgh.

Lewis, Matthew Gregory

1834   *Journal of a West India Proprietor, Kept During a Residence in the Island of Jamaica.* Reprinted 1969, New York: Negro Universities Press.

Licensed Beverage Industries

1946   *Beverage Distilling Industry: Facts and Figures 1934–1945.* New York.

Lieber, Charles

1998   "Hepatic and Other Medical Disorders of Alcoholism: From Pathogenesis to Treatment." *Journal of Studies on Alcohol* 59(1): 9–26.

Ligon, Richard
1673   *A True and Exact History of the Island of Barbadoes.* 2nd ed. London.
Lyttleton, Edward
1689   *The Groans of the Plantations.* London.
Lobdell, Richard
1996   "Patterns of Investments and Credit in the British West Indian Sugar Industry, 1838–1897." In *Caribbean Freedom: Economy and Society from Emancipation to the Present*, ed. H. Beckles and V. Shepherd, 319–29. Princeton: Markus Weiner.
Lock, Charles, Benjamin Newlands, and John Newlands
1888   *Sugar: A Handbook for Planters and Refiners.* London.
Long, Edward
1774   *The History of Jamaica; or, General Survey of the Antient and Modern State of That Island.* 3 vols. Reprinted 1970, London: Frank Cass.
Look Lai, Walton
1993   *Indentured Labor, Caribbean Sugar: Chinese and Indian Migrants to the British West Indies, 1838–1918.* Baltimore: Johns Hopkins University.
Lucas, Nathaniel
1955   "The Lucas Manuscript Volumes." *Journal of the Barbados Museum and Historical Society* 22(3):111–26.
MacAndrew, Craig, and Robert Edgerton
1969   *Drunken Comportment: A Social Explanation.* Chicago: Aldine Publishing.
Mackenzie, Charles
1830   *Notes on Haiti Made During a Residence in That Republic.* 2 vols. Reprinted 1971, London: Frank Cass.
Madiou, Thomas
1847   *Histoire d'Haïti: Années 1492–1807.* 4 vols. Reprinted 1985, Port-au-Prince: Editions Henri Deschamps.
Mahy, George, and D. Beverley Barnett
1997   "Mental Health." In *Health Conditions in the Caribbean.* Scientific publication no. 561. Washington, D.C.: Pan American Health Organization.
Malenfant, Colonel
1814   *Des colonies, et particulièrement de celle de Saint-Domingue; mémoire historique et politique.* Paris.
Malik, Yogendra
1971   *East Indians in Trinidad: A Study in Minority Politics.* London: Oxford University Press.
Mancall, Peter
1995   *Deadly Medicine: Indians and Alcohol in Early America.* Ithaca: Cornell University Press.

Manning, Patrick

1982   *Slavery, Colonialism, and Economic Growth in Dahomey, 1640–1960.* Cambridge: Cambridge University Press.

Maples, Thomas

1991   "Gin and Georgian London." *History Today* 41: 42–47.

Marsden, Peter

1788   *An Account of the Island of Jamaica; with Reflections on the Treatment, Occupation, and Provisions of the Slaves.* Newcastle.

Marshall, Mac, ed.

1979   *Beliefs, Behaviors, and Alcoholic Beverages: A Cross-Cultural Survey.* Ann Arbor: University of Michigan Press.

Marshall, Mac, and Leslie B. Marshall

1975   "Opening Pandora's Bottle: Reconstructing Micronesians' Early Contacts with Alcoholic Beverages." *Journal of the Polynesian Society* 84: 441–65.

Marshall, Woodville

1996   "Metayage in the Sugar Industry of the British Windward Islands, 1838–1865." In *Caribbean Freedom: Economy and Society from Emancipation to the Present,* ed. H. Beckles and V. Shepherd, 64–79. Princeton: Markus Weiner.

Martin, Samuel

1765   *An Essay Upon Plantership.* London.

Marx, Robert F.

1968   *Wine Glasses Recovered from the Sunken City of Port Royal: 1 May, 1966–31 March, 1968.* Kingston, Jamaica: Jamaican National Trust Commission.

Maspons Franco, Juan

1932   *La reorganización de la industria alcoholera y reforma del sistema tributario de los impuestos del emprestito de $35.000.000.* Havana, Cuba: P. Fernández y Cia.

Mather, Cotton

1708   *Sober Considerations, on a Growing Flood of Iniquity.* Boston.

Mathieson, William Law

1967   *British Slave Emancipation, 1838–1849.* New York: Octagon Books.

McClelland, D. C., W. N. Davis, E. Wanner, and R. Kalin

1966   "A Cross-Cultural Study of Folktale Content and Drinking." *Sociometry* 29: 308–33.

McCusker, John

1989   *Rum and the American Revolution: The Rum Trade and the Balance of Payments of the Thirteen Continental Colonies.* New York: Garland Publishing.

1990   "Distilling and Its Implications for the Atlantic World of the Seventeenth and Eighteenth Centuries." In *Production, Marketing, and Consumption of Alcoholic Beverages since the Late Middle Ages,* ed. E. Aerts, L. Cullen, and R. Wilson, 7–19. Leuven, Belgium: Leuven University Press.

2000   "The Business of Distilling in the Old World and the New World during the Seventeenth and Eighteenth Centuries: The Rise of a New Enterprise and Its Connection with Colonial America." In *The Early Modern Atlantic Economy*, ed. J. McCusker and K. Morgan, 186–224. Cambridge: Cambridge University Press.

Métraux, Alfred

1959   *Voodoo in Haiti*. Trans. H. Charteris. London: Andre Deutsch.

Meyer, Jean, Jean Tarrade, Annie Rey-Goldzeiguer, and Jacques Thobie

1991   *Histoire de la France coloniale: Des origines à 1914*. Paris: Armand Colin.

Miller, Joseph C.

1976   *Kings and Kinsmen: Early Mbundu States in Angola*. Oxford: Clarendon Press.

Millspaugh, Arthur

1931   *Haiti under American Control, 1915–1930*. Boston: World Peace Foundation.

Mintz, Sidney W.

1974   *Caribbean Transformations*. New York: Columbia University Press.

1985   *Sweetness and Power: The Place of Sugar in Modern History*. London: Penguin Books.

Mintz, Sidney W., and Richard Price

1992   *The Birth of African-American Culture: An Anthropological Perspective*. Boston: Beacon Press.

Moore, Brian

1995   *Cultural Power, Resistance, and Pluralism: Colonial Guyana, 1838–1900*. Montreal: McGill-Queen's University Press.

Mora de Tovar, Gilma Lucia

1988   *Aguardiente y conflictos sociales en la Nueva Granada durante el siglo xviii*. Bogotá, Colombia: Universidad Nacional de Colombia, Centro Editorial.

Moreau de St.-Méry, M. L. E.

1797–98 *Description topographique, physique, civile, politique et historique de la partie française de l'isle Saint-Domingue*. 2 vols. Philadelphia.

1798   *A Topographical and Political Description of the Spanish Part of Saint Domingo*. 2 vols. Philadelphia.

Moreno Fraginals, Manuel

1978   *El ingenio: Complejo económico social Cubano del azúcar*. 3 vols. Havana, Cuba: Editorial de Ciencias Sociales.

1996   "Plantations in the Caribbean: Cuba, Puerto Rico, and the Dominican Republic in the Late Nineteenth Century." In *Caribbean Freedom: Economy and Society from Emancipation to the Present*, ed. H. Beckles and V. Shepherd, 330–40. Princeton: Markus Weiner.

Mouer, Daniel, and Frederick H. Smith

2001   "Revisiting Mapps Cave: Amerindian and Probable Slave Occupation of a Sinkhole and Cavern, St. Philip Parish, Barbados." In *Proceedings of the 18th*

Annual Meeting of the International Association of Caribbean Archaeology, 301–7. St. George's, Grenada; Basse-Terre, Guadeloupe: l'Association Internationale d'Archéologie de la Caraibe.

Moussette, Marcel

1996   "The Site of the Intendant's Palace in Québec City: The Changing Meaning of Urban Space." *Historical Archaeology* 30(2): 8–21.

Murray, Gerald F.

1996   *El colmado: Una exploración antropológica del negocio de comidas y bebidas en la República Dominicana*. Santo Domingo, República Dominicana: Fondo para el financiamiento de la microempresa.

Nardin, Jean-Claude

1969   *La mise en valeur de l'île de Tobago*, 1763–1783. Paris: Mouton.

Nash, R. C.

1985   "Irish Atlantic Trade in the Seventeenth and Eighteenth Centuries." *William and Mary Quarterly* 42(3): 329–56.

Newman, Peter

1964   *British Guiana: Problems of Cohesion in an Immigrant Society*. London: Oxford University Press.

Nicholls, David

1979   *From Dessalines to Duvalier: Race, Colour and National Independence in Haiti*. Cambridge: Cambridge University Press.

Noel-Hume, Ivor

1988   *Martin's Hundred*. New York: Alfred A. Knopf.

Ober, Frederick

1880   *Camps in the Caribbees: The Adventures of a Naturalist in the Lesser Antilles*. Boston.

Oldmixon, John

1741   *The British Empire in America*. 2nd ed. 2 vols. London.

Ortiz, Fernando

1947   *Cuban Counterpoint: Tobacco and Sugar*. Trans. H. de Onís and reprinted 1995. Durham: Duke University Press.

Owens, Joseph

1979   *Dread: The Rastafarians of Jamaica*. London: Heinemann.

Pack, A. J.

1995   *Nelson's Blood: The Story of Naval Rum*. Annapolis: Naval Institute Press.

Pairault, M. E.-A.

1903   *Le rhum et sa fabrication*. Paris: Gauthier-Villars.

Pan, Lynn

1975   *Alcohol in Colonial Africa*. Vol. 22. Helsinki, Finland: Finish Foundation for Alcohol Studies.

Pares, Richard

1963   *War and Trade in the West Indies 1739–1763*. London: Frank Cass.

Parrinder, Edward Geoffrey

1961   *West African Religion: A Study of the Beliefs and Practices of Akan, Ewe, Yoruba, Ibo, and Kindred Peoples*. London: Epworth Press.

Parry, J. H., Philip Sherlock, and Anthony Maingot

1987   *A Short History of the West Indies*. 4th edition. London: Macmillan.

Pegram, Thomas

1998   *Battling Demon Rum: The Struggle for a Dry America, 1800–1933*. Chicago: Ivan R. Dee.

Pérez, Louis A., Jr.

1992   *Slaves, Sugar, and Colonial Society: Travel Accounts of Cuba, 1801–1899*. Wilmington, Delaware: Scholarly Resources Inc.

1999   *On Becoming Cuban: Identity, Nationality, and Culture*. Chapel Hill: University of North Carolina Press.

Pérez-López, Jorge F.

1991   *The Economics of Cuban Sugar*. Pittsburgh: University of Pittsburgh Press.

Peytraud, Lucien Pierre

1984   *L'esclavage aux antilles française avant 1789, d'après des documents inédits des archives colonials*. 2 vols. Paris: Edition et Diffusion de la Culture Antillaise.

Phillippo, James

1843   *Jamaica: Its Past and Present State*. Reprinted 1969, London: Dawsons.

Phillips, Ulrich B.

1914   "A Jamaica Slave Plantation." *American Historical Review* 19(3): 543–58.

Pigafetta, Filippo

1591   *A Report of the Kingdom of Congo, and of the Surrounding Countries; Drawn Out of the Writings and Discourses of the Portuguese, Duarte Lopez, by Filippo Pigafetta, in Rome*. Trans. and ed. M. Hutchinson, 1881. Reprinted 1969, New York: Negro Universities Press.

Pinckard, George

1806   *Notes on the West Indies*. 3 vols. London.

Pitman, Frank Wesley

1926   "Slavery on British West India Plantations in the Eighteenth Century." *Journal of Negro History* 11(4): 584–668.

Pluchon, Pierre

1982   *Histoire des Antilles et de la Guyane*. Toulouse: Privat.

Pope, Peter

1997   "Fish into Wine: The Historical Anthropology of Demand for Alcohol in Seventeenth Century Newfoundland." In *The Changing Face of Drink: Substance, Imagery, and Behaviour*, ed. J. S. Blocker and C. K. Warsh, 43–64. Ottawa: Les Publications Histoire Sociale.

Postma, Johannes

1990   *The Dutch in the Atlantic Slave Trade, 1600–1815.* Cambridge: Cambridge University Press.

Powell, Colin

1995   *My American Journey.* New York: Random House.

Poyer, John

1808   *The History of Barbados, from the First Discovery of the Island, in the Year 1605, till the Accession of Lord Seaforth, 1801.* London.

Price, Neil

1988   *Behind the Planter's Back: Lower Class Responses to Marginality in Bequia Island, Saint Vincent.* London: Macmillan.

Price, Richard, and Sally Price

1991   *Two Evenings in Saramaka.* Chicago: University of Chicago Press.

Price-Mars, Jean

1945   "Toussaint-Louverture." *Revue de la Société d' Histoire et de Géographie d' Haiti* 16(57): 1–33.

Puckrein, Gary

1984   *Little England: Plantation Society and Anglo-Barbadian Politics, 1627–1700.* New York: New York University Press.

Ragatz, Lowell Joseph

1927   *Statistics for the Study of British Caribbean Economic History 1763–1833.* London: Bryan Edwards Press.

1928   *The Fall of the Planter Class in the British Caribbean, 1763–1833.* New York: Century Company.

Ratekin, Mervyn

1954   "The Early Sugar Industry in Española." *Hispanic American Historical Review* 34: 1–19.

Rawlin, William

1699   *The Laws of Barbados Collected in One Volume.* London.

Regenten of Surinam

1788   *Essai historique sur la colonie de Surinam.* Trans. S. Cohen and ed. J. Marcus and S. Chyet, 1974. Cincinnati: American Jewish Archives.

Renard, Rosamunde

1996   "Immigration and Indentureship in the French West Indies, 1848–1870." In *Caribbean Freedom: Economy and Society from Emancipation to the Present,* ed. H. Beckles and V. Shepherd, 161–68. Princeton: Markus Weiner.

1996   "Labour Relations in Post-Slavery Martinique and Guadeloupe 1848–1870." In *Caribbean Freedom: Economy and Society from Emancipation to the Present,* ed. H. Beckles and V. Shepherd, 80–92. Princeton: Markus Weiner.

Rice, Prudence

1996   "Peru's Colonial Wine Industry and Its European Background." *Antiquity* 70(270): 785–801.

1997   "Wine and Brandy Production in Colonial Peru: A Historical and Archaeological Investigation." *Journal of Interdisciplinary History* 27(3): 455–80.

Rivera, Mayra

1999   "David Defeats Goliath in Puerto Rico." *Exchange, the Quarterly Newsletter of the American Medical Association Office of Alcohol and Other Drug Abuse.* Winter: 5–6.

Robertson, Reverend

1732   *A Detection of the State and Situation of the Present Sugar Planters of Barbados and the Leeward Islands.* London.

Robinson, Albert

1915   *Cuba, Old and New.* New York: Longmans, Green, and Company.

Rochefort, Charles de

1681   *Histoire naturelle et morale des isles Antilles de l'Amérique.* Rotterdam.

Rodriguez, José Angel

1990   "Venezuelan Rums in the Nineteenth Century." In *Production, Marketing, and Consumption of Alcoholic Beverages since the Late Middle Ages,* ed. E Aerts, L. Cullen, and R. Wilson, 56–67. Leuven, Belgium: Leuven University Press.

Rorabaugh, W. J.

1979   *The Alcoholic Republic: An American Tradition.* New York: Oxford University Press.

Rose-Rosette, Robert

1990   *Essai d'approche du punch martiniquais élément du société.* Fort-de-France, Martinique: Editorions Trois Rivieres.

Roughley, Thomas

1823   *The Jamaica Planter's Guide.* London.

Rouse, Irving

1992   *The Tainos: Rise and Decline of the People Who Greeted Columbus.* New Haven: Yale University Press.

Rudé, George

1971   "Mother Gin and the London Riots of 1736." In *Paris and London in the Eighteenth Century: Studies in Popular Protest,* ed. G. Rudé, 201–21. New York: Viking Press.

Rush, Benjamin

1790   *An Inquiry into the Effects of Ardent Spirits upon the Human Body and Mind with an Account of the Means of Preventing and of the Remedies for Curing Them.* Boston.

Sandoval, Fernando

1951   *La industria del azúcar en Nueva España, investigación y publicación costea-*
        dos. Mexico: Universidad Nacional Autónoma de Mexico.

Sauer, Carl Ortwin

1966   *The Early Spanish Main.* Berkeley: University of California Press.

Saugera, Éric

1995   *Bordeaux, port négrier: Chronologie, économiè, idéologie, XVIIe–XIXe siècles.*
        Paris: Karthala.

Schaefer, James M.

1976   "Drunkenness and Cultural Stress: A Holocultural Test." In *Cross-Cultural*
        Approaches to the Study of Alcohol: An Interdisciplinary Perspective, ed. M.
        Everett, J. Waddell, and D. Heath, 287–322. The Hague: Mouton.

Schnakenbourg, Christian

1977   "Statistiques pour l'histoire de l'économie de plantation en Guadeloupe et
        Martinique." *Bulletin de la société d'histoire de la Guadeloupe,* no. 31. Basse-
        Terre: Guadeloupe.

Schomburgk, Robert H.

1848   *The History of Barbados.* London.

Schumpeter, Elizabeth

1960   *English Overseas Trade Statistics, 1697–1808.* Oxford: Clarendon.

Scott, Rebecca

1985   *Slave Emancipation in Cuba: The Transition to Free Labor, 1860–1899.*
        Princeton: Princeton University Press.

Shephard, Charles

1831   *An Historical Account of the Island of Saint Vincent.* Reprinted 1971, London:
        Frank Cass.

Sheridan, Richard

1957   "The Molasses Act and the Market Strategy of the British Sugar Planters."
        Journal of Economic History 17(1): 62–83.

1974   *Sugar and Slavery: An Economic History of the British West Indies, 1623–1775.*
        Barbados: Caribbean Universities Press.

Silvester, Giles

1651   "A Breife Discription of the Ilande of Barbados." Author cited as anonymous in
        1967 reprint, *Colonising Expeditions to the West Indies and Guiana, 1623–1667,*
        ed. V. T. Harlow. Millwood, New York: Kraus.

Simpson, George Eaton

1970   *Religious Cults of the Caribbean: Trinidad, Jamaica, and Haiti.* Rio Piedra:
        University of Puerto Rico Press.

Singh, Kelvin

1994   *Race and Class Struggles in a Colonial State: Trinidad, 1917–1945.* Calgary:
        University of Calgary Press.

Sloane, Hans

1707–25 *A Voyage to the Islands Madera, Barbados, Nieves, S. Christophers, and Jamaica.* 2 vols. London.

Smith, Delores E., and Lynn Blinn Pike

1994 "Relationship between Jamaican Adolescents' Drinking Partners and Self-Image: A Cross-Cultural Perspective." *Adolescence* 29(114): 429–38.

Smith, Frederick H.

1998 "Disturbing the Peace in Barbados: Constant Silvester of Constant Plantation in the Seventeenth-Century." *Journal of the Barbados Museum and Historical Society* 44: 38–53.

Smith, Raymond

1956 *The Negro Family in British Guiana: Family Structure and Social Status in the Villages.* London: Routledge & Paul.

Southey, Thomas

1827 *Chronological History of the West Indies.* 3 vols. London: Longman, Rees, Orme, Brown, & Green.

Staden, Hans

1557 "Veritable History and Description of a Country Belonging to the Wild, Naked, and Terrible, Eaters of Men's Flesh, Situated in the New World, America." Marbourg: Kolben. Trans. M. Alexander and reprinted 1976 in *Discovering the New World.* New York: Harper Row.

Stedman, John

1790 *Narrative of a Five Years Expedition Against the Revolted Negroes of Surinam.* Trans. and ed. R. Price and S. Price, 1988. Baltimore: Johns Hopkins University.

Stein, Robert Louis

1988 *The French Sugar Business in the Eighteenth Century.* Baton Rouge: Louisiana State University Press.

Stevenson, Robert Louis

1965 *Treasure Island.* New York: Signet Classic.

Sturge, Joseph, and Thomas Harvey

1838 *The West Indies in 1837; Being the Journal of a Visit to Antigua, Montserrat, Dominica, Saint Lucia, Barbados, and Jamaica.* London.

Tarrade, Jean

1972 *Le commerce colonial de la France à la fin de l'ancien régime: L'evolution du régime de l'exclusif de 1763 à 1789.* Paris: Presses Universitaires de France.

1992 "Le commerce entre les Antilles françaises et les possessions espagnoles d' Amérique à la fin du XVIIIe siècle." In *Commerce et plantation dans la Caraïbe, XVIIIe et XIXe siècles*, ed. P. Butel. Bordeaux: Maison des Pays Ibériques.

Taylor, Douglas

1938   *The Caribs of Dominica*. Bureau of American Ethnology, bulletin 119, Anthropological Papers, no. 3. Washington D.C.

1946   "Kinship and Social Structure of the Island Carib." *Southwestern Journal of Anthropology* 2: 180–212.

1949   "The Interpretation of Some Documentary Evidence on Carib Culture." *Southwestern Journal of Anthropology* 5: 379–92.

1950   "The Meaning of Dietary and Occupational Restrictions among the Island Carib." *American Anthropologist* 52(3): 343–49.

Taylor, William

1979   *Drinking, Homicide, and Rebellion in Colonial Mexican Villages*. Stanford: Stanford University Press.

Thomas, Sir Dalby

1690   *An Historical Account of the Rise and Growth of the West India Colonies*. London.

Thome, James, and J. Horace Kimball

1838   *Emancipation in the West Indies. A Six Months' Tour in Antigua, Barbadoes, and Jamaica, in the Year 1837*. New York: American Anti-Slavery Society.

Thornton, John

1992   *Africa and Africans in the Making of the Atlantic World, 1400–1680*. Cambridge: Cambridge University Press.

Tucker, Katherine, and Thomas Hedges

1993   "Food Shortages and an Epidemic of Optic and Peripheral Neuropathy in Cuba." *Nutrition Reviews* 51(12): 349–58.

Turnbull, David

1840   *Travels in the West. Cuba; with Notices of Porto Rico, and the Slave Trade*. Reprinted 1969, New York: Negro Universities Press.

Turner, Mary

1996   "Chinese Contract Labour in Cuba, 1847–1874." In *Caribbean Freedom: Economy and Society from Emancipation to the Present*, ed. H. Beckles and V. Shepherd, 132–40. Princeton: Markus Weiner.

Turner, Victor

1969   *The Ritual Process: Structure and Anti-Structure*. Ithaca: Cornell University Press.

Underwood, A. J. V.

1935   "The Historical Development of Distilling Plant." *Transactions of the Institution of Chemical Engineers* 13: 34–62.

United States Department of Health and Human Services

1992   "Toxic Hypoglycemic Syndrome–Jamaica, 1989–1991." *Morbidity and Mortality Weekly Report* 41(4): 53–56.

University of Florida, Latin American Collection

1731–1925   Gale-Morant Papers. Papers relating to York Plantation and Gale's Valley Plantation. George A. Smathers Library. Gainesville, Florida.

Unwin, Tim

1991   *Wine and the Vine: An Historical Geography of Viticulture and the Wine Trade.* London: Routledge Press.

Vernon, Diane

1980   "Bakuu: Possessing Spirits of Witchcraft on the Tapanahony." *New West Indian Guide* 54(1): 1–38.

Vertovec, Steven

1992   *Hindu Trinidad: Religion, Ethnicity and Socio-Economic Change.* London: Macmillan.

Von Braunschweig, Hieronymus

1527   *The Boke of Distyllacyon of Herbes.* Reprinted 1973, London: Da Capo Press.

Wagner, Michael

1977   "Rum, Policy, and the Portuguese: Or, the Maintenance of Elite Supremacy in Post-Emancipation British Guiana." *The Canadian Review of Sociology and Anthropology* 14(4): 406–16.

Walduck, Thomas

1947   "T. Walduck's Letters from Barbados, 1710." *Journal of the Barbados Museum and Historical Society* 15(1): 27–51.

Ward, J. R.

1988   *British West Indian Slavery, 1750–1834: The Process of Amelioration.* Oxford: Clarendon Press.

1991   "The Profitability of Sugar Planting in the British West Indies 1650–1834." *Economic History Review* 31(2):197–213.

Warner, Jessica, and Frank Ivis

1999   "'Damn You, You Informing Bitch': Vox Populi and the Unmaking of the Gin Act of 1736." *Journal of Social History*, Winter: 299–330.

Watters, David

1994   "Mortuary Patterns at the Harney Site Slave Cemetery, Montserrat, in Caribbean Perspective." *Historical Archaeology* 28(3): 56–73.

Watters, David, and Desmond Nicholson

1982   Highland House, Barbuda: An Eighteenth-Century Retreat." *The Florida Anthropologist* 35(4): 223–42.

Watts, David

1987   *The West Indies: Patterns of Development, Culture, and Environmental Change since 1492.* Cambridge: Cambridge University Press.

Welsh, James

1589   "A Voyage to Benin Beyond the Country of Guinea." Reprinted 1978 in *Richard Hakluyt, Voyages*, 6:291–97. 8 vols. London: Everyman's Library.

Whistler, Henry

1654   "An Account of Barbados in 1654: Extracted from Henry Whistler's Journal of the West India Expedition." *Journal of the Barbados Museum and Historical Society* 5(4): 184–85.

Whitehead, Neil

2002   *Dark Shamans: Kanaimà and the Poetics of Violent Death*. Durham: Duke University Press.

1997   *The Discoverie of the Large, Rich, and Bewtiful Empyre of Guiana by Sir Walter Ralegh*. Transcribed, annotated, and introduced by N. Whitehead. Norman: University of Oklahoma Press.

Williams, David

1989   "The Impact of the Roman Amphorae Trade on Pre-Roman Britain." In *Centre and Periphery: Comparative Studies in Archaeology*, ed. T. Champion, 142–50. London: Unwin Hyman.

Williams, Eric

1944   *Capitalism and Slavery*. Reprinted 1994, Chapel Hill: University of North Carolina Press.

1984   *From Columbus to Castro: The History of the Caribbean 1492–1969*. New York: Vintage Books.

Williams, Joseph J.

1932   *Voodoos and Obeahs: Phases of West Indian Witchcraft*. New York: Dial Press.

Wilson, Peter J.

1973   *Crab Antics: The Social Anthropology of English-Speaking Negro Societies of the Caribbean*. New Haven: Yale University Press.

Wolfgang, Lori

1997   "Charting Recent Progress: Advances in Alcohol Research." *Alcohol Health and Research World* 21(4): 277–87.

Woodcock, Henry Iles

1867   *A History of Tobago*. Reprinted 1971, London: Frank Cass.

World Health Organization

1999   *Global Status Report on Alcohol*. Geneva.

Worrell, DeLisle

1982   *The Economy of Barbados, 1946–1980*. Bridgetown, Barbados: Central Bank of Barbados.

Wray, Leonard

1848   *The Practical Sugar Planter*. London.

Yawney, Carole

1979   "Drinking Patterns and Alcoholism in Trinidad." In *Beliefs, Behaviors, and Alcoholic Beverages: A Cross-Cultural Survey*, ed. M. Marshall, 94–108. Ann Arbor: University of Michigan Press.

Young, William

1807   *The West India Common-Place Book: Compiled from Parliamentary and Official Documents; Shewing the Interest of Great Britain in its Sugar Colonies.* London.

Zavala, Silvio Arturo

1939–46   *Fuentes para la historia del trabajo en Nueva España.* 8 vols. Ed. Silvio Zavala and Maria Castelo. Mexico: Fondo de Cultura Económica.

Index

Page numbers in *italics* refer to illustrations.

Maritime life, 27, 138–39, 157

Marketing, of rum, 233–37

Markets, metropolitan, 60, 71

Maroon societies, 192

Marronage, 160, 167

Martin, Samuel, 41–42, 51, 52–53, 54–55

Martinique, 235; French conquest of, 67; rum/sugar exports from, 209–10, *210,* 211–12, *212, 213,* 213–14; tafia exports from, 60, 63, 66, 68–69, 70, 261n.109

—rum trade in: early, 13–14, 15, 17–20, *19,* 24; nineteenth-century, 56, 209–10, *210,* 211–12, *213,* 213–14, 218; twentieth-century, 225–27

Masculinity, 236, 243, 244–45

Mather, Cotton, 31

Mauritius, 200, 201, 207

McCusker, John, 2, 49, 52, 55, *55,* 251n.30

Medicine: distilled spirits as, 24, 25–26, 27, 40, 77, 142–43, 167, 168; Galenic principles of, 25–26. *See also* Alcoholism; Health; Illness

Men: in British Guiana, 240; East Indian, 241; in rum shops, 244–45; young urban, 240. *See also* Gender; Masculinity

Mental health, alcoholism and, 242–43

Métayer. *See* Sharecropping (métayer)

Methodists, 169, 173, 174, 181, 185, 188, 240

Methuen Treaty, 72, 121

Métraux, Alfred, 114, 191

Mexico, 220; as New Spain, 11, 32

Middle Ages, 71–72

Military life: British, 76–77, 91, 101–2, 136–38, 143, 146–49, 157, 222–23, 236; mortality rates and, 146–49

Miller, Joseph, 101

Mintz, Sidney, 2, 41, 76, 79, 108, 109, 110, 173, 251n.31

Missionaries, Christian, 1, 7–8, 10, 36–37, 38, 200–201, 202, 240, 257n.179; in Haiti, 182; in Hawaii, 196; Jesuit, 30, 35; Low Church, 167, 181, 191; Portuguese, 98; in Puerto Rico, 181; temperance advocated by, 168, 169–76, 178–80, 181–82, 193; twentieth-century, 222; Wesleyan, 126. *See also specific individuals*

Mobbie (drink), 7, 8, 119–20, 121, 249n.7, 250n.21

Modiford, Thomas, 15

Molasses, 17–18, 22, 31, 61, 255n.133; in claying, 44, 50–51, 64; in eighteenth century, 42, 43–44, 45–46, *47, 48,* 50–51, 55, 56, 63–66, 67; Molasses Act on, 64–65, 66, 83; in nineteenth century, 205–6, 207, 209, 211–12, *212,* 217, 218, 219; in rum making, early, 17–18, 22, 31, 255n.133; to rum ratios, 55, *55;* in twentieth century, 222, 223, 225, 227–28, 229, 230

Montserrat, 23, 190, 193

Moore, Brian, 186

Moravians, 169, 170, 173

Moreau de St.-Méry, M.L.E.: on drunkenness, 128–29; on hospitality, 124; on slaves, 112, 113–14, 156, 160, 165; on temperance, 60, 126, 134, 136, 141, 160; on wealthy whites, 131

Mortality rates: binge drinking, 149; military, 146–49; in Puerto Rico, 238; slave, 146, 149–54, *151, 153,* 167

Mount Pelée, eruption of, 225

Murray, Gerald, 239

Muscavado sugar, 50–51, 218

Muslim religion, 96, 241

Myalists, 189–90

Napoleon I, 209

Napoleon III, 211

Nationalism, modern, 235

Native Americans, 30, 31, 57

Navigation Act of 1663 (British), 62, 121

Navigation Acts (U.S.), 204

Nearchus, General, 251n.31

Nelson, Horatio, 143

New England, 28–32, 63, 64, 65, 205, 255nn.133–34

New Spain. *See* Mexico

New World: drinks, alcoholic, 12–16, 251n.33, 251n.35; rum making, 13–17; sugar making in, 251n.30

New York, Haitian vodou in, 247

Nineteenth century: alcohol and, 168; concentrated rum making in, 54, 260n.64; Cuba in, 178–79, 215–19, *216;* drinking patterns, 168–76, *174;* economics, 194–221, 232; molasses in, 205–6, 207, 209, 211–12, *212,* 217, 218, 219;

Price, Richard, 108, 109, 110, 192

Price, Sally, 192

Pringle-Polgreen, Rachel, 106, *107*

Prohibitions/restrictions, alcohol: in Africa, 221, 222; British Caribbean, 214; in Canada, 222; in Cuba, 59; early, 31, 32–33, 256n.143; on excessive drinking, 133; French, 56, 61, 62–63, 208, 225–26; nineteenth-century, 176–77, 181; on obeah rituals, 112–13; Prohibitory Act (Britain) as, 88; slaves and, 31, 58, 105–6, 129, 273n.89; by Spain, 57–59, 261n.88; Spanish Caribbean, 215–16; television advertising and, 237; twentieth-century, 180, 181; U.S. and, 180, 181, 222, 229, 230. *See also* Duties; Tariffs, protective; Taxes; Temperance/temperance movements; Trade restrictions

Proof, alcohol, 52–55, *55*, 260n.64

Protestant reformers, 178, 181

Puckrein, Gary, 21

Puerto Rico, 180–81, 214, 217, 221, 227, 229–32; Bacardi rum and, 219, 229, 232; duties on rum from, 230; exports from, 229–32; missionaries in, 181; modern, 238; mortality rates in, 238; Spanish colonists in, 12, 59; taxes in, 229–30; U.S. and, 181

Pulque, 59

Punch, rum, 80–81, 122–25, 144, 155, 272n.38

Punishment, of slaves, 159–61, *161*

Racism, 196

Ragatz, Lowell, 198–99

Rastafarians, 190–91

Rations, rum, 76–77, 91, 101–2, 136, 222

Reagan, Ronald, 231

Rebellion rituals, 161–65. *See also* Uprisings/revolts, slave

Reexport trade. *See* Exports

Reformers. *See* Prohibitions/restrictions, alcohol

Religion. *See* Africa; Spiritual world; *specific religions*

Rémy-Amérique, 234

Restrictions. *See* Prohibitions/restrictions, alcohol

Réunion, 212, 227

Revolts. *See* Uprisings/revolts, slave

Rhum, 17, 60; agricole, 215, 225, 227, 235; agricole v. industriel, 56, 214, 227; guildive, 56; industriel, 226

Riots, East Indian, 184

Rites of passage: Carib, 36–37, 256n.163; funeral/burial, 98, 101–2, 114–16, 188, 192, 193, 270n.145

Rituals: African, 188–93, 247; blood and, 163–64, 165, 166, 185–86, 190; dirt in, 163–64, 165, 189; rum in, 192–93

Robertson, Robert, 122

Robinson, Albert, 179, 180

Rochefort, Charles de, 12–13, 15, 16, 17, 18–19, 120

Rodney, Sir George, 91

Rodriguez, José, 219

Ron (Spanish Caribbean), 17

Rorabaugh, W. J., 26, 29, 31, 204–5

Roughley, Thomas, *50*, 53, 104, 128

Royal African Company, 196

Rum, 1, 3, 4–5; birthplace/cradles of, 13–15, *16*, 16–17; Caribs and, 33–40; concentrated, 54, 260n.64; Dutch and, 13–14, 16, 29–30, 252n.44; early, in Barbados, 13–14, 15, *16*, 16–17, 18, 19, 20, *21*, 21–23, 26, 40, 253n.76; early, in British Caribbean, 23, 40, 71; early, in French Caribbean, 17–20, *19*; elite class and, 122–25; emergence of, 1, 6, 10–17; emergence of, in Atlantic World, 27–33, 40, 255n.117, 255nn.133–34; emergence of, in British Caribbean, 15–17, 19; emergence of, in French Caribbean, 12, 14–15, 17, 252n.36; emergence of, in Spanish Caribbean, 10–12, 17; in England, 31, 71–84, *74*, *82*, *84*, *86*, *89*, 90, 92–93, 94, 255n.134; fire/danger and, 156–57; flavored Indian, 195; health and, 142–54; as "hot," 25–26, 142, 144–45, 148; illegal trade/smuggling of, 33, 59, 60, 89, 91, 187, 214, 230, 241–42; as kill devil, 16, 19, 31, 62, 121, 122, 123, 155; Long on, 42, *50*, 54, 60, 85, 86, 106, 121, 126–27, 142, 143, 144, 148–49, 258n.24; modern, in French Caribbean, 56; modern, varieties of, 235, 237; naming of, 16–17; "new," 145–46, 148,

129, 154; health of, 142–46, 149–54, *151, 153,* 167; Islam/Muslims and, 96; Labat on, 24, 25, 103, 104, 105, 119, 120–21, 142; lead poisoning in, 147, 152, 153, 167, 241; Long on, 126–27, 162; Moreau de St.-Méry on, 112, 113–14, 156, 160, 165; plantation compared with urban, 130; punishment in, 159–61, *161;* rebellion rituals/celebrations, 161–65, 171; restriction of alcohol sold to, 31, 58, 105–6, 129, 273n.89; rum as drink of, 80, 120–21; rum as medicine/dietary supplement for, 25, 26, 103, 142–43; rum prototypes made by, 11, 12–13; rum shops, 105–7, *107;* rum as trade goods/wages for, 95–97, 102–7, 171–72, 175, 193; thievery and, 105; uprisings by, 76, 157, 163–67, 174; vulnerability and, 156, 157, 167; water as drink of, 120; whites on drinking by, 126–30; women and, 128, 152–54. *See also* Emancipation, slave; Plantations
Sloane, Hans, 18, 28, 45, 114–15, 123, 155, 250n.12
Smith, Raymond, 240
Smuggling, 60, 89, 91
Social change, 168, 192, 221
Social disorder, 58
Social drinking: in Africa, 102; in British Caribbean, 124–25, 134; India and, 183–84, 185–86; modern, 243–46; slaves and, 95–96, 99–102, 108–17, 270n.145
Soil quality, 42
Soldiers/sailors. *See* Military life
South America, 220
Southeast Asia, 222
Soviet Union, 231–32, 238, 242
Spain, 10–11, 12, 32, 59; alcohol interests in, 56, 57–60; Bourbon reforms in, 59; brandy from, 56, 57–58, 59, 60, 121, 122; restrictions by, 57–59, 261n.88; Spanish-American War and, 181, 229; Spanish Succession War and, 58; wine and, 56, 57–60, 121, 122, 216
Spanish-American colonies, 32–33, 57–61, 256n.143, 261n.88
Spanish Caribbean: eighteenth-century, 41, 56–60; emergence of rum in, 10–12, 17; nineteenth-century, 194, 207, 214–20, *216,*

232; prohibitions in, 215–16; rum making in, 56–60, 227–32; twentieth-century, 227–32, *228*
Spiritual world: alcohol and, 15, 35–36, 38–39, 95–96, 99–102, 108–17, 118, 134, 141, 155–56, 157, 163–67, 168, 188–93, 256n.161, 257n.181, 270n.145; funeral rites and, 98, 101–2, 114–16, 188, 192, 193, 270n.145; obeah as, 108, 109, 112–13; possession in, 191–93; slaves and, 95–96, 99–102, 108–17, 118, 141, 155–56, 157, 163–67, 270n.145; vodou as, 108, 113–14, 166, 191–92, 193, 246–47. *See also* Missionaries, Christian; *specific religions*
Spoeri, Felix, 122
Spooner, Charles, 153–54
Stedman, John, 105, 159
Stevenson, Robert Louis, 139, 275n.149
Stills/still houses: continuous, 197; early, *16,* 17, 18–20, *19;* eighteenth-century, 42, 43, 44, 46, 47–48; steam-heated, 197; technological advances in, 197–98, 214, 217–18. *See also* Distillation, alcohol
Stores: company, 172, 178, 179, 193 (*see also* Rum shops); grocery (colmados), 239
Sugarcane. *See* Sugar production
Sugar Duties Act of 1846, 200–201
Sugar production, 1, 249n.1; arrack from, 195; beet sugar compared with, 201, 208–9, 221, 223, 227; boiling process, 43–44, *44,* 52, 106, 120; British Caribbean, in nineteenth-century, 198–204, *199, 204;* in Cuba, 216–17; early alcoholic/fermented drinks from, 11–13, 251n.31, 251n.33, 252n.35; emergence of rum and, 10–17, *16,* 40, 251n.33, 251nn.30–31; juice, 43, 45, 56; Mintz on, 41, 251n.31; muscavado, 50–51, 218; in New World, 251n.30; nineteenth-century, 194–204, *199, 204,* 206, *206, 208,* 208–12, *210, 212,* 214–15, 216–18; origins of, 251n.31; peneles sugar and, 17; rum as byproduct of, 2, 4–5, 10–23, *16, 19,* 41, 249n.1, 251nn.30–31; rum canes in, 45; sugar duties and, 200–201; technological advances in, 217–18, 223; twentieth-century, 221, 222, 223–25, *224,* 227–28, 229, 232. *See also* Plantation(s); Rum making

FREDERICK H. SMITH is assistant professor of anthropology at the College of William and Mary. He is the author of several journal articles, including "European Impressions of the Island Caribs' Use of Alcohol in the Early Colonial Period" forthcoming in *Ethnohistory* and "Spirits and Spirituality: Enslaved Persons and Alcohol in Western Africa and the British and French Caribbean" in *Journal of Caribbean History*.